THE
PRESIDENCY
OF THE UNITED STATES

A Student Companion

THE PRESIDENCY
OF THE UNITED STATES

A Student Companion

SECOND EDITION

Richard M. Pious

OXFORD
UNIVERSITY PRESS

Oxford University Press

Oxford   New York
Athens   Auckland   Bangkok   Bogotá   Buenos Aires   Cape Town
Chennai   Dar es Salaam   Delhi   Florence   Hong Kong   Istanbul   Karachi
Kolkata   Kuala Lumpur   Madrid   Melbourne   Mexico City   Mumbai   Nairobi
Paris   São Paulo   Shanghai   Singapore   Taipei   Tokyo   Toronto   Warsaw

and associated companies in
Berlin   Ibadan

Copyright © 2001 by Richard M. Pious

Published by Oxford University Press, Inc.
198 Madison Avenue, New York, New York   10016
www.oup.com

Oxford is a registered trademark of Oxford University Press

Library of Congress Cataloging-in-Publication Data

Pious, Richard M.
Presidency of the United States : a student companion / Richard M. Pious.—2nd ed.
p.cm. — (Oxford student companions to American government)
Rev. ed. of: The young Oxford companion to the Presidency of the United States. c1994.
Includes bibliographical references and index.
ISBN 0-19-515006-6
1. Presidents—United States—Encyclopedias, Juvenile. 2. Vice-Presidents—United States—
Encyclopedias, Juvenile. I. Pious, Richard M., 1994– Young Oxford companion to the
presidency of the United States. II. Title. III. Series.

E176.1.P64 2001
973'.09'9--dc21   2001036136

9 8 7 6 5 4 3 2 1

Printed in the United States of America
on acid-free paper.

On the cover: *(top left) A campaign banner for Theodore Roosevelt;
(top right) President John F. Kennedy; (bottom)* President's House,
an 1848 lithograph based on a watercolor by Augustus Kollner.

Frontispiece: *George Washington takes the oath of office at
Federal Hall in New York City in 1789.*

CONTENTS

PREFACE
TO THE SECOND EDITION

When the first edition of this *Companion* was published, the Office of President was occupied by Bill Clinton. He reshaped the institution to fit his own style, and he expanded Presidential powers. In particular, Clinton extended the war powers and diplomatic powers of the Presidency, with an invasion of Haiti that removed a repressive regime, a successful mediation attempt to end religious conflict in Northern Ireland, leadership of NATO in curtailing Serbian atrocities in Kosovo, and an unsuccessful effort to end the conflict between Israel and the Palestinians. During Clinton's second term, however, his Presidency was compromised by a constitutional crisis brought on by his sexual escapades in the Oval Office. His impeachment by the House of Representatives marked only the second time a sitting President has been called to account in this manner.

The election of 2000 very nearly involved a constitutional crisis of great magnitude. For weeks, while the Florida election results were in doubt, federal and state courts had to consider how and if to intervene. The Florida Supreme Court ordered state judges to conduct recounts of the ballots, but the court's order was overturned by the United States Supreme Court. The Court backed the decision of the Secretary of State in Florida, Kathleen Harris, to certify the original election results, which gave the state's electoral votes to George W. Bush. If, however, a recount had given the popular vote—and the electoral vote—to Al Gore Jr., and if the Republican-controlled state legislature had contradicted that result, then the issue would have been settled by a Republican Congress. Had that occurred, the principle of popular choice for Presidential electors would have been overturned by the state legislature and Congress,

with incalculable damage to the people's regard for the Presidency.

What is clear, once again, is that the fundamental basis for Presidential governance in our country does not rest either on majority vote or majority support of public opinion, nor does it rest on maintaining majorities in Congress. The Presidency is a constitutional office, and its power consists of effective interpretation and use of the Constitution. That has always been its irreducible core, and so it remains today.

This second edition of *The Presidency of the United States: A Student Companion* has been updated completely to reflect the changes that have occurred in and around the Oval Office since 1993.

• New articles have been added for George W. Bush and Richard Cheney.

• Articles on Bill Clinton and Al Gore are fully updated, including Clinton's impeachment and the 2000 election.

• Other new articles include three important overviews of African Americans, Women, and Hispanic Americans in the Executive Branch, Third parties in American politics, Presidential perks, and more.

• Dozens of articles such as Executive privilege, Electoral college, Impeachment, Censure, and Secretary of State have been lengthened to reflect important events of recent years.

• An expanded Further Reading section, fully updated appendixes, and new Web sites for Presidential Historic Sites and Libraries will make research accurate and easy.

The Presidency has been a constitutional office for more than 200 years, but in spite of its constancy it is always changing. This *Companion*'s second edition offers you the very latest developments.

HOW TO USE THIS BOOK

The articles in this *Companion* are arranged alphabetically, so you can look up words, concepts, or names as you come across them in other readings. You can then use the SEE ALSO listings at the end of an article to read about related subjects. In some cases, you may find that the *Companion* deals with information under a different article name than what you looked up. In these cases, the book will refer you immediately to the proper article. For example, if you look up Executive Protective Service, you will find the notation "SEE Secret Service, U.S." If you cannot find a separate article on a particular subject, look in the index, which will guide you to the relevant articles. All people are listed alphabetically by last name; for example, the entry for John Adams is listed as Adams, John, under *A*.

You can also use this *Companion* topically, by reading all the articles that deal with a particular aspect of the Presidency. Below is a grouping of topics and the suggested order in which articles can be read.

Biographies: There are articles on all the Presidents and Vice Presidents of the United States and selected First Ladies. The biographical dates used throughout this book are generally accepted by scholars; readers may find that some dates vary in "standard sources." You can find statistical information about the Presidents and Vice Presidents in chronological order by consulting the table in Appendix 2.

Powers: If you want to know about the constitutional powers of the President, you can read articles such as Appointment power, Commander in chief, Creation of the Presidency, and Veto power. Articles on checking and balancing Presidential power include the following: Censure, resolutions of; Checks and balances; Ethics, Presidential; Impeachment; and War Powers Resolution (WPR).

Election and succession: A number of articles deal with Presidential nominations and elections, including Congressional caucus; Debates, Presidential; and Ticket, for example.

Regarding succession, see such articles as Assassinations, Presidential; Disability, Presidential; Inauguration, Presidential; Transitions, Presidential; and 25th Amendment. Appendix 1 contains a table of election results for all Presidential elections.

Presidential advisers: If you want to know about the staff agencies, advisers, and executive departments that help the President perform his functions, you can look up Brains Trust; Cabinet; and White House Office, for example. You can also look up the names of individual offices, such as Attorney general of the United States.

Decisions: To read about Presidential decision making, see such articles as Cuban Missile Crisis; Decision making, Presidential; Gulf of Tonkin Resolution; and Monroe Doctrine.

Policies: The major domestic programs of 20th-century Presidents are described in the following articles: Fair Deal; Great Society; New Deal; New Freedom; New Frontier; and Square Deal.

Perks of office: How do Presidents live, how much are they paid, and what are their fringe benefits? These questions are answered in the following articles: Air Force One; Camp David; Children of Presidents; Ex-Presidency; "Hail to the Chief"; Salary, Presidential; Secret Service, U.S.; and White House.

Theories about the Presidency: Four articles explore theories about Presidential power developed by historians, constitutional scholars, and political scientists: Hidden-hand Presidency; Imperial Presidency; Modern Presidency; and Postmodern Presidency.

Further Reading: If you want to know more about any of the topics presented in this *Companion*, you can use the FURTHER READING entries at the end of each article, which include citations of scholarly books and articles written by academic specialists. There is also a Further Reading guide at the end of the book, which lists more general sources and some more accessible to younger readers.

THE PRESIDENCY OF THE UNITED STATES
A Student Companion

Adams, Abigail
FIRST LADY

☆ *Born: Nov. 11, 1744, Weymouth, Mass.*
☆ *Wife of John Adams, 2nd President*
☆ *Died: Oct. 28, 1818, Braintree, Mass.*

WIFE OF John Adams, second President of the United States, mother of John Quincy Adams, sixth President, and an early champion of women's rights, Abigail Adams spent much of her life in towns on the outskirts of Boston. She had no formal schooling and her spelling was poor, but she was widely read and learned to read and write French. In October 1764 she married John Adams, a young law student. She strongly supported his criticisms of British colonial policies. During the first 10 years of their marriage they had four children. Then revolutionary politics separated the couple for most of the next decade. During the Revolution, Abigail Adams ran the family farm and several business enterprises. In 1784 she rejoined her husband in France, then in 1785 traveled with him to London, where he was the American minister to Great Britain.

Abigail wrote numerous letters to her husband, relatives, and friends, among them leaders of the Revolution such as Thomas Jefferson. Her letter writing was not only a form of communication but also a form of expression through which she could develop her ideas and influence the leaders of the new American nation.

Among those things she wrote was an eloquent statement on women's equality. "I desire you would Remember the ladies," she wrote to her husband in 1776 while he was attending the Continental Congress in Philadelphia, "and be more generous and favourable to them than your ancestors." She added that "if

perticuliar [sic] care and attention is not paid to the Laidies [sic] we are determined to foment a Rebellion, and will not hold ourselves bound by any Laws in which we have no voice, or Representation." But her plea was unavailing: at the end of the Revolution women had fewer rights in law and politics than they had been given by colonial governments.

In November 1800, in the last year of her husband's Presidency, Abigail Adams became the first Presidential wife to occupy the White House in Washington, D.C. More than two decades after her death, in 1840, her grandson Charles Francis Adams began publishing her letters, which became an inspiration to many women seeking greater equality.

FURTHER READING

Butterfield, L. H., et al., eds. *The Book of Abigail and John: Selected Letters of the Adams Family 1762–1784.* Cambridge: Harvard University Press, 1975.
Levin, Phyllis Lee. *Abigail Adams: A Biography.* New York: St. Martin's, 1987.
Nagel, Paul C. *The Adams Women: Abigail and Louisa Adams, Their Sisters and Daughters.* New York: Oxford, 1989.
Withey, Lynne. *Dearest Friend: A Life of Abigail Adams.* New York: Free Press, 1981.
Woloch, Nancy. "Abigail Adams." In *The Reader's Companion to American History,* edited by Eric Foner and John Garraty. Boston: Houghton Mifflin, 1991.

Adams, John
2ND PRESIDENT

☆ *Born: Oct. 19, 1735, Braintree, Mass.*
☆ *Political party: Federalist*
☆ *Education: Harvard College, A.B., 1755*
☆ *Military service: none*
☆ *Previous government service: Continental Congress, 1774–78; committee that drafted Declaration of Independence, 1776; wrote first draft of Massachusetts Constitution, 1779; minister to the Netherlands, 1780–84; minister to Great Britain, 1785–87; Vice President, 1789–97*
☆ *Elected President, 1796; served, 1797–1801*
☆ *Died: July 4, 1826, Quincy, Mass.*

JOHN ADAMS was the first President to occupy the White House and the first to be defeated for reelection and turn over his office to a member of an opposition party. Adams was one of the most experienced men ever to become President. As a young man, he taught school in Worcester, Massachusetts, and studied law, becoming a lawyer in Boston in 1758. He played a major role in the struggle for independence. On the principle that there should be "no taxation without representation," Adams led the opposition to the Stamp Act of 1765, which required the purchase of a stamp (effectively a tax) for all public documents. He showed his fierce independence, however, when he defended several British soldiers accused of killing four people in the Boston Massacre in 1770; most were acquitted.

As a member of the Second Continental Congress in 1775, Adams seconded the nomination of George Washington as commander of the Continental Army. The following year he seconded the motion for independence, introduced by Richard Henry Lee, that "these colonies are, and of a right ought to be, free and independent states." He then convinced Thomas Jefferson to draft the Declaration of Independence. He was, as Jefferson said, "the pillar of support" in the debate leading to its adoption.

Adams helped draft the Massachusetts Constitution of 1780. In 1781 and 1782 he helped negotiate the treaty with the British ending the war and then a commercial treaty with the Netherlands and a large loan to the United States.

In 1785 Adams was named minister to Great Britain. Two years later, while still in London, he published his book *A Defence of the Constitutions of Government of the United States of America,* which called for a balanced constitution. The people would be represented in the lower house of the legislature, "the rich, well born and able" would serve in the upper house, and a chief executive would act as a monarch to balance the interests of the upper and lower classes.

Adams received the second highest total of electoral college votes (behind George Washington) in the Presidential election of 1789, and so he assumed the post of Vice President. "My country has in its wisdom contrived for me the most insignificant office that ever the invention of man contrived or his imagination conceived," Adams observed. But he was instrumental in devising procedures for the new Senate, and he cast several important tie votes to pass Washington's legislative measures. He was one of the organizers of the Federalist party during his second term and was the choice of President Washington and most party leaders to run for President in 1796. He defeated Thomas Jefferson, 71 electoral votes to 68. Under the rules then in effect, Jefferson, as the runner-up, became Vice President, although he was the leader of the opposition party, the Democratic-Republicans.

During his Presidency, Adams faced intrigues within his own party as Alexander Hamilton moved to influence his cabinet and his policies. The Jay Treaty, which Adams had helped negotiate with Great Britain in 1795, allowed British ships to seize American cargoes bound for France. The French, in retaliation, decreed that French warships would follow the same policy against American ships bound for Britain, and they then seized 317 American merchant vessels in 1796. A diplomatic mission sent by Adams was refused a hearing by the French unless bribes were paid to French agents (who were referred to as X, Y, and Z) and the United States agreed to lend France $10 million. Adams refused and made the affair public. "Millions for War but not one cent for Tribute" became the slogan of Federalists calling for war.

Adams ignored pressure from Alexander Hamilton and his followers in the Federalist party and instead sought a diplomatic solution, while Congress passed laws enlarging the navy and preparing war measures. Bowing to party pressure, Adams appointed George Washington commander in chief of the army, in effect ceding his constitutional powers. Congress created the Navy Department, organized the Marine Corps, and canceled all treaties with France. Three new frigates, the *United States*, the *Constitution*, and the *Constellation*, were launched in 1797 and 1798 and soon put to service in a naval war with France. They were responsible for a number of American victories in the Caribbean. Although Congress had not declared this war, it did vote funds for it, and the Supreme Court held that the war was constitutional. With French emperor Napoleon's navy bottled up by the British fleet, and many French ships sunk by Admiral Horatio Nelson in the Battle of the Nile in 1798, France could not easily retaliate. Finally a diplomatic solution in 1799 averted further war. The decision to talk rather than continue fighting led to a final split between Adams and the Hamilton wing of the Federalist party. In 1800 Napoleon and Adams agreed to the Treaty of Montfortaine, which released the United States from its revolutionary war treaties with France.

During the conflict Adams assented to the passage of the Alien and Sedition Acts (1798), which made it a crime to publish anything "with the intent to defame" the President or the government. The sedition law was invoked in 25 cases and used by his party to arrest editors from the opposition ranks. Ten editors were convicted by Federalist judges and juries. But public opinion opposed the prosecutions. Madison and Jefferson worked to get the Virginia and Kentucky legislatures to pass resolutions that the laws were unconstitutional and would not be enforced.

Although Adams retained enough support from moderate Federalists to win his party's nomination for a second term, the split in his party led to his defeat by Thomas Jefferson in the election of 1800. Adams's final act in office, on the morning of March 4, 1801, was to send to the Senate his nomination of John Marshall to be chief justice of the United States.

SEE ALSO

Burr, Aaron; Jefferson, Thomas; Washington, George

FURTHER READING

Adams, James Truslow. *The Adams Family.* Boston: Little, Brown, 1930.
Brown, Ralph Adams. *The Presidency of John Adams.* Lawrence: University Press of Kansas, 1975.
Ellis, Joseph J. *Passionate Sage: The Character and Legacy of John Adams.* New York: Norton, 1993.

Adams, John Quincy
6TH PRESIDENT

☆ *Born: July 11, 1767, Braintree, Mass.*
☆ *Political party: Federalist, Democratic-Republican, Whig*
☆ *Education: Harvard College, A.B., 1787*
☆ *Military service: none*
☆ *Previous government service: minister to the Netherlands, 1794; minister to Prussia, 1797; Massachusetts Senate, 1802; U.S. Senate, 1803–8; minister to Russia, 1809–14; negotiator of Treaty of Ghent, 1814; minister to Great Britain, 1815–17; U.S. secretary of state, 1817–25*
☆ *Elected President, 1824; served, 1825–29*
☆ *Subsequent government service: U.S. House of Representatives, 1830–48*
☆ *Died: Feb. 23, 1848, Washington, D.C.*

JOHN QUINCY ADAMS spent much of his youth accompanying his father,

John Quincy Adams

John Adams, on diplomatic missions. He was educated in Amsterdam, Leipzig, London, Leiden, and Paris. In 1781, at the age of 14, he served as private secretary to Francis Dana, the American envoy to Russia. The following year he served as secretary to the American emissaries negotiating peace with Great Britain. After graduating from Harvard in 1787 and becoming a lawyer, he served as the American envoy to the Netherlands in 1794, and Washington wrote to Vice President Adams that his son "is the most valuable public character we have abroad." In 1797 he served as minister to Prussia during his father's Presidency and negotiated a commercial treaty with Prussia.

Adams returned home shortly after his father left the White House in 1801 and served in the U.S. Senate. He supported Jefferson's purchase of Louisiana and voted for Jefferson's Embargo Act of 1807. Both of these acts alienated the Federalists in Massachusetts and induced Adams to resign from the Senate a year early. He then joined the Democratic-Republicans and, after teaching at Harvard for two years, accepted the position of minister to Russia. He declined James Madison's offer of a Supreme Court appointment in 1810. He was one of three American commissioners who negotiated an end to the War of 1812 on terms favorable to America by negotiating the Treaty of Ghent (1814) with Great Britain.

Adams capped his career as a diplomat with eight years of service as James Monroe's secretary of state. He performed brilliantly, negotiating a treaty with Great Britain in 1818 to extend the U.S.–Canadian border along the 49th parallel; arranging future arbitration of the disputed Oregon boundary; and obtaining Florida from Spain in return for a renunciation of U.S. claims on Texas. His policy of benevolent neutrality, a "tilt" to the former colonies and away from Spanish efforts to reconquer them, assured the success of Latin American independence movements without leading to war with Spain. The Monroe Doctrine, which warned European states

Figures from Roman mythology represent the "Triumph of America" in this engraving celebrating the Treaty of Ghent, which ended the War of 1812. John Quincy Adams, as one of the commissioners appointed to negotiate the treaty, helped secure favorable American terms.

against interference in the Western Hemisphere, was largely Adams's work: President Monroe was willing to accept a joint declaration with the British to warn the French, Spanish, and Russians against attempts to dominate the Americas, but Adams insisted that the United States issue the doctrine unilaterally. Adams is considered by many to be the greatest secretary of state in American history.

Meanwhile, the Federalist party had disappeared, and in the misnamed Era of Good Feelings, as Monroe's Presidency was known, only the "National Republicans" under President Monroe remained. In the Presidential election of 1824, Adams was one of four regional candidates from this party. Andrew Jackson received a plurality of the popular vote (he got the most votes, but fewer than 50 percent), defeating Adams 153,000 to 114,000 in states where electors were chosen by popular vote. Jackson's 99 electoral college votes put him ahead of Adams's 84, Senator William Crawford's 41, and Representative Henry Clay's 37.

Because no one had received a majority of the electoral college votes, the election went to the House of Representatives, where each state would have one vote. Crawford had meanwhile suffered a stroke and was not in serious contention. Clay, who had come in fourth, was ineligible in the House election according to the 12th Amendment. But Clay was Speaker of the House and threw his influential support to Adams, who received a winning 13 votes to only 7 for Jackson and 4 for Crawford on the first ballot. Jackson's followers claimed there had been a "corrupt bargain." It is believable that a bargain had been involved—because Adams named Clay his secretary of state only three days after the election.

Adams's Presidency was tainted by the questions surrounding his election and the violent opposition of the Jacksonians. He had no personal following among the people or in Congress and accomplished little. He backed Clay's "American system," which called for protective tariffs that would raise the prices of foreign goods to encourage U.S. industry, land sales to encourage settlement of the West, and enlargement of foreign markets for American agricultural products. Adams also proposed the creation of a national university and naval academy, new scientific missions to explore American coastal waters and lands, and expeditions to the South Seas. His proposals were scornfully ignored in Congress. Adams, Clay, and Secretary of the Treasury Richard Rush did manage to get Congress to pass measures subsidizing canals, harbors, and roads. Adams was more successful in foreign affairs. Together with Secretary of State Clay, he negotiated commercial treaties that improved trade with a number of European nations and with Mexico.

The midterm elections of 1826 gave a large majority in Congress to anti-Adams factions. Meanwhile, Andrew Jackson organized his followers and in 1828, running under the label Democrat or Democratic-Republican, defeated Adams, who ran on the ticket of the National Republicans.

Adams was elected to the U.S. House of Representatives in 1830 and served there for 18 years. He was a tireless opponent of slavery and offered a plan for its gradual elimination. In 1841 he argued a case, *United States* v. *Amistad,* before the Supreme Court that resulted in overturning the convictions of the African crew members who had mutinied aboard the slave ship *Amistad.* He died in 1848 of a stroke, shortly after making an impassioned speech in the House against extending slavery to the Western territories won in the Mexican-American War.

SEE ALSO

Jackson, Andrew; Monroe Doctrine; Monroe, James

FURTHER READING

Adams, James Truslow. *The Adams Family.* Boston: Little, Brown, 1930.
Hargreaves, Mary. *The Presidency of John Quincy Adams.* Lawrence: University Press of Kansas, 1985.
Richards, Leonard. *The Life and Times of Congressman John Quincy Adams.* New York: Oxford, 1988.

Advice and consent, Senatorial

S E E Appointment power; Checks and balances

African Americans in the executive branch

DESPITE THE ABOLITION of slavery in 1865 and the extension of the vote in 1870, African Americans remained largely outsiders in American democracy. Post–Civil War Reconstructionist politics was full of fierce dispute over the role blacks should have in the political system: many Republicans worked to empower African Americans politically while reactionary Democrats sought to rebuild the antebellum South. Presidents began appointing African Americans to positions within the executive branch during the late 19th century. Former U.S. senator Blanche K. Bruce served as registrar of the Treasury, and the abolitionist Frederick Douglass was appointed U.S. minister to Haiti. Republican Presidents also appointed southern blacks as postmasters and to other federal patronage positions.

John Mercer Langston was elected clerk of a town in rural Ohio in 1855, making him the first black elected to public office. In organizing black political clubs around the country and helping to shape the post–Civil War Republican party's progressive relationship toward blacks, Langston had an important role in mobilizing African Americans. He was twice suggested as a candidate for Republican Vice President.

African Americans shifted political allegiance to the Democratic party during the Great Depression and New Deal in the 1930s. Under President Franklin D. Roosevelt, high-level African-American appointees in several agencies met regularly in what was popularly known as the Black Cabinet to discuss racial policy. Mary McLeod Bethune was the founder of the National Council of Negro Women in 1935, and Roosevelt appointed her director of the Division of Negro Affairs of the National Youth Administration in 1936, a position she held until 1944. Along with the rest of the Black Cabinet, Bethune forced politicians to see African Americans as a significant population of voters who deserved representation.

Another member of the Black Cabinet, Robert Weaver, became the first African American appointed to the Presidential cabinet, when Lyndon Johnson named him as secretary of housing and urban affairs in 1966.

The first African American to run for President was Jesse Jackson. Although he lost the Democratic party nomination in 1984 and 1988, his campaigns proved that a black candidate could command a large audience and reflect a broad range of political interests. In 1984 Jackson garnered 21 percent of the popular vote in the primaries, and in 1988 his campaign registered more than 2 million new voters.

Jackson also opened the door for future black Presidential hopefuls. In 1996 Colin Powell, the first African

American to serve as chairman of the Joint Chiefs of Staff (1989–93), made a Presidential bid but ultimately decided not to run. Alan Keyes, a former member of Ronald Reagan's administration and a U.S. ambassador to the United Nations Social and Economic Council, also made two bids for the Republican nomination, in 1996 and 2000.

Spiro Agnew (right) with Richard Nixon in December 1968, after winning the election.

Agnew, Spiro T.
VICE PRESIDENT

☆ *Born: Nov. 9, 1918, Baltimore, Md.*
☆ *Political party: Republican*
☆ *Education: Johns Hopkins University, 1937–40; Baltimore Law School, LL.B., 1947*
☆ *Military service: U.S. Army, 1943–45; Bronze Star*
☆ *Previous government service: county executive, Baltimore County, 1962–66; governor of Maryland, 1966–68*
☆ *Vice President under Richard Nixon, 1969–73*
☆ *Died: Sep. 17, 1996, Berlin, Md.*

SPIRO AGNEW played no substantive role in the policies of the Nixon administration, but he was its spokesman, launching strident attacks against Nixon's political enemies. A speech he gave in Des Moines, Iowa, in 1969 attacked the "instant analysis" that news commentators offered after Presidential addresses. In a 1970 speech in San Diego he characterized opponents of the administration as "nattering nabobs of negativism." Agnew's favorite target was what he referred to as the "Eastern establishment." He called this group "effete snobs" and "limousine liberals," claiming they had lost touch with the interests of working Americans, whom he and Nixon referred to as the "New American Majority." Agnew campaigned in 1972 against the "permissiveness"

of American society, a social issue that drove millions of Democrats to desert their liberal nominee, George McGovern, and give the Republican ticket one of the largest landslides in American history.

In 1973 Agnew was prosecuted for taking bribes from Baltimore land developer Lester Matz between 1962 and 1971 and failing to report the income on his federal tax returns. On October 9, 1973, he pleaded no contest; he was declared guilty and fined $10,000. Agnew was spared a jail sentence as part of a plea bargain with the prosecutors in which he resigned his office. He later became a public relations representative and lobbyist and then retired to California. In 1981 a civil suit brought by taxpayers in Maryland led to a judgment against Agnew that required him to pay the state of Maryland $248,735 in compensation for the bribes he had taken when he was governor and Vice President.

SEE ALSO

Ford, Gerald R.; Nixon, Richard M.; Vice President

FURTHER READING

Agnew, Spiro T. *Go Quietly... Or Else.* New York: Morrow, 1980.
Cohen, Richard M., and Jules Witcover. *A Heartbeat Away: The Investigation and Resignation of Spiro T. Agnew.* New York: Viking, 1974.
Witcover, Jules. *White Knight: The Rise of Spiro Agnew.* New York: Random House, 1972.

Air Force One

AIR FORCE ONE is the designation of the plane on which the President flies. Since 1989 the President has usually flown on one of two Boeing 747s, each able to carry 80 passengers and 23 crew members to any point on the globe. Each plane is outfitted as a mobile command center and is linked to all U.S. military and national security communications networks.

The planes are coated in silver and have blue trim, and they carry the Presidential seal on their sides. They are operated by the Special Missions Fleet of the 89th Military Airlift Wing at Andrews Air Force Base. Expenses for *Air Force One* come out of the Defense Department budget, unless the President is on a campaign trip, in which case the political party's national committee or campaign committee foots the bill.

Marine One is the designation of the VH-3 helicopter that transports the President from the helipad on the South Lawn of the White House to local destinations or to the hangar at Andrews Air Force Base in Maryland where he boards *Air Force One*. Marine Helicopter Squadron One usually consists of eight craft, located at a base just down the Potomac River from the White House. *Marine One* is often used to take the President and his guests to his rural retreat at Camp David in nearby Maryland.

The cost of operating *Air Force One* is $40,243 per hour of flight. Each year the Pentagon spends approximately $185 million on travel expenses for the President and his top aides, according to the House Post Office Committee's Subcommittee on Human Resources.

FURTHER READING

Patterson, Bradley. *The Ring of Power.* New York: Basic Books, 1988.
TerHorst, Jerold F. *The Flying White House: The Story of Air Force One.* New York: Coward, McCann & Geoghegan, 1979.

Jimmy Carter boards Air Force One *for a peace mission to Egypt and Israel in 1979.*

Amnesty, Presidential

THE CONSTITUTION (Article 2, Section 2) gives the President the power "to grant reprieves and pardons for offences against the United States except in cases of impeachment." This power is exercised by Presidential proclamation.

In 1795 President George Washington issued an amnesty to all participants in the Whiskey Rebellion, which involved a protest by farmers in Pennsylvania against paying federal taxes. President Abraham Lincoln's proclamation of December 8, 1863, offered a full pardon to Confederates (rebels), on condition that they take an oath to support the Constitution, laws, decisions of the Supreme Court, and proclamations of the President of the United States. On May 29, 1865, President Andrew Johnson issued a proclamation excluding certain groups of rebel leaders from amnesty but pardoning most other participants in secessionist activities. Decrees of July 4,

1868, and December 25, 1868, provided for full pardons for all who had participated in "the rebellion." This action led to the return from exile in England of several members of Confederate President Jefferson Davis's wartime cabinet. All told, more than 200,000 people were covered by these Civil War amnesties.

In 1946 President Harry S. Truman issued an amnesty covering 1,500 draft resisters in World War II. Six years later he granted amnesty to 9,000 individuals who had deserted from the military during the Korean War. The power of amnesty was also used by Presidents Gerald Ford and Jimmy Carter for more than 10,000 individuals who had resisted the draft during the Vietnam War.

SEE ALSO

Carter, Jimmy; Ford, Gerald R.; Johnson, Andrew; Lincoln, Abraham; Pardon power; Washington, George

FURTHER READING

Adler, David Gray. "The President's Pardon Powers." In *Inventing the American Presidency*, edited by Thomas E. Cronin. Lawrence: University Press of Kansas, 1989.

Appointment power

THE CONSTITUTION (Article 2, Section 2) gives the President the power to nominate and, with the advice and consent of the Senate, appoint officers of the United States. The Constitution also provides that Congress by law may vest the appointment of "inferior Officers" in the President alone, in the courts of law, or in the heads of departments. Presidents also appoint and promote all military officers subject to Senate consent.

The President appoints (with Senate consent) 1,000 top officials, who bear titles such as secretary, under secretary, deputy secretary, and assistant secretary of the departments. These officials collectively are the President's "administration." The other million or so federal civilian employees are considered "inferior officers," and almost all of them are appointed by heads of departments under civil service regulations.

To preserve the principle of separation of powers—the balance among the executive, legislative, and judicial branches—no member of Congress can be an officer of the United States while he or she serves in the Congress. Legislators are often appointed to a President's administration after leaving Congress, however.

Presidents since John Adams have chosen mostly members of their own political party for executive office, though Congress by law can require that appointments to regulatory commissions be evenly divided between Democrats and Republicans. Some Presidents, such as John F. Kennedy, chose several members of the opposition party for key positions in order to gain public and congressional support. Customarily, the Senate allows the President to pick whomever he wants for his administration, even if the Senate is controlled by the opposition party. The Senate usually does not consider the politics of nominees but restricts itself to their character. The Senate cannot attach formal conditions to its consent. It does not tell nominees what they must do once in office.

Prior to the 1950s only seven cabinet nominations were turned down. More recently, Dwight Eisenhower's nomination of Lewis Strauss for secretary of commerce in 1959 and George Bush's nomination of John Tower for secretary of defense in 1989 were defeated. Some nominees will withdraw before a Senate vote if the President senses they will be defeated; President Jimmy Carter withdrew the nomination of Theodore Sorensen for the position of director of

Janet Reno, the first woman attorney general, was appointed by President Clinton in 1993.

This 1966 cartoon shows Lyndon Johnson making appointments in a game of "White House Solitaire."

Central Intelligence in 1977, and President Clinton withdrew his first two nominees for attorney general, Zoë Baird and Kimba Wood, because of Senate opposition in 1993. In 1962 Congress refused to create the Department of Urban Affairs because President Kennedy made it known that he intended to appoint Robert Weaver to head it—and he would have been the first African American in the cabinet. By 1967 President Lyndon B. Johnson won congressional approval for the department and then for Weaver's appointment.

Presidents also nominate justices of the U.S. Supreme Court and judges of the lower federal courts. In each term a President appoints, on average, two Supreme Court justices. On at least 60 occasions sitting justices have offered suggestions for filling vacancies, and senators often provide advice. Of the 148 nominations through 2001, 119 were approved, 11 rejected, and 17 withdrawn. When a President's party controls the Senate, more than 90 percent of his Supreme Court nominations are typically approved; when the opposition controls the Senate, the approval rate for justices drops to 50 percent.

Presidents often place their appointment powers at the disposal of important members of Congress. Senators often

provide names of people from their state to the President for nomination as federal district judges as well as for positions in federal government regional offices located within their state; the President then makes the formal nomination. Moreover, the practice of "senatorial courtesy" enables the senator of a state affected by a Presidential nomination to declare that the nominee is "personally obnoxious"—in which case the Senate will take no action on a Presidential nomination. The Senator must be of the President's party and the Presidential nomination must be to a position in which power is exercised within the senator's home state.

The Constitution authorizes the President to make recess appointments when the Senate is not in session. Such appointments last only until the end of the next session of the Senate and do not require Senate consent. If the head of a department vacates the office, Congress by law has provided that Presidents may make an interim, or temporary, appointment without the consent of the Senate if the Senate had previously consented to the new appointee for another position. The interim appointee may serve for 30 days in the new position without Senate consent.

SEE ALSO
Cabinet

FURTHER READING

Abraham, Henry J. *Justices, Presidents, and Senators: A History of the U.S. Supreme Court Appointments from Washington to Clinton.* Lanham, Md.: Rowman & Littlefield, 1999.
Fisher, Louis. *Constitutional Conflicts between Congress and the President.* Princeton, N.J.: Princeton University Press, 1985.
Harris, Joseph. *The Advice and Consent of the Senate.* Berkeley: University of California Press, 1953.
MacKenzie, G. Calvin. *The Politics of Presidential Appointments.* New York: Free Press, 1981.

Approval rating, Presidential

SEE Public opinion, Presidents, and the media

Arthur, Chester Alan

21ST PRESIDENT

☆ Born: Oct. 5, 1829, Fairfield, Vt. (or Waterville, N.Y.)
☆ Political party: Republican
☆ Education: Union College, B.A., 1848; read law in New York City, 1853
☆ Military service: quartermaster general and brigadier general of New York, 1861–62
☆ Previous government service: collector of the Port of New York, 1871–78; Vice President, 1881
☆ Succeeded to Presidency, 1881; served, 1881–85
☆ Died: Nov. 18, 1886, New York, N.Y.

CHESTER ALAN ARTHUR was a loyal follower of the corrupt Conkling political machine, or organization, in New York State who owed his political positions to connections and party loyalty. Ironically, it was this machine politician who, as President, presided over the creation of the first merit system for the civil service, or government employees.

Arthur was the son of a clergyman. After graduating from Union College he taught school briefly, then studied law. His law practice involved several cases in which he defended fugitive slaves and other African Americans. He obtained a large financial settlement for a black woman named Lizzie Jennings who had been put off a horsecar (a bus pulled by horses) in New York City because of her race. He served in the Civil War as a general of the New York volunteer troops.

Arthur became active in New York State Republican politics in an era of spoils—the awarding of jobs according to political connections—and corruption. He was named collector of the Port of New York by President Ulysses S. Grant, a position in which he dominated patronage in New York on behalf of Senator Roscoe Conkling. He controlled 1,000 jobs, which he gave to party regulars. President Rutherford B. Hayes forced him out as a reform measure.

At the Republican convention of 1880 Arthur was one of the leading Stalwarts supporting Ulysses Grant's third-term bid. After James G. Blaine's Half-Breed wing of the party (so-called because their opponents did not consider them "real" Republicans but quasi-Democrats) helped James Garfield win the nomination, Arthur was put on the ticket to regain the support of the Stalwart faction.

As Vice President, Arthur could cast the deciding vote in the Senate, which was sometimes deadlocked on straight-party votes because there were 37 Democrats opposed by an equal number of Republicans. When President Garfield appointed someone to the post of collector of New York without consulting Arthur, the two men had a parting of the ways.

Although Arthur had always been a political hack, upon succeeding to the Presidency after Garfield's assassination in 1881 he promised that he would avoid the excesses of patronage appointments that had marked his career. He overhauled the cabinet entirely, replacing all but one of Garfield's secretaries with his own. He took action against fraud in the post office. His first message to Congress called for the creation of a civil service system, and over the opposition of his Stalwart colleagues he strongly supported the Pendleton Act of 1883, which created a civil service commission and began the principle of hiring on merit rather than party affiliation. He classified 14,000 federal positions, 10 percent of the total, as subject to the merit system. He vetoed a large rivers and harbors bill that Republicans had passed. He also vetoed the Chinese Exclusion Act of 1882, which would have kept workers from China out of the country for 20 years but then signed the measure when the exclusion was limited to 10 years.

Arthur is considered the father of the "steel navy," replacing the "floating washtubs" of the Civil War with modern, state-of-the-art steam warships. This program would give the United States the fifth largest navy in the world by the turn of the century. His major mistake was in foreign affairs, when he signed a treaty with Nicaragua to build a canal, in violation of an existing U.S. treaty with the British. The Senate refused to act on it, and President Grover Cleveland later withdrew it.

"It would be hard to better President Arthur's administration" was Mark Twain's verdict. But Roscoe Conkling had broken with him over civil service reform and other issues, and Grant devoted his energies to blocking Arthur's bid for an elected term of his own. With the knowledge that he was dying of Bright's disease, Arthur did not put up much resistance to James G. Blaine's attempt to win the Republican nomination in 1884. Arthur returned to New York City to practice law but died soon after leaving office.

SEE ALSO

Garfield, James A.

FURTHER READING

Doenecke, Justin D. *The Presidencies of James A. Garfield and Chester A. Arthur.* Lawrence: University Press of Kansas, 1981.

Howe, George F. *Chester A. Arthur.* New York: Frederick Ungar, 1935.

Articles of Confederation

THE ARTICLES of Confederation was the document that organized a "perpetual Union" among the 13 states that had declared independence from Great Britain. The Articles were in effect between March 1, 1781, and March 4, 1789, when they were superseded by the Constitution of the United States of America.

The Articles of Confederation and Perpetual Union, as they were formally called, made no mention of a President or an executive branch of government. In November 1777 the draft of the Articles that the Continental Congress submitted to the states for ratification specifically rejected a plan for an executive proposed by James Dickinson and the Committee of Thirteen the year before. The Dickinson draft would have provided for a "Council of State" appointed by Congress and for other officers "for managing the general affairs of the United States." The council would have exercised broad powers:

The Spirit of Liberty protects a Chinese laborer from the mob in this cartoon by Thomas Nast. Responding to public demands to limit Chinese immigration, Chester Arthur signed the Chinese Exclusion Act in 1882.

command of the military, administration of finances and diplomacy, and "the Execution of such Measures as may be resolved on by the United States."

The Articles of Confederation provided instead for a "Committee of States" to "execute in the recess of Congress, such of the powers of Congress as the United States, in Congress assembled, shall by the consent of nine states, from time to time, think expedient to vest them with." The committee could not exercise military, diplomatic, or fiscal powers or make any decisions, to which the Articles required the assent of nine states.

Under the Articles, the president of the Continental Congress was simply the presiding officer of the legislature and had no executive functions. The importance of the office can best be understood by the fact that in the absence of the president, a clerk was designated to perform his duties. Presidents served one-year terms, and they were usually men whose talents matched their limited powers.

Until 1789 there was no executive branch of government. Beginning in 1776, ad hoc (a Latin phrase meaning "for the thing," or "temporary") or permanent congressional committees, supplemented by boards of officials operating under their direction, performed administrative duties. The Marine Committee dealt with the navy, the Board of War and Ordnance with the army, and the Committee of Secret Correspondence handled diplomacy. By 1781 several departments were created, among them Foreign Affairs, War, Marine, and Treasury, each with a single head. Neither the president of the Congress nor the Committee of States supervised these officials.

SEE ALSO

Creation of the Presidency; Executive branch

FURTHER READING

Burnett, Edmund C. *The Continental Congress.* New York: Norton, 1941.

Jensen, Merrill. *The Articles of Confederation.* Madison: University of Wisconsin Press, 1940.
Morris, Richard B. *The Forging of the Union, 1781–1789.* New York: Harper & Row, 1987.
Rakove, Jack. *The Beginnings of National Politics: An Interpretive History of the Continental Congress.* New York: Knopf, 1979.
Sanders, Jennings. *Evolution of the Executive Departments of the Continental Congress.* Chapel Hill: University of North Carolina Press, 1935.
Sanders, Jennings. *The Presidency of the Continental Congress.* Gloucester, Mass.: Peter Smith, 1961.

Assassinations, Presidential

PRESIDENTS ABRAHAM Lincoln, James A. Garfield, William McKinley, and John F. Kennedy were assassinated in office, and unsuccessful attempts were made against Presidents Andrew Jackson, Harry S. Truman, Gerald Ford, and Ronald Reagan. Attempts were made against Lincoln and Franklin D. Roosevelt when they were Presidents-elect.

Abraham Lincoln was shot by actor John Wilkes Booth on the night of April 14, 1865, while sitting in the Presidential box at Ford's Theatre. Booth and other conspirators were caught, tried, convicted, and sentenced to death. President Andrew Johnson refused to commute the sentences, and the conspirators were hanged.

James A. Garfield was shot to death at a railroad station in Washington, D.C., by a disappointed office seeker and religious fanatic, Charles Julius Guiteau, on July 2, 1881. William McKinley was

A poster offering rewards for the capture of John Wilkes Booth and his accomplices.

Spectators watch the hanging of the conspirators who arranged the assassination of Abraham Lincoln.

shot to death on September 6, 1901, by Leon Czolgosz, an anarchist, at the Pan-American Exposition in Buffalo, New York. John F. Kennedy was shot to death on November 22, 1963, while on a political trip to Dallas, Texas, by Lee Harvey Oswald. The Warren Commission, which investigated the Kennedy assassination, concluded that the President had been shot by Oswald acting alone, though some people have argued that at least one other gunman was involved.

In response to the Kennedy assassination, Congress enacted a law on August 28, 1965, making it a federal (no longer merely a state) crime to kill, kidnap, or assault the President, Vice President, or President-elect or to threaten these officials with death or bodily harm. The penalty for killing the President is life imprisonment or death. The punishment for an attempt on the President's life is imprisonment for a term up to life. Since passage of the law, attempts on the President's life have fallen under the primary jurisdiction of the Federal Bureau of Investigation and other federal law enforcement officials, not under the jurisdiction of the local police departments in the place where an attempt was made on the President's life.

SEE ALSO

Ford, Gerald R.; Garfield, James A.; Jackson, Andrew; Kennedy, John F.; Lincoln,

Abraham; McKinley, William; Reagan, Ronald; Roosevelt, Franklin D.; Secret Service, U.S.; Truman, Harry S.

FURTHER READING

McKinley, James. *Assassination in America.* New York: Harper & Row, 1977.

Assistants to the President

S E E White House Office

Attorney general of the United States

THE ATTORNEY general is the chief legal adviser to the President and head of the Department of Justice. The attorney general is a member of the President's "inner cabinet" of close advisers, along with the secretaries of defense, state, and Treasury, and is appointed by the President with the advice and consent of the Senate. The attorney general also serves as chief legal adviser to heads of executive branch departments, interpreting at their request the laws of the United States. The attorney general publishes interpretations of the Constitution in volumes known as the *Opinions of the Attorney General.*

The office of attorney general was created by Congress in the Judiciary Act of 1789, and at the request of President George Washington the first attorney general, Edmund Randolph of Virginia, served in the President's cabinet. In 1870 Congress created the Department of Justice and placed the attorney general at its head. Legal officers for the various executive departments were put under the supervision of the Department of Justice, as

John F. Kennedy (right) consults with his brother Robert, whom he appointed attorney general in 1961.

were U.S. attorneys, clerks, and marshals assigned to federal courts. At that time the solicitor general, the third-ranking official in the Department of Justice, was given the duty of arguing government cases before the Supreme Court, a duty that until then had been exercised by the attorney general.

Attorneys general administer the Justice Department to suit Presidential priorities. President John F. Kennedy even appointed his brother Robert, joking that he wanted his brother to get some legal experience as a government lawyer before entering private practice. President Richard Nixon appointed his campaign manager, John Mitchell, and President Ronald Reagan appointed one of his senior White House aides, Edmund Meese. Many attorneys general are appointed after having served in other cabinet or White House positions, or they move to other positions in the inner cabinet after their tour of duty at the Justice Department. Several have been subsequently named to the Supreme Court; the two most influential in modern times were Chief Justice Harlan Fiske Stone and Justice Robert Jackson. Janet Reno, the county prosecutor in Dade County, Florida, appointed by President Bill Clinton in 1993, was the first woman attorney general.

SEE ALSO
Cabinet; Counsel, Office of; Office of Management and Budget

FURTHER READING
Baker, Nancy V. *Conflicting Loyalties: Law and Politics in the Attorney General's Office, 1789–1990.* Lawrence: University Press of Kansas, 1992.

Australian ballot

THE AUSTRALIAN ballot, invented in that country in 1858, is a ballot printed by the government with all candidates for each office listed, to be marked by voters in voting booths. This process permits a secret ballot. By 1892 the Australian ballot had been adopted by all the states.

Prior to the 1880s most states did not have secret balloting for President. Voters would tell election officials whom they favored or put ballots printed by political parties into a ballot box. Both systems made it difficult to preserve confidentiality. Using party ballots also made split-ticket voting (voting for a President of one party and members of the House or Senate from another) impossible. The Australian ballot reduced fraud and increased split-ticket voting, but it also reduced turnout because voters had to be able to read the ballot, which had not been the case with party ballots.

SEE ALSO
Election campaigns, Presidential

FURTHER READING
Hofstadter, Richard. *The Age of Reform: From Bryan to F.D.R.* New York: Vintage, 1955.
McCormick, Richard P. *The Presidential Game: The Origins of American Presidential Politics.* New York: Oxford, 1982.

Barkley, Alben
VICE PRESIDENT

☆ *Born: Nov. 24, 1877, Lowes, Ky.*
☆ *Political party: Democrat*
☆ *Education: Marvin College, B.A., 1897; studied law, Emory College, 1897–98; University of Virginia Law School, 1902*
☆ *Military service: none*
☆ *Other government service: Paducah County, Ky., prosecuting attorney, 1905–8; state judge, Paducah County Court, 1909–11; U.S. House of Representatives, 1913–27; U.S. Senate, 1927–49, 1955–56; Senate majority leader, 1937–46; Senate minority leader, 1947–49*

☆ *Vice President under Harry S. Truman, 1949–53*
☆ *Died: Apr. 30, 1956, Lexington, Va.*

ALBEN BARKLEY was the last of the Vice Presidents who did nothing in office. A major figure in Congress, responsible for pushing New Deal legislation through the Senate in the 1930s, Barkley was also a power broker at Democratic

national conventions, pressing for border-state interests such as appointments and government contracts. He was the keynote speaker at Democratic nominating conventions in 1932, 1936, and 1940. He was mentioned as a potential Vice President in 1940 and 1944, but personality differences with Franklin D. Roosevelt kept him off the ticket. When Harry Truman allowed the convention delegates to select their choice in 1948, Barkley was nominated, though he provided no regional balance on the ticket. Barkley's only duties during his Vice Presidential years involved helping Truman as a liaison with Congress on pending legislation. He spent most of his time courting his second wife. In 1952 Barkley gave some thought to running for President himself. But labor leaders declined to support him on the grounds of age (he was 75), and he decided not to run. Barkley was reelected to the U.S. Senate in 1954 and served until his death.

SEE ALSO
Roosevelt, Franklin D.; Truman, Harry S.

FURTHER READING
Barkley, Alben. *That Reminds Me.* Garden City, N.Y.: Doubleday, 1954.
Davis, Polly. *Alben Barkley: Senate Majority Leader and Vice President.* New York: Garland, 1979.
Libbey, James K. *Dear Alben: Mr. Barkley of Kentucky.* Lexington: University of Kentucky Press, 1979.

Brains Trust

BRAINS TRUST is the informal name for senior government officials who advise the President. A Brains Trust is different from a "kitchen cabinet" of Presidential friends, none of whom hold public office. The original Brains Trust was a group of advisers to New York governor and later President Franklin D. Roosevelt who helped him develop his New Deal program. Members included prominent Columbia University professors such as Adolph A. Berle, Jr., of the law school, Rexford G. Tugwell of the economics department, and Raymond Moley of the department of public law and government. It also included political adviser and speech writer Samuel Rosenman (who first told Roosevelt to recruit the professors) and Frances Perkins, industrial commissioner of New York State when FDR was governor of New York. Roosevelt appointed Perkins to the position of secretary of labor, and she was the first woman to serve in a President's cabinet.

SEE ALSO
Kitchen cabinet; New Deal; New Frontier; Roosevelt, Franklin D.

FURTHER READING
Rosen, Elliot A. *Hoover, Roosevelt and the Brains Trust.* New York: Columbia University Press, 1977.
Tugwell, Rexford G. *The Brains Trust.* New York: Viking, 1967.

Secretary of Labor Frances Perkins, the first woman cabinet member, supported equal wages and legal protection for women workers.

Breckinridge, John C.
VICE PRESIDENT

☆ *Born: Jan. 21, 1821, outside Lexington, Ky.*
☆ *Political party: Democrat*
☆ *Education: Centre College, B.A., 1839; College of New Jersey*

(Princeton), 1839; studied law, Transylvania University, 1840
☆ *Military service: U.S. Army, 1847–48; Confederate Army, 1862–64*
☆ *Previous government service: Kentucky House of Representatives, 1850–51; U.S. House of Representatives, 1851–55*
☆ *Vice President under James Buchanan, 1857–61*
☆ *Subsequent government service: U.S. Senate, 1861; Confederate secretary of war, 1865*
☆ *Died: May 17, 1875, Lexington, Ky.*

JOHN BRECKINRIDGE was a border-state Democrat who tried to preserve the Union. As James Buchanan's Vice President, he presided over the Senate with impartiality. Nominated for President by a group of pro-slavery Democrats in 1860, he carried all the cotton states and the border states of Delaware and Maryland, running third in the popular vote behind Abraham Lincoln and Stephen A. Douglas. He supported the peace convention organized by former President John Tyler in the spring of 1861, hoping it would avert secession. Appointed U.S. senator from Kentucky in 1861, he hoped to forge a compromise that would keep the South in the Union. When Kentucky came under military occupation in the fall of 1861, Breckinridge left the capital and accepted a commission as a major general in the Confederate Army, for which he was expelled from the Senate. Breckinridge distinguished himself in the Virginia campaigns of 1864 and became Confederate secretary of state in February 1865. At the end of the Civil War he fled to Cuba and then went to England. He returned to the United States after President Andrew Johnson proclaimed amnesty, or forgiveness, for important rebel leaders. He practiced law in Lexington, Kentucky, until his death.

SEE ALSO
Amnesty, Presidential; Buchanan, James; Lincoln, Abraham; Tyler, John

FURTHER READING
Davis, William C. *Breckinridge: Statesman, Soldier, Symbol.* Baton Rouge: Louisiana State University Press, 1974.

Buchanan, James
15TH PRESIDENT

☆ *Born: Apr. 23, 1791, Cove Gap (near Mercersburg), Pa.*
☆ *Political party: Democrat*
☆ *Education: Dickinson College, B.A., 1809*
☆ *Military service: volunteer of dragoons, 1812*
☆ *Previous government service: Pennsylvania House of Representatives, 1814–16; U.S. House of Representatives, 1821–31; minister to Russia, 1832–33; U.S. Senate, 1834–45; U.S. secretary of state, 1845–49; minister to Great Britain, 1853–56*
☆ *Elected President, 1856; served, 1857–61*
☆ *Died: June 1, 1868, near Lancaster, Pa.*

JAMES BUCHANAN was a loyal Democrat; as President he did all he could to hold his party together by adopting a conciliatory position on slavery. As a Northerner, he opposed slavery in principle, but he was willing to protect the rights of slaveholders under the Constitution. His inability to see that his first responsibility was to the Union rather than to sectional compromise cost him his office and created the conditions for the Civil War.

James Buchanan was the oldest son of a Scotch-Irish merchant in Mercersburg, Pennsylvania. After graduating first in his class from Dickinson College, he became a successful lawyer. An engagement to Anne Caroline Coleman was broken off by her family, and she committed suicide; Buchanan never married, becoming the country's only bachelor President. After serving during the War of 1812 in the defense of Baltimore, he went into politics, moving from his affiliation as a Federalist in the Pennsyl-

vania legislature in 1814 to the National Republicans in the 1820s as a member of the U.S. House of Representatives. He then switched to the Democrats in 1828. He became a loyal follower of President Andrew Jackson, who rewarded him by making him U.S. minister to Russia, where he negotiated the first commercial treaty between the two nations. Buchanan then served for 11 years in the Senate. He declined President Martin Van Buren's offer to serve as attorney general.

After a long career in Congress, Buchanan was a "favorite son" candidate at the Democratic convention in 1844 but lost the nomination to James K. Polk. He then served as Polk's secretary of state, successfully negotiating the end of a dispute with Great Britain over the Oregon boundary and bringing Texas into the Union. His offer to purchase Cuba was rejected by Spain, however. Buchanan did not get along with Polk, who thought his secretary of state was too ambitious and wished to replace him.

Buchanan was defeated by Lewis Cass for the Democratic nomination for President in 1848. He retired to private life but almost won the nomination in 1852. During Franklin Pierce's Presidency (1853–57) he served as minister to Great Britain. His participation in drafting the Ostend Manifesto, threatening war with Spain if it did not sell Cuba to the United States, made him popular with Southern Democrats.

Buchanan was nominated for President by the Democrats in 1856 as a noncontroversial choice: he had been out of the country during the bruising battles over the Kansas-Nebraska Act. Though his predecessor had been a weak and ineffectual President, the prosperity of the nation made it seem likely to party leaders that they could retain the White House with a candidate who appealed to both sections. Buchanan defeated Republican candidate John C. Frémont and

American party (also known as the Whig and Know-Nothing party) candidate Millard Fillmore, though he did not receive a majority of the popular vote. Buchanan's base of support was the slave states: he won all except Maryland, which voted for Fillmore.

Buchanan became a "doughface" President—a term for a Northerner with Southern leanings. Buchanan's cabinet, like Pierce's, was balanced between North and South but seemed to many people to have a Southern tilt. Bolstered by the Supreme Court decision in *Dred Scott* v. *Sandford* (1857) that African Americans—whether slave or free—were not citizens and had no legal rights that could be protected by federal courts, Buchanan enforced the Fugitive Slave Act and incensed the Northern wing of his party.

In his first year as President, Buchanan dealt with a challenge to federal authority in Utah. The governor, Mormon spiritual leader Brigham Young, refused to obey federal laws and defied federal officials in the state. Buchanan sent in troops, removed Young, and appointed a new governor. Buchanan reported to Congress that "the authority of the Constitution and the laws has been fully restored and peace prevails throughout the territory."

Buchanan's greatest failure involved the sectional split over slavery. His party split over his support for a Southern attempt to bring Kansas into the Union as a slave state, with abolitionists such as Stephen Douglas opposing him. In a referendum, Kansas voters overwhelmingly adopted an antislavery constitution and compelled Buchanan and Congress to admit Kansas into the Union as a free state early in 1861. Minnesota and Oregon also came into the Union as free states. Northern sentiment swung sharply against Buchanan, and many anti-Buchanan Democrats won in the midterm elections of 1858, among them

Stephen Douglas in the Senate contest in Illinois. Buchanan was now fatally weakened, with no following in Congress.

After the election of Abraham Lincoln in November 1860, South Carolina seceded from the Union. Buchanan denounced the secession but did nothing to enforce the laws of the United States, hoping for a peaceful solution. In his message to Congress in December, Buchanan observed that a state had no constitutional right to secede from the Union, but he argued that no state could be compelled to remain. He warned the Northern states that if they did not repeal their laws obstructing the execution of the Fugitive Slave Act, "it is impossible for any human power to save the Union." He defended his inaction against secession by arguing, "The Union rests upon public opinion, and can never be cemented by the blood of its citizens shed in civil war."

Although seven states in the lower South seceded and formed the Confederacy on February 20, 1861, eight other border and Southern slave states remained in the Union, awaiting the results of efforts to compromise. Buchanan's goal was to keep these states from seceding. When he sent a ship, *Star of the West,* to reinforce Fort Sumter, South Carolina, with 200 troops, shore batteries fired on the vessel and forced it to withdraw. Yet Buchanan

did nothing to provoke the remainder of the slave states, lest they leave the Union. To advance Buchanan's notion of a compromise, a peace convention was held in Richmond, Virginia, under the chairmanship of former President John Tyler, but even before his inauguration Abraham Lincoln rebuffed the compromise proposals introduced there.

After leaving office Buchanan supported the Union cause during the Civil War. He died on June 1, 1868, at Wheatland, his Pennsylvania estate.

SEE ALSO

Lincoln, Abraham

FURTHER READING

Klein, Philip Shriver. *President James Buchanan: A Biography.* University Park: Pennsylvania State University Press, 1962.
Smith, Elbert B. *The Presidency of James Buchanan.* Lawrence: University Press of Kansas, 1975.

Budget, Presidential

THE PRESIDENTIAL budget is the request that the President submits to Congress for legal authority to spend federal funds. Fourteen days after the Monday on which Congress convenes each January, the President is required by the Budget and Accounting Act of 1921 to submit to Congress the budget of the U.S. government, along with a message outlining his budget priorities. The budget covers the fiscal, or business, year (from October 1 to September 30) and is named for the calendar year in which it ends. The FY 2000 budget, for example, covers the period from October 1, 1999, through September 30, 2000. (Prior to passage of this law, departments submitted requests for funds directly to Congress, bypassing the President entirely.)

Presidential budget requests are prepared by the Office of Management and

James Buchanan greets Japanese emissaries at a formal White House reception in 1860.

Money for all military equipment and personnel must be approved by Congress. Since the end of the cold war, the defense budget has undergone large cuts.

Budget (OMB), based in part on spending justifications submitted to it by each executive branch department and independent agency of government. The OMB evaluates all agency spending requests according to White House priorities.

The Budget of the United States provides data on past expenditures and current spending authority for each agency, but it is only a set of recommendations to Congress for future spending. The Constitution (Article 1, Section 9) provides that "no Money shall be drawn from the Treasury but in Consequence of Appropriations made by law." This provision gives Congress the final word on spending money. Presidents have at times asserted a power to impound funds, or to refuse to spend money appropriated by Congress.

According to provisions of the Budget and Impoundment Control Act of 1974, the House and Senate Budget Committees set overall spending targets and guidelines in 13 categories (such as defense, natural resources, and the environment) by passing a concurrent budget resolution. (A concurrent resolution is a motion passed simultaneously by both houses of the Congress.) Congressional appropriations committees (and some other standing committees that are permitted by congressional rules to authorize spending) modify each Presidential spending request according to their own priorities. They then convert them into budget authority—permission to withdraw funds from the Treasury—in the form of an appropriation or other law, which they report to each chamber of Congress. These appropriations and other spending bills must be passed in identical form by both chambers of Congress. The Treasury uses these appropriations laws to set limits on the "checking accounts" maintained by each agency. The OMB monitors the spending by each agency to see that it does not exceed the allowable limits.

Since the 1930s the Presidential budget has usually projected a deficit, or an excess of expenditures over revenue. In 1986 Congress passed the Gramm-Rudman-Hollings Act, which required the President to pare the projected deficits in his budget from $180 billion to zero by fiscal year 1991 or face mandatory "sequesters" (or holdbacks by the OMB) of funds to meet the targets. In 1988, the zero-deficit deadline was pushed back to fiscal year 1993.

In 1990, with a projected deficit of $318 billion, there was no way to make the sequesters required by the law without making deep cuts in the defense budget and in social welfare programs. Instead, President George Bush and congressional leaders agreed at a "budget summit" meeting held at Andrews Air Force Base in October 1990 to scrap the Gramm-Rudman-Hollings deficit targets. They decided instead to try to limit overall spending, with the assumption that within a few years increases in revenues would produce a balanced budget.

To implement their agreement, Congress passed the Budget Enforcement Act of 1990, which provided for caps on government spending. The law provided that any tax cuts in the President's budget would have to be accompanied by an equal amount of spending reductions. Similarly, any spending increases would have to be offset by equivalent tax increases. In 1995, a Republican-dominated Congress failed to pass a balanced-budget amendment to the Constitution or a measure allowing the President to veto individual items in appropriations bills.

SEE ALSO

Impoundment; Office of Management and Budget

FURTHER READING

Carroll, Richard J. *An Economic Record of Presidential Performance: From Truman to Bush.* Westport, Conn.: Praeger, 1995.

Savage, James D. *Balanced Budgets & American Politics.* Ithaca, N.Y.: Cornell University Press, 1988.

Wildavsky, Aaron. *The Politics of the Budgetary Process.* 5th ed. Boston: Little, Brown, 1992.

Bureau of the Budget

S E E Office of Management and Budget

Burr, Aaron

VICE PRESIDENT

☆ *Born: Feb. 6, 1756, Newark, N.J.*
☆ *Political party: Democratic-Republican*
☆ *Education: College of New Jersey (Princeton), B.A., 1772; read law with Tapping Reeve, Litchfield, Conn., 1783*
☆ *Military service: Continental Army, 1776–79*
☆ *Previous government service: attorney general of New York State, 1789–91; U.S. Senate, 1791–97; New York State Assembly, 1797–98*
☆ *Vice President under Thomas Jefferson, 1801–5*
☆ *Died: Sept. 14, 1836, Port Richmond, Staten Island, N.Y.*

AARON BURR practiced law in New York City before entering government service. Elected to the U.S. Senate in 1790, he was defeated for reelection in 1796, then served two terms in the New York State Assembly from 1797 to 1798. He was a founder of the Society of St. Tammany, a political club that won control of the state legislature in 1800. The Republican majority in the legislature delivered New York State's electoral college vote to Thomas Jefferson in 1800 (in those days Presidential electors in New York and some other states were chosen not by the voters, but by the state legislators), and Burr was himself elected Vice President.

Aaron Burr was at the center of two of the most unusual episodes in American political life. One involved the Presidential election of 1800. At that time, electors in the electoral college cast two ballots for President. Jefferson and Burr ran on the same ticket, and so each received the same number of votes in the electoral college. Even though it had been clearly understood by members of their party that Jefferson was running for President and Burr was running for Vice President, the tie vote meant that the election would have to be settled by the House of Representatives, with each state having one vote. Burr then conspired with the opposition Federalists, who controlled a number of state delegations, in an effort to block Jefferson and win the Presidency for himself.

Fortunately for Jefferson, one of his political enemies, Alexander Hamilton, hated Aaron Burr even more—perhaps because Burr had defeated Hamilton's father-in-law in the Senate election of 1790. Hamilton broke the deadlock in the House, and on the 36th ballot Jefferson won the election. Soon afterward, the 12th Amendment to the Constitution was adopted, giving each elector a separate ballot to cast for President and Vice President.

Because of Burr's conspiracy against him in the election, Jefferson gave him nothing to do during his term of office, and he dropped him from the ticket in 1804. The same year, Burr lost the New York gubernatorial election. He fled west after killing Alexander Hamilton in a duel at Weehawken, New Jersey, on July 11, 1804, over Hamilton's remarks during the election campaign that Burr was "dangerous" and "despicable."

Burr then became involved in a second bizarre situation. With several hundred armed followers, Burr traveled down the Mississippi River toward New Orleans. No one knew what he intended to do: get Western territories to secede from Union control; attack Mexico or a Central American country and carve out an empire for himself; or charter ships in New Orleans and sail back to the nation's capital and try to seize power. President Jefferson took no chances. He had Burr arrested in the West and transported back to Virginia to face trial for attempting to take some of the Louisiana Territory away from the Union. Although Burr was eventually acquitted of the charges, his political career was finished, and he spent the next several years in Europe before returning to New York City, where he practiced law from 1812 until his death in 1836.

SEE ALSO

Electoral college; Jefferson, Thomas; Ticket; 12th Amendment

FURTHER READING

Fleming, Thomas J. *Duel: Alexander Hamilton, Aaron Burr, and the Future of America.* New York: Basic Books, 1999.
Kennedy, Roger G. *Burr, Hamilton, and Jefferson: A Study in Character.* New York: Oxford, 2000.
Lomask, Milton. *Aaron Burr.* 2 vols. 1979. Reprint, New York: Farrar, Straus & Giroux, 1982.
Parmet, Herbert S., and Marie Hecht. *Aaron Burr: Portrait of an Ambitious Man.* New York: Macmillan, 1967.

Bush, George

41ST PRESIDENT

☆ *Born: June 12, 1924, Milton, Mass.*
☆ *Education: Yale College, B.A., 1948*
☆ *Political party: Republican*
☆ *Military service: U.S. Navy, 1942–45; Distinguished Flying Cross, three Air Medals*
☆ *Previous government service: U.S. House of Representatives, 1967–71; U.S. ambassador to the United Nations, 1971–73; chief, U.S. Liaison Office, People's Republic of China, 1974–75; director of Central Intelligence, 1976–77; Vice President, 1981–89*
☆ *Elected President, 1988; served, 1989–93*

GEORGE BUSH was the first Vice President to move directly to the White House by election since Martin Van Buren did so in 1836. His term was marked by few domestic initiatives, but he took bold action in foreign affairs, using the military to depose Panamanian dictator Manuel Noriega in 1989 and to repel Iraq's invasion of Kuwait in 1991.

Bush came from a politically and socially connected family: his father was Prescott Bush, an investment banker and U.S. senator from Connecticut (1953–63). His mother was Dorothy Walker Bush, a member of the family that donated the Walker Cup, one of amateur golf's most prestigious tournaments. Bush grew up in the affluent town of Greenwich, Connecticut, and attended Phillips Academy in Andover, Massachusetts, one of the finest prep schools in the nation.

During World War II, Bush enlisted in the navy and became its youngest pilot at age 19, flying Grumman Torpedo bombers in the Pacific from the aircraft carrier *San Jacinto.* On one mission his plane was hit by enemy fire. He and his crew bailed out; although the other two crew members died, Bush was saved by a U.S. submarine. He flew 58 combat missions and was rotated back home in 1944.

After his war service Bush married Barbara Pierce and attended Yale University, where he was captain of the championship baseball team and a member of the secret society Skull and Bones. He founded his own oil company in Houston, which soon merged with another to form the Zapata Petroleum Corporation.

After making a small fortune in oil exploration, George Bush turned to

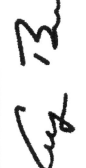

Republican politics in Texas. In 1962 he became Harris County Republican party chairman. Two years later he won the Republican Senate nomination but was defeated by the Democratic incumbent. He was elected to the U.S. House of Representatives from Houston in 1966 and was reelected in 1968. Bush served on the Ways and Means Committee, which deals with tax matters. In 1970 he was defeated for the Senate again.

After serving as U.S. ambassador to the United Nations, Bush was appointed by President Richard Nixon to be chair of the Republican National Committee in 1973. His tenure in office occurred after the Watergate scandal, and he spent much of his time insisting that the White House, not the Republican National Committee, was responsible for any criminal violations. President Gerald Ford appointed Bush to serve as chief of the U.S. Liaison Office to the People's Republic of China and then to be director of Central Intelligence.

Bush ran for President in 1980, but he was defeated by Ronald Reagan in the Republican primaries. Bush ended his campaign before the convention and was rewarded for his efforts to achieve party unity by receiving the Vice Presidential nomination.

As Vice President, Bush chaired the Task Force on Regulatory Relief, which took a pro-industry position on most issues: it watered down proposals from the Occupational Safety and Health Administration (OSHA) on toxic substances in the workplace, delayed Transportation Department requirements that air bags be installed in cars, and delayed Environmental Protection Agency proposals to reduce lead in gasoline and remove asbestos from the workplace. Bush presided over the crisis management team at the White House and the drug interdiction task force. When President Reagan underwent cancer surgery in 1985, the powers of the Presidency were transferred to Bush for several hours under the provisions of the 25th Amendment.

Bush defeated Senator Robert Dole and the Reverend Pat Robertson for the Republican Presidential nomination in 1988. He chose Dan Quayle, junior Republican senator from Indiana, as his running mate. In the general election, running against Massachusetts Democratic governor Michael Dukakis, Bush repeatedly promised voters, "Read my lips, no new taxes." He told them he opposed abortion and gun control, embracing a conservative social agenda. Bush won the election with 54 percent of the popular vote and 426 electoral votes to Dukakis's 111. Bush entered office facing large Democratic majorities in the House and Senate.

In his inaugural address, President Bush promised to "make kinder the face of the nation and gentler the face of the world" and called for more cooperation between Democrats in Congress and Republicans in the White House. In his first year in office he followed a conciliatory line. He moved quickly past a dispute over the nomination of former senator John Tower to be secretary of defense (Tower was rejected by the Senate) and settled on the appointment of the less controversial Richard Cheney. He made a relatively noncontroversial Supreme Court appointment of the low-keyed David Souter. Bush concluded bipartisan negotiations over the budget by agreeing to the possibility of an increase in taxes, even though that meant repudiating his campaign promises and alienating the conservatives in his own party.

In foreign affairs President Bush initially tried to avoid any major new international crisis, preferring not to confront either Libya or Syria over support for terrorists. Similarly, he took a soft line on China after its leaders ordered a massacre of leaders of the democracy movement at Tiananmen Square in Beijing in 1989. He invaded Panama in 1989 to seize its dictator, Manuel Noriega, and then put him on trial for drug trafficking, securing a conviction in 1992. In Central America, Bush all but abandoned military pressure on the Sandinista government of Nicaragua, a revolutionary government with strong ties to the Soviet Union and Cuba. He opted instead to support an agreement for free elections that produced a non-Sandinista government. The results of his conciliatory approach to Congress and international adversaries were high standings in the polls and a reputation for skill in managing foreign affairs.

In the second year of Bush's term the collapse of Soviet control over the nations of Eastern Europe made it seem as if no international crisis would occur for the remainder of his term. The President signed an agreement with Soviet president Mikhail Gorbachev that greatly reduced the number of North Atlantic Treaty Organization (NATO) and Warsaw Pact (the Soviet-bloc nations of Eastern Europe) troops and tanks in Europe. In August, however, Iraq invaded and annexed Kuwait. Bush sent more than 500,000 troops into the Persian Gulf, escalated his rhetoric against Iraqi dictator Saddam Hussein, and obtained a U.N. resolution approving the use of force against Iraq. Public approval for his handling of the crisis diminished, however, and many other nations urged more time for sanctions (trade restrictions) and diplomacy to work. Eventually, he received authorization from Congress to use force against Iraq, and the combined forces of the United States and several European and Arab nations waged a quick and successful military campaign. The effort forced Iraq to withdraw from Kuwait, but Saddam Hussein remained in power.

Bush began his third year with the highest ratings since public opinion poll-sters began gauging Presidential popularity. Bush's popularity went into the 90 percent range, yet he offered almost no new domestic programs to Congress, refusing to capitalize on his standing with the public. He pressured the Soviet Union to accelerate its pace of economic and political reform, a strategy that culminated in a strategic arms reduction agreement signed in Moscow in August 1991. He pressured Israel and its Arab neighbors to come to an international peace conference, which began meeting early in 1992. He dropped sanctions on South Africa and refused to call for sanctions on China to protest human rights violations. Both moves were unpopular with Democrats in Congress.

Bush supported Mikhail Gorbachev's program of Perestroika, or economic and political restructuring, in the Soviet Union and led a coalition of Western nations that opposed a coup attempt against Gorbachev in August 1991. But Bush opposed the efforts of some republics within the Soviet Union to secede. Gorbachev was succeeded in power by Boris Yeltsin, and the Soviet Union was transformed into the Commonwealth of Independent States at the beginning of 1992. Bush then began to work with Yeltsin and his team of free-market reformers on programs of aid, trade, and nuclear disarmament.

In domestic affairs Bush continued his conservative stance. He scuttled a compromise civil rights measure sponsored by Republican moderates in the Senate, setting up a major dispute with Democrats and civil rights organizations, but eventually he signed a version of the bill into law. He pushed hard for a defense budget that contained funding of major new strategic weapons programs, but his budget had little money for domestic initiatives—even for his much-trumpeted educational initiatives. The White House lobbied hard in the Senate for approval of Bush's Supreme Court nomination of Clarence Thomas, a black conservative. Although Bush won most of his highly publicized confrontations with Congress, his legislative success record remained one of the lowest of any modern President, even as his popularity with the public continued to hover in the 70 percent range.

In his fourth year Bush continued his emphasis on foreign affairs. He put more pressure on Israel to end its construction of new settlements in the West Bank by linking continued American foreign aid to Israeli policies regarding that disputed territory. He insisted that Iraq dismantle its strategic weapons and won United Nations sanctions against Libya until that nation agreed to turn over terrorists for trial in the 1988 bombing of a Pan Am passenger jet. He vetoed a Democratic bill to end "most favored nation" treatment of China (a policy giving it the lowest tariffs on goods exported to the United States), and his veto was sustained. At the end of 1992 he sent marines and other military personnel into Somalia to provide protection for relief workers alleviating the famine in that country. In early 1993 the United States and Russia signed a nuclear arms reduction agreement.

In domestic affairs Bush was more confrontational with Congress, using or threatening to use his veto power on a wide range of legislation. He fired the director of the National Endowment for the Arts as a result of a dispute over federal funding of so-called "pornographic" art. He reiterated his position calling for an end to abortion. He refused to pledge American adherence to proposed new pollution controls that had gained worldwide backing. He insisted that the budget limitations on domestic spending (agreed to in 1990) remain in place, in spite of pressure to spend the "peace dividend" (money not spent on defense) on social programs. He blocked a range

of Democratic economic measures with vetoes, all of which were sustained. Meanwhile, the President's popularity slid from better than 70 percent into the low 40s. By early spring President Bush had the lowest rating in the polls of any first-term President in his fourth year in office since Herbert Hoover.

Bush's weak political position, due in large part to a severe recession that began in the fall of 1991, brought conservative political commentator Pat Buchanan into the primary races against him. But Buchanan was quickly vanquished by Bush, who received the Republican nomination. In the November election, Bush was defeated by Arkansas governor Bill Clinton, who won 43 percent of the popular vote to Bush's 38 percent. Independent candidate Ross Perot received 19 percent. After leaving the White House, Bush made his home in Houston, Texas.

SEE ALSO

Director of Central Intelligence; Ford, Gerald R.; Nixon, Richard M.; Quayle, J. Danforth; Reagan, Ronald

FURTHER READING

Campbell, Colin, and Bert Rockman, eds. *The Bush Presidency: First Appraisals.* Chatham, N.J.: Chatham House, 1991.
Duffy, Michael, and Dan Goodgame. *Marching in Place: The Status Quo Presidency of George Bush.* New York: Simon & Schuster, 1992.
Parmet, Herbert S. *George Bush: The Life of a Lone Star Yankee.* New York: Scribner, 1997.
Thompson, Kenneth W., ed. *The Bush Presidency: Ten Intimate Perspectives of George Bush.* Lanham, Md.: University Press of America, 1997.

Bush, George W.

43RD PRESIDENT

☆ *Born: July 6, 1946, New Haven, Conn.*
☆ *Political party: Republican*
☆ *Education: Yale University, B.A.,*

1968; Harvard University, M.B.A., 1975
☆ Military Service: Texas Air National Guard, 1968–73
☆ Previous government service: governor of Texas, 1994–2001
☆ Elected President, 2000; served, 2001–

GEORGE W. BUSH was elected to the Presidency eight years after his father's defeat by Bill Clinton in 1992. He grew up in the booming oil town of Midland, Texas, and as a young man worked in the oil industry. He lost a race for Congress in 1978. In 1989 he was part of a group that purchased the Texas Rangers baseball team, and he served as managing director until he became governor of Texas. Bush was the first Texas governor to win a second consecutive four-year term.

Governor Bush persuaded the legislature to pass tort reform and limit frivolous lawsuits and pass welfare reform to require recipients to go for job training. He opposed the elimination of aid to illegal immigrants and focused on improving the quality of Texas education. He was able to work with Democrats as well as Republicans, gaining a reputation for bipartisanship on issues important to him.

Bush became the front-runner for the Republican Presidential nomination and defeated John McCain in the primaries. Running against Al Gore, Jr., Bush proclaimed himself a "compassionate conservative." His program called for large tax cuts focused on the wealthy, new drug benefits in Medicare to appeal to the elderly, and an overhaul of Social Security to provide young contributors with the opportunity to invest some of their contributions in the stock market. In foreign affairs, Bush strongly supported constructing an anti-missile system and was skeptical about Amer-

ica's role in peacekeeping and nation-building abroad. His addition of Dick Cheney on the ticket and his promise that he would appoint an experienced team to assist him assuaged voters worried about his lack of national experience. His call to restore "honor and dignity" to the White House was heeded by the voters, and Bush was elected narrowly with 48 percent of the vote, slightly less than Gore received, and 271 electoral college votes, after a contest marred by inaccurate vote counts in Florida and a lengthy set of legal challenges by Gore.

SEE ALSO
Cheney, Richard; Electoral college

FURTHER READING
Minutaglio, Bill. *First Son: George W. Bush and the Bush Family Dynasty.* New York: Times Books, 1999.

President George W. Bush sits at his desk in the Oval Office for the first time on Inaugural Day, January 20, 2001. His father, former President George Bush, shares the moment.

Cabinet

THE CABINET is a Presidential advisory group composed of the secretaries of the executive branch departments and other invited officials. At the Constitutional Convention delegates assumed that the

President might convene the heads of departments for advice, but the cabinet was never mentioned in the original Constitution. The 25th Amendment, however, gives the cabinet certain duties regarding succession to the Presidency in cases of Presidential disability.

George Washington created the cabinet in 1789 when he invited the secretaries of state, Treasury, and war and the attorney general to meet informally with him. At first these officials met the President with other advisers, such as the chief justice of the United States, and it was not until 1791 that the cabinet met separately with the President. The secretary of the navy was added in 1798 by President John Adams, and the postmaster general in 1829 by Andrew Jackson. Other secretaries were added when their departments were created; the postmaster general was dropped in 1970 when the post office department became the U.S. Postal Service, an independent agency. Richard Nixon was the first Vice President to sit regularly with the cabinet (Coolidge had done so occasionally).

From 1791 onward Washington frequently convened his secretaries to debate the most important issues of his administration, and the term *cabinet* gained currency in 1793 during a crisis with the French government, when it met in a small room almost every day for nearly a year. Secretary of the Treasury Alexander Hamilton and Secretary of State Thomas Jefferson were the major figures in the first cabinet. Their disagreements over foreign policy led them to create the Federalist and Republican parties. By 1795 Washington understood that his cabinet and administration should be united on the major principles of foreign and domestic policy. By 1801, when Thomas Jefferson became President, it was understood that the cabinet would consist of appointees who supported his principles. Because the Democratic-Republican

party retained power until 1828, it became the practice for a new President to retain some of his predecessor's secretaries and to consult with them before taking any action. Presidents often counted the opinion of the cabinet as equal to their own, creating a system of cabinet government. Cabinet government ended with the election of Andrew Jackson in 1828. Jackson established new rules: the President convenes cabinet meetings at his pleasure; the cabinet has no right to be consulted or convened; Presidential appointees serve as his subordinates and take direction from him; and the President may fire secretaries who disagree with his instructions. Because of a dispute with the cabinet over its ostracism of the wife of Secretary of War John Eaton in 1829, Jackson did not convene a meeting for two years and instead relied on a group of informal advisers known as the "kitchen cabinet." But in 1831 he finally bowed to pressure from members of his own party to meet with his secretaries.

Jackson dropped the prior practice of polling the secretaries for their positions on issues and then following the majority. President Lincoln was reported to have taken a vote in which he was the only person to favor a certain course of action. He then announced, "The ayes have it." After the Civil War the cabinet

President George Washington with the first cabinet (left to right): Washington, Secretary of War Henry Knox, Secretary of the Treasury Alexander Hamilton, Secretary of State Thomas Jefferson, and Attorney General Edmund Randolph.

met regularly twice a week and was used primarily to give the President advice on patronage—the awarding of government jobs on the basis of political ties—and party politics and to coordinate legislative and budget proposals to Congress from the executive departments.

Until the 1930s there was only a handful of examples of a President making major decisions without first consulting the cabinet. These include the Emancipation Proclamation issued by President Lincoln, who gathered his cabinet and said, "I do not wish your advice about the main matter. That, I have determined for myself." Nor did Woodrow Wilson consult his cabinet on most issues, including the decision that the United States should enter World War I. Recent Presidents have convened their cabinets irregularly, one or two times a month at best. John F. Kennedy thought that cabinet meetings were a waste of time, asking, "Why should the Postmaster General sit there and listen to a discussion of the problems of Laos?" Kennedy held only six meetings in three years.

Today cabinets provide the President with political advice, serve as sounding boards for his ideas, and enable secretaries to coordinate their public statements on administration policy. Presidents also use cabinet meetings for symbolic purposes: Jimmy Carter used his first meeting to order that high officials use fewer limousines.

The "inner cabinet" consists of the secretaries of state, defense, and Treasury and the attorney general. These positions are usually the most prestigious, and the opinions of these secretaries carry the most weight with the President. The President sees these officials often, together or individually. The "outer cabinet" consists of the secretaries of the clientele agencies such as the Departments of Agriculture, Commerce, Interior, and Labor. These secretaries deal with issues that concern constituencies such as union workers, farmers, and business executives. Presidents spend little time with these secretaries and often use the White House staff and agencies of the Executive Office of the President to supervise their work.

SEE ALSO

Attorney general of the United States; Brains Trust; Departments, executive; Executive branch; Executive Office of the President; Kitchen cabinet; Modern Presidency; Office of Management and Budget; Patronage, Presidential; Removal power; Secretary of defense; Secretary of state; Succession to the Presidency; 25th Amendment

FURTHER READING

Fenno, Richard. *The President's Cabinet.* Cambridge: Harvard University Press, 1959.

Calhoun, John C.
VICE PRESIDENT

☆ *Born: Mar. 18, 1782, Mount Carmel, S.C.*
☆ *Political party: Democratic-Republican, Democrat*
☆ *Education: Yale College, B.A., 1804; Tapping Reeve Law School, 1805*
☆ *Military service: none*
☆ *Previous government service: South Carolina House of Representatives, 1809–10; U.S. House of Representatives, 1811–16; U.S. secretary of war, 1817–24*
☆ *Vice President under John Quincy Adams, 1825–29, and Andrew Jackson, 1829–32*
☆ *Subsequent government service: U.S. Senate, 1833–44, 1845–50; U.S. secretary of state, 1844–45*
☆ *Died: Mar. 31, 1850, Washington, D.C.*

JOHN C. CALHOUN was the choice of various factions of his party for the Vice Presidency in 1824. His Southern background provided a balance to the newly elected President from Massachusetts, John Quincy Adams. Calhoun played virtually no role in the Adams adminis-

John C. Calhoun resigned as Andrew Jackson's Vice President because he believed federal policies were damaging to his home state, South Carolina.

tration, however. In 1828, even though the Presidency went to Adams's bitter rival Andrew Jackson, Calhoun was elected Vice President a second time.

Calhoun and Jackson soon differed on a variety of issues, but the most important rift between them involved the marriage of the secretary of war, John Eaton, to Peggy O'Neale. Because the new Mrs. Eaton was considered too scandalous for Washington society, Calhoun's wife led a campaign among cabinet wives to freeze her out. Jackson was furious. He began to favor Martin Van Buren as his successor instead of Calhoun. The Vice President retaliated by opposing Jackson's plan to destroy the Bank of the United States—an organization that Calhoun had played a key role in chartering while a member of the House in 1816. The final rift between the two men occurred when it was revealed that Calhoun, as secretary of war, had sought the censure of Jackson for his controversial invasion of Florida in 1818.

In 1832, in protest against a new tariff law passed by Congress that many Southerners believed discriminated against their region (because higher tariffs would force them to pay more for imported goods and because Northern industries could also raise prices of goods to the South), Calhoun resigned from the Vice Presidency. He was the first Vice President to do so.

Calhoun returned home and South Carolina promptly elected him U.S. senator. Calhoun induced the South Carolina legislature to pass an ordinance of nullification, which declared that the new tariff law would not be enforced in that state. President Jackson made it clear that he would use military force if necessary to collect the tariffs, or duties, in Southern ports, and the state backed down.

In his 1850 book *Disquisition on Government,* Calhoun argued that states should be allowed to nullify, or ignore, laws passed by Congress and that no national laws should go into effect unless a majority of the members of Congress from each region of the country approved. If a majority from any region dissented, that would be enough to kill the measure. Calhoun's ideas for amending the Constitution went nowhere. By 1850 he predicted that there would be a civil war within 12 years.

Calhoun ended his career by serving as John Tyler's secretary of state in 1844, then returning to the Senate in 1845, where he served until his death.

SEE ALSO

Adams, John Quincy; Jackson, Andrew; Monroe, James; Tyler, John

FURTHER READING

Celsi, Teresa. *John C. Calhoun and the Roots of War.* Englewood Cliffs, N.J.: Silver Burdett, 1991.
Niven, John. *John C. Calhoun and the Price of Union.* Baton Rouge: Louisiana State University Press, 1988.
Wilson, Clyde N., ed. *The Essential Calhoun.* New Brunswick, N.J.: Transaction Publishers, 1992.

Campaign Fund, Presidential Election

THE PRESIDENTIAL Election Campaign Fund is an account administered by the U.S. Treasury that provides funds to Presidential candidates in the nominating contest and the general election.

The fund is authorized by the Revenue Act of 1971, which allows each taxpayer to allocate a dollar of his income taxes to the Treasury's Presidential election account. The allocation does not increase the amount of tax a person pays. The law went into effect with the 1976 election.

To be eligible for federal funds, candidates must agree to abide by the reporting requirements and spending limitations of the Federal Election Campaign Act of 1971 and the amendments of 1974. Candidates qualify for federal funds during the nominating contest if they raise $5,000 in each of 20 states through individual contributions of $250 or less. Once qualified, they receive matching funds from the Treasury for all contributions of $250 or less, up to the limits established by law.

In the general election, candidates who agree not to accept any private contributions are eligible for Treasury funding of their campaigns, up to the legal limits. In addition, the two major parties receive $11 million each for their national conventions. They may accept private donations for "party building" activities such as voter registration drives, which in reality go toward Presidential campaign activities.

Candidates who choose not to accept public funding for their primary or general election campaigns have no spending limits. Since the law was enacted, the only two serious contenders for the Presidency who did not accept federal funds were John Connally, who spent millions in 1980 and won just a single delegate to the Republican national convention, and independent Ross Perot, who spent $60 million of his own funds and received almost 20 percent of the popular vote in 1992.

SEE ALSO
Election campaigns, Presidential; Primaries, Presidential

Campaigns, Presidential election
SEE Election campaigns, Presidential

Camp David

CAMP DAVID is a Presidential weekend retreat in Maryland's Catoctin Mountains. Originally a military base, it was turned over to the White House during the Great Depression and was named Shangri-La by President Franklin D. Roosevelt. President Dwight Eisenhower renamed it Camp David for his grandson David. It consists of 180 forested acres, protected by a ring of three fences and marine guard patrols. It is maintained by 150 naval personnel and, when the President is in residence, by 250 other support staff. It contains a number of residence cabins for the President and his guests, who often include foreign heads of state. Camp David also has a heated pool, skeet range, tennis courts, and horseshoe pit. It has a conference center where administration officials can meet with the President when

Dwight Eisenhower with his family at Camp David. Mamie Eisenhower (far right) holds her grandson David, for whom the camp was named.

he is on a "working vacation." Expenses for Camp David are part of the Navy Department budget.

SEE ALSO
Camp David peace talks

Camp David peace talks

FROM SEPTEMBER 4 to 17, 1978, President Jimmy Carter held meetings at Camp David with Anwar Sadat, president of Egypt, and Menachem Begin, prime minister of Israel. These negotiations led to a peace treaty between Israel and Egypt. The proceedings were kept secret and the delegations from both nations remained at Camp David throughout the sessions, ensuring no premature newspaper leaks about the substance of the talks.

President Carter negotiated separately with Sadat and Begin, shuttling between their cabins. Carter and his diplomatic team then produced drafts of agreements and modified them to take each side's objections into account. Carter oversaw every aspect of the negotiations.

Carter's own position adhered to United Nations Resolution 242, which instructed Israel to withdraw from occupied Arab territory and Arab nations to recognize and make peace with Israel. Carter's proposals included Israeli withdrawal from the Sinai Peninsula and Gaza Strip, an autonomous "homeland" for Palestinians in Gaza and the West Bank, an end to Israeli settlements in the West Bank, and a five-year transitional period in which the final status of the West Bank would be determined. In return, there would be an end to the Egyptian economic boycott of Israel and full recognition. Egypt would also give Israel navigation rights through the Suez Canal and Straits of Tiran. The borders existing before the 1967 Arab–Israeli war would be restored.

Sadat was willing to go along with most of these proposals, but he also wanted reparations from Israel for the occupation of Egyptian territory and for oil it had taken from the Sinai. Israel was willing to withdraw from the Sinai and insisted that most of it be demilitarized but wished to keep some military facilities in the area as well as some of its settlements. Israelis would give the Palestinians administrative self-rule but wanted to retain the right to buy land and settle on the West Bank. Israel also expressed interest in a mutual defense treaty with the United States, an idea rebuffed by Carter.

The main disagreements were between Carter and Begin. Carter argued that international borders could not be changed, while Begin insisted that the 1967 war gave Israel the right to change its frontiers. Carter claimed that West Jerusalem was part of the West Bank; Begin insisted it was an integral part of Israel. Carter wanted a freeze on Israeli settlements; Begin resisted. The Israeli leader insisted that Carter honor a pledge made by President Gerald Ford: that the United States would coordinate with Israel any American proposal for a peace settlement before submitting it to the Arabs. Carter rejected this approach to the negotiations.

Begin made a number of concessions to Carter. These included agreeing to the principle of Egyptian sovereignty in the Sinai and to complete Israeli withdrawal

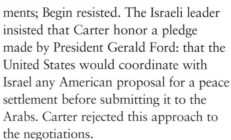

Jimmy Carter greets Anwar Sadat (left) and Menachem Begin outside a cabin at Camp David.

from all military facilities and all settlements in the Sinai.

Sadat and Carter were in substantial agreement on most issues, and the two men became close friends as the conference proceeded. Sadat made a number of concessions to Carter, which alienated some of his own delegation, including his foreign minister (who resigned at the end of the conference). They believed that Sadat had made too many concessions to the Americans and had been outmaneuvered by the Israelis.

On September 17, the Camp David Accords were signed. The accords included a *Framework for Peace in the Middle East* and a *Framework for Conclusion of a Peace Treaty between Egypt and Israel*, together with *Accompanying Letters* exchanged between President Carter and the two leaders. Israel withdrew from Arab territories and dismantled settlements in the Sinai Peninsula and Gaza. It recognized the principle that there were Palestinian rights to be negotiated in the future. Egypt made peace with the Jewish state and formally recognized it. It agreed to limit its military presence in the Sinai and recognized that Israel had legitimate security interests subject to negotiation.

Carter appointed Robert Strauss, former chairman of the Democratic National Committee, as a Presidential special envoy to the Middle East to implement the agreement. After intensive negotiations, Sadat and Begin traveled to Washington and signed a peace treaty on March 26, 1979. For their efforts, the two men shared the Nobel Peace Prize.

SEE ALSO

Carter, Jimmy

FURTHER READING

Lenczowski, George. *American Presidents and the Middle East.* Durham: Duke University Press, 1990.
Quandt, William. *Camp David: Peacemaking and Politics.* Washington, D.C.: Brookings Institution, 1986.

Carter, Jimmy

39TH PRESIDENT

☆ *Born: Oct. 1, 1924, Plains, Ga.*
☆ *Political party: Democrat*
☆ *Education: U.S. Naval Academy, B.S., 1946*
☆ *Military service: U.S. Navy, 1947–53*
☆ *Previous government service: chair, Sumter County, Ga., Board of Education, 1955–62; Georgia Senate 1963–66; governor of Georgia, 1971–75*
☆ *Elected President, 1976; served, 1977–81*

PROMISING A "government as good as the people," Jimmy Carter was elected in 1976 as a Washington outsider by voters fed up with the Watergate scandal and the weak economy. Carter shed many of the trappings of the "imperial" Presidency and pursued a foreign policy emphasizing human rights and peaceful solution of international conflict. But his unpopular Panama Canal Treaty and rocketing inflation and interest rates made him a one-term President.

Born in the small town of Plains, Georgia, James Earl Carter, Jr., was the first American President to be born in a hospital. He graduated from Plains High School as valedictorian in 1941, and in 1946 he graduated from the U.S. Naval Academy in the top tenth of his class. He served as an ensign on an experimental nuclear submarine with Captain (later Admiral) Hyman Rickover, the father of the nuclear navy. In 1953, after the death of his father, Carter resigned his commission to take over his family's peanut farm, which he turned into a thriving business.

Carter became a deacon and Sunday school teacher in the Plains Baptist Church, then chairman of the Sumter County School Board, where he peacefully promoted racial desegregation of the schools. As a state senator, Carter fought local segregationist groups, and he defeated racist opponents to win reelection to the senate. He encouraged blacks to join the Plains Baptist Church.

In 1966 Carter ran for governor but lost to arch-segregationist Lester Maddox. Carter's loss led him to become a born-again Christian. In the 1970 Democratic gubernatorial primary Carter declared his opposition to busing as a means of overcoming racial segregation in schools, leading the *Atlanta Constitution* to call him an "ignorant, racist, backward, ultra-conservative, rednecked South Georgia peanut farmer." With evangelical and fundamentalist Christian support, he won the election.

Although elected with segregationist support, Carter was a progressive, especially on race relations. Carter reorganized the state government and consolidated many independent agencies into a few efficient departments. He increased minority hiring in state government by 50 percent, and he promoted environmental and educational programs. But he worked poorly with traditional politicians in the state legislature, gaining a reputation as an arrogant and isolated governor.

Carter began a steady rise in national Democratic politics, however. He became chair of the Democratic Governors' Campaign Committee in 1972 and campaign chair for the Democratic National Committee in 1974—a year in which the party scored major successes in congressional elections. By 1975 Carter was spending most of his time making speeches and traveling from one state to another seeking financial support and media attention.

Carter portrayed himself as an outsider who could clean up the mess in Washington. He promised never to lie to the American people, implicitly contrasting himself to politicians like Richard

Nixon in the Watergate scandal. He called for "a government that is as honest and decent and fair and competent and truthful and idealistic as are the American people." Carter won the Iowa Presidential caucuses on January 19, 1976, and propelled himself to the forefront of the Democratic field. When he won the New Hampshire primary a few weeks later, funds poured into his campaign. He won a number of other primaries and gained sufficient votes for a first-ballot nomination at the national convention. He defeated the incumbent President, Gerald Ford, in the general election by a narrow margin, due in large measure to a split in the opposition ranks between moderate Republicans and conservatives who had favored Ronald Reagan. The high unemployment rate and Ford's pardon of Nixon also worked in Carter's favor.

Although Carter took office with large Democratic majorities in Congress, he was unable to get them to support much of his program. His opposition to some rivers and harbors projects early in his term was fiercely resisted by his own party's congressional leaders, as was his 1978 veto of a public works measure on the grounds that it would be inflationary. Although Congress passed his proposal to create a department of energy, his comprehensive energy program was revised. When it did pass, it proved unpopular with the public because it emphasized conservation and higher prices. He cut back on federal aid to urban areas, causing a backlash among liberal Democrats. His decision to cancel the B-1 bomber upset party conservatives. When Congress transformed his tax reform plan into new favors for special interests, Carter referred to them as "a pack of ravenous wolves." Carter did have some successes: he got Congress to divide the Department of Health, Education, and Welfare into two new departments, one

A Carter campaign souvenir symbolizes his family peanut business.

for education and the other for health and human services; the minimum wage was raised; and Congress deregulated the airline, trucking, and railroad industries. It also established a "Superfund" to clean up toxic waste sites.

In foreign affairs, too, Carter took actions that were unpopular. In 1977, although more than three-fourths of the American people wanted to keep the Panama Canal Zone, Carter negotiated two treaties with Panama that called for the United States to give up sovereign rights in the Panama Canal Zone and to turn over operation of the canal to Panama by the turn of the century. The Senate consented to the treaties by only a bare margin. In 1978 Carter presided over the Camp David peace accords between Israel and Egypt, which resulted in a treaty between the two nations the following year. In 1979 Carter recognized communist China and canceled a defense treaty with the anticommunist government on Taiwan—actions that upset Southern conservatives. He began an emphasis in American foreign policy on human rights, cutting off foreign aid to certain Latin American nations with repressive regimes. The second Strategic Arms Limitation Treaty (SALT II) with the Soviet Union was signed on June 18, 1979, but the Soviet invasion of Afghanistan put Senate consent to the treaty in doubt and Carter withdrew it from the Senate. Nevertheless, both governments adhered to its terms.

Carter's popularity fell during much of his term as inflation increased to more than 15 percent and the unemployment rate, after dropping early in his term, rose again to more than 6 percent. Interest rates rose to the 20 percent range, which made it difficult for people to purchase homes and consumer goods. The seizure of American diplomats in the embassy in Iran by "student" militants on November 4, 1979, and Carter's inability to obtain their release by diplomatic means also caused his popularity to sink. An April 1980 attempt to rescue the hostages ended in failure with the death of eight U.S. servicemen in a helicopter crash in the Iranian desert. The abortive mission seemed to many Americans to symbolize U.S. military weakness in the post-Vietnam era. In July 1980 Carter's popularity slid to 20 percent in the polls—lower even than Nixon's during the Watergate scandal.

In the 1980 Democratic nominating contest, Senator Edward M. Kennedy almost defeated Carter, and much of Kennedy's liberal platform was adopted by the convention in a repudiation of the Carter Presidency. With the Democrats split, Republican conservative Ronald Reagan defeated Carter in a three-way race that also involved independent candidate John Anderson. On the day Carter's successor was inaugurated, the Iranian government released the 52 hostages they had held for 444 days. President Reagan asked Carter to fly to Germany to greet the returning hostages.

After his election defeat, Carter returned to Georgia. He gave courses in public affairs at Emory University, participated in the creation and work of the Carter Presidential Center in Atlanta, an organization devoted to human rights and humanitarian causes around the world. Carter became involved in monitoring elections in a number of foreign nations, which aided in their transformation from dictatorship to democracy.

SEE ALSO

Camp David peace talks; Ford, Gerald R.; Mondale, Walter F.; Reagan, Ronald

FURTHER READING

Brinkley, Douglas. *The Unfinished Presidency: Jimmy Carter's Journey beyond the White House.* New York: Viking, 1998.
Carter, Jimmy. *Keeping Faith: Memoirs of a President.* New York: Bantam, 1982.

Fink, Gary M., and Hugh Davis Graham. *The Carter Presidency: Policy Choices in the Post–New Deal Era.* Lawrence: University Press of Kansas, 1998.

Glad, Betty. *Jimmy Carter, In Search of the Great White House.* New York: Norton, 1980.

Hargrove, Erwin C. *Jimmy Carter as President: Leadership and the Politics of the Public Good.* Baton Rouge: Louisiana State University Press, 1988.

Morris, Kenneth E. *Jimmy Carter: American Moralist.* Athens: University of Georgia Press, 1996.

Thompson, Kenneth W. *The Carter Presidency: Fourteen Intimate Perspectives of Jimmy Carter.* Lanham, Md.: University Press of America, 1990.

Caucuses, Presidential nominating

NOMINATING CAUCUSES are one method used to select delegates to Presidential nominating conventions. Republicans select almost one-quarter and Democrats almost one-third of their national convention delegates from states that use nominating caucuses. Until the 1970s caucuses were administered as follows: Members of local political party organizations met in precinct, or district, caucuses to choose delegates to county or congressional district conventions. They made their choices by majority vote. The conventions, in turn, chose delegates to a state convention, which would select delegates to the national nominating convention. The delegates were not pledged to a particular Presidential candidate. This system produced uncommitted state delegations who would vote for whomever the party bosses told them to at the national convention.

In 1972 the Democratic party's McGovern-Fraser Commission reformed caucus procedures by requiring that precinct meetings be open to all registered Democrats. The Republicans then adopted similar rules. Caucuses have since been transformed into contests between the Presidential candidates. The delegates selected to the national convention from caucus-convention states are now declared supporters of particular candidates. Delegates from these states to the national convention are allotted in the Democratic party to each Presidential contender according to the rule of proportional representation; if three-quarters of the precincts vote for candidate A and one-quarter for candidate B, then three-quarters of the convention delegates will cast their convention ballots for candidate A and one-quarter for candidate B. In the Republican party a winner-take-all system is often used, so that with a similar caucus result all of the state's delegates would vote for candidate A.

The precinct caucus usually takes place in a meeting hall, such as a high school gymnasium or auditorium. The people attending nominate their choices for delegates to the district conventions; each slate of delegates consists of supporters of a different Presidential candidate. Some caucuses provide for an open vote, which is often taken by having those attending move to different corners of the room to demonstrate support for competing slates of delegates. This method is known as "grouping." In some states, however, party rules allow a secret ballot.

The precinct caucus is run as a meeting, in which the deliberations are supposed to influence the eventual outcome, though many attending have already made up their minds. Although the turnout of registered voters in caucuses is lower than the turnout in primaries, some states have turnouts of 10 to 15 percent.

Because the Iowa caucuses, which usually occur in the first week of February, are the first contest for convention delegates, they have assumed great importance in the Presidential contest. The winner in Iowa receives more media coverage than other contenders and a boost in campaign contributions. Candidates who fare badly in Iowa may be forced to drop out of the race.

SEE ALSO

Election campaigns, Presidential; Nominating conventions, Presidential; Primaries, Presidential

FURTHER READING

Ceaser, James. *Presidential Selection.* Princeton, N.J.: Princeton University Press, 1979.
Shafer, Byron. *Quiet Revolution.* New York: Russell Sage, 1984.
Wayne, Stephen. *Road to the White House.* New York: St. Martin's, 1992.

Censure, resolutions of

CONGRESS MAY pass resolutions of censure to condemn the President for improper, illegal, or unconstitutional conduct. Although the Constitution makes no mention of censure, four Presidents have been involved in incidents involving the censure power of Congress.

Andrew Jackson was censured by the Senate for dismissing his secretary of the Treasury, William J. Duane, in a dispute over the Second Bank of the United States. On December 26, 1833, Senator Henry Clay introduced a resolution of censure, which was adopted on March 28, 1834, by a vote of 26 to 20. The Senate resolved that Jackson had acted in a way "not conferred by the Constitution and laws, but in derogation of both." Jackson protested that Congress had only the power of Presidential impeachment— the power to accuse and try a President for serious crimes—not of censure. Therefore, he said, the censure resolution was unconstitutional, and if Congress were serious about dealing with his conduct, it would have used the impeachment mechanism. The Senate refused to enter Jackson's protest in its journal of proceedings. In 1837, with Jackson's party in control of the Senate, the original resolution was expunged, or deleted.

In 1843 President John Tyler was censured by the House of Representatives after it failed to impeach him for vetoing bills passed by the Whig congressional majority. Former President John Quincy Adams chaired a select committee that reported that Tyler had misused his veto power. Tyler, like Jackson, responded with a letter to the House defending his conduct. The House refused to enter it into its journal and the matter was dropped.

President James Buchanan was investigated in 1860 by a congressional committee chaired by Representative John Covode for alleged improprieties involving appointments and contracts for government printing. The Covode committee's work might have led to censure, but President Buchanan sent a message of protest to the House. No resolution of censure was voted.

In 1998, after President Bill Clinton admitted having lied about his affair with a White House intern, House Democrats drafted a resolution of censure. By a nearly party-line vote, the Republican majority defeated the censure resolution and instead impeached the President, who was later acquitted by the Senate.

SEE ALSO

Buchanan, James; Impeachment; Jackson, Andrew; Tyler, John

Senator Henry Clay sews up the mouth of President Andrew Jackson in this cartoon. In 1834, the Senate passed a resolution of censure against Jackson, but it was later expunged, or deleted, from the records.

Ceremonial Presidency

AS HEAD of state, the President represents the American people on many ceremonial occasions. The Constitution, however, mentions none of the President's ceremonial functions, nor does it assign to the President the role of head of state. Some of the President's ceremonial functions are required by law, but most of them have come to be regarded as customary.

Presidents light the national Christmas tree, preside over the Easter egg roll on the White House lawn, and throw out the first ball to open the major league baseball season. They hold receptions to honor Americans who have won international prizes, such as the Nobel Prize. They greet returning astronauts after important missions.

Presidents issue proclamations to draw attention to national priorities, such as National Poison Prevention Week and National Safety Belt Use Day. They give out the Presidential Medal of Freedom, the nation's highest civilian award. Charities such as the American Cancer Society receive Presidential recognition each year. Presidents (or more often Vice Presidents, secretaries of state, or former Presidents) attend funerals of foreign heads of state. They issue memorial statements commemorating the death of prominent Americans and lead the nation in honoring the war dead by laying wreaths at the Tomb of the Unknown Sol-

The Easter egg roll at the White House in 1898. Today, the President still presides over the annual event.

dier on Memorial Day and Veterans Day. Lincoln's Gettysburg Address is the most famous eulogy in American history. With congressional approval, Presidents proclaim national holidays, as George Washington did in 1789 when he created Thanksgiving Day and Ronald Reagan did in 1983 when he declared the third Monday in January to be Martin Luther King, Jr., Day. They also issue proclamations each year celebrating national holidays such as Thanksgiving and the Fourth of July.

SEE ALSO
Gettysburg Address

FURTHER READING
Hinckley, Barbara. *The Symbolic Presidency.* New York: Routledge, 1990.

Checks and balances

THE CONSTITUTION divides the powers and responsibilities of the federal government among the legislative, executive, and judicial branches. Constitutional provisions enable each branch of government to check abuses of power and resist encroachments on its own powers by the other branches, thereby balancing the power of the three branches. James Madison, writing in *The Federalist Papers,* a series of newspaper articles defending the new Constitution, referred to the concept as "a defensive power."

The Presidential check on Congress is the power to veto legislation it passes. Congress can override a veto only by a two-thirds vote. The veto power was used extensively by Presidents John Tyler, Andrew Johnson, Rutherford B. Hayes, Grover Cleveland, Harry S. Truman, Richard Nixon, and Gerald Ford. The principal Presidential check on the judiciary is the appointment power, which

The power of the President (Harry S. Truman) is weighed against the power of the Constitution in this 1952 cartoon.

can change the direction of the federal courts, as it did under Ronald Reagan and George Bush. A secondary Presidential check on the judiciary is the power to pardon people convicted of offenses against the United States.

Principal congressional checks against the President include the power to override the veto. Congress also has the power to impeach and remove the President for bribery, treason, or other high crimes and misdemeanors. Only three Presidents, Andrew Johnson, Richard Nixon, and Bill Clinton, have ever been involved in impeachment proceedings.

The Senate can check Presidential appointments of executive officials, federal judges, and Supreme Court justices by withholding its approval, and it can block implementation of a treaty negotiated by the President if more than one-third of the membership disapproves.

Article 1, Section 8 of the Constitution gives Congress the power to pass laws dealing with the powers of the Presidency. The War Powers Act of 1973, for example, specifies conditions under which the President may use force in hostilities. The Budget and Impoundment Control Act of 1974 permits the President to delay spending funds, subject to congressional approval.

The principal judicial check against the President is the power of judicial review, which allows the Supreme Court and other federal courts to declare a Presidential action unconstitutional, as the Supreme Court did when President Truman seized steel mills to ensure the production of steel for defense industries during the Korean War. To safeguard the justices against Presidential retribution,

federal judges and Supreme Court justices of the United States serve on "good behavior" for life—unless they resign or commit a major offense—and cannot be removed except by the congressional impeachment process.

SEE ALSO

Appointment power; Creation of the Presidency; Impeachment; Pardon power; Pocket veto; Removal power; Steel seizure; Treaty powers; Veto power

FURTHER READING

Ritchie, Donald A. *The U.S. Constitution.* New York: Chelsea House, 1989.

Cheney, Richard
VICE PRESIDENT

☆ Born: Jan. 30, 1941, Lincoln, Neb.
☆ Political party: Republican
☆ Education: University of Wyoming, B.A., 1965; M.A., 1996
☆ Military service: none
☆ Previous government service: Office of Economic Opportunity, 1969–71; assistant director, Cost of Living Council, 1971–73; deputy assistant, White House Staff, 1974–75; White House chief of staff, 1975–76; U.S. representative from Wyoming, 1979–89; secretary of defense, 1989–93

DICK CHENEY was captain of his football team and married his high school sweetheart, one of the team cheerleaders. Cheney worked in the oil business, then entered Richard Nixon's administration as a staff assistant. Rising through the ranks, he became White House chief of staff. After serving in Congress as one of its most conservative members, he became secretary of defense. He presided over two successful military campaigns, Operation Just Cause in Panama and Operation Desert Storm in the Persian Gulf.

Cheney's nomination as Vice Presidential candidate in 2000 added experi-

ence and maturity to the ticket headed by George W. Bush. Cheney was expected to be a forceful proponent of conservative views on social policy and hawkish views on national defense.

SEE ALSO
Bush, George W.

Chief of staff, White House

SEE White House Office

Children of Presidents

THIRTY-FIVE PRESIDENTS of the United States and their wives, through Bill and Hillary Clinton, had 89 boys and 61 girls. Six had no children: George Washington, James Madison, Andrew Jackson, James Polk, James Buchanan, and Warren Harding. Presidents with large families living in the White House included John Tyler, Benjamin Harrison, and Theodore Roosevelt. All the Presidential children were born in the United States except for George Washington Adams (son of John), who was born in Berlin; Herbert Clark Hoover, Jr., and Allen Henry Hoover, both born in London; and Franklin D. Roosevelt, Jr., born at the Roosevelt vacation home on Campobello Island, New Brunswick, Canada.

Theodore Roosevelt's children kept a small zoo and a pony on the White House grounds. His daughter Alice once interrupted a White House meeting, and Roosevelt said, "I can be President of the United States, or I can control Alice. I cannot possibly do both." John F. Kennedy's daughter, Caroline, was also known for her antics in the Oval Office,

Caroline Kennedy plays under her father's desk in the Oval Office with her cousin, Kerry Kennedy.

and his son John-John made the Presidential desk his secret hiding place. The Kennedy children also had a small zoo as well as a tree house and a playground with a slide and tunnel. The Kennedys established a nursery school in the White House, which Caroline and nine other children attended. Jimmy Carter's daughter, Amy, went to a public school in the District of Columbia. She took advantage of the White House movie theater and used a telescope on the White House roof.

Some children of Presidents have grown up to have distinguished government careers of their own. John Quincy Adams was a secretary of state and the sixth President of the United States. Robert Todd Lincoln served as secretary of war for President James Garfield. Franklin D. Roosevelt, Jr., served as under secretary of commerce for President Lyndon Johnson after several terms in the U.S. House of Representatives. Other Presidential sons who served in the House include Charles Francis Adams (son of John Quincy), John Scott Harrison (son of William Henry), David Tyler (son of John), and James Roosevelt (son of Franklin). Robert Taft, Sr. (son of William Howard), was a U.S. senator and a candidate for the Republican Presidential nomination. Other sons who were involved in Presidential politics include John Van Buren, who declined the Free Soil nomination in favor of his father, Martin; John Scott Harrison, who declined the Whig nomination in 1856; and Robert Todd Lincoln, who was defeated at Republican conventions in 1884 and 1888.

A number of Presidential children have served in the armed forces. Frederick D. Grant graduated from West Point. During the Spanish-American War, James Webb Cook Hayes, son of former President Rutherford B. Hayes, won a Medal of Honor in the Philippines. Aviator Quentin Roosevelt, son of Theodore, was shot down and killed in a dogfight in France in World War I. Roosevelt's two other sons, Archibald Roosevelt and Theodore Roosevelt, Jr., also served in that war, and Theodore, Jr., was killed in the Normandy campaign during World War II. The four sons of Franklin D. Roosevelt—James, Elliott, Franklin, and John—also served in World War II. John Eisenhower graduated from West Point and served in the Korean War, turning down an opportunity to leave the combat zone offered by President Harry Truman, who finally ordered him to a different command.

In recent years the children of Presidents have gravitated to the media and entertainment fields. Margaret Truman

became a mystery writer. Lynda Bird Johnson went into magazine publishing. Ron Reagan, Jr., was a ballet dancer and then host of a talk show; his sisters, Maureen Reagan and Patti Davis, wrote books about the First Family. Caroline Kennedy became a lawyer and wrote a best-selling book about the Bill of Rights. Several of George Bush's children have been involved in business and politics. His sons George W. and Jeb have served as governors, and George W. became the 43rd President.

Several Presidential children have been married at the White House. These include Maria Hester Monroe, John Adams (son of John Quincy), Elizabeth Tyler, Nellie Grant, Alice Roosevelt (daughter of Theodore), Jessie Woodrow Wilson and Eleanor Wilson (who married her father's secretary of the Treasury), Lynda Bird Johnson, and Tricia Nixon.

SEE ALSO
First Lady

Cleveland, Grover
22ND AND 24TH PRESIDENT

☆ *Born: Mar. 18, 1837, Caldwell, N.J.*
☆ *Political party: Democrat*
☆ *Education: common school; read law, 1855–59*
☆ *Military service: none*
☆ *Previous government service: ward supervisor, Erie County, N.Y., 1863; assistant district attorney, Erie County, 1863–65; Erie County sheriff, 1871–73; mayor of Buffalo, 1882; governor of New York, 1883–84*
☆ *Elected President, 1884; served, 1885–89; elected, 1892; served, 1893–97*
☆ *Died: June 24, 1908, Princeton, N.J.*

GROVER CLEVELAND began his political career as Erie County sheriff in

Quentin Roosevelt, son of Theodore, rides a pony with the help of a White House policeman.

New York, and after a meteoric rise became the first Democratic President elected after the Civil War and the only President to be married in the White House. In dealing with Congress and state governors, he was the strongest President since Abraham Lincoln.

The son of a Presbyterian minister, Cleveland helped support his family by working in a local grocery store beginning at age 14. He worked on his uncle's farm in Buffalo, then studied law. He became assistant district attorney of Erie County during the Civil War, hiring a substitute to fight for him for $300 when he was drafted, a frequent and legal procedure at the time. In 1865 he was defeated in his first election bid when he ran for district attorney of Erie County.

Nine years later he was elected mayor of Buffalo. As mayor, and then as governor of New York, he ran honest administrations and vetoed patronage (political appointments) and pork barrel measures (special projects for the benefit of particular constituents) of the city council and state legislature. He also vetoed progressive legislation that would have held down transit fares and regulated transit workers' hours.

Cleveland won the Democratic nomination in 1884 because of his record as a reformer. As the keynote speaker at the convention put it, Cleveland was known primarily for "the enemies he has made," particularly the corrupt Democratic Tammany Hall political machine in New York City. He defeated the Republican candidate, James G. Blaine, in a vicious campaign marked by the defection of Republican reformers known as the Mugwumps to the Cleveland camp. (The Mugwumps took their name from the Algonquian Indian Mugquump; like him, they were trying to become chiefs.)

Blaine's followers charged that Cleveland had an illegitimate child. Cleveland denied that the child was his but paid child support anyway. "Ma, Ma, where's my pa? Gone to the White House, ha ha ha!" became the Republican theme. Cleveland defused the issue by advising his campaign allies, "Tell the truth." The issue of morality was raised and disposed of by one supporter who said,"We are told that Mr. Blaine has been delinquent in office but blameless in public life, while Mr. Cleveland has been a model of official integrity but culpable in personal relations. We should therefore elect Mr. Cleveland to the public office which he is so well qualified to fill, and remand Mr. Blaine to the private station which he is admirably fitted to adorn." The election was close; Cleveland won the electoral college vote, 219 to 182.

As President, Cleveland was a conservative in budget matters and a reformer when it came to patronage and the civil service. He expanded the classified "merit appointment" list of the civil service by 85,000 positions. His cabinet and other high-level appointments owed less to patronage and politics and more to merit; his new secretary of the navy, William Whitney, built a modern steel navy that proved its worth to future Presidents. He vetoed 200 of the 1,700 private pension bills Congress passed for veterans of the Civil War, arguing that many of these claims were fraudulent. He also vetoed measures to relieve farmers in the West from drought because he did not believe that the national government had the responsibility under the Constitution to solve the problems of people in need. Like most other Democrats, Cleveland favored lower tariffs (taxes on imported products), arguing that they would benefit consumers, but could not get Congress to pass his proposals. He used federal troops to protect Chinese workers in the Western states after white coal miners had killed and

Grover Cleveland was married to Frances Folsom in the Blue Room in 1886. He is the only President to have been married in the White House.

injured 500 of them in a race riot in Wyoming.

Although Cleveland's administration was free of scandal and corruption, he was not all that popular. In 1888, running against a high-tariff candidate, Republican Benjamin Harrison, he won a majority of the popular vote but lost in the electoral college, in part because he failed to carry New York.

After leaving the White House, Cleveland practiced law in New York City for four years, a period he termed the happiest in his life. In 1892, Cleveland was nominated by the Democrats a third time, and he won the rematch with Harrison. Cleveland ran on a platform of good government, lower tariffs, and a return to using only gold (rather than silver) to back the paper currency issued by the U.S. Treasury. His victory made him the only American President to serve two nonconsecutive terms.

Early in his second term Cleveland had an operation for cancer of the mouth, which was performed in secrecy on a yacht in New York Harbor. The surgery was not revealed to the public for 25 years.

Cleveland's eventful second term was a contrast to his first. The Panic of 1893 led to calls from populists and pro-

gressives for national government programs to regulate the banks, but Cleveland turned a deaf ear. He refused to inflate the currency and forced repeal of the Silver Purchase Act, which had guaranteed that the government would purchase a set amount of silver from mine owners each year. This led to a contraction in the supply of money that worsened already hard times in the West. He bought gold for the Treasury from financiers J. P. Morgan and Augustus Belmont that returned them large profits. He refused to compromise with high-tariff interests in the Northeast, leading to an erosion of his support.

Labor unrest added to Cleveland's troubles. When Jacob S. Coxey led "Coxey's army," a group of unemployed men, to the capital to demand public service jobs, Cleveland had them dispersed by the police. When Pullman railway car workers went on strike in 1894, Cleveland won a court injunction and then sent 2,000 federal troops into Illinois to break the strike. At the behest of Attorney General Richard Olney, a former railroad lawyer himself, the socialist leader Eugene V. Debs, head of the American Railway Union, was jailed for his role in organizing a boycott of Pullman cars in support of the strikers.

In foreign affairs Cleveland refused to accept a petition from a white settlers' government that Hawaii be annexed by the United States, accurately describing the local "Committee of Safety" as unrepresentative of the native population and not elected by it. In 1895 he insisted that the British government accept an American determination of the boundary between Venezuela and British Guyana. Ultimately, the British and Venezuelans negotiated an end to their boundary dispute, and arbitration upheld most of the British claim. Cleveland refused to intervene in the Cuban revolt against Spanish rule, leaving the problem for his successor. When there was talk in Congress of declaring war against Spain, Cleveland let it be known that as commander in chief he would refuse to use the military to fight such a war. He also rejected the idea that the United States buy Cuba from Spain. Instead, he proposed that the Spanish offer "genuine autonomy" to the Cubans.

By 1896 Cleveland's leadership was repudiated by his own party. A coalition of populists and silver Democrats, who were interested in aid to farmers, regulation of business, and increased use of silver coins as currency, dominated the party convention. It turned away from conservative policies and nominated the fiery populist William Jennings Bryan.

Cleveland moved to Princeton, New Jersey, and became a trustee of Princeton University. When he died in 1908 he was buried in Princeton Cemetery, close to the grave of former Vice President Aaron Burr.

SEE ALSO

Harrison, Benjamin

FURTHER READING

Nevins, Allan. *Grover Cleveland: A Study in Courage*. New York: Dodd, Mead, 1932.
Welch, Richard E. *The Presidencies of Grover Cleveland*. Lawrence: University Press of Kansas, 1988.

Clinton, Bill

42ND PRESIDENT

☆ *Born: Aug. 19, 1946, Hope, Ark.*
☆ *Political party: Democrat*
☆ *Education: Georgetown University, B.S., 1968; Rhodes scholar, Oxford University, 1968–70; Yale University, J.D., 1973*
☆ *Military service: none*
☆ *Previous government service: attorney general of Arkansas, 1977–79; governor of Arkansas, 1979–81, 1983–92*
☆ *Elected President, 1992; served 1993–2001*

BILL (WILLIAM JEFFERSON) CLINTON was only the second Democrat to win the Presidency since 1968. Like Jimmy Carter, he had been a Southern governor identified with the moderate rather than the liberal wing of his party. He was also the first President from the "baby boom" generation (born between 1946 and 1960).

Clinton's father was killed in an automobile accident three months before he was born, and he was adopted by his mother's second husband. Throughout his school years he was considered a leader. Selected for the Boys Nation Leadership Camp in 1963, he shook hands with John F. Kennedy at the White House. He worked for Arkansas senator J. William Fulbright as an intern during his college years at Georgetown University and won a Rhodes scholarship to study at Oxford University. In 1969 he organized two anti–Vietnam War rallies in London.

In 1972 Clinton worked for George McGovern as codirector of his Presidential campaign in Texas. That fall Clinton entered Yale Law School. He taught at the University of Arkansas law school from 1974 to 1976, becoming only the second future President to teach constitutional law (the first was Woodrow Wilson).

Clinton became active in Arkansas Democratic politics. After losing a race for the U.S. House of Representatives in 1974, he was elected attorney general of Arkansas in 1976 and then governor in 1978 with more than 60 percent of the vote. He raised taxes and was defeated for a second term, becoming the youngest ex-governor in U.S. history. He was again elected governor in 1982 and served until 1992. He was elected president of the National Governors Association and was instrumental in founding the Democratic Leadership Conference, an organization devoted to moving the Democratic party away from its liberal orientation toward a centrist position, designed to win back voters in the southern and border states in Presidential elections.

In the spring of 1991, when President Bush's popularity stood at 91 percent in the aftermath of the Persian Gulf War, Clinton began his run for the 1992 Presidential nomination. He defeated a weak field of contenders in the primaries despite allegations that he had engaged in extramarital affairs, had smoked marijuana, and had avoided military service during the Vietnam War.

In a three-candidate race (involving the independent candidacy of Texas billionaire Ross Perot) Clinton positioned himself as the one best equipped to manage the economy. His selection of Tennessee Democratic senator Al Gore as his running mate added strength to the ticket and took away the Republican advantage in the southern and border states.

Clinton broke new ground in campaign strategy. He appeared on a late-night television show wearing sunglasses and played the saxophone in a successful attempt to appeal to younger voters. He followed up with many appearances on daytime television and radio talk shows.

Clinton won his first election with 42 percent of the popular vote, against 37 percent for Bush and 19 percent for Perot. He won 370 electoral college votes, compared with 160 for Bush.

In his first term, Clinton cut the annual deficits in half, laying the groundwork for growth, as well as lower unemployment and inflation. His bill to provide health insurance to all Americans was defeated after health insurers lobbied against it in Congress. Questions about his character continued to dog Clinton, especially his role in a scandal involving a failed savings and loan institution in Arkansas. In the 1994 midterm elections, Republicans won control of Congress for the first time in 40 years, putting an end to Clinton's legislative agenda. Thereafter his threat to veto Republican measures enabled him to negotiate with House Speaker Newt Gingrich and Senate majority leader Robert Dole on welfare reform and environmental policy.

Clinton won reelection over former senator Bob Dole with almost half the vote of the electorate, but the Congress, which in the 1994 midterm elections had become controlled by Republicans, remained in the hands of the opposition party. Two years into his second term, Clinton had failed to win enactment of his major health care initiatives but otherwise had compiled a respectable legislative record by cooperating with the Republicans or outmaneuvering them. He reoriented the Democratic party toward the center by balancing the budget, winning crime control measures (crime rates plunged during his terms), and cooperating with the Republicans to end "welfare as we know it" by providing incentives for states to reform their programs to get recipients into jobs.

Clinton's administration also downsized the federal departments as part of a "reinventing government" initiative. Clinton worked hard to improve race relations by appointing minorities to high positions in his administration and beginning a national dialogue on race.

A saxophone pin indicated support for Bill Clinton in the 1992 election.

He appointed women to the highest positions in government, including for the first time secretary of state and attorney general. He presided over one of the longest periods of economic expansion in the 20th century, with low rates of interest, inflation, and unemployment and high rates of economic growth. In consequence, the stock market reached new highs, and so did his job approval rating in the polls.

Throughout his Presidency, Clinton remained a centrist, attacked by conservatives for his defense of affirmative action programs and abortion rights and attacked by liberals for his willingness to cut domestic programs.

In foreign affairs, Clinton acted cautiously. He pulled U.S. troops out of Somalia after they came under attack; negotiated with North Korea to halt its development of nuclear weapons; and allowed former President Jimmy Carter to negotiate an agreement with Haiti's military rulers that allowed for a peaceful occupation of Haiti. In other diplomatic efforts, Clinton worked to secure peace agreements between Protestants and Catholics in Northern Ireland and between Israelis and Palestinians in the Middle East.

Clinton and other Western leaders made the decision to launch air attacks in Bosnia against the Serbs, which led to the Dayton Accords. Then in 1999 NATO leaders acted militarily against Serbia for its repression of the Kosovars, a decision that required Clinton to use all his negotiating skills to lessen the confrontation between NATO and the Russians and between his administration and the Chinese.

Clinton also backed a "Partnership for Peace" that would eventually permit Eastern European nations to join NATO without antagonizing Russia. Twenty years after the end of the Vietnam War, he established diplomatic relations with the communist government of Vietnam. Despite its human rights violations, Clinton refused to sever U.S. commercial relations with China.

Clinton showed leadership in international trade issues. He led the United States into the North American Free Trade Agreement (NAFTA) with Canada and Mexico against the opposition of a majority of his party and made $20 billion available to Mexico during the transition to a free-trade zone. He won congressional approval for the 1994 General Agreement on Tariffs and Trade (GATT), which lowered tariffs and provided for a World Trade Organization (WTO). Both NAFTA and the WTO led to an increase in world trade.

In January 1998 the news media reported that Clinton had had an affair with White House intern Monica Lewinsky. At first the President denied the allegation, but by late August he had admitted to having an "improper relationship" with her. Independent Counsel Kenneth Starr submitted a referral to the House of Representatives outlining possible "high crimes and misdemeanors," and the House subsequently voted to impeach Clinton for perjury and obstruction of justice committed during the investigation of his sexual relationships with Paula Jones and Monica Lewinsky. The vote was highly partisan, with most Democrats defending the President and most Republicans voting for impeachment.

In February 1999 the crisis ended when the Senate failed to muster the two-thirds vote needed to convict—or, for that matter, failed to secure even a majority. Clinton remained in office, but he was unable to pursue much of his legislative agenda because of the impeachment crisis and the conflict in the Balkans.

SEE ALSO
Bush, George; Gore, Albert, Jr.

FURTHER READING

Campbell, Colin, and Bert A. Rockman, eds. *The Clinton Presidency: First Appraisals.* Chatham, N.J.: Chatham House, 1995.

Drew, Elizabeth. *On the Edge: The Clinton Presidency.* New York: Simon & Schuster, 1994.

Maraniss, David. *First in His Class.* New York: Simon & Schuster, 1995.

Posner, Richard A. *An Affair of State: The Investigation, Impeachment, and Trial of President Clinton.* Cambridge: Harvard University Press, 1999.

Renshon, Stanley A. *High Hopes: The Clinton Presidency and the Politics of Ambition.* New York: Routledge, 1998.

Clinton, George

VICE PRESIDENT

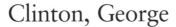

☆ *Born: July 26, 1739, Little Britain, N.Y.*

☆ *Political party: Democratic-Republican*

☆ *Education: no formal education*

☆ *Military service: New York Militia, 1775–77; Continental Army, 1777*

☆ *Previous government service: governor of New York, 1777–95, 1801–4; New York State Assembly, 1800–1801*

☆ *Vice President under Thomas Jefferson, 1805–9, and James Madison, 1809–12*

☆ *Died: Apr. 20, 1812, Washington, D.C.*

GEORGE CLINTON was the first governor of New York, serving during and after the revolutionary war. He also served as a brigadier general during the war. He was a strong governor whose conduct in office served as a model for the delegates at the Constitutional Convention who wanted a strong executive. Clinton himself presided over the New York State Convention called to consider ratification. He opposed ratification of the Constitution in 1788 because he believed in strong state government and a weak national government. Like most of the early Anti-Federalists, he followed Thomas Jefferson and James Madison into the Republican party,

opposing President George Washington and Alexander Hamilton. He served again as governor of New York between 1801 and 1804. Clinton received some electoral college votes in 1789, 1792, and 1796, but not enough to win the Presidency or Vice Presidency.

In 1804 President Thomas Jefferson barred Vice President Aaron Burr from gaining the Republican party's renomination, and the Republicans nominated Clinton to take Burr's place on the ticket. Jefferson and Clinton defeated the Federalist candidates, Charles Cotesworth Pinckney and Rufus King. In 1808 Clinton was again nominated to serve as Vice President, and he was reelected on the Republican ticket led by James Madison.

Like most 19th-century Vice Presidents, Clinton did little in office. His most important act occurred in 1812, while he was presiding over the Senate: he cast the tiebreaking vote against the bill to recharter the Bank of the United States. He retained his hold on the Vice Presidency in 1812 but died in office before his third term began.

SEE ALSO

Burr, Aaron; Jefferson, Thomas; Madison, James

FURTHER READING

Kaminski, John P. *George Clinton: Yeoman Politician of the New Republic.* Madison, Wis.: Madison House, 1990.

Coattails, Presidential

PRESIDENTIAL COATTAILS is a term that refers to the ability of a Presidential candidate to bring out supporters who then vote for his party's candidates for other offices. In effect, the other candidates are said to ride on his coattails. In the 19th century voters cast their ballots by taking a ticket provided by a party worker and putting it in the ballot box. The party-column ballot listed all candidates of the party in a single column and allowed the voter to mark off the party box at the top, which encouraged straight-party voting and the coattails effect. Straight-party voting was the norm, and winners in Presidential elections often had long coattails. They almost always began their term with majorities in the House and Senate.

In modern times voting machines have replaced the party-column ballot with the office-column ballot: candidates are grouped by office rather than party. Often there is no way to cast a party-line vote, and each office must be voted on separately. The proportion of voters choosing House and Presidential candidates of different parties increased from 13 percent in 1952 to more than 40 percent in the elections of 1972, 1980, and 1988. Consequently, Presidential coattails have been virtually eliminated in most elections, and a number of Presidents—including Richard Nixon, Ronald Reagan, and George Bush—have begun their terms with one or both chambers of Congress controlled by the opposition party.

Presidents may suffer from a "reverse coattail" effect, in which more votes are cast for their party's candidates for the House or Senate than are cast for them. In 1976, for example, Jimmy Carter won the White House and obtained a total of 40,828,587 votes, but Democratic candidates for the House that year received 41,749,411 votes. In 1992 almost all Democrats elected to Congress won more votes than the party's Presidential candidate, Bill Clinton.

There is also the "negative coattail" effect, in which an unpopular Presidential candidate may hurt candidates on the party's ticket running for lower offices. Barry Goldwater's poor showing in the Presidential election of 1964 led to the defeat of dozens of Republicans in the House of Representatives, leaving President Lyndon Johnson a large Democratic majority to pass his programs.

SEE ALSO

Election campaigns, Presidential; Johnson, Lyndon Baines

FURTHER READING

Calvert, Randall, and John Ferejohn. "Coattail Voting in Recent Presidential Elections." *American Political Science Review* 7 (June 1983): 407–19.
Campbell, James, and Joe Sumners. "Presidential Coattails in Senate Elections." *American Political Science Review* 84 (June 1990): 513–24.

Colfax, Schuyler
VICE PRESIDENT

☆ Born: Mar. 23, 1823, New York, N.Y.
☆ Political party: Republican
☆ Education: grammar school
☆ Military service: none
☆ Previous government service: U.S. House of Representatives, 1855–69; Speaker of the House, 1863–69
☆ Vice President under Ulysses S. Grant, 1869–73
☆ Died: Jan. 13, 1885, Mankato, Minn.

SCHUYLER COLFAX worked as a journalist in Indiana before winning election to the U.S. House of Representatives in 1854. Colfax's nickname in the House was Smiler because of his genial manner. He was chosen Speaker of the House during the Civil War and by 1868 was frequently mentioned as a Republican candidate for President. Colfax supported Ulysses S. Grant and was rewarded with the Vice Presidential nomination.

Colfax served one undistinguished term as Grant's Vice President, and the Republicans declined to renominate him. After the Republican convention of 1872, the Credit Mobilier financial scandal erupted: directors of the Union Pacific railroad had given stock in their Credit Mobilier company to several members of Congress, including Colfax when he had been Speaker. There were some calls for his impeachment, but his term of office was ending and no action was taken. He spent the last years of his life as a public speaker.

FURTHER READING

Smith, Willard, II. *Schuyler Colfax: The Changing Fortunes of a Political Idol.* Indianapolis: Indiana Historical Bureau, 1952.

Commander in chief

ARTICLE 2, SECTION 2, of the Constitution refers to the President as "Commander in Chief of the Army and Navy of the United States, and of the Militia of the several states, when called into the actual service of the United States." This clause is the only mention the Constitution makes of Presidential war powers.

Harry Truman meets General of the Army Douglas MacArthur on Wake Island in October 1950.

By it the President becomes, in Alexander Hamilton's phrase, "first general and admiral," and no one may be placed over him by Congress. Nor can he be outvoted by his cabinet, his senior military commanders, or the National Security Council. Final military decisions rest solely with the President, as with Harry Truman when he alone ordered atomic bombs dropped on Japan in 1945.

The President issues orders through the chain of command that runs (by act of Congress) through the secretary of defense and the Joint Chiefs of Staff to the military theater (on-site, or field) commanders. The President's power to command troops, to assign them duties, and to move them anywhere he deems fit is generally not restricted by the courts.

It is not expected that the President will personally take command of troops, though like George Washington during the Whiskey Rebellion he may review them to determine their combat readiness. And like Abraham Lincoln during the Civil War, he may visit senior commanders near the theater of operations. He may also, as Woodrow Wilson did in World War I, temporarily place American forces under a foreign commander.

The President is not himself a member of the armed forces even in his capacity as commander in chief. To preserve the principle of civilian control of the military, it is a custom, adhered to by all candidates beginning with Washington, that a member of the armed forces will resign before running for President or taking the oath of office. Ulysses S. Grant, for example, did so in 1868, and Dwight Eisenhower did so in 1952.

The President's most important role as commander in chief is to defend the United States, its territories and possessions, and its armed forces against attack, and he need not wait for Congress to declare war to do so. The President also supervises the establishment of military rule in theaters of war, proclaims and enforces martial law (military rule) and establishes military courts in conquered territories, establishes military governments to rule these territories, and can proclaim armistices and cease-fires and conduct peace negotiations with the enemy. The President does not have the power to permanently acquire territory, but he may govern by Presidential decree until Congress acts. The Panama Canal Zone was governed in

DECEM. 26 1776.

THE HERO WHO DEFENDED THE MOTHERS   WILL PROTECT THE DAUGHTERS.

As a war hero, George Washington was well qualified to be the nation's commander in chief. Here the President-elect greets a crowd in New Jersey.

this manner from 1905 to 1912. The President may seize enemy property according to the rules of international law, but he may not seize or take control of property in the United States to pursue his war aims, except under provision of laws passed by Congress.

The President does not have absolute power to choose his military subordinates. Congress by law determines the ranks and qualifications for commissioned officers, and the Senate must consent to the appointment of all officers. The President's power to dismiss officers from the service is confined in peacetime to dismissal after a court-martial, or trial, but he can dismiss any officer from a particular command by naming someone else in his or her place. In wartime the President has an absolute power of dismissal.

Thirteen presidents had no military experience: John Adams, Thomas Jefferson, John Quincy Adams, Martin Van Buren, Millard Fillmore, Grover Cleveland, William Taft, Woodrow Wilson, Warren Harding, Calvin Coolidge, Herbert Hoover, Franklin D. Roosevelt, and Bill Clinton. Another, Abraham Lincoln, served briefly in an Illinois volunteer regiment and was reprimanded twice for breaches of discipline. Of these Presidents, John Adams, Lincoln, Wilson, and Roosevelt presided over serious con-

flicts (the naval war with France, the Civil War, and World Wars I and II), and historians do not regard their lack of military experience as a handicap in functioning as commander in chief.

SEE ALSO

War powers; War Powers Resolution

Congressional caucus

THE CONGRESSIONAL caucus was a method of nominating Presidential candidates used by the Federalist party in 1800 and the Democratic-Republican party between 1800 and 1824.

Each party's congressional caucus consisted of its U.S. senators and representatives. At the end of the congressional session in the Presidential election year, the party members met at the Capitol or a local tavern or boardinghouse. A vote was taken, and the candidate receiving a majority would be declared the party nominee for President. A "committee of correspondence and arrangements" would then send word to party newspapers, which would announce the caucus decision to the public.

No congressional caucus was held in 1789, when George Washington was "nominated" by the public by acclamation at huge outdoor rallies. For the second Presidential election, a number of Republicans met in Philadelphia on October 16, 1792, to choose a candidate for Vice President. They decided to back George Clinton rather than Aaron Burr. A similar meeting took place in June 1796, at which time Thomas Jefferson and Burr were chosen as Republican nominees for President and Vice President. In both cases the caucuses were "mixed" because many politicians who were not members of Congress attended the sessions.

The first full-fledged congressional caucus was held by the Federalists on May 3, 1800, when they nominated John Adams for reelection as President and Charles Cotesworth Pinckney to be Vice President. The Republicans held their first nominating caucus on March 11, 1800, and chose Jefferson for President and Aaron Burr as his running mate. The Republicans held their first pure congressional caucus (limited to members of Congress) on February 25, 1804. Jefferson was renominated for President. The dispirited Federalists did not even hold a caucus that year.

Federalist representatives from eight states held an informal meeting in New York City in July 1808, but no formal caucus was held. Some Federalist party leaders caucused in 1812 and secretly agreed to back Clinton against James Madison, exploiting a split in the Republican party rather than nominating their own candidate.

Through 1824 Republican congressional caucuses nominated candidates, but from 1808 on, many of the representatives backing candidates not expected to win the nomination absented themselves, so the caucuses were really gatherings of the front-runner's supporters rather than a deliberative body. Proxy votes (a form of absentee ballot) for missing legislators were permitted in 1816 and 1824. The caucus of 1820 involved only 50 members of Congress, and it was not considered "expedient" to take a vote because James Monroe was the President and had no opposition to his renomination from within his party.

The congressional caucus was discredited in the election of 1824 by Andrew Jackson, who referred to it as "King Caucus" because of its allegedly corrupt and undemocratic proceedings. Tennessee and Maryland instructed their congressional delegations to boycott any caucus proceeding. Several state legislatures favorable to Jackson or John Quincy Adams held their own caucuses to "nominate" their choices. When the congressional caucus was convened on February 14, 1824, only 66 members of Congress, representing only 14 of 22 states, attended. Almost all of those who attended were backers of William H. Crawford. Adams and Jackson simply ignored the congressional caucus and its endorsement.

The caucus system fell into disuse because the Republican party disintegrated under Jackson's onslaught in 1828. That year several state legislatures "nominated" Jackson by passing resolutions recommending him to the electorate.

The caucus system had shortcomings. It did not provide any representation for states that had not elected Republicans to Congress. It was poorly attended. State party leaders did not take part. But in some respects the caucus worked well for the Republicans while it lasted. It provided "peer review"—the judgment of people who knew the candidates personally and had worked with them—for the cabinet secretaries and congressional leaders running for President.

SEE ALSO
Adams, John; Adams, John Quincy; Burr, Aaron; Clinton, George; Jackson, Andrew; Jefferson, Thomas; Madison, James; Monroe, James; Washington, George

FURTHER READING
Stanwood, Edward. "The Defeat of King Caucus." Chap. 11 in A *History of the Presidency*. Boston: Houghton Mifflin, 1898.
Thompson, C. S. *The Rise and Fall of the Congressional Caucus*. New Haven: Yale University Academical Department, 1902.

Conventions

SEE Nominating conventions, Presidential

Coolidge, Calvin

30TH PRESIDENT

☆ *Born: July 4, 1872, Plymouth, Vt.*
☆ *Political party: Republican*
☆ *Education: Amherst College, B.A., 1895*
☆ *Military service: none*
☆ *Previous government service: Northampton, Mass., City Council, 1898–1900; Northampton city solicitor, 1901; clerk of the Northampton courts, 1905–6; Massachusetts State Assembly, 1907–9; mayor of Northampton, 1910–11; Massachusetts Senate, 1911–15; president, Massachusetts Senate, 1913–15; lieutenant governor of Massachusetts, 1916–19; governor of Massachusetts, 1919–21; Vice President, 1921–23*
☆ *Succeeded to Presidency, 1923; served, 1923–29*
☆ *Died: Jan. 5, 1933, Northampton, Mass.*

CALVIN COOLIDGE succeeded to the Presidency in the midst of the Teapot Dome scandal, which involved corruption in the sale of leases on naval oil reserves to private investors. His firm resolve to investigate corruption, and his firing of Attorney General Harry Daugherty for refusing to respond to investigations of corruption, did much to restore public confidence in the Republican party. Coolidge did little, but he was immensely popular.

Coolidge was born in a small town in Vermont, where he worked in his father's general store and on his own farm. He graduated from Amherst College and two years later became a lawyer. He then became active in Republican politics, moving from local office to become president of the Massachusetts Senate, then lieutenant governor, and finally governor.

Calvin Coolidge gained national attention while governor for his handling of the Boston police strike of September 1919. The police force demanded union recognition, and when it went out on strike, looting and rioting occurred in the downtown stores. Coolidge ordered the state militia into the city to restore order, and on September 11 he took control of the police department. He backed the Boston mayor's refusal to reinstate the striking police officers. In a message to Samuel Gompers, president of the American Federation of Labor, he argued, "There is no right to strike against the public safety by anybody, anywhere, any time." That sentence brought him immediate acclaim and a large reelection margin.

Coolidge went on to campaign for the Republican Presidential nomination in 1920, but he lacked the support of Massachusetts senator Henry Cabot Lodge. The convention denied him the nomination, but the rank-and-file delegates selected him as Warren Harding's running mate. Coolidge had no part in the scandals that occurred during Harding's administration. He presided over the Senate and was the first Vice President to attend cabinet sessions.

After learning of President Harding's death on August 3, 1923, Coolidge was sworn in as President by his father, the justice of the peace in Plymouth, Vermont. He was the first President from New England since Franklin Pierce. Coolidge became a very popular President because of his unusual public diffidence—it was hard for anybody, anywhere, at any time, to get a word out of Silent Cal. In the spring of 1924, when the Teapot Dome scandal broke, he appointed a special prosecutor and new attorney general to investigate the scandals, using the slogan "Let the guilty be punished."

That summer Coolidge won the Republican nomination on the first ballot, at the first convention to be broadcast on the radio. With his smashing election victory over Democrat John W. Davis and Progressive Robert La Follette, he became the second President, after

In March 1925, Coolidge met with members of the Sioux Indian Republican Club of the Rosebud Reservation.

Theodore Roosevelt, to win a term in his own right after completing the term of his deceased predecessor.

"The business of America is business," Coolidge had observed as Vice President, and once in the White House his priorities were to reduce government expenditures, lessen government regulation of corporations, promote subsidies for industries and protect them with high tariffs (taxes on imported products), and cut taxes. He vetoed 50 liberal spending bills passed by a coalition of progressive Republicans and Democrats. He used surpluses to reduce the national debt. He refused to take action in the coal strike of 1927. He got Congress to cut the income tax and inheritance tax. These policies fueled a boom in the stock market.

In foreign policy Coolidge continued the Republican opposition to American participation in the League of Nations. He won Senate approval of a treaty that provided for American adherence to the World Court, but the reservations attached by the Senate proved unacceptable to other nations and Coolidge dropped the issue. He moderated American disputes over the oil and mineral policy of the revolutionary government of Mexico. He sent marines into Nicaragua to preserve order at the request of its government, repulsing rebels led by Augusto Sandino. He negotiated the

Kellogg-Briand Pact of 1927, which renounced war as an instrument of national policy, though it did little good in the next decade.

In 1927 Coolidge issued an announcement: "I do not choose to run for President in 1928." After leaving office he wrote an autobiography and with the proceeds lived in comfortable retirement.

SEE ALSO
Harding, Warren G.

FURTHER READING
McCoy, Donald R. *Calvin Coolidge: The Quiet President.* New York: Macmillan, 1967.
White, William A. *A Puritan in Babylon.* New York: Macmillan, 1938.

Council of Economic Advisers

THE COUNCIL of Economic Advisers (CEA) is a three-member unit of the Executive Office of the President that provides the President with economic advice. It was established by the Employment Act of 1946; its members are appointed by the President. The CEA provides the President with economic advice on policies to stimulate growth, maintain price stability, and provide for full employment and advises on issues of international economics. It conducts research on economic problems and prepares the annual *Economic Report of the President,* which, accompanied by the President's economic message, is transmitted to Congress each January.

The CEA helps make fiscal policy—decisions on the relationship between revenues and expenditures—through its forecasts of future economic performance and the revenues the government is likely to receive. These estimates are used to prepare the President's budget and tax requests to Congress. The CEA often projects lower revenues than the Treasury Department does as well as higher spending levels than the Office of Management and Budget does. Such discrepancies sometimes lead to conflicts within the Presidential advisory system.

Some members of the CEA offer the President expert nonpolitical advice. The first chair of the CEA, Edwin Nourse, observed in a letter to President Harry Truman that "there is no occasion for the Council to become involved in any way in the advocacy of particular measures." Truman had no use for this approach and fired Nourse. He appointed as CEA chair a highly partisan Democrat, Leon Keyserling, who was not even a professional economist but was willing to defend the administration's policy proposals. Gardner Ackley, who chaired the CEA under President Lyndon Johnson, concluded, "If his economic advisor refrains from advice on the gut questions of policy, the President should and will get another one."

The CEA may also play a major role in planning new domestic programs. Its members chaired or participated in task forces that created many of John Kennedy's New Frontier and Lyndon Johnson's Great Society programs, including the War on Poverty. In the administrations of Gerald Ford, Jimmy Carter, Ronald Reagan, and George Bush, CEA members served on task forces dealing with deregulation of industry, energy policy, and international economic negotiations.

In 1993 President Bill Clinton appointed the first woman to chair the CEA: Laura D'Andrea Tyson, an expert in revitalizing American industry and in trade negotiation.

SEE ALSO

Executive Office of the President; Office of Management and Budget

FURTHER READING

Flash, Edward S. *Economic Advice and Presidential Leadership.* New York: Columbia University Press, 1965.

Hargrove, Erwin C., and Samuel A. Morley, eds. *The President and the Council of Economic Advisers.* Boulder, Colo.: Westview, 1984.

Pfiffner, James, ed. *The President and Economic Policy.* Philadelphia: Institute for the Study of Human Issues, 1986.

Council on Environmental Quality

THE COUNCIL on Environmental Quality (CEQ) is the unit of the Executive Office of the President that recommends to the President national policies to preserve and improve environmental quality. It also analyzes changes and trends in the environment, reviews government programs to determine their effects on environmental policy, conducts research relating to ecological systems and environmental quality, assists the President in the preparation of the annual environmental quality report to Congress, and oversees implementation of the National Environmental Policy Act of 1969 and the Environmental Quality Improvement Act of 1970.

The CEQ was established by the National Environmental Policy Act of 1969. It replaced the Environmental Quality Council, which had been created by President Richard Nixon's executive order in June 1969. The CEQ consists of three members appointed by the President with the advice and consent of the Senate. The chair of the CEQ also serves as chair of the President's Commission

Exposure to hazardous chemicals is one concern of the Council on Environmental Quality.

on Environmental Quality, an advisory group consisting of private citizens.

SEE ALSO
Executive Office of the President

Counsel, Office of

THE OFFICE of Counsel is the unit within the White House Office that provides legal advice to the President and his aides on policy and personal matters, including conflict of interest and ethics laws. The Office of Counsel consists of approximately 20 lawyers and is headed by the White House counsel, who is appointed by the President.

Duties of the counsel include handling requests for Presidential pardons and commutation of sentences; advising the President on which gifts he may accept for the nation; ensuring compliance with campaign finance laws during election campaigns; and responding to subpoenas from Congress for information and, when necessary, invoking executive privilege (the right of the President to withhold information about his activities from Congress or the courts). The White House counsel advises the President whether to sign or veto legislation and supervises compliance with the War Powers Resolution, a law that requires the President to report to Congress when he introduces U.S. armed forces into hostilities or situations that might lead to hostilities. The counsel's office prepares a handbook on procedures to be followed in case of Presidential disability, according to the provisions of the 25th Amendment to the Constitution. The office reviews data on appointments with the White House Personnel Office and the Office of Government Ethics and may show copies of Federal Bureau of Investigation reports and tax-compliance sum-

maries prepared by the Internal Revenue Service to Senate committees reviewing Presidential nominations.

The White House counsel interviews candidates for District of Columbia judgeships, reviews the nominations made by the attorney general for federal judgeships, and is a principal adviser to the President on Supreme Court nominations.

At the end of a President's term, the White House counsel handles legal matters in connection with the establishment of a Presidential library and the disposition of the Presidential papers.

SEE ALSO
Appointment power; Ethics, Presidential; Office of Government Ethics; Pardon power; White House Office.

Court-packing plan

COURT PACKING was an attempt by President Franklin D. Roosevelt to increase the size of the Supreme Court in order to make additional appointments of justices who would support his programs. The size of the court is not fixed by the Constitution but is set by Congress in Judiciary Acts and has varied from 6 to 10 members.

In 1935, in the case of *Schechter* v. *United States,* the Supreme Court invalidated Roosevelt's New Deal industrial recovery program; the same year, in *Carter* v. *Carter Coal Products,* it struck down a federal tax on coal producers. In 1936, in *United States* v. *Butler,* it struck down the Agricultural Adjustment Act. Between 1935 and 1937 the Court struck down 76 laws passed by Congress, almost all of them regulating the economy.

Four justices, Willis Van Devanter, James McReynolds, George Sutherland, and Pierce Butler, were ardent opponents of the New Deal. Three justices had voted to uphold Roosevelt's program: Louis D. Brandeis, Harlan Fiske Stone, and Benjamin Cardozo. Chief Justice Charles Evans Hughes and Associate Justice Owen Roberts were swing voters; they sometimes upheld New Deal legislation, but they had voted to strike down several laws that they believed delegated too much power to New Deal agencies. None of these justices had been appointed by Roosevelt, who was the first President since James Monroe to serve a term without making any appointments.

On February 5, 1937, President Roosevelt sent to Congress a bill that would have added a new justice for every sitting justice 70 years of age or older. This bill would have given the President six new appointments, enough to ensure a majority in favor of his programs. Many members of his own party were dubious about the wisdom of interfering with the high court's independence. Chief Justice Hughes lobbied hard against the measure, providing statistics to Congress indicating that the Court had no trouble keeping up with its work load, which was the reason Roosevelt had offered for increasing the size of the court.

In the midst of the struggle over the plan, Justices Hughes and Roberts voted to support several New Deal measures, including the Wagner Labor Relations Act and the Social Security Act. These votes were dubbed "the switch in time that saved nine." Public support for the court-packing plan diminished.

Realizing that his proposal was in trouble, Roosevelt accepted a compromise worked out by supporters in Congress. The President would make one additional appointment each year for every justice 75 or older. But it was too late to stem defections by congressional Democrats. On July 22, 1937, Roosevelt's court-packing plan was voted down by the Senate, 70 to 20. Although the Court never again struck down New

Deal economic legislation, the negative vote on the court-packing plan led to the creation of a coalition of southern Democrats allied with Republicans in the so-called Conservative Coalition. Roosevelt had very few legislative successes after 1937, in large measure because of the opposition of that coalition.

SEE ALSO

Appointment power; New Deal; Roosevelt, Franklin D.

FURTHER READING

Baker, Leonard. *Back to Back: The Duel between FDR and the Supreme Court.* New York: Macmillan, 1967.

Leuchtenburg, William. "The Origins of Franklin D. Roosevelt's 'Court-Packing Plan.'" *Supreme Court Review* (1966): 347–400.

Leuchtenburg, William. *The Supreme Court Reborn: The Constitutional Revolution in the Age of Roosevelt.* New York: Oxford, 1996.

Nelson, Michael. "The President and the Court: Reinterpreting the Court-packing Episode of 1937." *Political Science Quarterly* 103, no. 2 (1988): 267–93.

Creation of the Presidency

THE OFFICE of President of the United States was created at the Constitutional Convention of 1787. The framers had three options: to create a weak executive to administer the departments of government, whose powers would come solely from laws passed by Congress; to create a stronger executive that would be able to check and balance Congress; or to establish an executive with its own constitutional grants of power.

The Virginia Plan (designed by George Mason and James Madison of Virginia), with which delegates began their work, envisioned a weak plural executive that would be elected by Congress and subject to recall by a majority

Gouverneur Morris, a delegate to the Constitutional Convention from Pennsylvania, was an advocate for strong Presidential powers.

of state governors or state legislatures. In contrast, Alexander Hamilton proposed a supreme governor to be elected by the people or their delegates for life, with an absolute veto over laws passed by the legislature and armed with "Supreme Executive Power." The Constitutional Convention settled on a middle course, providing for an executive branch that could check the legislature. Eventually, it also accepted language that would allow the President to exercise vast constitutional powers on his own prerogative, without requiring Congress to pass laws giving him authority to act in many diplomatic or military matters.

Convention deliberations began with Robert Morris's motion, which carried unanimously, to make George Washington the presiding officer. It was obvious that delegates expected Washington to lead the new government. All deliberations about the powers of the executive were also debates about powers to be accorded to Washington. "The first man put at the helm will be a good one," Benjamin Franklin acknowledged; "nobody knows what sort may come afterwards."

The Virginia Plan created a "National Executive" consisting of several officials elected by Congress who would be vested with "general power to execute National laws," but it specified neither the length of the term nor the powers of the office. No person holding an executive office would be eligible to serve in Congress simultaneously, and Congress could not change the salary of the President during his term. Both of these provisions were designed to promote the separation of the executive and legislative branches that later appeared in the Constitution. The executive would have a check on laws passed by Congress, but that power would be shared by a Council of Revision consisting of members of the high court, called the "supreme tribunal." Congress could,

however, pass a law over the veto. The members of the executive could be impeached, or tried for crimes, by the "supreme tribunal."

After two weeks of debate these provisions were replaced by an article that called for a single executive officer, chosen for a seven-year term by Congress, ineligible for reelection, with powers derived solely from laws passed by Congress and the ability to veto laws (though the veto could be overridden by a two-thirds vote of each house of Congress).

The Committee on Detail added several constitutional powers for the "President" (as the committee now referred to the executive). These powers sometimes were modified by floor debate and on other occasions by the Committee on Postponed Matters when the delegates could not come to an agreement. The President was to appoint officers not otherwise provided for by the Constitution, give Congress information on the state of the Union and recommend measures for its consideration, receive foreign ambassadors, grant reprieves and pardons to people convicted of crimes, convene Congress on extraordinary occasions, take care that the laws be faithfully executed, command the armed forces, and command the militia when it was called into federal service. The Constitution also provided for an oath of office. The Committee on Detail also provided that the House could impeach the President on the grounds of "treason, bribery or corruption" and the trial would be held by the Supreme Court.

The Committee on Postponed Matters turned the trial of a President over to the Senate. It also dropped the vague charge of "corruption," and the convention substituted for it the phrase "other High Crimes and Misdemeanors," which referred to serious abuses of Presidential power. The convention also raised the number of senators needed for conviction

Delegates to the Constitutional Convention gather to sign the final version of the Constitution. The delegates worked for 17 weeks and agreed to many compromises before the final document was drafted.

from a majority to two-thirds. After the Committee on Detail assigned the power to make treaties to the Senate rather than to the President, James Madison dissented, arguing that the President alone should have the power. The delegates referred the issue to the Committee on Postponed Matters, which split the difference: it decided that the President, with the advice and consent of two-thirds of the Senate, would make treaties. The committee also removed the power to appoint judges from the Senate and gave it to the President, subject to the advice and consent of the Senate.

Throughout the conventions proponents of a strong Presidency argued for a short term of four years, no restrictions on eligibility for reelection, and a method that would remove selection from the legislature and make the President accountable to the people. At times an electoral college was proposed and once even briefly accepted, but on most occasions the convention rejected the idea and returned to legislative selection of the President. Eventually, the Committee on Postponed Matters incorporated the electoral college into the final draft of the Constitution. Its proposal to have the Senate elect a President in the event of an electoral college deadlock was changed after debate to a House contingency election; because the House was popularly elected, it was considered the more democratic chamber.

The Committee on Postponed Matters also provided that the President be 35 years old, a natural-born citizen (or a citizen at the time of the Constitution's adoption), and a resident of the United States for at least 14 years. The convention approved Charles Pinckney's motion that no religious test should be required or be part of the oath of office.

The Committee on Postponed Matters suggested the opening language of Article 2, that "the Executive Power of the United States shall be vested in a President of the United States." This wording made it clear that the powers of the office, especially the enumerated, or specified, powers that followed, were derived from the Constitution, not from legislation that might be passed by Congress. Thus Congress could not modify or rescind these powers, though Article 1, Section 8, would permit Congress to pass all laws "necessary and proper" for the President to carry out his constitutional powers. Moreover, the phrase "Executive Power" could itself be an open-ended grant of power that might be interpreted expansively by Presidents to include powers not specifically mentioned in the Constitution, such as the power to remove officials from office and the power to direct executive department secretaries.

At the Constitutional Convention the Committee on Style was chaired by Gouverneur Morris, an ally of Washington and a strong proponent of Presidential power. He left the "Executive Power" provision of Article 2 intact but provided in Article 1 that Congress could exercise only the legislative powers "herein granted." The difference in language between Article 1 and Article 2 is taken by proponents of a strong Presidency to mean that the executive power may consist of more than the specific powers that follow in Article 2. The Committee on Style left the Constitution at key points ambiguous, incomplete, and undefined. Much of the subsequent history of the Presidency would involve the incumbent's claim that he had the power to act, refuted by critics' claims that his exercise of power was unconstitutional.

The unsettled issue of Presidential power was to trouble many of the delegates to state conventions to ratify the Constitution. "Your President may easily become a King," thundered Patrick Henry of Virginia, and he predicted "there will be no checks, no real balances in this government." James Monroe gloomily foresaw a President who might be reelected for life. In Paris, Thomas Jefferson noted tartly that "their President seems a bad edition of a Polish King" because he could be reelected indefinitely and commanded the armed forces. The Virginia and North Carolina conventions submitted proposed constitutional amendments to limit tenure in office to 8 years in any 16-year period.

Defenders of Article 2 tried to minimize the scope of Presidential powers that the Constitution had granted. They pointed out that the President could not become a king because there was no established church or aristocracy in the United States. The President did not appoint the Senate and was unlikely to combine with it in a conspiracy to usurp congressional power. He had no royal prerogatives, or privileges, and his limited diplomatic authority was subject to Senate approval. He would be nominated and elected by the electoral college to a short term in office and would remain accountable to the people.

SEE ALSO
Appointment power; Articles of Confederation; Checks and balances; Commander in chief; Electoral college; Eligibility for the Presidency; Executive power; Impeachment; Madison, James; Term of office; Treaty powers; Veto power; War powers; Washington, George

FURTHER READING
Bowen, Catherine Drinker. *Miracle at Philadelphia*. Boston: Little, Brown, 1966.
Cronin, Thomas, ed. *Inventing the American Presidency*. Lawrence: University Press of Kansas, 1989.
Thach, Charles. *The Creation of the Presidency*. Baltimore, Md.: Johns Hopkins University Press, 1922.

Cuban Missile Crisis

THE CUBAN Missile Crisis was a confrontation between the United States and the Soviet Union in October 1962 that threatened all-out nuclear war. The dispute involved the Soviet placement of intermediate-range ballistic missiles in Cuba.

On October 15, 1962, President John F. Kennedy received a briefing from intelligence advisers informing him that the Soviet Union was installing intermediate-range ballistic missiles, medium-range bombers, in Cuba and sending more than 10,000 troops to that island nation. The Executive Committee of the National Security Council (known as Ex Comm) gave Kennedy four options. He could do nothing, use quiet diplomacy and not publicize the presence of the missiles, take the weapons out with an air strike, or impose a naval blockade against Cuba.

The "do nothing" option was not feasible because Congress had already passed a joint resolution backing military action if offensive weapons were found in Cuba, and Republicans were using the possibility of the existence of such weapons against Democrats in the upcoming midterm (1962) congressional elections. Six members of the Ex Comm favored an air strike. Kennedy decided against it because he thought American allies in Europe would not approve until other alternatives had been tried. Attorney General Robert Kennedy argued against bombing, calling the tactic "a Pearl Harbor in reverse." The State Department legal adviser argued that bombing would be a violation of international law. Moreover, there were logistical concerns. The bombing could not be done by a single "surgical" strike; 500 or more missions would be required, destroying hundreds of targets to prevent missiles or aircraft from attacking the United States. The magnitude of the operation would lead to high casualties (provoking international outrage) and losses among the Soviet military, which might bring on military action by its forces against the United States.

Secretary of Defense Robert McNamara points to a map of Cuba during a briefing about the Cuban Missile Crisis at the State Department.

On October 17 Kennedy decided on a blockade, or "quarantine," as his advisers called it, because a blockade—preventing ships from coming in or out of a port—is prohibited under international law unless a nation is at war. It would begin only with further shipments of missiles but if necessary could expand to cover civilian goods. Implementing it in stages would permit time for diplomacy to work. The quarantine would take place near American waters, where the United States had overwhelming naval superiority.

On October 22 Kennedy gave a televised speech to the nation in which he called the presence of the missiles "a change in the status quo [present situation] which cannot be accepted by this country if our courage and our commitments are ever to be trusted again, by friend or foe." He described the threat to the United States, saying that "the purpose of these bases can be none other than to provide a nuclear strike capability against the Western Hemisphere." He announced the quarantine and warned the Soviet Union that "it will be the policy of the United States Government to regard any missile launched from Cuba against any nation in the Western Hemisphere as an attack upon the United States by the Soviet Union, requiring a full retaliatory response." Soviet ships attempting to enter Cuban waters would be subject to search in international waters, and if Soviet ships tried to run the blockade, Kennedy would order American ships to fire on them. The following day the Council of the Organization of American States unanimously backed Kennedy's quarantine.

For several days Soviet ships headed toward the blockade line and work on missile sites in Cuba accelerated. Then the ships stopped dead in the water, leading the members of the Ex Comm to think that the crisis was over. But one ship started again toward Cuba, and a Soviet air-defense missile battery shot down an American U-2 reconnaissance plane flying over Cuba, heating the crisis up again.

The crisis was finally resolved by negotiations between President Kennedy and Soviet chairman Nikita Khrushchev. Khrushchev offered to remove the missiles if the President would pledge that the United States would not invade Cuba. Kennedy hinted, through Attorney General Robert Kennedy, that if the Soviets ended the crisis, the United States would remove intermediate-range missiles from bases in Turkey. On October 28, the Soviets agreed to withdraw their missiles (and accepted verification by United Nations observers). The United States ended the quarantine and pledged not to invade Cuba.

The Soviets withdrew 42 missiles and 42 long-range bombers as well as 5,000 troops. They also removed weapons that the United States did not know were on the island: 9 short-range missiles equipped with nuclear warheads, which would have been used in case of an American invasion, and 36 nuclear warheads for use on the medium-range Soviet missiles. The short-range missiles could have been fired by local commanders, without authorization from Moscow, a possibility of which the American side was completely unaware. After the crisis ended, the Soviets kept in Cuba 37,000 of the 42,000 troops already there—a number far higher than American estimates during the crisis—as well as fighter planes and antimissile weapons. (The size of the Soviet commitments was not revealed to the American side until Soviet and American officials who had been involved in the crisis held a series of meetings between 1987 and 1992.)

American intermediate-range Jupiter missiles were withdrawn from Turkey and Italy. Kennedy pledged not to invade Cuba, but on December 14, 1962, he wrote to Khrushchev that the United States would require "adequate assurances that all offensive weapons are removed from Cuba and are not reintroduced, and that Cuba itself commits no aggressive acts against any of the nations of the Western Hemisphere." He thus left open the possibility that the United States might invade Cuba if these assurances were not received.

SEE ALSO

Kennedy, John F.; National Security Council

FURTHER READING

Allison, Graham. *Essence of Decision: The Cuban Missile Crisis.* Boston: Little, Brown, 1971.

Bright, James, and David Welch. *On the Brink: America and Soviets Reexamine the Cuban Missile Crisis.* New York: Hill & Wang, 1991.

Curtis, Charles
VICE PRESIDENT

☆ Born: Jan. 25, 1860, North Topeka, Kans.
☆ Political party: Republican
☆ Education: read law, 1879–82
☆ Military service: none
☆ Previous government service: county attorney, Shawnee County, Kans., 1885–91; U.S. House of Representatives, 1893–1907; U.S. Senate, 1907–13, 1915–29
☆ Vice President under Herbert Hoover, 1929–33
☆ Died: Feb. 8, 1936, Washington, D.C.

CHARLES CURTIS had an Indian grandparent and was born on an Indian reservation in Kansas. He dropped out of high school to study law privately and was admitted to the bar in 1879. After serving as county attorney for Shawnee County, he served seven terms in the House of Representatives. Elected to the U.S. Senate in 1906, he was defeated for reelection in 1912 but then elected again in 1914. His congressional career involved a steady rise in influence; though he authored few bills, his mastery of legislative politics made him a natural leader in efforts to pass Republican programs. He became Senate whip in 1915 and majority leader in 1924. President Calvin Coolidge was unimpressed with Curtis and rebuffed his efforts to win the Vice Presidential nomination in 1924.

Curtis ran for the Republican Presidential nomination in 1928 as a favorite son from Kansas. Herbert Hoover, the eventual nominee, chose Curtis as his running mate in a bid for party unity and to attract votes from Midwestern farmers. The ticket was the first in American history on which both candidates came from states west of the Mississippi.

Curtis played next to no role in the Hoover administration, because the President never asked him to join in cabinet meetings or gave him any assignments, and their relationship was always strained. Curtis was nominated for a second term as Vice President in 1932, but after the ticket was defeated he retired from politics to practice law in Washington, D.C.

FURTHER READING

Ewy, Marvin. *Charles Curtis of Kansas: Vice President of the United States, 1929–1933.* Emporia: Kansas State Teachers College, 1961.

Dallas, George
VICE PRESIDENT

☆ *Born: July 10, 1792, Philadelphia, Pa.*
☆ *Education: College of New Jersey (Princeton), B.A., 1810*
☆ *Political party: Democrat*
☆ *Military service: none*
☆ *Previous government service: diplomatic mission to Russia, 1813; lawyer, Bank of the United States, 1815–17; U.S. Senate, 1831–32; attorney general of Pennsylvania, 1833–35; ambassador to Russia, 1837–39*
☆ *Vice President under James K. Polk, 1845–49*
☆ *Subsequent government service: ambassador to Great Britain, 1856–60*
☆ *Died: Dec. 31, 1864, Philadelphia, Pa.*

IN 1844 the Democratic national convention unanimously chose Silas Wright of New York to be its Vice Presidential nominee, but for the first and only time in American history, a candidate declined a major party nomination. George Dallas was nominated to take his place.

During his term Dallas broke several tie votes in the Senate in favor of tariff cuts. He also backed President James K. Polk's expansionist policies in Oregon and in the Southwest during the Mexican-American War. Polk broke with Dallas when he refused to accept Dallas's suggestions for judicial and other appointments, and he kept Dallas off the ticket in 1848. In gratitude for his support for the annexation of Texas, the city of Dallas was named for him in 1846. Dallas closed out his government career as ambassador to Great Britain from 1856 to 1860 under President James Buchanan.

FURTHER READING

Belohlavek, John M. *George Mifflin Dallas: Jacksonian Patrician.* University Park: Pennsylvania State University Press, 1977.

Dark horse

A DARK HORSE is a candidate for the Presidential nomination who trails far behind the favorites going into a national convention. The dark horse may be the second or third choice of many delegates but the first choice of few. The strategy of the dark horse is to block the favorite and create a deadlock among the front-runners.

James K. Polk was the first dark horse, winning the Democratic nomination in 1844 on the 9th ballot. Franklin Pierce won the Democratic nomination on the 49th ballot in 1852. In 1876 Rutherford B. Hayes won the Republican nomination on the 7th ballot. Recent Republican dark horses have included Warren G. Harding in 1920 and Wendell Willkie in 1940. All of these candidates except Willkie ultimately won the Presidency.

Changes in party rules have diminished the role of the nominating conventions in choosing Presidential candidates. Today they tend to function as events that officially record the preferences of voters in state primaries and caucuses. It is highly unlikely that a national convention will choose a dark-horse candidate in the future.

SEE ALSO

Caucuses, Presidential nominating; Nominating conventions, Presidential; Primaries, Presidential

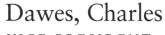

Dawes, Charles

VICE PRESIDENT

☆ *Born: Aug. 27, 1865, Marietta, Ohio*
☆ *Education: Marietta College, B.A., 1884; Cincinnati Law School, LL.B., 1886*
☆ *Political party: Republican*
☆ *Military service: U.S. Army, 1918–19*
☆ *Previous government service: comptroller of the currency, 1898–1902; director, Bureau of the Budget, 1921–23*
☆ *Vice President under Calvin Coolidge, 1925–29*
☆ *Subsequent government service: Commission to Santo Domingo, 1929; ambassador to Great Britain, 1929–32; delegate to London Naval Conference, 1930; president, Reconstruction Finance Corporation, 1932*
☆ *Died: Apr. 23, 1951, Evanston, Ill.*

CHARLES DAWES was a successful banker and one of the most distinguished public servants the United States has ever produced. He began his career as a lawyer for utility companies in the Midwest. He was appointed comptroller of the currency in 1898 and served until 1902. That year, he organized the Central Trust Company of Illinois, remaining president until 1921 and serving as honorary chair until 1931.

Dawes was a brigadier general in World War I, directing supply efforts for American troops. He then served as the first director of the federal Bureau of the Budget, bringing businesslike methods to budgeting for cabinet departments. "Cabinet secretaries are Vice-Presidents in charge of spending, and as such are the natural enemies of the President," he concluded about his work. He was appointed by the Allied Reparations Commission in 1923 to help devise a financial plan for Germany. The Dawes Plan, a revised schedule of war reparations for Germany—payments to the victorious Allied nations—was adopted in 1924 to much international acclaim, and Dawes shared the Nobel Peace Prize for 1925 with British foreign secretary Sir Austen Chamberlain.

Calvin Coolidge chose Dawes to be his running mate in 1924, and the ticket swept to a huge victory. Dawes expected to be an active Vice President but was given no assignments by Coolidge. Dawes himself told Coolidge that he did not wish to attend cabinet meetings. The two men never established any rapport. As presiding officer of the Senate, Dawes attempted to overhaul its rules but met with failure. He wrote a diary of each day's events in office, *Notes as Vice President, 1928–29*, which was published in 1935. Coolidge blocked Dawes's efforts

71

★ D E A T H   I N   O F F I C E ★

to gain support of Republican politicians for the Presidential nomination in 1928.

President Herbert Hoover appointed Dawes ambassador to Great Britain in 1929 and made him president of the Reconstruction Finance Corporation in 1932, where he spearheaded attempts to combat the Great Depression. After leaving office Dawes served as chairman of City National Bank and Trust Company of Chicago.

FURTHER READING

Dawes, Charles. *Notes as Vice President, 1928–29.* Boston: Little, Brown, 1935.

Death in office, Presidential

S E E Garfield, James A.; Harding, Warren G.; Harrison, William Henry; Kennedy, John F.; Lincoln, Abraham; McKinley, William; Roosevelt, Franklin D.; Succession to the Presidency; Taylor, Zachary; 22nd Amendment

Debates, Presidential

TELEVISED DEBATES were held between the major candidates for President in 1960 and in every election since 1976. A panel of reporters acceptable to the candidates questions them, and they are given time to rebut their opponents' statements. Debates are also held between Vice Presidential candidates. Originally sponsored by the League of Women Voters and the television networks, Presidential debates are now organized by the Commission on Presidential Debates, a bipartisan group created by Congress.

Presidential debates attract huge television audiences: 107 million adults in 1960, 122 million in 1976, and more than 100 million in 1980 and 1984. Only 70 million people watched in 1988,

reflecting a decline in enthusiasm for the candidates. But in 1992, thanks to interest in independent candidate Ross Perot, the three Presidential debates attracted more viewers than ever before; more than 130 million Americans watched one or more. This was the first debate in which both major-party candidates appeared at the same time as an independent third candidate. The debates gave Perot's campaign a major boost, especially among independent voters. Debates raise voter interest and provide information about the candidates and their response under pressure. In close contests many voters wait for the debates before deciding for whom to vote. This is especially true of independents, voters not registered as members of a political party, and those without strong feelings for their party. Those who watch debates tend to vote on the basis of the issues, whereas those who do not watch are more likely to vote on the basis of personality. The media not only report on the debates but also announce the "winner." This verdict may also affect voter behavior as people jump on the "winner's" bandwagon.

Polls showed that in 1960 four million voters based their vote on the debates. Of these, John F. Kennedy won 72 percent, helping him into the White House. In 1980 Ronald Reagan gained ground with undecided voters and political independents, helping him defeat Jimmy Carter. In 1988 George Bush lost some of his lead after the first debate and neither gained nor lost any of his lead over Michael Dukakis after their second debate—a victory for Bush

Richard Nixon (left) and John F. Kennedy faced each other on October 13, 1960, for their third televised Presidential debate.

because Dukakis was trailing and needed to score a "knockout."

After the 1960 debates between Kennedy and Richard Nixon, none were held in 1964, 1968, and 1972 because in each instance one of the candidates was clearly ahead and felt he had nothing to gain. In 1976 debates resumed: President Gerald Ford wanted to debate because he was behind in the polls and had nothing to lose, and Jimmy Carter wanted debates because his lead had begun to slip. By 1984 debates had become an institution, and a candidate could not avoid them without making his refusal an issue in its own right.

Candidates can use debates to overcome negative perceptions about them, as Kennedy did when his performance changed people's opinions about his youth. Candidates can defuse issues in debates, as Ronald Reagan did when he joked, "I will not make an issue of my opponent's youth and inexperience." Debates can also torpedo a campaign, as when Walter Mondale announced in a 1984 debate against Reagan that if elected, he would raise taxes. In 1980 Ronald Reagan's performance against Jimmy Carter was aided by the fact that his campaign had obtained one of the "briefing books" that Carter used to prepare for the debates, so he knew what Carter would say and could prepare his rebuttals in advance.

SEE ALSO
Bush, George; Carter, Jimmy; Clinton, Bill; Ford, Gerald R.; Kennedy, John F.; Nixon, Richard M.; Reagan, Ronald

FURTHER READING
Jamieson, Kathleen, and David Birdsell. *Presidential Debates: The Challenge of Creating an Informed Electorate.* New York: Oxford, 1988.
Ranney, Austin, ed. *The Past, Present and Future of Presidential Debates.* Washington, D.C.: American Enterprise Institute, 1979.

Decision making, Presidential

A successful Presidential decision is one that wins White House, public, and congressional support. Politically, a decision that unites the President's party and divides the opposition is much better than a decision that splits his own party and unites his opponents. When President Bill Clinton attempted to end the military ban on homosexuals in his first week in office, he failed to gain a consensus within his own party and quickly agreed to a compromise. When he pushed for a family leave law (allowing workers to take time off from their jobs for a new baby or for a family emergency), Clinton unified his party, put the opposition on the defensive, and won a major victory early in his term.

Each Presidential decision, therefore, can be considered part of the game of politics. Decisions Presidents make not only affect the immediate problems they are trying to solve but also affect their power to make decisions on future issues, in much the same way that a move in chess or checkers affects the rest of the game. For example, when John Kennedy was negotiating with Soviet premier Nikita Khrushchev in the Cuban Missile Crisis, his decisions had an impact on Soviet-American relations long after the crisis was resolved. Kennedy's willingness to make a deal with the Soviets paved the way for the Test-Ban Treaty of 1963.

Some Presidents make decisions based on the national interest and then work out the strategy and tactics to get Congress and the bureaucracy to implement them; others seem to make decisions by determining what is best for them. When Jimmy Carter told Congress

An atomic bomb explodes over Nagasaki and brings an end to World War II. Truman decided to drop two atomic bombs after the Japanese refused to surrender.

he would veto bills containing unnecessary "pork barrel" public works projects, he was attempting to act in the national interest, yet he antagonized members of Congress (even members of his own party), who delayed working on much of his legislative program in retaliation until Carter gave in and approved their pet projects. Yet if a President does not lead the nation in the public interest, who else can or will? When President Clinton called for sacrifice from all Americans to reduce the deficit in his first address to Congress in 1993, he was not doing the popular thing, but most observers applauded him for acting in the national interest.

Some political scientists have argued that what is in the political interest of the President is in the interest of the entire nation. A President, in their view, should always do what is best for himself because that will result in the most viable public policy. This argument can be taken too far: few people would argue that Richard Nixon's actions in covering up the Watergate crimes of his aides was in the national interest. Moreover, the argument ignores the basic principles of the Constitution. Ours is a government of separate institutions sharing the power of decision in making public policy. If the President acts unilaterally and claims he has done so in

the public interest, what role is there for Congress or the courts? In any event, Congress does not accept the idea that the President's decisions are the last word on the public interest. And the Supreme Court, at times, has checked Presidential assertions of power, as it did when it ordered Harry Truman to return to their owners the steel mills he had seized during the Korean War.

Presidents do not always act rationally when they make decisions, nor do they always make decisions in their own interest, let alone the national interest. A President might ignore, discount, deny, or misinterpret information that contradicted his own beliefs. John Kennedy, in the first stages of the Cuban Missile Crisis, simply could not believe the Soviets would go back on their promises to him and place missiles in Cuba. The Soviets had several additional weeks to construct their missile facilities until reconnaissance photos convinced the skeptical President. A President might procrastinate to reduce the stress of having to make hard decisions, as George Bush did in dealing with the economy in his fourth year in office—a delay that cost him a second term, as his inaction became an election issue. Alternatively, a President might push his administration to meet self-imposed deadlines to make a decision and be done with it. And once the decision is made, the President might not reconsider it, even if he obtained important new information casting doubt on his original decision. Lyndon Johnson, for example, paid little attention to advisers, including top officials in the Central Intelligence Agency, who warned him that his escalation of the war in Vietnam could not lead to a military victory, once he had made his decision to use 500,000 troops. It was not until the chairman of the Joint Chiefs of Staff asked for an additional 200,000 troops that Johnson realized he could not win the war.

A President might miscalculate the costs and benefits of a decision, as Ronald Reagan did when he agreed to sell arms to Iran in return for the release of U.S. hostages held in Lebanon. His decision led to the release of three hostages —but three new hostages were taken so the Iranians could obtain even more arms from the United States.

A President might make decisions based on "lessons" of history when these lessons may not apply. Presidents Kennedy and Johnson compared the civil war in Vietnam to World War II. In their view, a communist victory in South Vietnam would result in other nations in Southeast Asia turning communist. Yet after 1975, when Vietnam was unified under communist rule, noncommunist nations in the area, such as Thailand, Burma, Malaysia, and Singapore, did not find their security threatened by the Vietnamese government.

A President must guard against "groupthink," a situation in which consensus, or agreement, is prized and dissenters are frozen out and their potential contributions minimized. Indeed, one tip-off that decision making is poor is early agreement among advisers on the nature of the problem and the preferred solution. If debate fails to cover the full range of options, and if there is no advocate for the unpopular options, the President is not well served. The President, in turn, must encourage debate and dissent, must seek advisers who will be candid with him, and must be suspicious of premature consensus. Lyndon Johnson was not happy with advisers who disagreed with him about the Vietnam War. He cut Vice President Hubert Humphrey out of his inner circle over the issue and replaced Defense Secretary Robert MacNamara when he became skeptical about the war. The role of Presidential staffers, when they perform their jobs correctly, is to explore all the options and let the President know the full range of choices, but no adviser can force a President to listen to unpleasant truths.

Successful Presidents, much like unsuccessful Presidents, make mistakes. The big difference is that successful Presidents know when to extricate themselves from failing policies, as Franklin Roosevelt did on many occasions with his New Deal domestic programs. Any army, it is said, can learn to advance; the best armies also know when and how to retreat. The same maxim applies to the White House: a decision to undo a bad decision may sometimes be the best decision of all.

Jimmy Carter during negotiations for the release of American hostages held in Iran. The hostages were released the day Carter's successor, Ronald Reagan, took office in 1981.

SEE ALSO

Camp David peace talks; Cuban Missile Crisis; National security adviser; Steel seizure; Treaty of Versailles; Watergate investigation

FURTHER READING

George, Alexander. *Presidential Decision-making and Foreign Policy.* Boulder, Colo.: Westview, 1980.
Neustadt, Richard. *Presidential Power and the Modern Presidents.* New York: Free Press, 1991.

Departments, executive

THE EXECUTIVE departments are the units of government that are under the

direct supervision of the President. These do not include independent regulatory commissions and other independent agencies, such as the Federal Reserve Board, which are insulated by law from Presidential control. Top departmental officials are appointed by the President with the advice and consent of the Senate. They serve at the President's pleasure, and he may remove them at his discretion. The President uses his executive power to issue orders to the heads of the departments, usually called secretaries, and their subordinates. Their legislative and budget requests to Congress and the rules and regulations they intend to issue are cleared by a Presidential agency, the Office of Management and Budget. The heads of the executive departments constitute the President's cabinet.

The Department of Foreign Affairs, later renamed the Department of State, was the first cabinet-level department, established by Congress in 1789. It was followed that same year by the Department of the Treasury and the Department of War. The Navy Department was organized in 1798, though naval affairs prior to that time were organized by the secretary of the navy, a post established in 1789. Although the position of attorney general was provided for by the Judiciary Act of 1789, the Department of Justice was not established until 1870, after the Department of the Interior in 1849. The Department of Agriculture was established in 1889 and the Department of Commerce and Labor in 1903, which split into separate departments of Commerce and Labor in 1913. In 1949 the Department of Defense consolidated the Air Force (founded 1943), War Department, and Navy Department. The Department of Health, Education, and Welfare was established in 1953 but was reorganized in 1980 into the Department of Health and Human Services and the Department of Education. The Depart-

ment of Housing and Urban Development was created in 1965, and the Department of Transportation in 1966. The Department of Veterans Affairs was created in 1988, replacing the Veterans Administration, an independent agency established in 1930.

SEE ALSO

Appointment power; Cabinet; Executive branch; Executive orders; Executive power; Patronage, Presidential; Removal power

FURTHER READING

United States Government Organization Manual. Washington, D.C.: Government Printing Office, 1992.

Director of Central Intelligence

THE DIRECTOR of Central Intelligence is the principal intelligence adviser to the President, the director of the Central Intelligence Agency (CIA), and a statutory adviser to the National Security Council (NSC). The position of DCI was established by the National Security Act of 1947 in order to provide a coordinating mechanism for providing foreign intelligence—information about the military and economic capabilities of other nations—to the President and to maintain civilian control over the compilation of intelligence estimates. National Security Decision Directive 276, issued by President Ronald Reagan in 1987, makes the DCI a member of the National Security Planning Group, a committee of the NSC that reviews and oversees the implementation of national security policies. The DCI also serves on the NSC crisis-monitoring committee and is generally a trusted inner-circle adviser to the President.

The DCI coordinates all the intelligence reports from the CIA, the intelligence agencies of the military services,

John F. Kennedy (left) awards the National Security Medal to Allen Dulles, his director of Central Intelligence, in 1961.

the Defense Intelligence Agency, the National Security Agency (which deals with codes and electronic intelligence), and the State Department's Bureau of Intelligence. Based on the information supplied by these agencies, the DCI provides the President with a daily briefing that summarizes these intelligence reports. He also oversees preparation of the National Intelligence Estimates, which deal with the military and diplomatic capabilities and intentions of foreign nations. The DCI is required by law to assist the President in complying with legal provisions requiring consultation with Congress when covert activities are implemented. Covert activities are actions in which the government does not acknowledge its involvement, such as attempts to overthrow anti-American governments in Latin America.

The DCI may assist the President in evading compliance with congressional consultation or reporting requirements by exploiting loopholes in the laws. For example, during the Iran-Contra affair in 1986, President Reagan did not inform Congress that funds from sales of arms to Iran were being sent to the Contra forces who opposed the Nicaraguan government. The DCI may also set up one or more fall guys to take the blame for covert operations away from the President, a system of protection for the White House known as "plausible denial"; the President states that he was unaware of the intelligence operation. This system may have been used to shield Presidents when CIA assassination plots against Cuban leader Fidel Castro and other world leaders were uncovered in the 1970s by two congressional committees and a national commission chaired by Vice President Nelson Rockefeller.

SEE ALSO
National security adviser; National Security Council

FURTHER READING
Powers, Thomas. *The Man Who Kept the Secrets.* New York: Knopf, 1979.
Richelson, Jeffrey. *The United States Intelligence Community.* Cambridge: Ballinger, 1984.
Turner, Stansfield. *Secrecy and Democracy.* Boston: Houghton Mifflin, 1985.

Disability, Presidential

PRESIDENTIAL DISABILITY is any condition in which the President is unable to exercise the powers and duties of his office. Ten Presidents have been disabled while in office. In six instances the disability resulted in the President's death. In 1841 William Henry Harrison was bedridden for a week before dying of pneumonia. Zachary Taylor was bedridden for five days before his death from an acute intestinal obstruction (or perhaps appendicitis) in 1850. Abraham Lincoln was unconscious for nine hours before dying of a gunshot wound in 1865. James Garfield was bedridden for 80 days and William McKinley for 8 days before they died from gunshot wounds. Warren Harding was incapacitated for four days before his death from food poisoning (or a heart attack).

Four Presidents recovered from major disabilities. Woodrow Wilson was incapacitated with a stroke for 280 days. During that time his wife communicated to government officials from his bedside, refusing to allow cabinet secretaries to see her husband while he was making his slow and only partial recovery. Dwight Eisenhower was incapacitated for 143 days by his first heart attack in 1955 and later convalesced from a stroke. He was also incapacitated briefly

Dwight Eisenhower leaves the hospital in a wheelchair after recovering from a heart attack.

during an operation for ileitis. Ronald Reagan was incapacitated for 20 hours while undergoing surgery after suffering a gunshot wound in 1981 and later while undergoing surgery for colon cancer.

The Constitution makes no mention of the procedures involved when a President is disabled and the Vice President must assume the duties of the office as acting President. After Eisenhower's heart attack, he wrote a letter to Vice President Richard Nixon stating that if he were again disabled, Nixon would serve as acting President until the President announced he was able to resume his duties. If Eisenhower could not communicate, then Nixon was to make the determination himself about taking over the duties. Presidents John F. Kennedy and Lyndon Johnson continued this arrangement, which was later superseded by the specific provisions of the 25th Amendment to the Constitution.

SEE ALSO

Succession to the Presidency; 25th Amendment

FURTHER READING

Gilbert, Robert E. *The Mortal Presidency.* New York: Basic Books, 1992.
Hansen, Richard. *The Year We Had No President.* Lincoln: University of Nebraska Press, 1962.
Moses, John, and Wilbur Cross. *Presidential Courage.* New York: Norton, 1980.

Doctor, White House

SEE Physician to the President

Double vacancy

SEE Succession to the Presidency

Eisenhower, Dwight David

34TH PRESIDENT

☆ *Born: Oct. 14, 1890, Denison, Tex.*
☆ *Political party: Republican*
☆ *Education: U.S. Military Academy, B.S., 1915; U.S. Army Command and General Staff School, 1925–26; Army War College, 1927–28; Industrial College of the Armed Forces, 1931–32*
☆ *Military service: U.S. Army: 2nd lieutenant, 1915; major (temporary), 1917; lieutenant colonel (temporary), 1918; major, 1918; Office of Assistant Secretary of War, 1929–33; Office of Army Chief of Staff, 1933–35; assistant military adviser, Commonwealth of the Philippines, 1935–39; colonel, 1939; chief of staff of 3rd Army, 1939–41; major general, 1941; War Plans Division, Army Staff, 1941–42; commander of U.S. forces in Europe, 1942; Allied commander for invasion of North Africa, 1942–43; Allied commander in chief, 1943–45; five-star general of the army and army chief of staff, 1945–47; Supreme Allied Commander, Europe, North Atlantic Treaty Organization, 1950–52*
☆ *Previous civilian government service: none*
☆ *Elected President, 1952; served, 1953–61*
☆ *Died: Mar. 28, 1969, Washington, D.C.*

DWIGHT D. EISENHOWER was the first Republican President elected after the Great Depression. A "middle of the road" leader, he retained most of the Democratic New Deal programs rather than attempt to repeal them. He continued Harry Truman's policy of containment against communism but sought unsuccessfully to engage the leaders of the Soviet Union in summit diplomacy to limit atomic weapons. Although he won two elections, he was unable to make the Republican party dominant in American politics.

Eisenhower was born in Texas and raised in Abilene, Kansas. He graduated

A 1952 campaign button.

from West Point in 1915, ranking 61st in a class of 168. During World War I he saw no action but spent the time in training camps. After the war he was posted for a time in the Canal Zone of Panama. He graduated at the top of his class from the Army Command and General Staff School, then went to the War College and the Industrial College of the Armed Forces. He then worked as an aide to General Douglas MacArthur, army chief of staff, in Washington and later in the Philippines, returning to the United States as a lieutenant colonel in 1939. In the spring of 1941, with the rank of colonel, he distinguished himself in training maneuvers commanding the Third Army, winning promotion to brigadier general.

During World War II, Eisenhower was named chief of operations of the army in 1942 with the rank of major general. He was then named commanding general of the European theater of operations, a promotion that jumped him over 350 more senior officers. He commanded the forces that invaded North Africa in November 1942 and defeated the Axis powers by May 1943; he commanded the Italian campaign in 1943 that led to an armistice with the Italians; and he was named Supreme Commander of Allied Forces in Europe on January 17, 1944. He made the decision to go ahead with the invasion of Normandy, France, on June 6, 1944 (D Day), in spite of bad weather that might have imperiled the operation. He later called it the most difficult decision he ever made. He achieved the highest rank in the American military, five-star general of the army, in December 1944. After the war he served as army chief of staff, helping President Truman organize the new Department of Defense.

In 1948 Eisenhower retired from the army, declined offers from both political parties to run for President, and served two years as president of Columbia University, the only civilian position (other than the U.S. Presidency) he ever held. His account of the war, *Crusade in Europe,* was a best-seller. In 1950 President Truman recalled him to active duty to serve as the first commander of supreme headquarters, Allied Powers in Europe (SHAPE), the military arm of NATO (the North Atlantic Treaty Organization, an alliance of the United States, Canada, and Western European nations), a position he held for two years.

Although both parties considered him for the 1952 Presidential nomination, Eisenhower chose to enter the Republican contest and gained the support of the liberal and moderate wings of the party. He won a bitter nomination fight over Republican conservatives, led by "Mr. Republican," Senator Robert Taft of Ohio. His victory was due in part to the efforts of Senator Richard Nixon, who helped organize the California convention delegation for Eisenhower. Nixon was rewarded with the Vice Presidential nomination.

With the Republican campaign slogan "I like Ike" and a series of effective television commercials, Eisenhower won a landslide victory over Democratic nominee Adlai Stevenson. His coattails brought in a Republican Congress.

Eisenhower concentrated on foreign affairs. "I shall go to Korea," Eisenhower had promised the American people, and one of his first acts was to honor that pledge and end the Korean War. The final truce agreement was signed on July 27, 1953. The following year he refused a French request to use American military might against North Vietnamese forces and instead supported the Geneva Accords that ended French involvement in Indochina. Between 1954 and 1955 Eisenhower shored up the American position in Asia by concluding a mutual defense agreement with the Nationalist

As a general in World War II, Eisenhower consults with French general Charles de Gaulle in Normandy.

Chinese government on Taiwan, providing military assistance to the South Korean government, cementing a strategic alliance with Japan, and giving American support to an anti-communist regime organized with U.S. assistance in South Vietnam. The United States, along with Great Britain and France, also sponsored the Southeast Asian Treaty Organization (SEATO), an alliance of the United States, Great Britain, France, and several Asian nations, including Pakistan and Thailand, to resist communist expansion.

There were foreign policy successes in other parts of the world as well. In 1953 the Central Intelligence Agency (CIA) organized a coup that brought down an anti-American government in Iran. Then the Eisenhower administration organized the Central Treaty Organization, a military alliance between several Middle Eastern nations and the United States. In 1954 the CIA organized a coup against Jacobo Arbenz, the leftist president of Guatemala, and installed a pro-American leader. In 1956 Eisenhower insisted that France and Great Britain withdraw their troops from Egypt and end their attempt to topple Egyptian leader Gamal Abdel Nasser.

Eisenhower did not confront Soviet military power directly. When Soviet forces crushed East German workers in 1953 and a full-scale revolution in Hungary in 1956, the United States made no move to respond. In dealing with the Soviets, Eisenhower showed respect for their military might and preferred peaceful negotiation. In 1955 he held a summit meeting with Soviet leader Nikita Khrushchev in Geneva. There he made an "open skies" proposal to allow each

nation's air force to fly over the other's territory in order to conduct peaceful surveillance and reduce the military threat on both sides. The Soviets turned him down.

In domestic affairs Eisenhower expected Congress to take the initiative. He proposed combining the New Deal social agencies into a Department of Health, Education, and Welfare, which Congress approved, as well as an increase in Social Security payments and the minimum wage. He proposed only one major new additional domestic program, the interstate highway system. Eisenhower concluded the St. Lawrence Seaway agreement with Canada, which benefited U.S. ports on the Great Lakes by improving their access to the Atlantic Ocean in winter months. He proposed a constitutional amendment to allow 18-year-olds to vote, but Congress took no action on it. In the 1954 midterm elections Congress went back to the Democrats, which forced Eisenhower to adopt a bipartisan stance in domestic and foreign policy. Rather than claiming credit as a Republican, he worked closely with Democratic leaders to gain their support.

The least successful aspect of Eisenhower's first term involved his failure to stand up forcefully to Senator Joseph McCarthy (Republican–Wisconsin). McCarthy had charged that some members of the State Department and the army were part of a communist conspiracy. Though almost all his allegations proved unfounded, his mean-spirited investigation severely hurt morale in many government agencies. Eisenhower was slow in responding to McCarthy, though some have argued that he played a "hidden hand," working with Vice President Nixon and Senate majority leader Lyndon Johnson in maneuvers designed to weaken the senator. Eventually the Senate censured McCarthy for his unfair tactics of smear and innuendo.

Although Eisenhower suffered a heart attack in 1955 and had an operation to relieve an intestinal blockage the following year, his health was good enough for a second term. He was reelected over Adlai Stevenson in a landslide victory in 1956. But Congress remained in the hands of the Democrats, the first time a President had been elected without winning either House since Zachary Taylor's victory in 1848. Eisenhower's second term was marked by health problems; he had a stroke in 1957. Alaska and Hawaii were admitted to the Union in 1959. Eisenhower used federal troops to enforce federal court orders desegregating the public schools in Little Rock, Arkansas, but gave tepid support to other civil rights initiatives, leading congressional Democrats to pass their own civil rights measures in 1957 and 1960.

In 1957 Eisenhower announced the Eisenhower Doctrine, approved by Congress, that assured stability to nations threatened by communist subversion or aggression. In July 1958, to back up this doctrine, U.S. Marines landed in Lebanon to bolster the government against threats of civil war. When communist China starting shelling the islands of Quemoy and Matsu and threatened to invade them, Eisenhower ordered the U.S. Navy to escort Nationalist Chinese ships to resupply the islands.

In 1957 the Soviets launched a Sputnik satellite into outer space, challenging the United States for technological dominance and leading many Americans to

Nikita Khrushchev (right), premier of the Soviet Union, talks with Eisenhower at Camp David during his 1959 visit to the United States.

think that the nation needed new leadership. With unemployment rising and the nation entering a recession, the midterm elections of 1958 led to a stunning loss for the Republicans in Congress and in gubernatorial elections. The Democrats, now controlling both houses, assumed control of domestic policy-making. They held hearings on shortcomings in national preparedness, science, education, and the space program, and they passed the National Aeronautics and Space Act of 1958 as well as a law that provided federal funding for science and foreign language education.

Eisenhower's foreign policy began to suffer setbacks as well. In 1959 Fidel Castro assumed power in Cuba, and it soon became apparent that he was establishing the first communist regime in the Western Hemisphere. Then in 1960 Eisenhower planned a summit meeting with the Soviets to advance his arms limitations proposals. On May 1, 1960, shortly before the summit, the Soviets shot down an American U-2 reconnaissance plane over their territory; Eisenhower denied that the plane had been over Soviet territory, then had to admit the truth when the Soviets displayed the captured American pilot, Gary Francis Powers. The Soviets insisted that Eisenhower apologize for these flights, and when he refused, they broke up the summit conference. Khrushchev withdrew an invitation for Eisenhower to visit the Soviet Union. Later, Eisenhower toured the Far East but was forced to cancel a visit to Japan because of anti-American sentiment.

Eisenhower was popular throughout his two terms and probably would have won the next election had he not been the first President forbidden by the 22nd Amendment to stand for a third term. Although he campaigned for Republican nominee Richard Nixon in 1960, Nixon was defeated by Democrat John F.

Kennedy, who ran a campaign highly critical of the Eisenhower administration.

After the election, Eisenhower delivered a famous farewell address in which he warned the American people of the potential dangers involved in the "military industrial complex" that had been created to produce weapons for the armed forces.

After retiring to private life in 1961, Eisenhower published his Presidential memoirs and lived at his farm at Gettysburg, Pennsylvania. He died of heart failure in 1969.

SEE ALSO

Health, Presidential; Hidden-hand Presidency; Kennedy, John F.; Nixon, Richard M.; Succession to the Presidency; Truman, Harry S.; 22nd Amendment

FURTHER READING

Ambrose, Stephen. *Eisenhower, The President.* New York: Simon & Schuster, 1984.
Eisenhower, Dwight D. *Mandate for Change, 1953–56.* Garden City, N.Y.: Doubleday, 1963.
Eisenhower, Dwight D. *Waging Peace, 1956–1961.* Garden City, N.Y.: Doubleday, 1965.
Greenstein, Fred. *The Hidden Hand Presidency.* New York: Basic Books, 1982.

Election campaigns, Presidential

INITIALLY, CANDIDATES for President "stood" for election—they did not "run" for the office—so they would not be accused of being too ambitious for power. In 1789 and 1792 George Washington had no opponent and was selected unanimously by the electoral college without campaigning.

Since 1796 there have been contests between candidates belonging to different political parties, and for many years the party managers did the campaigning while the candidates remained at home.

In 1840 William Henry Harrison took a short "tour" but did not discuss issues or seek votes. In 1844 James K. Polk began the custom of sending "letters" to his supporters on issues such as the tariff, though he did not make speeches on political subjects. In 1852 Winfield Scott became the first candidate to campaign. By 1860 it was expected that the candidate who trailed would campaign: Stephen Douglas campaigned throughout the South and Midwest while Abraham Lincoln stayed home in Springfield, Illinois.

In 1876 Rutherford B. Hayes began the practice of responding to his party's nomination with an "acceptance letter" that dealt with the candidate's position on the issues. He confined himself to a "front porch" campaign, in which supporters would visit him, and his discussions with them would then be reported by the wire services and appear in newspapers. Hayes later advised James Garfield to "sit cross-legged and look wise until after the election," something his successor managed to do quite well on his farm in Mentor, Ohio. That election, in 1880, started the custom in which the challenger campaigned while the incumbent seeking reelection remained at home. In 1892 Grover Cleveland held a "notification" ceremony before thousands of his supporters in New York's Madison Square Garden, but he did not take to the campaign trail.

In the 19th century there usually was no need for a popular Presidential candidate to campaign: in 1896 Democrat William Jennings Bryan went to 27 states, made 600 speeches to 5 million people, and got crushed by Republican William McKinley, who ran a front-

Franklin D. Roosevelt (right) and John Nance Garner campaign from the observation car of their train during the 1932 election.

Harry Truman displays a copy of the Chicago Daily Tribune, *which mistakenly proclaimed the victory of Thomas Dewey in the 1948 election.*

porch campaign. In 1904 Theodore Roosevelt thought it improper for an incumbent President to go on the campaign trail. Instead, he wrote hundreds of letters to party leaders, making patronage appointments to secure their support. He won by the greatest landslide since 1832 yet hardly ever left his home in Oyster Bay, New York.

The first incumbent President to stump for votes was William Howard Taft in the election of 1912. He made an 18,000-mile, 400-speech tour. His Democratic opponent, Woodrow Wilson, also toured the nation, making this the first election in which both major-party candidates campaigned.

Just as candidates began to take to the campaign trail, their speeches were eclipsed by new ways of communicating with voters. In 1916 Wilson used newspapers, magazines, billboards, and motion pictures in his campaign for reelection. In 1924 Calvin Coolidge began the use of radio in campaigns when he spoke to more than a million listeners. In 1928 Alfred E. Smith used the radio to reach 8 million people, though his strident speeches could not keep him from being crushed by Herbert Hoover. In 1932 Hoover, in turn, was defeated by Franklin D. Roosevelt, who broadcast a series of radio "chats" to the voters from his Hyde Park, New York, home.

Perhaps the greatest victory on the campaign trail was won by Harry Truman in 1948, who did it the old-fashioned way, speech by speech. In April, when surveys showed only 30 percent of the public approved of his Presidency, pollsters did not give him a chance. Fifty leading campaign analysts predicted that Republican Thomas E. Dewey would win by 376 electoral college votes. Truman boarded a train named the *Ferdinand Magellan* and traveled 31,000 miles, delivering 271 speeches. The press started referring favorably to Truman's "whistle stop" campaign. Truman struck hard at the "Do-Nothing 80th Congress." "Give 'em hell, Harry," a supporter yelled out in Seattle. "I'm going to give 'em hell," he responded. His opponent, Dewey, aboard the *Victory Special,* rode 16,000 miles, made 13 major speeches, and briefly spoke on 43 other occasions. Ahead in the polls, Dewey spoke in generalities, telling a crowd in Arizona, "Our future lies before us." Referring to the Grand Old Party, the nickname of the Republicans, Democrats said that "GOP with Dewey leading it means Grand Old Platitudes." On election night—despite the *Washington Post*'s forecast that he would lose, Truman told his aides that he had won, then went to bed. He awoke the next morning and received Dewey's concession telegram. When he returned to the capital, a sign on the Washington Post building said, "Mr. President, we are ready to eat crow whenever you are ready to serve it."

In 1952 Dwight Eisenhower pioneered the use of television commercials. "Eisenhower answers Mr. and Mrs. America" was a series in which the candidate answered questions from a moderator. "To think that an old soldier should come to this," Eisenhower lamented between takes. He also made several 30-minute speeches on issues, which went over with the audience like lead balloons, but he defeated his Democratic opponent handily.

By the 1960s political TV commercials dominated Presidential campaigns. Candidates used private polls to find

Left: A campaign umbrella supporting the candidacy of William McKinley and Garret Hobart in 1896. Above: An Al Smith license plate from 1928.

"The Exciting New Game of the Kennedys" was produced for the 1960 election.

In this campaign block puzzle, Benjamin Harrison's name is placed above that of Grover Cleveland, his opponent in the 1888 election.

A poster from Democrat William Jennings Bryan's 1900 campaign.

A 1952 Republican cookie cutter in the shape of the GOP elephant.

positions on issues that would demonstrate their leadership qualities to the electorate. John F. Kennedy, for example, used surveys conducted at the state level in his 1960 campaign to emphasize issues that would enhance his image as a leader ready to move the nation forward. "Issues are only a means to establish personal qualities with voters," Republican media adviser Robert Teeter later observed. By the 1970s, candidates were using focus groups of voters to pretest campaign commercials. Groups of voters, gathered in small settings, would preview speeches and commercials: themes that appealed to them would be retained; those that fell flat would be dropped.

Candidates experimented with new ways to reach the voters. The network campaign commercials of the 1960s gave way to commercials geared to specific states in the 1970s and to particular racial and ethnic audiences in the 1980s.

In the 1980s, 30-second attack commercials and quick "sound bites" were combined with sentimental ads such as Ronald Reagan's "Morning in America."

In the 1992 election voters did not respond to carefully crafted commercials, which seemed too slick and contrived. Radio and television stations participated in the Adwatch and Truth Test public service programs, in which they scrutinized advertisements for "fairness," making attack advertisements more of a liability than an asset. Appearances on staid network news programs gave way to appearances on television talk shows and entertainment programs such as "Arsenio Hall" (on which Bill Clinton played the saxophone) and "Larry King Live" (on which Ross Perot made his campaign announcements). In these forums candidates seemed more spontaneous, and voters felt they could make a judgment about character.

Increasingly, voters have used the Presidential debates to obtain information about candidates. More than one-third of the electorate usually waits until the debates are concluded before deciding for whom to vote.

To reach voters concerned primarily about issues, candidates prepared short books, such as Clinton's *Putting People First—A National Economic Strategy for America* and George Bush's *Agenda for American Renewal,* which were distributed free to voters who called toll-free telephone numbers. Campaigns also established computer "bulletin boards" to reach voters who subscribed to on-line information services.

SEE ALSO

Campaign Fund, Presidential Election; Caucuses, Presidential nominating; Congressional caucus; Dark horse; Debates, Presidential; Federal Election Commission; Nominating conventions, Presidential; Primaries, Presidential; Ticket

FURTHER READING

Boller, Paul F., Jr. *Presidential Campaigns.* Rev. ed. New York: Oxford, 1996.

Brown, Clifford W., Jr., Lynda W. Powell, and Clyde Wilcox. *Serious Money: Fundraising and Contributing in Presidential Nomination Campaigns.* New York: Cambridge University Press, 1995.

Campbell, James E. *American Campaign: U.S. Presidential Campaigns and the National Vote.* College Station: Texas A&M University Press, 2000.

Jamieson, Kathleen Hall. *Dirty Politics: Deception, Distraction, and Democracy.* New York: Oxford, 1992.

Jamieson, Kathleen Hall. *Packaging the Presidency: A History and Criticism of Presidential Campaign Advertising.* 3rd ed. New York: Oxford, 1996.

Kolbert, Elizabeth. "Test-marketing a President." *New York Times Magazine,* August 30, 1992.

McCormick, Richard M. *The Presidential Game: The Origins of American Presidential Politics.* New York: Oxford, 1982.

Melder, Keith. *Hail to the Candidate: Presidential Campaigns from Banners to Broadcasts.* Washington, D.C.: Smithsonian Institution Press, 1992.

Shields-West, Eileen. *The World Almanac of Presidential Campaigns.* New York: World Almanac, 1992.

Troy, Gil. *See How They Ran: The Changing Role of the Presidential Candidate.* New York: Free Press, 1991.

Electoral college

THE ELECTORAL college, which consists of the electors of the President of the United States, is elected by the states. Each state has the same number of electors as its congressional delegation: members of the House (allotted on the basis of state population) plus two senators. The method of choosing electors is determined by state election laws. At first many states left the decision to their legislatures; other states permitted the people to choose the electors. By 1832 all states except South Carolina had switched to popular election of Presidential electors, and that state joined the others in 1856.

There is no constitutional requirement that all the electors of a state vote for a single candidate, but all states except Michigan in the 1890s and Maine in modern times have provided for a winner-take-all system: the candidate who receives a majority of the popular vote in the state receives all the state's electoral votes, and the other candidates receive nothing. Maine has adopted a "congressional district" system that chooses electors based on the plurality (the most votes but not necessarily a majority) in each district. This means that a candidate might win 3 rather than all 4 electoral votes if he or she loses in one of the districts. (The winner of the statewide vote in Maine also receives the two "senatorial" electors.)

On a date fixed by Congress the people vote in each state (and the District of Columbia) for members of the

As president of the Senate, Vice President Richard Nixon announces his own defeat by John F. Kennedy in the 1960 election.

electoral college. Although the names of the Presidential candidates appear on the ballot, the voters actually cast their ballots for a slate of electors pledged to vote for that candidate. After the popular voting, on a date fixed by Congress (currently, the first Monday after the second Wednesday in December), the winning electors meet in their respective state capitals to cast one ballot for President and one ballot for Vice President. (The electoral college never meets in a single place to cast ballots because the framers of the Constitution feared that the electors could be coerced or bribed more easily in one location.) The ballots from each state are sent to Congress. The outgoing Vice President of the United States (who is the president of the Senate) counts the ballots in the presence of Congress and announces the name of the next President. In 1960 Richard Nixon, president of the Senate, announced that he had lost the election to John F. Kennedy. In 1968, outgoing Vice President Hubert Humphrey announced that Nixon had defeated him for the Presidency.

The delegates to the Constitutional Convention thought that in most elections the electoral college would be dominated by electors from the large states, who would vote for candidates from their own states. In that situation, none of the five leading candidates would amass the necessary majority of votes to be elected. In the event of a deadlock, the election would go to the House of Representatives, where each state's delegation would cast a single vote for one of the top five contenders. In a sense, the electoral college was expected to function as a nominating body and the House as the final arbiter. (The 12th Amendment to the Constitution, adopted in 1804, restricts the House's choice to the top

three candidates.) The Vice President would be chosen by the Senate from among the top two candidates in the event of an electoral college deadlock.

The cumbersome system of contingency elections provided by the Constitution would give the large states the chance to "nominate" candidates for President, while all states, large and small, would have an equal voice in the final selection. This compromise between large and small states is at the heart of the original electoral college scheme.

The framers thought that electors would operate as free agents, diligently searching to find the best candidates for President. But since 1796 electors have been the agents of political parties supporting candidates already seeking the office. The electoral college has become a registering device for the preferences of the voters. Only a few electors have ever violated their pledges and voted for someone else, and none of these "faithless electors" have ever influenced the outcome of an election by doing so.

There have been two elections in which the electoral college deadlocked and contingency elections were held. In 1800 Thomas Jefferson was the Presidential candidate and Aaron Burr the Vice Presidential candidate of the Republicans. At that time each elector cast two ballots for President; the top candidate was elected President and the runner-up assumed the Vice Presidency. Jefferson and Burr each received the same number of electoral college votes for President, and because neither received a majority, the election went to the House, which elected Jefferson. To forestall that possibility in future elections, the 12th Amendment, adopted for the election of 1804, provided that the electoral college cast separate ballots cast for President and Vice President.

In 1824 no candidate received a majority of ballots cast for President, and the House elected John Quincy Adams in a contest marked by charges of corruption.

In 1876 close contests in several southern states led both parties to claim victory, and therefore the Democratic and Republican electors sent their ballots to the Capitol. It took a special commission set up by Congress to decide which party had won the statewide vote and therefore which party's ballots should be counted. In what was effectively a deal to end military occupation of the South, the southern Democrats accepted the commission's finding that the electoral votes of the Republicans would be counted, thus ensuring the election of Republican President Rutherford B. Hayes, who needed all the contested votes cast in his favor to defeat his Democratic opponent, Samuel Tilden, by a single electoral vote. In turn, federal troops were quickly withdrawn from southern states and Reconstruction policies were ended.

In several elections the candidate with the most popular votes has been defeated: Andrew Jackson in 1824; Samuel Tilden in 1876; and Grover Cleveland in 1888.

In other situations, small shifts in the popular vote could have had major effects on the electoral vote. In 1976, if a total of 9,245 votes had shifted to Gerald Ford in Ohio and Hawaii, he would have been elected President, even though he would have received 1.7 million fewer votes than Jimmy Carter. In 1988, a shift of 547,000 votes in 11 states would have shifted the election from George Bush to Michael Dukakis, even though Bush would have retained a margin of 5 million votes.

In the election of 2000, Vice President Albert Gore won the popular vote but narrowly lost the electoral college to Texas governor George W. Bush. Gore objected to the vote count in Florida,

Observers inspect ballots in West Palm Beach, Florida, after the 2000 election. A hand recount of disputed ballots was started, but halted after a U.S. Supreme Court decision that accepted the original count.

where Bush was certified as winning by 500 votes, but where 175,000 ballots were eliminated by voting machines that could not determine for whom the ballots had been cast. These "undercounted" ballots came disproportionately from districts that favored Gore. He demanded a hand recount of the disputed ballots to determine the intention of the voters, but Bush sued to stop the recount. By a vote of 5 to 4, in *Bush* v. *Gore,* the U.S. Supreme Court prohibited a recount because not enough time remained to ensure the equal protection of all voters. Florida's electors, and with them the Presidency, then went to Bush.

In the 1970s several constitutional amendments to abolish the electoral college were introduced in Congress, and on several occasions they have passed the House or Senate, but none have received the two-thirds vote necessary for adoption.

SEE ALSO

Adams, John Quincy; Burr, Aaron; Hayes, Rutherford B.; Humphrey, Hubert H.; Jackson, Andrew; Jefferson, Thomas; Johnson, Andrew; Kennedy, John F.; Nixon, Richard M.

FURTHER READING

Longley, Lawrence D., and Alan G. Braun. *The Politics of Electoral College Reform.* New Haven: Yale University Press, 1975.
Pierce, Neal R., and Lawrence D. Longley. *The People's President.* Rev. ed. New Haven: Yale University Press, 1981.
Schlesinger, Arthur M., Jr., and Fred L. Israel, eds. *Running for President.* New York: Simon & Schuster, 1993.

Eligibility for the Presidency

IN ARTICLE 2, Section 1, the Constitution sets forth the eligibility requirements for the President. These requirements were modified by the 12th Amendment in 1804. To serve as President, one must be a natural-born citizen (an American citizen born abroad whose parents were citizens at the time meets this requirement), 35 years of age upon assuming office, and 14 years a resident of the United States (though not necessarily the 14 years immediately preceding the election). The Constitution bars any religious test for federal office and does not contain any racial or gender restrictions.

The 12th Amendment, which provides for separate electoral college ballots for President and Vice President, requires that the Vice President have the same qualifications for office as the President does.

SEE ALSO
12th Amendment

Emancipation Proclamations

DURING THE Civil War, President Abraham Lincoln issued two Presidential proclamations that freed slaves from states in secession.

At the beginning of the Civil War Lincoln wanted the border states to remain in the Union, and so he resisted pressure from abolitionists to issue an order ending slavery everywhere in the nation. In September 1861 he ordered General John C. Frémont to revoke a military proclamation that had freed the slaves of Missourians who supported the Confederacy. In 1862 Congress passed several acts confiscating the slaves of rebels, measures that Lincoln did not support or enforce. He preferred to compensate slaveholders for the slaves who were freed. After the Union victory at Antietam, however, Lincoln decided on a bolder course. "The moment came," Lincoln said, "when I felt that slavery must die that the Union might live." On September 23, 1862, Lincoln issued a proclamation stating that as of the new year, all slaves within rebelling states "shall be, then, thenceforward and forever free."

On January 1, 1863, using his authority as commander in chief, Lincoln issued the Emancipation Proclamation, declaring that the slaves in areas "in rebellion against the United States" were free as of that date. It specifically exempted border states such as Tennessee, Kentucky, and Missouri, the western part of Virginia, and parts of Louisiana in order to retain the support of Unionists in those areas. (Tennessee, although exempted, ended slavery of its own volition.)

There was no mention of compensation in the Emancipation Proclamation. Lincoln described it as a war measure: it enabled Union armies to obtain the services of former slaves. The proclamation was a political triumph for Lincoln. It was opposed by the Democrats, who argued that it violated Lincoln's 1860 pledge never to interfere with slavery in states where it existed. It also seemed to violate the 5th Amendment: the Supreme Court had

When Lincoln issued his Emancipation Proclamation, he claimed it was a war measure: former slaves would be recruited into the Union Army.

ruled in the 1857 *Dred Scott* case that slaves were property, and Lincoln had emancipated slave owners' property without due process of law or compensation. Emancipation was, of course, popular with abolitionists in the North. And because of Lincoln's policy, African Americans remained strong supporters of the Republican party into the 1930s.

The emancipation of all slaves was attained with the passage of the 13th Amendment in 1865. Lincoln's refusal to compensate slave owners for their property was embodied as constitutional policy in the 14th Amendment, ratified in 1868.

SEE ALSO

Lincoln, Abraham

FURTHER READING

Franklin, John Hope. *The Emancipation Proclamation.* Garden City, N.Y.: Doubleday, 1963.

Ethics, Presidential

PRESIDENTS AND their appointees are supposed to have high ethical standards, avoiding conflicts of interest between their public duties and private affairs. Concerns about ethics fall into three general categories: personal gain, conflict of interest, and misuse of public funds.

Presidents place their financial assets in a "blind trust," a legal arrangement under which a trustee, chosen by the President, handles the President's personal financial affairs. During his term the President has no knowledge of the trustee's investment decisions, allowing him to make decisions without thinking of personal gain.

To avoid misusing public funds, modern Presidents pay for political activities out of their own pockets or through their political parties. Party

national committees pay for such expenses as public opinion polls and the President's appearances at political events. Similarly, members of the administration are expected to reimburse the government for transportation and related expenses when they use government vehicles for personal or political trips. Sometimes officials misuse this privilege or blur the line between public and private or political business.

Restrictions on officials began in 1789, when the secretary of the Treasury was forbidden by law from investing in government securities. In 1853 Congress passed the first conflict-of-interest statute, but its criminal penalties were rarely enforced. Most Presidents in the 19th century, especially James Buchanan and Ulysses S. Grant, did not enforce ethical standards.

In modern times President Dwight Eisenhower was forced to dismiss his chief of staff, Sherman Adams, for accepting presents from a Boston financier. Jimmy Carter's director of the Office of Management and Budget, Bert Lance, resigned over charges involving his conduct as a banker in Georgia, though the charges were eventually dropped. In 1986 two officials of Ronald Reagan's administration, Michael Deaver and Lyn Nofziger, were prosecuted for violating a ban on lobbying the government for one year after leaving government service. Deaver was found guilty of perjury and Nofziger of violating

Photographers greet members of the Senate committee investigating the Teapot Dome scandal in 1924. The secretary of the interior, Albert Fall, had leased naval oil reserves at Teapot Dome, Wyoming, to an oil producer after receiving bribes from him.

the one-year ban, but his conviction was overturned on appeal. In 1987 Attorney General Edwin Meese was investigated by independent counsel for his efforts to help a friend build an oil pipeline between Iraq and Jordan. A 1988 report indicated that Meese had violated federal law, but not for personal gain. Meese was not prosecuted, but he resigned as attorney general.

In 1965 President Lyndon Johnson issued Executive Order 11222, which ordered officials to avoid actions that gave the appearance of using their offices for private gain, giving preferential treatment to any individual or organization "affecting adversely the confidence of the public in the integrity of government" or making decisions outside official channels. President Jimmy Carter established strict standards for appointees, including disclosure of financial assets, divestiture or sale of assets that might create conflicts of interest, and restrictions on private employment after officials leave government, including a one-year prohibition on lobbying. These provisions were incorporated into the Ethics in Government Act of 1978, which established an Office of Ethics in the White House to monitor compliance with reporting provisions and to issue advisory opinions to government personnel.

The Presidential Transition Effectiveness Act of 1988 covers ethics issues during changes of administration. It provides that transition aides who make conduct investigations and make recommendations about policy in government departments and agencies must fill out disclosure forms, so that the public will know the names, recent employment history, and "sources of funding" (if not paid for by transition funds) of such transition officials. During the transition to Bill Clinton's administration, rules for transition staff included a six-month ban on subsequent lobbying of government agencies by staffers involved with these agencies.

President Clinton ordered the strictest code of ethics for political appointees ever instituted. By executive order, he prohibited officials from lobbying their former departments for five years after leaving government service (an increase from the one-year ban in the 1978 law), although they could lobby other government agencies after one year. In addition, high officials in many departments, including U.S. trade negotiators, would also be banned for life from representing the interests of foreign governments and political parties, though they would be free to represent foreign corporations and interest groups after five years (an increase from the three-year ban in existing law). These rules covered the top 1,100 government officials. An additional 3,500 top executive branch officials are prohibited from lobbying federal agencies for one year after they leave government service.

SEE ALSO

Carter, Jimmy; Cleveland, Grover; Clinton, Bill; Executive Office of the President; Grant, Ulysses S.; Independent counsel; White House Office

FURTHER READING

Eastland, Terry. *Energy in the Executive: The Case for the Strong Presidency.* New York: Free Press, 1992.
Roberts, Robert North. *White House Ethics: The History of the Politics of Conflict of Interest Regulation.* Westport, Conn.: Greenwood Press, 1988.

Executive agreements

A PACT OR understanding with a foreign government reached by the President or a Presidential agent is called an executive agreement. The agreement may be written or oral. Unlike a treaty, it does not require the advice and consent of the Senate.

Although executive agreements are not mentioned in the Constitution, Presidents claim the power to enter into such agreements based on their executive power, their duty to receive ambassadors from other nations, their power as commander in chief, and their duty to take care that the laws be faithfully executed.

The first known executive agreement involved a 1792 postal arrangement with Canada, negotiated by the American and Canadian postmasters general. The vast majority have involved agreements between departments of government and their foreign counterparts in agriculture, health, trade, communications, the environment, science, and defense.

Executive agreements have been crucial in foreign affairs. There are many examples: the Bagot-Rush agreement to limit American and British naval forces on the Great Lakes (1817); a coalition between the United States and several European powers to crush the Boxer rebellion in China (1900); the so-called Gentlemen's Agreement to regulate Japanese immigration to the United States (1905); and an armistice with Imperial Germany (1918). Agreements have been made to exchange U.S. destroyers for British naval bases (1940); to end the fighting in Germany and establish the status of Berlin (1945); to end the Korean War (1953); to end U.S. involvement in the Vietnam War (1973); to implement a strategic arms limitation agreement with the Soviet Union (1979); to secure the release of U.S. diplomats from Iran (1981); and to forge a coalition to defeat Iraqi aggression against Kuwait (1990).

There are nearly 10 times as many executive agreements as there are treaties; on average, only 30 treaties but more than 250 agreements have been concluded each year since the 1960s. The majority of the executive agreements have been authorized by Congress in advance or ratified by Congress after being put into effect, and most require subsequent laws by Congress to be implemented.

Only about 5 percent of executive agreements are negotiated and implemented without any congressional role. Some of these are major American commitments to the defense of other nations or agreements to lease military bases in other countries, pacts that in effect create military alliances without any congressional participation.

In 1969 Congress passed the National Commitments Resolution, which stated that a national commitment of the United States could not be made by executive agreement but only by "affirmative action taken by the executive and legislative branches of the U.S. Government by means of a treaty, statute, or concurrent resolution of both Houses of Congress specifically providing for such commitment."

Presidents do not accept this interpretation of a national commitment, arguing that executive agreements are binding obligations of the United States. The courts have imposed some limits on executive agreements: they cannot be inconsistent with prior congressional legislation; agreements that affect prior laws passed by Congress must be implemented by new congressional legislation; and they cannot impair the constitutional rights of American citizens.

Some executive agreements have been kept secret, especially those involving the Department of Defense and intelligence agencies. In 1972 Congress passed the Case Act, which provided that the secretary of state must transmit the text of any executive agreement to Congress within 60 days. Secret agreements must be submitted to the House Foreign Affairs and Senate Foreign Relations Committees, which keep them secret unless released from that obligation by the President. In 1977 the time limit under the Case Act was reduced by Congress to 20 days.

SEE ALSO
Treaty powers

FURTHER READING
Fisher, Louis. *The Constitution between Friends*. New York: St. Martin's, 1978.

Executive branch

THE DEPARTMENTS and agencies that take political direction from the President, including the 14 cabinet-level departments, constitute the executive branch of the federal government. "The executive branch" is not a phrase found in the Constitution, but it is favored by Presidents because it assumes that these departments are under their sole direction. The Constitution, however, provides that officials of the departments are to take direction not only from the President but also from laws passed by Congress.

Top officials in the executive branch, generally referred to as "the administration," are appointed by the President with the advice and consent of the Senate, and they serve at the pleasure of the President. The President uses his Executive Office agencies to supervise their budgets, their legislative requests to Congress, and the regulations they make and enforce.

Independent regulatory agencies (such as the Federal Trade Commission), units of government that are insulated by Congress from political direction (such as the Federal Reserve Board), as well as several agencies that perform functions for Congress (such as the Congressional Budget Office) are not part of the executive branch. Presidential appointment and removal powers over officials in these agencies may be limited by Congress, and the President may not provide them with political direction.

SEE ALSO
Appointment power; Budget, Presidential; Cabinet; Executive Office of the President; Removal power

FURTHER READING
Pyle, Christopher H., and Richard M. Pious. *The President, Congress, and the Constitution*. New York: Free Press, 1984.

Executive Office Buildings

THE TWO Executive Office Buildings near the White House provide offices for the Executive Office of the President and some units of the White House Office.

The Old Executive Office Building, located next to the White House on Pennsylvania Avenue, provides office space for much of the Vice Presidential staff, the White House Office, and the National Security Council staff, as well as for the Office of Management and Budget and the Council of Economic Advisers. It also contains the White House Library and Research Center.

Built in 1875, the building housed the State, War, and Navy departments until 1947. It was designed in French

A crowd gathers in front of the Old Executive Office Building to watch an airplane take off in 1910.

Second Empire style, with ornate stone-work, including dormer windows, tiers of columns, a green copper mansard roof, and two dozen chimneys. It has 553 rooms and 440,250 square feet of office space. It was completely renovated and redecorated during Ronald Reagan's administration.

The New Executive Office Building, completed in 1968, houses the remaining Presidential agencies, such as the Office of Personnel Management. It is a 10-story structure of red brick with 307,000 square feet of office space. It is located one block from the Old Executive Office Building, off Pennsylvania Avenue on Jackson Place. Although modern in style, its rooflines were designed to harmonize with the mansard style.

Executive Office of the President

THE EXECUTIVE Office of the President (EOP) assists the President in supervising the executive branch. It was created by President Franklin D. Roosevelt in Reorganization Act No. 1, submitted to Congress in 1939. At various times the EOP has included agencies to improve the management and administration of the executive departments, such as the Council on Personnel Administration in the 1940s; economic advisory boards, such as the International Economic Policy Board of the 1970s; agencies for national security, such as the Board of Consultants on Foreign Intelligence Activities in the 1950s; and agencies for emergency preparedness, such as the Office of Civil and Defense Mobilization in the 1960s.

Sometimes the EOP has contained agencies that should have belonged in the departments but have been given "Presidential status" to signal their importance to the administration. Such agencies include the Disarmament Agency in the 1950s, the Office of Economic Opportunity (which administered antipoverty programs) in the 1960s, and the Office of Drug Abuse Policy in the 1970s.

In 1992 the offices within the EOP had a total of 2,000 employees and spent $200 million each year. These offices included the White House Office, which provides the President with assistance in communicating with Congress, special interest groups, and the general public; the Office of Management and Budget, which prepares the Budget of the United States, oversees departmental requests for legislation from Congress, assists the President with veto messages, and ensures that new government regulations are in accordance with Presidential priorities; the Council of Economic Advisers, which prepares the economic report of the President and gives advice on economic policy; the National Security Council, which provides advice to the President on foreign policy and military matters; the Office of the U.S. Trade Representative, which negotiates trade policies with other nations; the Council on Environmental Quality, which develops regulatory policies for clean air and water; the Office of Science and Technology Policy, which recommends new government programs in science; the Office of Policy Development, which provides long-range studies for new domestic legislation; the Office of the Vice President, which assists the incumbent with speeches and scheduling of activities; and the Office of Administration, which provides management support for the other agencies.

SEE ALSO

Council of Economic Advisers; Council on Environmental Quality; Executive Office Buildings; National Security Council; Office of Administration; Office of Management and Budget; Office of Science and Technology Policy; Office of U.S. Trade Representative; Vice President; White House Office

FURTHER READING

Burke, John P. *The Institutional Presidency.* Baltimore, Md.: Johns Hopkins University Press, 1992.
Cronin, Thomas, ed. *The Presidential Advisory System.* New York: Harper & Row, 1969.
Johnson, Richard. *Managing the White House.* New York: Harper & Row, 1974.
Nathan, Richard. *The Administrative Presidency.* New York: Wiley, 1986.

Executive orders

EXECUTIVE ORDERS are regulations issued by the President. Provided that they are based either on his constitutional powers or laws passed by Congress, they have the force of law. Federal courts will enforce them just as if they had been enacted by Congress, provided that they do not conflict with federal laws. An executive order that carries out a law may later be revoked by new legislation. An executive order can be nullified, or canceled, if the Supreme Court or lower federal courts find that it is unconstitutional. For instance, in 1952 the Supreme Court ruled that President Harry Truman's seizure of the steel mills during the Korean War violated the due process clause of the Constitution because the President had seized property without being given statutory authority by Congress.

Executive orders are filed in the Department of State after the President issues them. Between 1789 and 1907 Presidents issued approximately 2,400 such orders. Since 1907 the orders have been filed chronologically, and each is given a number, with more than 13,000 numbered between 1908 and 1991.

The first executive order, issued by George Washington on June 8, 1789, instructed the heads of departments to make a "clear account" of matters in their departments. Since then, the orders have been used to regulate the civil service, to determine holidays for federal workers, to recognize federal employee unions, to institute security programs, and to classify government documents as top secret or secret. They have been used to designate public lands as Indian reservations and for environmental protection. They are also used to organize federal disaster assistance efforts. Executive orders have been used by each President beginning with Dwight Eisenhower to organize the intelligence agencies at the beginning of his term in office and to set up other aspects of White House operations.

President Franklin D. Roosevelt used executive orders to create agencies without going through Congress. In 1944 Congress prohibited funding such agencies. In 1968 Congress prohibited the creation of Presidential commissions, councils, or study groups that were not authorized by Congress. President Richard Nixon tried to dismantle several agencies by executive order. This action was blocked by the federal courts because Congress had not abolished them by law.

Executive orders have been used to assert Presidential war powers in the

By executive order, Franklin Roosevelt called for the internment of Japanese Americans on the West Coast during World War II. This photo of a Japanese family awaiting relocation was taken by Dorothea Lange in 1942.

Civil War and all subsequent wars. Franklin Roosevelt seized defense plants to ensure production of aircraft in World War II. He also used a series of executive orders to establish a curfew for Japanese Americans on the West Coast, to exclude them from certain areas, and finally, to intern them in camps in the desert until 1944.

Executive orders have often been used for civil rights enforcement. Harry Truman issued an executive order in 1948 ending racial segregation in the armed forces. John Kennedy issued an executive order banning racial discrimination in newly constructed public housing and another banning pay discrimination against women by federal contractors. He issued orders prohibiting racial discrimination in federally funded libraries, hospitals, and other public facilities. Richard Nixon required government contractors to institute affirmative action hiring programs for women and members of minority groups.

SEE ALSO

Executive branch; Executive power; Imperial Presidency; Steel seizure

FURTHER READING

Fisher, Louis. *President and Congress.* New York: Free Press, 1972.

Executive power

ARTICLE 2 of the Constitution opens with the words, "The executive power shall be vested in a President of the United States." Presidents take the term *executive power* to mean a general responsibility to direct the bureaucracy.

The Presidential claim is controversial because the Constitution confers neither the title nor the powers of "chief executive" on the President, nor does it assign the President any powers to make a budget or remove other government officials. It does not explicitly say that the President can issue orders to heads of departments. Instead, it provides that he may "require the opinion in writing, of the principal officer in each of the departments, on any subject relating to the duties of their respective offices."

When Andrew Jackson asserted that he could give orders to the secretary of the Treasury, his claim led to a split within his own party and the rise of an opposition party known as the Whigs, who challenged the prerogatives of "King Andrew the First." The Whigs sought to minimize, if not entirely eliminate, Presidential control of the departments. Senator Daniel Webster countered that the Founding Fathers did not intend to make the President administrative chief. He argued that "the executive power" meant no more than the specific powers that appear after it in Article 2—most of which had nothing to do with administering the government. "I do not regard the declaration that the executive power shall be vested in a President as being any grant at all," Webster concluded. The Whigs believed that Presidents could not remove cabinet secretaries without the consent of Congress, nor could they control policy in the departments. Instead, the Whigs believed that Congress should make policy.

Modern Presidents, beginning with Theodore Roosevelt, have argued that the "executive power" constitutes an affirmative grant of power that allows them to supervise the executive departments' budget and legislative requests to Congress. Presidents Herbert Hoover and Franklin D. Roosevelt both argued that the principle of accountability to the people in a democracy requires that Presidents have absolute control over operations of the departments, that they be considered the "chief executive," and that they be able to issue orders to officials in the departments. Only with such

This cartoon labels Andrew Jackson "King Andrew the First" and criticizes his use of Presidential power.

powers, they concluded, could Presidents be fairly held accountable for the actions of officials in their administrations.

The conflict between Congress and the President over power to run the departments remains unsettled, in large part because of specific powers the Constitution grants to Congress in Article 1. The legislature creates all the departments, determines their powers, and creates all the offices (and the salaries that go with them)—all by passing laws. It also reorganizes the government bureaucracy to create new agencies or abolish existing ones.

Congress authorizes government programs, determines the powers and duties of all officials, and can prohibit activities of which it disapproves. Congress appropriates all funds for departments, and officials can spend only the money appropriated by its laws. Congress oversees the activities of the agencies to ensure that officials have obeyed the laws and spent money lawfully. Congress makes the rules that govern the civil and military personnel in the bureaucracies. The Supreme Court has stated the principle that officials are expected, in performing routine duties, to obey the laws of the United States rather than orders that the President might issue, if such orders conflict.

In modern times Presidents have vastly increased their executive powers.

Since 1921 they have submitted an annual budget to Congress, rather than permitting departments to request funds directly. Since 1926 they have had the power to remove officials from departments. Since the late 1930s the Executive Office of the President has enabled the President to dominate personnel selection, program development, and legislative requests made to Congress by the departments. In the 1940s the President was given authority by Congress to formulate and then implement reorganization plans, subject only to prior congressional consent. By the 1970s Presidents were implementing new management techniques in the departments. In the 1980s they were approving or disapproving all departmental agency regulations prior to final adoption. They had indeed become "chief executives."

SEE ALSO

Appointment power; Budget, Presidential; Cabinet; Commander in chief; Departments, executive; Executive branch; Executive Office of the President; Executive orders; Executive privilege; Impoundment; Modern Presidency; Office of Management and Budget; Removal power; War powers

FURTHER READING

Pyle, Christopher H., and Richard M. Pious. *The President, Congress, and the Constitution.* New York: Free Press, 1984.

Executive privilege

EXECUTIVE PRIVILEGE is the claim made by the President that the Constitution permits Presidents and their advisers to withhold information from Congress and the courts. The Constitution says nothing about secrecy in the executive branch and does not contain the phrase "executive privilege." Presidents claim the privilege by arguing that it is a functional necessity: the advice they receive and the deliberations in their administration will not be candid and truthful if they are subject to subsequent congressional and judicial scrutiny.

In the 19th century Presidents tried to withhold information about diplomatic and military ventures, but all eventually provided Congress with the information it sought. When President George Washington refused to give Congress information about the Jay Treaty with Great Britain, it was because he claimed such information should be submitted only to the Senate, which must consent to all treaties.

The modern practice of withholding information was instituted by President William Howard Taft, whose Executive Order 1062 provided that the President could order heads of departments not to furnish information to Congress if it were "incompatible with the national interest." Prior to World War II, refusals to furnish Congress with information were rare. During the war, however, President Franklin D. Roosevelt refused to turn over some Federal Bureau of Investigation files to congressional committees, and President Harry Truman ordered that congressional requests for personnel files be submitted to him for a final decision about compliance.

The term *executive privilege* was invented by Dwight Eisenhower's administration in the 1950s. In 1954 the President refused to turn over military personnel records to the Permanent Investigations Subcommittee of the Senate Government Operations Committee, headed by Senator Joseph McCarthy. Most of Congress took Eisenhower's side because McCarthy—without any evidence to back up his allegations—was questioning the loyalty of career military and diplomatic officers, charging them with being communists or communist sympathizers. Then, in 1958, Attorney General William Rogers argued that

Eisenhower need not disclose candid advice from his assistants nor provide Congress with any documents relating to Presidential activities.

Other Presidents have also used executive privilege against Congress. President John F. Kennedy ordered General Maxwell Taylor, the White House military adviser, to refuse to testify before a House committee investigating the failure of an American-backed invasion of Cuba in 1961. Richard Nixon refused to supply documents to the House Armed Services Committee when it investigated bombing raids on North Vietnam that occurred without prior Presidential authorization.

The most important use of executive privilege occurred during the Watergate crisis. President Nixon refused to turn over tapes made of conversations in the Oval Office to the Select Senate Committee on Campaign Activities, which was investigating the Watergate crimes. A federal appeals court upheld Nixon's refusal, agreeing that he did not need to supply evidence about Watergate crimes to a congressional committee whose mandate from Congress was to consider changes in campaign financing laws.

In a second case, the Supreme Court denied the President's contention that he did not have to turn over evidence to

The jury in the case of United States v. Nixon *listens to the tapes recorded by Richard Nixon in the White House. The Supreme Court ruled that Nixon could not use executive privilege to withhold information in a criminal investigation.*

federal courts investigating Watergate crimes. Grand juries (which issue indictments, or formal accusations) and juries on federal cases, the Supreme Court held, are entitled to all the evidence in a criminal case. No one, not even a President, may withhold evidence from the courts. While agreeing with Nixon that there is "a valid need for protection of communications" between Presidents and those who advise them, the Supreme Court insisted that the President was required to turn over evidence to the federal judge trying the case. The judge would then decide whether or not Nixon's claim was valid and whether or not the evidence could be introduced at a trial. In *United States* v. *Nixon* (1974) the Supreme Court concluded that it was up to the courts, not the President, to weigh the balance between legitimate national security interests that might require information to be kept secret and the right of juries to obtain information about crimes.

The *United States* v. *Nixon* case recognized for the first time the Presidential claim that there may be, under certain circumstances, a right of executive privilege. But it left the final decision about the validity of the claim to the federal courts.

During the impeachment of Bill Clinton, the White House claimed that the President and his aides were shielded by executive privilege, that his lawyers were shielded by attorney-client privilege, and that Secret Service agents were shielded by "protective privilege." The federal courts rejected all of these claims, relying on the settled law in the *United States* v. *Nixon* case that, absent a national security issue, the President and his aides are required to provide evidence of criminal wrongdoing to grand juries.

SEE ALSO

Checks and balances; Executive orders; Nixon, Richard M.; Watergate investigation

FURTHER READING

Berger, Raoul. *Executive Privilege: A Constitutional Myth*. Cambridge: Harvard University Press, 1974.
Cox, Archibald. "Executive Privilege." *University of Pennsylvania Law Review* (June 1974): 1,383–1,438.
Rozell, Mark J. *Executive Privilege: The Dilemma of Secrecy and Democratic Accountability*. Baltimore, Md.: Johns Hopkins University Press, 1994.
Schlesinger, Arthur M., Jr. *The Imperial Presidency*. Boston: Houghton Mifflin, 1973.

Executive Protective Service

S E E Secret Service, U.S.

Ex-Presidency

IN THE 19th century former Presidents received no pensions or regular retirement income, but often Congress passed special acts providing funds for them or for their widows or for paying off their debts. The Office of the Ex-Presidency was created as a formal entity by Congress in 1958, when it passed the Former Presidents Act. This law provided former Presidents with an annual pension of $25,000, to be adjusted upward to equal the salary of cabinet secretaries ($143,800 in 1993).

The Presidential Transition Act of 1963 provides ex-Presidents with an additional $1 million to cover expenses for the first six months out of office. During that time the General Services Administration provides them with office space, funds to pay staff, and travel expenses. For the remainder of their lives they are given free mailing privileges, use of an official residence at 716 Jackson Place, near the White

Jimmy Carter does volunteer work at a Milwaukee housing project sponsored by Habitat for Humanity in 1989.

Ronald Reagan on horseback at his California ranch.

House, the privilege of addressing the Senate, and Secret Service protection for themselves and their immediate families. The pension for Presidential widows was set at $10,000 in 1958 and was increased to $20,000 in 1971. However, widows under age 60 who remarry forfeit this pension. All widows are granted free use of the mails, and since 1968 widows have received lifetime Secret Service protection. Presidential children are guarded by the Secret Service until the age of 16.

In 1957 the cost of providing for former Presidents was $74,836, which was paid toward the upkeep of Presidential libraries. By 1987 that cost had grown to $16,202,000 for Presidential libraries, $1,234,000 for office allowances, and $9,843,965 for Secret Service protection, for a total of $27,279,965. In constant dollars the amount spent to support ex-Presidents had increased more than seven times.

To reduce these costs, the Presidential Libraries Act of 1986 provided that Presidents leaving office after 1989 would have to use private funds to operate as well as build their Presidential libraries, and it imposed new size and space limits on the size of Presidential museums operated with federal funds.

SEE ALSO

Libraries, Presidential; Secret Service, U.S.; Transitions, Presidential

FURTHER READING

Chambers, John Whiteclay, II. "Presidents Emeritus." *American Heritage,* June/July 1979, 16–22.

Fairbanks, Charles
VICE PRESIDENT

☆ *Born: May 11, 1852, Unionville Center, Ohio*
☆ *Political party: Republican*
☆ *Education: Ohio Wesleyan University, B.A., 1872*

☆ *Military service: none*
☆ *Previous government service: U.S. Senate, 1898–1904*
☆ *Vice President under Theodore Roosevelt, 1905–9*
☆ *Died: June 4, 1918, Indianapolis, Ind.*

CHARLES FAIRBANKS was a lawyer who became active in Republican state politics in Indiana. He was named the temporary chair and keynote speaker at the Republican national convention in 1896. The following year he was elected to the U.S. Senate, where he chaired several important committees and served on a diplomatic commission that settled the Canadian-Alaskan boundary.

Fairbanks was nominated to run for Vice President on Theodore Roosevelt's ticket in 1904 to provide geographic balance and secure the electoral votes of Indiana. A conservative, he exercised no influence in the progressive Roosevelt administration. He later supported William Howard Taft against Roosevelt in the 1912 Presidential election. The Republicans again nominated him for Vice President in 1916 on a ticket headed by Supreme Court Justice Charles Evans Hughes.

Fair Deal

THE FAIR DEALwas the slogan that President Harry S. Truman applied to the 21-point program that he presented to Congress on September 5, 1945, to convert the economy from wartime to peacetime status. The message to Congress emphasized passage of the Full Employment Act to provide jobs for American servicemen and servicewomen returning from World War II. When Congress passed the Employment Act of 1946 (dropping "Full" from the title), it converted the measure from a guarantee of employment into a bill creating an economic advisory system for the President.

In 1949, after winning reelection, Truman presented a State of the Union address that again referred to a Fair Deal program. He called for protecting the civil rights of black Americans by establishing a fair employment commission. He also proposed federal aid to education, more funding for public housing, national health insurance, an expansion of Social Security benefits, an increase in the minimum wage, new land reclamation and public power programs, and a program of technical assistance to underdeveloped nations.

SEE ALSO

Truman, Harry S.

FURTHER READING

Hamby, Alonzo. *Beyond the New Deal.* New York: Columbia University Press, 1973.

Federal Election Commission

THE FEDERAL Election Commission (FEC) is a bipartisan independent regulatory agency that administers federal campaign finance laws. It was established by the Federal Election Campaign Act Amendments of 1974 in the aftermath of the Watergate scandals, when illegal corporate contributions to Presidential campaigns were uncovered by a Senate investigation. The FEC consists of six commissioners appointed by the President with the advice and consent of the Senate. No more than three commissioners can be members of the same political party.

The FEC provides information about campaign finance laws to the candidates and the public. It issues regulations about, and monitors compliance with, campaign funding limitations established by law. The FEC monitors the operation of the

A 1992 campaign poster for H. Ross Perot. Perot accepted no public funding for his campaign but spent $60 million of his own money.

Treasury Department's Presidential Election Campaign Fund, which provides matching public funding to Presidential candidates who qualify in the nominating period by raising $5,000 in each of 20 states. The fund also provides money for national nominating conventions of the major parties and gives public funds to the Presidential nominees of the two major parties and qualifying minor parties.

SEE ALSO

Campaign Fund, Presidential Election; Election campaigns, Presidential

FURTHER READING

Mutch, Robert E. *Campaigns, Congress, and the Courts—The Making of Federal Campaign Finance Law.* New York: Praeger, 1988.

Sorauf, Frank J. *Money in American Elections.* Glenview, Ill.: Scott Foresman, 1988.

Fillmore, Millard

13TH PRESIDENT

☆ Born: Jan. 7, 1800, Cayuga County, N.Y.
☆ Political party: Whig
☆ Education: six months of grade school; read law, 1822
☆ Military service: none
☆ Previous government service: New York State Assembly, 1829–33; U.S. House of Representatives, 1833–35, 1837–43; New York State comptroller, 1847–48; Vice President, 1849–50
☆ Succeeded to Presidency, 1850; served, 1850–53
☆ Died: Mar. 8, 1874, Buffalo, N.Y.

MILLARD FILLMORE was the third and last Whig President, succeeding Zachary Taylor, who died in office. He was the first and only successor to the Presidency to appoint an entirely new cabinet. His support of the Compromise of 1850 preserved the Union for another decade but destroyed his own political career.

Fillmore was born on a frontier farm in upstate New York. He was apprenticed to a cloth maker at age 14,

Sheet music dedicated to the Know-Nothing party. Millard Fillmore ran on the Know-Nothing ticket in 1856 and lost the election.

then became a schoolteacher. He read law with a county judge and became a lawyer in East Aurora, New York. He served three terms in the New York legislature, sponsoring legislation to close the debtors prison.

Fillmore began his career in national politics as an opponent of Andrew Jackson, joining the Whig party during his first term in the House of Representatives in 1833 and becoming party congressional leader in 1841. He opposed the spoils system, under which government posts were filled according to the recommendations of party bosses, and was in favor of national funding for internal improvements. Two of the tariff bills he wrote as chair of the Ways and Means Committee were vetoed by President John Tyler, but a third was approved in 1842. Fillmore lost the Whig nomination for Vice President in 1844 and was defeated in an election for New York governor that same year. In 1847 he was elected New York State's first comptroller. Fillmore received the Vice Presidential nomination in 1848 to appease northern Whigs opposed to the nomination of slaveholder Zachary Taylor. As Vice President, he presided fairly and firmly in the Senate over the intense debates between northern abolitionists and southern slaveholders. When Fillmore became President, he broke his political alliance with New York State Whig party boss Thurlow Weed and appointed a completely new cabinet, including Daniel Webster as secretary of state. He reversed Taylor's opposition to Henry Clay's Compromise of 1850, a measure designed to effect a compromise over extension of slavery into the newly acquired territories. It admitted California to the Union as a free state, permitted slavery in the New Mexico and Utah territories, abolished slavery in the District of Columbia, and strengthened the fugitive slave law to allow Southern slaveholders to use northern state courts and police in efforts to retrieve runaway slaves. Fillmore approved the compromise to avoid sectional conflict. His major accomplishment in foreign policy was the decision to send a fleet commanded by Commodore Matthew C. Perry to Japan, which resulted in an 1854 treaty that opened up that nation to U.S. trade. As a result of his sectional compromises, Fillmore was discredited among northern Whigs, and after 53 ballots he lost the bid for his party's Presidential nomination in 1852 to General Winfield Scott, the third war hero the Whigs had nominated for the Presidency. But the party destroyed itself over the slavery issue, and Fillmore turned the White House over to Democrat Franklin Pierce; he then retired to Buffalo to practice law.

Fillmore's 1856 Presidential campaign on the Know-Nothing ticket was an embarrassment; the party was opposed to foreigners and was strongly anti-Catholic, though Fillmore refused to endorse these prejudices in the campaign. He ran as a nationalist, attempting to preserve the Union from sectional divisions. He received 21 percent of the vote, a record for a third-party candidate until 1912. But after the election the party disappeared and he retired from politics.

Fillmore became active in local affairs in upstate New York. A man who had received only six months of schooling in his life, he had begun his political career in New York by developing the public school system. In later life he founded the University of Buffalo (becoming its first chancellor) and the Buffalo Fine Arts Academy.

FURTHER READING

Smith, Elbert B. *The Presidencies of Zachary Taylor and Millard Fillmore.* Lawrence: University Press of Kansas, 1988.

Fireside chat

A FIRESIDE CHAT is a Presidential address to the nation characterized by a warm, intimate, and informal tone. It is designed to build confidence in the President's policies. The tradition of the fireside chat was begun by President Franklin D. Roosevelt on March 12, 1933, speaking to the nation by radio shortly after his inauguration, in the midst of the Great Depression. He discussed the banking crisis, the bank holiday he had declared on March 6 and its results, and his plan to reopen banks the next day. Entitled "An Intimate Talk with the People of the United States on Banking," it was delivered in plain English to ordinary people. As the humorist Will Rogers put it, Roosevelt took up the subject of banking and "made everyone understand it, even the bankers." The talk was successful in preventing a run on deposits and restored stability to the banking system.

The term *fireside chat* was first used by a CBS radio executive to promote an audience for Roosevelt's second address. Roosevelt gave 30 such addresses during his Presidency. Many of the chats described the bills that Roosevelt had gotten Congress to pass to deal with the Depression. Other chats offered lessons in democracy.

President Jimmy Carter gave a televised fireside chat in 1977, complete with roaring fire in the Oval Office, and wore a cardigan sweater instead of the customary suit. That gesture earned him the nickname Jimmy Cardigan.

SEE ALSO

Carter, Jimmy; Public opinion, Presidents, and the media; Roosevelt, Franklin D.

FURTHER READING

Biuhite, Russell D., and David W. Levy, eds. *The Fireside Chats of Franklin D. Roosevelt*. Norman: University of Oklahoma Press, 1991.

Franklin Roosevelt prepares to deliver a fireside chat in 1934.

First Lady

INITIALLY, THE President's wife was referred to as Lady (as in "Lady Washington") or Mrs. President. The term *First Lady* was coined by Mary Clemmer Ames in an 1877 magazine article describing the inauguration of President Rutherford B. Hayes. It was popularized by a play about Dolley Madison entitled *The First Lady in the Land*, produced in New York City in 1911.

All Presidents except for James Buchanan married. Five remarried after the death of their first wife, and one (Ronald Reagan) remarried after a divorce. Some wives died before their husband reached the White House, including Martha Jefferson, Rachel Jackson, Hannah Van Buren, and Ellen Arthur. Presidents who were unmarried while in office relied on hostesses to assist them at state dinners, receptions, and other social functions. These include Martha Jefferson Randolph, daughter of Thomas Jefferson; Emily Donelson, niece of

Mary Todd Lincoln, who suffered from depression, was severely attacked by the press.

Andrew Jackson; Angelica Van Buren, daughter-in-law of Martin Van Buren; Harriet Lane, niece of James Buchanan; Martha Patterson, daughter of Andrew Johnson; and Mary Arthur McElroy, sister of Chester Arthur.

In the 19th century few First Ladies had much formal education and none had careers, with the exception of Abigail Fillmore, a teacher. Most occupied themselves by managing the White House, hosting its social functions, and raising their family. The first to attend school was Anna Harrison, wife of William Henry Harrison; the first to attend college was Lucretia Garfield, who graduated from Hiram College. "Lemonade" Lucy Hayes did charity work and promoted the temperance (anti-alcohol) movement; Caroline Harrison, wife of Benjamin Harrison, raised money for Johns Hopkins University and pressed it to accept women into the medical school.

The wedding of Grover Cleveland and Frances Folsom, which took place in the White House on June 2, 1886, marked the first time a President was married in the executive mansion. Press coverage of that event made the First Lady a nationally known figure. Edith Roosevelt (wife of Theodore) was the first to hire a social secretary to assist her in her duties. Woodrow Wilson's first wife, Ellen, was the first to take a public position on a bill being considered by Congress; his second wife, Edith, served as a liaison between her husband and the rest of government after he suffered a stroke in 1919.

Eleanor Roosevelt was the first Presidential wife to have a significant career; she was a teacher, journalist, and Democratic party activist. Others with careers include Jacqueline Kennedy (journalism and publishing), Patricia Nixon (teaching and government service), Lady Bird Johnson (communica-

tions), Nancy Reagan (acting), and Hillary Clinton (law), though none pursued their careers in the White House as Mrs. Roosevelt had done.

Lady Bird Johnson was the first wife to campaign alone on behalf of her husband in a Presidential campaign. Rosalynn Carter was the first to play an active role within the White House Office, acting as a staff aide to the President. She testified before Congress on legislation, supported the Equal Rights Amendment, was active in promoting mental health initiatives in government, met foreign heads of state as her husband's representative, and attended cabinet meetings. Nancy Reagan sponsored a "Just Say No" campaign against drug use. Barbara Bush, who dropped out of Smith College in her sophomore year to marry George Bush and raise a family, was active in organizing a campaign against illiteracy.

Hillary Clinton, a graduate of Yale Law School, was a partner in a large corporate law firm in Little Rock while her husband, Bill Clinton, served as governor of Arkansas. She also chaired the board of the Children's Defense Fund. During the transition to the Clinton administration, she used her influence to bring large numbers of women into high levels of government. She was given an office in the West Wing and was put in charge of a task force on health care reform, but after a bill embodying her plan failed to pass Congress, she backed

Lady Bird Johnson plants a tree on the White House grounds. As First Lady, she sponsored a beautification project to improve the look of cities and highways.

away from a visible role in policy-making. She preferred instead to assume a more traditional role in public while retaining her place as one of the President's most important advisers.

Traditionally, First Ladies took responsibility for furnishing the family quarters, assisted by the White House Curator, who is responsible for the maintenance and restoration of its public rooms with authentic period furniture; for hosting White House social functions, including choosing the menu and entertainment; and for representing the President on ceremonial occasions. Today they also serve as confidential advisers and policy formulators.

The First Lady earns no salary and holds no formal office. She employs more than 20 aides and has an office in the East Wing of the White House to answer mail, deal with the media, and supervise social functions. She uses her West Wing office to work on policies of interest to her.

SEE ALSO

Adams, Abigail; Kennedy, Jacqueline; Madison, Dolley; Roosevelt, Eleanor; White House

FURTHER READING

Boller, Paul F., Jr. *Presidential Wives*. New York: Oxford, 1988.
Caroli, Betty Boyd. *First Ladies*. Expanded ed. New York: Oxford, 1995.
Gould, Lewis L., ed. *American First Ladies: Their Lives and Their Legacy*. 2nd ed. New York: Routledge, 2001.
Gould, Lewis L. "First Ladies." *American Scholar* (Autumn 1986): 528–35.
Gould, Lewis L. "Modern First Ladies and the Presidency." *Presidential Studies Quarterly* 20 (Fall 1990): 677–82.

Flag, Presidential

THE PRESIDENTIAL flag denotes the presence of the President of the United States. It is displayed on the Presidential

yacht and limousines and on ceremonial occasions at the White House. It may also be displayed when the President gives an address and when he meets with foreign heads of state.

The first official Presidential flag was adopted by President Woodrow Wilson on May 29, 1916. Against a field of blue, the Presidential seal in bronze and a large white star in each corner were placed. On October 25, 1945, President Harry Truman increased the number of stars to 48, one for each state. The number was increased to 50 in 1959 by President Dwight Eisenhower to take into account the admission of Alaska and Hawaii to the Union.

SEE ALSO

Seal, Presidential

The Presidential flag flies near John F. Kennedy's casket in front of the Capitol.

Ford, Gerald R.

38TH PRESIDENT

☆ Born: July 14, 1913, Omaha, Nebr.
☆ Political party: Republican
☆ Education: University of Michigan, B.A., 1935; Yale University Law School, LL.B., 1940
☆ Military service: U.S. Navy, 1942–45
☆ Previous government service: U.S. House of Representatives, 1949–73; House minority leader, 1965–73; Vice President, 1973–74
☆ Succeeded to Presidency, 1974; served, 1974–77

GERALD FORD was the first Vice President ever to serve without having been popularly elected (he was appointed under the provisions of the 25th Amendment), and he was the first to succeed a

President who resigned from office. His pardon of Richard Nixon for all Watergate crimes and his weak performance in dealing with the economy contributed to his election defeat in 1976.

Ford was originally named Leslie King, Jr. When he was two years old, his parents divorced; he took the name of his stepfather, Gerald Rudolph Ford, when his mother remarried. He was an Eagle Scout and in high school was a star football player and member of the student council. While an undergraduate at the University of Michigan, Ford played football, and after graduation he received offers from the Detroit Lions and Green Bay Packers. Instead he went to Yale Law School and while there coached boxing, was the assistant football coach, and occasionally modeled for magazines. After receiving his law degree, Ford served as a lieutenant commander in the navy during World War II. He received 10 battle stars for action in the Pacific theater and almost lost his life when a typhoon hit the Third Fleet on December 18, 1944. After the war Ford briefly practiced law, and in 1948 defeated an incumbent Republican and won election to the U.S. House of Representatives from Grand Rapids, Michigan. During the campaign he married Betty Bloomer Warren. He served 12 terms in the House, never receiving less than 60 percent of the vote, and became Republican leader in 1965. He frequently sparred with President Lyndon Johnson, who once remarked that Ford had "played too much football with his helmet off." Ford opposed most of Johnson's Great Society programs, including aid to education and Medicare for the elderly.

After the resignation of Vice President Spiro Agnew as part of a plea bargain involving tax evasion charges, Ford was tapped by President Nixon for the Vice Presidency on October 12, 1973. He was sworn in, after receiving

Gerald Ford confers with National Security Adviser Brent Scowcroft at the Helsinki Conference in 1975.

congressional approval, on December 6, 1973.

When Nixon resigned on August 9, 1974, Ford succeeded to the Presidency. "Our long national nightmare is over," he told a nation numbed by the Watergate scandal. On September 8 he gave Nixon a "full, free and absolute" pardon for all Watergate crimes. "I do believe, with all my heart and mind and spirit, that I, not as President but as a humble servant of God, will receive justice without mercy if I fail to show mercy," he told the American people in a televised address. Ford's popularity plummeted because of the pardon, and it never recovered. Many Americans believed there had been a secret deal, or at least an "understanding," between Nixon and Ford, that Ford would issue a pardon if he were appointed Vice President and later succeeded Nixon in the White House.

Ford recommended to Congress that Nixon be paid $850,000 in transition expenses, which also upset public opinion. Congress allocated only $200,000 to Nixon. Ford appeared before a congressional committee to discuss the pardon, becoming the first President ever to appear before Congress for questioning. In September 1974 Ford offered Vietnam War deserters Presidential clemency if they participated in a work program. The contrast with the unconditional pardon given to Nixon seemed outrageous to many people.

Ford's domestic program was stalled by the Democratic Congress. As a result of the 1974 midterm elections, Democrats gained 43 House and 3 Senate seats to provide them with almost veto-proof margins. One-quarter of Ford's vetoes were overridden, a figure much higher than the 7 percent that other Presidents averaged. His anti-inflation effort, called Whip Inflation Now (WIN), was ignored, although the inflation rate dropped from 12 to 5 percent. His energy conservation program was derailed. Democrats passed their own education, public works, and housing measures. Ford vetoed many Democratic spending measures on domestic programs in 1976, but the vetoes were unpopular with Democrats and independent voters.

In foreign affairs, Ford's most notable achievements included an arms agreement with the Soviet Union on strategic weapons. In addition, the Helsinki Conference of 35 nations signed a pact in 1975 that recognized the borders of all states in Europe. It conferred legitimacy on Soviet expansionism after World War II but also required all nations to adhere to universal standards of human rights— provisions that eventually would make Soviet rule in Eastern Europe more difficult to sustain. In October 1975 Secretary of State Henry Kissinger helped put in place an interim peace agreement between Egypt and Israel in the Sinai Peninsula.

In 1975 the North Vietnamese army overran South Vietnam and put an end to the Vietnam War. President Ford ordered U.S. armed forces to evacuate Americans and South Vietnamese allies. Seven laws prohibited the use of the armed forces in Vietnam, and Ford went before a joint session of Congress to urge their repeal. After Congress deadlocked and did nothing, Ford ordered the evacuations anyway. He asked Congress to allocate almost half a billion dollars to settle 140,000 refugees from Indochina in the United States—one of his few legislative successes. Later, he sent the military to rescue crewmen of the merchant ship *Mayaguez* from Cambodian custody, losing 43 servicemen in the incident.

On September 22, 1975, Ford was almost assassinated by Sarah Jane Moore as he emerged from the St. Francis Hotel in San Francisco. The pistol was deflected by a bystander and Ford was not hit by the bullet.

In 1976 Ford was challenged by Ronald Reagan in the Republican primaries and barely defeated him for the nomination. The Republican platform, however, was written by conservatives and repudiated much of the Ford-Kissinger foreign policy of détente, or relaxation of tensions with the Soviet Union. During the general election campaign, Ford made a major slip in a debate when he asserted that "there is no Soviet domination of Eastern Europe." Although he seemed to have meant that the Soviets could not crush the Polish, Hungarian, and Czechoslovak peoples' longing for freedom, his poor choice of words gave the Democrats a chance to argue that Ford simply did not have the brains to be President. Ford was defeated by Jimmy Carter in a close election, receiving slightly less than 49 percent of the vote.

After retiring from the White House, Ford wrote his memoirs and saw to the construction of his Presidential library in Ann Arbor and museum in Grand Rapids, Michigan. In 1980 there was an effort to put Ford on the Reagan ticket as Vice President, but Ford insisted on a virtual "co-Presidency" in which he would share Presidential powers, and the effort was aborted by the Reagan camp.

SEE ALSO

Agnew, Spiro T.; Carter, Jimmy; Nixon, Richard Milhous; Pardon power; 25th Amendment; Watergate investigation

FURTHER READING

Ford, Betty, with Chris Chase. *The Times of My Life.* New York: Harper & Row, 1978.

Ford, Gerald. *A Time to Heal.* New York: Harper & Row, 1979.

Hartmann, Robert. *Palace Politics: An Inside Account of the Ford Years.* New York: McGraw-Hill, 1980.

Witcover, Jules. *Crapshoot: Rolling the Dice on the Vice Presidency.* New York: Crown, 1992.

Garfield, James A.

20TH PRESIDENT

☆ *Born: Nov. 19, 1831, Orange, Ohio*

☆ *Political party: Republican*

☆ *Education: Williams College, B.A., 1856*

☆ *Military service: 42nd Ohio Infantry, 1862–63*

☆ *Previous government service: Ohio Senate, 1859–61; U.S. House of Representatives, 1863–80; member of electoral commission, 1876*

☆ *Elected President, 1880; served, 1881*

☆ *Died: Sept. 19, 1881, Elberon, N.J.*

JAMES A. GARFIELD served the second-shortest term of any President (the shortest was served by William Henry Harrison). In the four months before he was shot, he accomplished next to nothing, but his death by a disappointed office seeker spurred the Congress several years later to pass a civil service reform bill.

Garfield was born on the Ohio frontier. He was a canal sailor, a teacher, and a farmer. After graduating from Williams College he became a professor of ancient languages and literature at Hiram Eclectic Institute.

Garfield entered Republican politics and was elected to the Ohio legislature. During the Civil War he headed a volunteer company that consisted of many of his former students. He distinguished himself with his bravery at the Battle of Chickamauga, receiving a promotion to major general.

Garfield served as a member of the House of Representatives for 17 years. He was a radical Republican who voted for the impeachment of Andrew Johnson and later was one of the two House Republicans to serve on the electoral commission that decided the disputed election of 1876 in favor of Rutherford B. Hayes.

James Garfield was a true dark horse Presidential candidate, one whose name first emerged at the convention itself. He received not a single vote on the first ballot for the Republican nomination in 1880. At the national convention he headed the faction supporting Secretary of Treasury John Sherman and opposing ex-President Ulysses S. Grant and Senator James G. Blaine. The three-way race deadlocked, and on the 36th ballot Garfield was nominated as a compromise candidate. He defeated the Democratic candidate, Civil War hero General Winfield Scott Hancock, by a tiny popular majority, though his electoral college margin was more substantial.

Garfield and Secretary of State Blaine, leaders of the Half-Breed faction of the Republican party (so called because their opponents thought they were half-Democrat), struggled against Senator Roscoe Conkling and other "Stalwart" Republicans over appointments to positions in his administration. Eventually, Garfield appointed his own man as collector of the Port of New York, signaling his victory. He also started an investigation of corruption in the post office department, which involved the awarding of certain mail routes to political favorites who then submitted inflated claims for payment.

On July 2, 1881, while standing at a railway station in Washington, D.C., Garfield was shot by Charles Julius Guiteau, who wanted to become an ambassador and had been rebuffed by Blaine. Guiteau, evidently insane, shouted, "I am a Stalwart. Arthur is now President of the United States," implying that Vice President Chester Arthur would get jobs for the Stalwarts. For 11 weeks Garfield hung between life and death while the cabinet debated questions about Presidential succession, including whether Arthur should assume office as acting President while Garfield lay ill. Garfield died on September 19 and was succeeded by Arthur; his assassin was found guilty of murder and hanged.

SEE ALSO

Arthur, Chester Alan; Assassinations, Presidential; Hayes, Rutherford B.; Succession to the Presidency

FURTHER READING

Doenicke, Justus D. *The Presidencies of James A. Garfield and Chester A. Arthur.* Lawrence: University Press of Kansas, 1981.

Garner, John Nance
VICE PRESIDENT

☆ Born: Nov. 22, 1868, Red River County, Tex.
☆ Political party: Democrat
☆ Education: Vanderbilt University, 1888
☆ Military service: none
☆ Previous government service: Texas House of Representatives, 1899–1902; U.S. House of Representatives, 1903–33; House minority leader, 1929–31; Speaker of the House, 1931–33
☆ Vice President under Franklin D. Roosevelt, 1933–41
☆ Died: Nov. 7, 1967, Uvalde, Tex.

JOHN NANCE GARNER, known as "Cactus Jack" because of his prickly humor, was a contender for the Democratic Presidential nomination in 1932. He received the Vice Presidential nomination as a reward for delivering the Texas delegation to Franklin D. Roosevelt.

Garner helped Roosevelt deal with Congress in the early days of the New Deal. But Roosevelt gave him no other

duties, and he spent much of his time at his ranch in Uvalde, Texas, taking target practice on a spittoon on his front porch. It was there that he described the Vice Presidency as "not worth a pitcher of warm spit."

In his second term, Garner opposed Roosevelt's attempt in 1937 to "pack" the Supreme Court—Roosevelt wanted to appoint additional justices sympathetic to his social and economic policies—and his attempt to "purge" Democrats in Congress who opposed the New Deal program in the 1938 elections. When Roosevelt decided to run for a third term, Garner objected to this violation of the unwritten two-term custom that had prevailed since George Washington. His own campaign for the 1940 Presidential nomination went nowhere, and he retired from politics permanently.

SEE ALSO
New Deal

FURTHER READING
Timmons, Bascom. *Garner of Texas.* New York: Harper, 1948.

Gerry, Elbridge
VICE PRESIDENT

☆ Born: July 17, 1744, Marblehead, Mass.
☆ Political party: Democratic-Republican
☆ Education: Harvard College, A.B., 1762
☆ Military service: none
☆ Previous government service: judge, Massachusetts General Court, 1772–74; signer of Declaration of Independence, 1776; Continental Congress, 1776–81, 1783–85; U.S. House of Representatives, 1789–93; governor of Massachusetts, 1810–11
☆ Vice President under James Madison, 1813–14
☆ Died: Nov. 23, 1814, Washington, D.C.

AS A DELEGATE to the Constitutional Convention, Elbridge Gerry was a strong proponent of states' rights. He spoke

against popular election of either the President or the Senate. He also wanted to restrict the size of the army to 3,000 in times of peace. He refused to sign the final draft of the Constitution because it did not provide a Bill of Rights.

Gerry was elected to Congress in 1789 and served two terms. In 1797 President John Adams sent Gerry, along with John Marshall and Charles Cotesworth Pinckney, on a diplomatic mission to France. Three French diplomats, known as X, Y, and Z, insisted on bribes and a $10 million loan as compensation for alleged American "insults." The mission ended in failure when the Americans refused these demands and published details of the so-called XYZ affair in American newspapers. A naval war with France ensued.

As governor of Massachusetts, Gerry invented the gerrymander, a system of redrawing state legislative and congressional districts to benefit members of his party. The term *gerrymander* was a combination of *Gerry* and *salamander,* a reference to the odd shapes of the districts that resulted.

In 1812 Gerry ran for Vice President as James Madison's running mate on the Republican ticket and won the election. He strongly supported the War of 1812, although opposition in his native Massachusetts was strong and the Federalist party, which controlled state governments in New England, refused to help the war effort. Gerry died in office in 1814.

Gettysburg Address

ON NOVEMBER 19, 1863, President Abraham Lincoln gave a short speech in Gettysburg, Pennsylvania, commemorating the Battle of Gettysburg and dedicating a national cemetery for fallen Union soldiers. Lincoln's speech is the most famous address ever given by an American President, and it is one of the most eloquent expressions of democratic ideals ever uttered. He wrote it in the White House, though he made a few changes on the train ride to Gettysburg.

He was preceded at the podium by the noted orator Edward Everett, who had spoken for nearly two hours. Lincoln's speech, by contrast, took only a few minutes. Lincoln observed, "The world will little note nor long remember what we say here, but it can never forget what they did here." Although the crowd gave Lincoln only perfunctory applause, Everett was more appreciative. He told Lincoln, "My speech will soon be forgotten; yours never will be. How gladly would I exchange my hundred pages for your twenty lines."

"Now we are engaged in a great civil war," Lincoln said, testing whether "any nation, conceived in liberty, and dedicated to the proposition that all men are created equal, can long endure." He urged Americans to resolve "that these dead shall not have died in vain; that this nation, under God, shall have a new birth of freedom; and that government of the people, by the people, and for the people, shall not perish from the earth." By emphasizing the equality of Americans, a value not mentioned even in the Constitution, Lincoln had provided a vision of the United States that could justify the carnage of the Civil War and would reshape the meaning of American politics for generations to follow.

SEE ALSO

Emancipation Proclamations; Lincoln, Abraham

FURTHER READING

Wills, Garry. *Lincoln at Gettysburg.* New York: Simon & Schuster, 1992.

Gore, Albert, Jr.

VICE PRESIDENT

☆ Born: Mar. 31, 1948, Washington, D.C.
☆ Political party: Democrat
☆ Education: Harvard College, A.B., 1969; Vanderbilt University Graduate School of Religion, 1971–72; Vanderbilt University Law School, LL.B., 1974
☆ Military service: U.S. Army, 1969–71
☆ Previous government service: U.S. House of Representatives, 1977–85; U.S. Senate, 1985–1993
☆ Vice President under Bill Clinton, 1993–2001

AL GORE, JR.'s father was for 32 years a Democratic representative and senator from Tennessee. Al, Jr., was raised in a Washington hotel owned by his family and attended St. Alban's School for Boys, where he won varsity letters in football, basketball, and track. He graduated from Harvard and later Vanderbilt Law School. After serving as an army journalist in Vietnam, he worked as a reporter and editorial writer for the *Nashville Tennessean*.

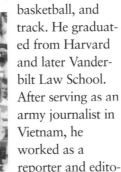

Al Gore (right) and wife, Tipper, join hands with Bill and Hillary Clinton to greet a cheering crowd during the 1992 campaign.

As a senator from Tennessee, Gore compiled a consistently liberal voting record. But he broke with the party leadership as only one of 10 Democratic senators to vote to authorize President George Bush to use military force against Iraq in the Persian Gulf War of 1991.

Gore ran unsuccessfully for the Democratic Presidential nomination in 1988. In 1992 he added tremendous strength to Bill Clinton's ticket in the border and Southern states.

As Vice President, Gore led the National Performance Review that recommended more businesslike methods in the bureaucracy and downsizing the federal work force. He played a major role in shaping policies regarding the "information superhighway," particularly in proposing new telecommunications regulations, and environmental issues. Clinton relied on Gore as his chief liaison with Democratic party leaders in Congress.

In 1996 Gore was renominated and reelected on Clinton's ticket. In his second term, he continued to play a major role in developing communications and high-technology policies for the government. During the Clinton impeachment crisis, Gore emerged as one of the President's chief defenders. Gore himself had to weather allegations that his fund raising in the 1996 campaign had violated campaign finance laws. The charges could not be proved, though, and in spite of the resulting drop in his poll ratings, Gore defeated former senator Bill Bradley for the Democratic Presidential nomination in 2000. Distancing himself from Clinton, Gore proposed protection for Social Security and Medicare, targeted tax cuts to encourage savings and education, health care for all children younger than five years old, and improvements in public education. His selection of Joe Lieberman, the first Jewish candidate on a major ticket, as running mate was lauded by most Americans, because Lieberman had been a strong critic of Clinton's behavior. In a tight race, Gore was defeated in the electoral college count by George W. Bush (although Gore won a majority of the popular vote), in spite of the peace and prosperity of the Clinton years.

SEE ALSO

Clinton, Bill; Electoral college

FURTHER READING

Gore, Al. *Earth in the Balance.* Boston: Houghton Mifflin, 1992.
Turque, Bill. *Inventing Al Gore: A Biography.* Boston: Houghton Mifflin, 2000.

Grant, Ulysses S.

18TH PRESIDENT

☆ *Born: Apr. 27, 1822, Point Pleasant, Ohio*
☆ *Political party: Republican*
☆ *Education: U.S. Military Academy, B.S., 1843*
☆ *Military service: U.S. Army: lieutenant, 1843; regimental quartermaster, 1846–48; 1st lieutenant, 1848; brevet captain, 1848; captain, 1853–54; 1st Illinois Volunteers: colonel, 1861; Galena Illinois Company: brigadier general, 1861; major general, 1862–63; lieutenant general and commander of all Union armies, 1864–65; general of the armies of the United States, 1866*
☆ *Previous civilian government service: interim U.S. secretary of war, 1867–68*
☆ *Elected President, 1868; served, 1869–77*
☆ *Died: July 23, 1885, Mount McGregor, N.Y.*

ULYSSES S. GRANT was an excellent general but a mediocre politician. He won the Civil War, but his Presidency was a failure because Grant surrounded himself with corrupt men who embroiled his administration in one scandal after another.

Grant was born on a farm and studied at local schools until obtaining an appointment to West Point, where he graduated 23rd in a class of 39. He fought under Zachary Taylor in the Mexican-American War, winning citations for bravery in several battles. In 1854 he resigned as captain of infantry and went back to farming, this time in Missouri. In 1860 he was a clerk at a leather goods store run by his father and brothers. When the Civil War broke out, he organized a local militia, then became colonel of an Illinois militia regiment, rising to the rank of major general.

Grant achieved great success in the Western campaigns, forcing Confederate forces to retreat from forts Henry and Donelson on the Tennessee and Cumberland rivers. He then won the Battle of Shiloh, and by July 4, 1863, the garrison at Vicksburg, Mississippi, surrendered. Grant was promoted to major general after this victory and became lieutenant general when he won a victory at Chattanooga. Lincoln later made him commander of all the Union armies. In May 1864 he began the final campaign of attrition against General Robert E. Lee in Virginia, and a year later, on April 9, 1865, Lee surrendered to Grant at Appomattox Court House. In 1866 Grant was named general of the armies, a rank that had been achieved by no one other than George Washington. He demobilized his armies, then became involved in civilian politics.

In the words of Woodrow Wilson, President Ulysses Simpson Grant "combined great gifts with great mediocrity." At first it seemed as if Grant were an astute politician at the end of the Civil War: he supported a strong military presence in the South to protect the rights of newly freed blacks, endearing himself to the radical Republicans in Congress. When President Andrew Johnson tried to replace Secretary of War Edwin Stanton in order to wrest Reconstruction policy from Congress, Grant accepted an appointment as interim secretary of war. But when Congress restored Stanton to the position, Grant turned his office back over to Stanton. Grant's refusal to support Johnson's actions gained him the unanimous first-ballot Republican nomination for President in 1868, and he won a narrow

Ulysses Grant at a battle camp during the Civil War.

popular vote victory over Democrat Horatio Seymour in the election.

But Grant was not politically astute. His first mistake was in naming several cronies from his home state to his cabinet. Several cabinet secretaries and other high-level officials became implicated in financial scandals. Resignations included those of his secretary of the Treasury (for irregularities in revenue collection), his secretary of war (for corruption in purchasing contracts), and his attorney general and secretary of the interior (for the Credit Mobilier railroad scandal).

Grant knew nothing of high finance, and he was taken advantage of by his brother-in-law, who worked with financiers Jay Gould and Jim Fisk in a scheme to corner the market in gold. They convinced Grant not to sell any government gold on financial markets, no matter how high the price went, so that their own gold would become more valuable. Grant eventually realized that his relative was using him and ordered the sale of $4 million in Treasury gold. This action caused a crash in the price of gold and financial ruin for many investors, though Gould and Fisk made a great deal of money.

Grant managed to defuse criticism of the corruption in his administration by establishing the Civil Service Commission in 1871. He was renominated in 1872, again by a unanimous first ballot at the convention, and he defeated Democrat Horace Greeley by a landslide. Grant had a tougher time in his second term. A financial panic that began in 1873 helped Democrats gain control of the House of Representatives in 1874. However, Congress cut taxes and repealed an income tax law, which proved to be popular actions.

In foreign affairs, Grant's attempts to annex the Caribbean island of Santo Domingo were defeated by the Senate. The President's policy of remaining strictly neutral in the conflict between Cuban nationalists and the Spanish occupiers was upheld by Congress, when it voted down a resolution recognizing the revolutionary government proclaimed by the Cuban belligerents.

He tried for a third term in 1880 but lost the Republican nomination to James Garfield.

Grant spent his retirement writing popular articles about his military exploits. Mark Twain published Grant's best-selling memoirs just weeks after the ex-President's death on July 23, 1885.

SEE ALSO

Garfield, James A.; Johnson, Andrew

FURTHER READING

McFeely, William. *Grant: A Biography.* New York: Norton, 1981.

Great Society

THE GREAT Society was the phrase that President Lyndon B. Johnson gave to his domestic programs. Johnson spelled out his vision of the Great Society in a commencement speech at the University of Michigan on May 22, 1964. He called on the nation to move not only toward "the rich society and the powerful society, but upward to the Great Society," one that would "end poverty and racial injustice." The term came from the English socialist Graham Wallas, who wrote a book of that name in 1914; the term was also used by the

Cartoonist Thomas Nast depicts Uncle Sam falling into a barrel of scandals during Grant's administration.

Lyndon Johnson meets a member of the Job Corps. The program helped prepare inner-city teenagers for the job market.

English socialist Harold Laski in his 1931 book *Introduction to Politics.*

Johnson believed that low-income communities could be aided by providing a variety of social services to their residents. These services would enable them to obtain the education and training necessary to obtain jobs that would lift them from poverty. Programs for the poor included the following: Head Start, which provided preschool educational and health programs; the Job Corps and Neighborhood Youth Corps, along with the Vocational Education Act, which gave job training to inner-city teenagers; the Higher Education Act, which provided loans and scholarships to college students from low-income families; the Teachers Corps, Volunteers in Service to America (VISTA), VISTA Lawyers and Legal Services Program, which sent teachers, community organizers, and lawyers into poor neighborhoods; the Model Cities Program of 1966, which coordinated slum renewal and economic development; the Fair Housing Act of 1968, which barred racial discrimination in housing, provided more low-income housing, and experimented with rent-supplement payments to the poor; Medicaid and Neighborhood Health Services, which provided funding to hospitals and doctors serving the poor; and the Elementary and Secondary Education Act of 1965, which provided federal funding to schools and targeted the aid to low-income school districts.

Johnson created the Office of Economic Opportunity in 1964 in order to coordinate social programs in poor neighborhoods. It did so through community action programs that provided for participation by residents in the communities served, usually through the creation of public corporations with elected boards of directors to administer services. These community action programs came under fire at the local level from conservatives opposed to government services for the poor as well as from mayors who wanted local governments to administer such programs. By 1968 most of these programs had been reorganized to place them under the control of city officials.

Richard Nixon's administration attempted to abolish the Office of Economic Opportunity and gave departments such as Health, Education, and Welfare (HEW) and Housing and Urban Development (HUD) the responsibility to administer its programs. Ronald Reagan was an unabashed foe of these programs, campaigning in 1980 with the slogan "In the 1960s we fought a war against poverty and poverty won." During Reagan's Presidency many of these programs were abolished and others, including job training, housing, and community development programs, suffered significant cutbacks.

Democrats pointed out that the Great Society programs had significantly reduced the poverty rates in the 1960s, down from 19 percent to 12 percent of the population between 1964 and 1969. In the 1980s, by contrast, poverty rates increased to about 15 percent when conservative Republican administrations phased out Great Society programs. In the 1960s the income of young black families had risen more than 60 percent. In 1992 families with children headed by people younger than 30 had one-third less income, and young black families had half the income of their predecessors in 1972.

Democrats also noted that many Great Society programs benefited middle-class families. These included the College Work Study and Higher Education Act, which provided loans and work-study employment for college students, and the Medicare program, which provided health insurance for the elderly.

SEE ALSO

Johnson, Lyndon B.

FURTHER READING

Marris, Peter, and Martin Rein. *Dilemmas of Social Reform.* London: Routledge, 1967. Murray, Charles. *Losing Ground: American Social Policy, 1950–1980.* New York: Basic Books, 1984.

Gulf of Tonkin Resolution

THE GULF of Tonkin Resolution was passed by Congress in 1964 to support President Lyndon Johnson in taking measures to protect American armed forces in Indochina.

As requested by Johnson, Congress passed the resolution in response to incidents between American naval destroyers and North Vietnamese gunboats. According to the navy, on August 2, 1964, three North Vietnamese torpedo boats fired on the U.S.S. *Maddox.* Two of these gunboats were damaged by aircraft from the U.S.S. *Ticonderoga.* On August 4, the *Maddox* and the U.S.S. *Turner Joy* were on patrol in international waters when they came under attack, but they were not damaged. On August 5, in retaliation for these attacks, U.S. planes destroyed or damaged 25 patrol boats.

The resolution reads in part: "That the Congress approves and supports the determination of the President, as commander-in-chief, to take all measures necessary to repel any armed attack against the forces of the United States and to prevent further aggression. . . . The United States is, therefore, prepared, as the President determines, to take all necessary steps, including the use of armed forces." Congress passed the resolution virtually unanimously.

Johnson later used this resolution as justification for sending 500,000 troops into South Vietnam to defend it against communist armies attempting to overthrow the government. His administration claimed it was the "functional equivalent" of a declaration of war.

Congressional critics argued that Johnson had deceived Congress and the American people. An investigation by the Senate Foreign Relations Committee in 1968 revealed that the *Maddox* was on an intelligence mission, much closer to North Vietnam than the administration had revealed, and was sailing near South Vietnamese vessels that were attacking the North Vietnamese patrol boats at the time. The *Maddox* fired first in the August 2 incident. Critics argued that Johnson deceived Congress by using this minor incident as a pretext to get congressional authorization to escalate U.S. involvement in Vietnam.

SEE ALSO

Johnson, Lyndon B.; War powers

FURTHER READING

Herring, George C. *America's Longest War: The United States and Vietnam, 1950–1975.* New York: Knopf, 1986. U.S. Congress. Senate Committee on Foreign Relations. *The Gulf of Tonkin: The 1964 Incidents.* 90th Cong., 2nd sess., 1968.

"Hail to the Chief"

"HAIL TO THE CHIEF" is the march music played to announce the arrival or recognize the presence of the President of the United States. The music was first published in the United States in 1812, to the words of "Lady of the Lake" by Sir Walter Scott. It may have been composed by James Sanderson, a noted English songwriter, but because it is unknown in England, "Mr. Sanderson" is most likely a pseudonym for an American composer. "Hail to the Chief" was first played at the inauguration of President Martin Van Buren on March 4, 1837.

SEE ALSO

Marine Band, U.S.; "Ruffles and Flourishes"

FURTHER READING

Fuld, James J. *The Book of World-Famous Music.* 3rd ed. New York: Dover, 1985.
Kirk, Elise. *Music at the White House.* Urbana: University of Illinois Press, 1986.

Hamlin, Hannibal

VICE PRESIDENT

☆ Born: Aug. 27, 1809, Paris Hill, Maine
☆ Political party: Democrat, then Republican
☆ Education: secondary school; read law, 1832
☆ Military service: none
☆ Previous government service: Maine House of Representatives, 1836–41; U.S. House of Representatives, 1843–47; U.S. Senate, 1848–56, 1857–60; governor of Maine, 1856
☆ Vice President under Abraham Lincoln, 1861–65
☆ Subsequent government service: collector of Port of Boston, 1865–66; U.S. Senate, 1869–81; minister to Spain, 1881
☆ Died: July 4, 1891, Bangor, Maine

ORIGINALLY A "Jackson Democrat," a follower of Andrew Jackson, Hannibal Hamlin joined the new Republican party in 1856. He was nominated by the Republicans for the Vice Presidency in 1860 to provide regional balance on the ticket (Presidential candidate Abraham Lincoln was from Illinois). As a strong

antislavery voice, he also provided ideological balance to the more moderate Lincoln. As Vice President, Hamlin was closely associated with the radical wing of the Republican party in Congress, pressing its case with Lincoln and supporting congressional efforts to emancipate the slaves.

Although Hamlin had been loyal to Lincoln, in 1864 the President decided to drop him from the ticket and replace him with Tennessee loyalist Andrew Johnson in a move to widen the appeal of the Union cause in the border states. Lincoln named Hamlin collector of the Port of Boston in 1865. Hamlin later returned to the Senate and became a leading advocate of harsh Reconstruction measures in the South. He then served as U.S. minister to Spain.

SEE ALSO

Lincoln, Abraham

FURTHER READING

Hunt, H. Draper. *Hannibal Hamlin of Maine: Lincoln's First Vice President.* Syracuse: Syracuse University Press, 1969.

Harding, Warren G.

29TH PRESIDENT

☆ Born: Nov. 2, 1865, Blooming Grove, Ohio
☆ Political party: Republican
☆ Education: Ohio Central College, 1879–82
☆ Military service: none
☆ Previous government service: Ohio Senate, 1899–1903; lieutenant governor of Ohio, 1903–4; U.S. Senate, 1915–21
☆ Elected President, 1920; served, 1921–23
☆ Died: Aug. 2, 1923, San Francisco, Calif.

WARREN HARDING was a handsome, amiable man who looked like a President but hardly acted like one. He won election by a landslide but did nothing with

An 1860 campaign banner for Presidential candidate Abraham Lincoln and running mate Hannibal Hamlin.

his mandate. A conservative Republican, he favored a return to "normalcy" after Woodrow Wilson's New Freedom program of business regulation. Scandals rocked Harding's Presidency and contributed to his untimely death in office.

Harding grew up on a farm in Ohio. He worked on his father's newspaper, then became a reporter and publisher of the *Marion Star*. He lost a race for county auditor in 1892 but in 1899 won election to the state senate. After serving two terms he became lieutenant governor of Ohio in 1903. He lost the election for governor in 1909. Harding won Ohio's first direct primary nomination for U.S. senator and was elected in 1914. He voted for two constitutional amendments in the Senate, one prohibiting the sale and consumption of alcohol (though he was a heavy drinker) and the other establishing woman suffrage. He voted against the Treaty of Versailles at the end of World War I.

In 1920 Harding was a compromise choice when a deadlock developed at the convention between front-runners Leonard Wood and Frank Lowden. Harding won the nomination on the 10th ballot. He defeated Democratic candidate James Cox, the governor of Ohio, by a huge margin.

Harding's Presidential policies were pro-business: high tariffs (taxes on imports) to protect American industry, lower government expenditures, tax cuts for corporations, and an end to antitrust enforcement (the regulation or breakup of large financial empires that established business monopolies). Secretary of the Treasury Andrew Mellon, one of the wealthiest men in the United States, got Congress to reduce income taxes on millionaires by two-thirds. Harding was the first President to broadcast a radio address, when he dedicated the Francis Scott Key Memorial at Fort McHenry in Baltimore, Maryland, on June 14, 1922.

In foreign affairs Harding proposed an association of nations in place of the newly formed League of Nations, but his idea got no support at home or abroad. His secretary of commerce, Herbert Hoover, provided $20 million in emergency food relief for the Soviet Union in 1921 to avert a famine, saving as many as 10 million people. Harding concluded a treaty with Colombia that provided $25 million in reparations for the U.S. role in detaching Panama from that nation. Secretary of State Charles Evans Hughes organized the Naval Disarmament Conference of 1921–22, a successful effort to limit naval expenditures of major military powers. It resulted in treaties establishing ceilings on the total number of battleships owned by the United States, Great Britain, Japan, and several other nations.

Harding presided over one of the most corrupt administrations in U.S. history. If George Washington could not tell a lie, then Warren Harding could not tell a liar. The Ohio Gang from his state party took key positions; his main political adviser, the director of the Veterans Bureau, Charles Forbes, received tens of millions of dollars in bribes for the construction of veterans hospitals. Forbes was forced to resign and eventually spent two years in jail.

The biggest scandal of all involved naval oil reserves at Teapot Dome, Wyoming. The President and Secretary of the Navy Edwin Denby transferred control of naval petroleum reserves from the Navy Department to the Department of the Interior, headed by Albert Fall. Fall then leased the Teapot Dome reserve to oil producer Harry Sinclair after receiving at least $300,000 from him in bribes. (In 1927 the government canceled the leases and Fall went to prison.) Though Harding himself was not involved in these scandals, he was embarrassed by the way in which his friends betrayed his trust for personal gain. Harding's death, from a heart attack during a vacation trip in the West, released him from the White House before the scandals became public and before the full political effects of his corrupt administration could be visited upon him.

SEE ALSO

Coolidge, Calvin

FURTHER READING

Murray, Robert K. *The Harding Era: Warren G. Harding and His Administration.* Minneapolis: University of Minnesota Press, 1969.

Trani, Eugene P., and David L. Wilson. *The Presidency of Warren G. Harding.* Lawrence: University Press of Kansas, 1977.

Harrison, Benjamin

23RD PRESIDENT

☆ *Born: Aug. 20, 1833, North Bend, Ohio*
☆ *Political party: Republican*
☆ *Education: Miami University (Ohio), B.A., 1852*
☆ *Military service: 70th Regiment of Indiana Volunteers, 1861–65*
☆ *Previous government service: crier of the federal court, 1854; Indiana Supreme Court reporter, 1860–62; member, Mississippi River Commission, 1879; U.S. Senate, 1881–87*
☆ *Elected President, 1888; served, 1889–93*
☆ *Subsequent government service: chief counsel for Venezuela in arbitration of boundary dispute with British Guyana, 1898–99*
☆ *Died: Mar. 13, 1901, Indianapolis, Ind.*

BENJAMIN HARRISON was one of the few Presidents to be elected despite winning fewer popular votes than his opponent. He was an effective leader in international affairs, and his administration concluded commercial treaties with many nations and improved relations with Latin America. But the economy deteriorated during his Presidency, infla-

tion and joblessness increased, and labor unrest made him a one-term President.

Harrison was descended from a family of Ohio politicians that included his great-grandfather, Virginia governor Benjamin Harrison (a signer of the Declaration of Independence); his grandfather, President William Henry Harrison; and his father, Whig congressman John Scott Harrison. A lawyer by vocation, Benjamin Harrison became a member of the newly formed Republican party in the 1850s and held various state party positions. During the Civil War his regiment saw fierce fighting in Georgia, and Harrison led his men several times in successful charges against enemy positions. After the war he resumed the practice of law. He tried but failed to win the nomination for Indiana governor in 1872, then lost a close election for governor in 1876.

In 1880 Harrison chaired the Indiana delegation to the Republican national convention. His switch to Garfield decided the nomination. He declined a cabinet position in order to serve in the U.S. Senate for one term but was defeated for reelection. At the Republican convention of 1888, the delegates could not decide between Ohio's John Sherman and Indiana's Walter Gresham. Harrison was the compromise choice. Although he received 100,000 fewer popular votes than President Grover Cleveland, Harrison defeated Cleveland in the electoral college.

Harrison opened Oklahoma to settlement in 1889 under the Homestead Act, and in a single day 20,000 settlers claimed all the acreage available. During his term six states (Washington, Idaho, Montana, Wyoming, North Dakota, and South Dakota) entered the Union, completing the westward expansion of the nation.

Harrison almost secured the annexation of Hawaii as well. American

A tent city in Oklahoma in 1889. After Benjamin Harrison signed the Homestead Act to allow settlement in Oklahoma, homesteaders poured into the territory.

settlers and plantation owners overthrew the government of Queen Liliuokalani, established a new regime, and were recognized by U.S. minister John L. Stevens, who sent 150 marines to protect the new government. Harrison denied any interference in the internal affairs of the islands, but the Senate delayed until 1898 action on a treaty of annexation offered by the revolutionary government.

The most powerful man in the Harrison administration was Secretary of State James G. ("Jingo") Blaine, and its most notable accomplishments were in foreign affairs. The first Pan American Conference, a meeting of the nations of the Western Hemisphere, was held in 1889, leading to the formation of the Pan American Union. A dispute over trading privileges in Samoa resulted in an international conference and creation of a three-power protectorate (British, German, and American) so each could receive the same trading rights in the islands.

An October 16, 1891, riot in Valparaíso, Chile, involving sailors from the U.S.S. *Baltimore*, left 2 American sailors dead, 17 injured, and many others imprisoned. In a special message to Congress on January 25, 1892, Harrison warned of war. Blaine had sent an ultimatum to Chile on January 21 requiring an apology. Chile did so and paid a $75,000 reparation, even as Harrison's message was sent off, ending the crisis.

During Harrison's administration Congress was dominated by "Czar" Thomas Reed, the Speaker of the House, and several Republican senators. They included John Sherman, who in 1890 got Congress to pass the Sherman Anti-Trust Act. It was supposed to allow the government to bring lawsuits against organizers of business enterprises that acted to restrain competition, but it was not vigorously enforced. The concentration of trusts proceeded with no interference from Harrison's Justice Department. The Sherman Silver Purchase Act (1890) was designed to help the silver industry and to secure votes in the West and among farmers favoring cheap money by having the government buy silver and then increase the amount of coins in circulation. Pensions for Civil War veterans increased by 50 percent under the Pension Act of 1890, but the McKinley Tariff increased the rates on most imports of industrial goods and was so unpopular with farmers and consumers in the 1890 election that Congress went over to Democratic control. Two years later, with the country reeling from labor unrest, Harrison was defeated for reelection by Grover Cleveland.

Harrison returned to his law practice in Indiana and wrote two books, *This Country of Ours* and *Views of an Ex-President*. He served as counsel to Venezuela from 1898 to 1899 in its negotiation of a boundary dispute with Great Britain. He was a strong critic of U.S. colonial policies after the Spanish-American War.

SEE ALSO
Cleveland, Grover

FURTHER READING
Socolofsky, Homer E., and Allen B. Spetter. *The Presidency of Benjamin Harrison.* Lawrence: University Press of Kansas, 1987.

Harrison, William Henry

9TH PRESIDENT

☆ *Born: Feb. 9, 1773, Charles City County, Va.*
☆ *Political party: Whig*
☆ *Education: Hampden-Sydney College, 1787–89; Philadelphia College of Physicians and Surgeons, 1790*
☆ *Military service: U.S. Army, 1791–98, 1812–14*
☆ *Previous government service: secretary of Northwest Territory, 1798–99; nonvoting member of U.S. House of Representatives from Northwest Territory, 1800; governor of Indiana Territory, 1800–12; U.S. House of Representatives, 1817–19; Ohio Senate, 1819–21; U.S. Senate, 1825–28; U.S. minister to Colombia, 1828–29*
☆ *Elected President, 1840; served, 1841*
☆ *Died: Apr. 4, 1841, Washington, D.C.*

WILLIAM HENRY HARRISON was the first member of the Whig party to be elected President. He served the shortest time of any President, only 32 days. Harrison was born at Berkeley, his family's Virginia plantation, and intended to

study medicine to please his father. When his father died, however, he abandoned medicine for a military career, serving in the Northwest Territory and seeing action in the Battle of Fallen Timbers, in which the Indian Confederacy of the Northwest was defeated. He became governor of the Indiana Territory in 1800.

Harrison became a military hero, defeating the Shawnee Indians at the Battle of Tippecanoe on November 7, 1811, and again at the Battle of the Thames in Canada in October 1813. The death of the Shawnee chief Tecumseh in that battle secured the Northwest frontier of the United States. Harrison then moved to Ohio and served in the U.S. House of Representatives, the state legislature, and the U.S. Senate and as a diplomat. He was active in organizing the Whig party.

Although Democratic candidate Martin Van Buren won the election of 1836, Harrison was the most popular of the four Whig candidates who ran for the Presidency in that election. In 1839 the Whigs united to nominate Harrison and then added Democratic defector John Tyler to the ticket. They campaigned in 1840 with the slogan "Tippecanoe and Tyler, too." The

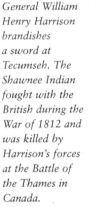

General William Henry Harrison brandishes a sword at Tecumseh. The Shawnee Indian fought with the British during the War of 1812 and was killed by Harrison's forces at the Battle of the Thames in Canada.

"The Tippecanoe or Log Cabin Quick Step" was a song dedicated to Whig candidate William Henry Harrison during the 1840 campaign.

Whigs did not adopt a party platform: they relied on songs, parades, and symbolism to appeal to the emotions rather than to the brains of the voters. They claimed that Harrison had grown up in a log cabin and hid his aristocratic plantation origins.

Harrison was nationally known as a war hero, but he had no record on political issues and his appeal was enormous. His election was more significant for the new style of politics it demonstrated than for his subsequent tenure in office because he served only one month before dying of pneumonia. He may have contracted the illness at his inaugural ceremony, which took place on the coldest inauguration day in American history. Harrison was the first President to die in office.

SEE ALSO

Tyler, John; Van Buren, Martin

FURTHER READING

Peterson, Norma Louis. *The Presidencies of William Henry Harrison and John Tyler.* Lawrence: University Press of Kansas, 1989.

Hayes, Rutherford B.
19TH PRESIDENT

☆ Born: Oct. 4, 1822, Delaware, Ohio
☆ Political party: Whig, then Republican
☆ Education: Kenyon College, B.A., 1842; Harvard Law School, LL.B., 1845
☆ Military service: Ohio Volunteers, 1861–65
☆ Previous government service: solicitor of Cincinnati, 1858; U.S. House of Representatives, 1865–68; governor of Ohio, 1868–72, 1876–77
☆ Elected President, 1876; served, 1877–81
☆ Died: Jan. 17, 1893, Fremont, Ohio

RUTHERFORD B. HAYES was the President who ended Reconstruction in the South. His honest administration restored the nation's faith in the Republican party after the corruption that occurred during the administration of Ulysses S. Grant.

Hayes never knew his father, who died before his birth. After graduating at the head of his class from Kenyon College and completing his legal studies at Harvard, Hayes practiced law in Cincinnati, Ohio, where he was active in the Whig party. He became a Republican in 1856. During the Civil War he commanded an Ohio regiment, fought in six major campaigns, and received a medal "for gallant and distinguished services." At the Battle of Winchester he captured an artillery position in hand-to-hand fighting. In the Battle of South Mountain he suffered a severe arm wound that ended his military career.

Hayes was then elected to the U.S. House of Representatives, where he supported the moderate wing of his party, which wished for conciliation with the South, rather than the radical Republicans, who intended to impose a harsh military occupation on the defeated region. He served three terms as governor of Ohio, providing honest and competent government. But Hayes failed in his efforts in 1868 to amend the state constitution to allow African Americans to vote. In 1876, as a dark horse candidate, Hayes defeated James G. Blaine for the Republican nomination for President. In his letter accepting the nomination, he pledged that he would not be a candidate for a second term.

Throughout his career Hayes managed to win one close election after another: it took 13 ballots for the Cincinnati city council to elect him solicitor; he won three Ohio gubernatorial contests by less than 1 percent margins; and his Presidential election followed a similar pattern. At first it appeared that Democrat Samuel J. Tilden was the winner. But Republicans challenged the results in

Florida, Louisiana, Oregon, and South Carolina. These states had 20 electoral votes—enough for Hayes to win the White House.

Hayes believed that many African Americans had been intimidated from voting and that fraud had been committed. In South Carolina, for example, the number of votes counted was larger than the state's population. The Republican Senate and Democratic House created a 15-member electoral commission to examine the returns from these states and to certify which electoral votes—Democratic or Republican—it would accept as valid. The commission awarded all 20 of the contested electoral votes from these states to Hayes by a party-line vote of 8 to 7. On March 2, 1877, the commission declared Hayes elected by 185 to 184 electoral college votes.

In what historians have termed the "great betrayal" of African Americans, the southern Democrats agreed to accept the election of Hayes in return for the withdrawal of all federal troops from Louisiana and South Carolina, thus ending Reconstruction. The troops were withdrawn within two months of Hayes's inauguration. Republicans abandoned black voters, and without federal protection, white supremacy in politics and the segregation of public accommodations soon occurred. Republicans also promised the South financing for a transcontinental railroad line to link southern and western markets.

Early in his Presidency Hayes lost any chance of popular support through his actions during the railroad strikes of 1877. Workers faced wage cuts on the Baltimore and Ohio Railroad and went on strike. At the request of the governor of West Virginia, Hayes sent federal troops to guard the mails and ensure the safety of trains. Rail strikes spread to Baltimore, Philadelphia, Pittsburgh, and

other cities. Eventually, the workers gave in to management, but the resentment against Hayes's use of troops led to the first congressional investigation of labor-management relations.

Hayes had campaigned for President as a reformer, distancing himself from the corrupt Grant administration. "He serves his party best who serves his country best," he said in his inaugural address. Once in office, he alienated members of his party by making merit appointments and reforming government departments. His secretary of the interior, Carl Schurz, rooted out corrupt practices in the Indian Bureau. In June 1877 Hayes issued an order that civil servants could not be assessed, or forced by the parties to make political contributions, but this order was disregarded. Because of the opposition of New York party leader Senator Roscoe Conkling, it took Hayes two years to secure the dismissal for mismanagement of Chester A. Arthur as collector of the Port of New York. But Conkling (whom he had defeated for the nomination in 1876) was able to thwart Hayes's efforts to obtain civil service legislation.

After the 1878 midterm election Democrats controlled both houses of Congress, and Hayes had little influence in the legislature. He often vetoed legislation passed by Congress. His most notable vetoes included the Bland-Allison Act, which required the resumption of silver coinage (Congress passed the bill over his veto); "riders" to appropriations bills sponsored by southern Democrats that would have nullified federal election laws protecting black voting rights in southern states; and a bill to exclude Chinese immigrants, on the grounds that it violated the Burlingame Treaty of 1868, an agreement between the United States and China that precluded the United States from a total exclusion of Chinese immigrants. Hayes bowed to anti-Chinese sentiment and negotiated a new treaty with China that limited immigration.

Hayes opposed a French scheme to build the Panama Canal, claiming it was a violation of the Monroe Doctrine. He sent a special message to Congress on March 8, 1880, stating that "the policy of this country is a canal under American control." He further proclaimed that the United States would insist on exercising "supervision and authority" over any canal that was built. When the French diplomat Ferdinand de Lesseps formed an "advisory committee" in the United States and paid the secretary of the navy, Richard W. Thompson, $25,000 to serve, Hayes put an end to this effort to buy influence in the capital by firing Thompson. De Lesseps tried to build his canal anyway but eventually abandoned the project.

In other foreign matters, Hayes ordered U.S. troops into Mexico to end raids by Indians, eventually obtaining cooperation from Mexican authorities so that troops could be withdrawn. He negotiated a treaty with Samoa that gave the U.S. Navy the use of the port of Pago Pago.

In 1880 Hayes honored his pledge not to seek reelection. He returned to his home in Fremont, Ohio, where he promoted educational reforms, especially for African-American industrial education in the South. From 1883 on, he served as president of the National Prison Association, an organization established to promote improvements in the correctional system.

SEE ALSO

Arthur, Chester Alan; Electoral college; Grant, Ulysses S.; Monroe Doctrine; Veto power

FURTHER READING

Davison, Kenneth E. *The Presidency of Rutherford B. Hayes.* Westport, Conn.: Greenwood, 1972.
Hoogenboom, Ari. *The Presidency of Rutherford B. Hayes.* Lawrence: University Press of Kansas, 1988.
Logan, Rayford. *The Betrayal of the Negro.* New York: Collier, 1965.

Health, Presidential

MANY PRESIDENTS have suffered illnesses prior to and during their terms of office. Four died in office of illness: William Henry Harrison caught pneumonia after delivering his inaugural address; Zachary Taylor and Warren Harding both died of heart disease while their performance in office was being harshly criticized; and Franklin Roosevelt died of a cerebral hemorrhage. In fact, 25 of the 35 deceased Presidents did not live as long as other people of their generation. White House "burnout" really does take the ultimate toll. The more active and successful the President, however, the less the "mortality gap"—the difference between the life expectancy of someone the President's age and the actual age at which the President dies.

In the 19th century medical problems were often poorly diagnosed and treated. Even after modern medicine permitted accurate diagnoses by the President's doctors, the custom until the 1950s was to keep such information confidential. But since Dwight Eisenhower's heart attack in 1955, the public has come to expect full disclosure, though often the condition of the President is still minimized by White House aides.

George Washington suffered more serious illnesses than any other President, including tuberculosis, smallpox, and pneumonia. In his first year in office, a cancerous tumor was removed from his thigh.

Andrew Jackson was in the worst medical condition of any President. One dueling wound had shattered his left shoulder, while another, a bullet that lodged in his left lung, caused bleeding throughout his life. He had chronic infections in his bronchial tubes. He also was partially blind, and his poor digestion and diarrhea from chronic dysentery left him emaciated. He took calomel, a medicine that gave him mercury poisoning and headaches, possibly contributing to his colossal temper.

Two Whig Presidents died in office from their illnesses. William Henry Harrison caught a chest cold at his inauguration, then became chilled at a cabinet meeting. He contracted pneumonia and jaundice. Purging and vomiting left him debilitated. He died of pneumonia, pleurisy, and septicemia. Zachary Taylor spent too much time in the sun at Fourth of July ceremonies in 1850. He became dehydrated and suffered cramps, fever, and vomiting before he died. Doctors today speculate that he might have had a perforation of the diverticulum of the colon or a ruptured appendix.

Franklin Pierce was an alcoholic and suffered from cirrhosis of the liver. Abraham Lincoln suffered periods of depression that made it impossible for him to function. He had hyperphoria in his left eye, a condition in which the eye rolled slightly upward, inducing headaches, indigestion, and nausea. He also suffered from diplopia, or double vision. He contracted smallpox just before giving the Gettysburg Address and was diagnosed with exhaustion in March 1865. Some doctors today believe that he had Marfan's syndrome, which might have induced fatal congestive heart failure. Grover Cleveland was diagnosed with cancer of the mouth and upper jaw in 1893. He kept it secret, telling his doctors, "If a rumor gets around that I'm dying, then the country is dead too." He did not even tell his pregnant wife. He had surgery on the *Oneida*, a yacht floating in

Franklin Roosevelt, disabled by polio, was photographed on crutches when he met with John W. Davis, the Democratic Presidential candidate, in 1924. After Roosevelt became President, the media avoided showing that he was disabled.

New York City's East River, on July 1, 1893, and a few days later was fitted with an artificial jaw. Cleveland's operation was finally revealed in 1917 in the *Saturday Evening Post*.

Woodrow Wilson suffered from the flu in April 1918, and bouts of coughing and shortness of breath remained with him. On September 26, 1919, he collapsed from exhaustion while on a nationwide speaking tour to promote the Treaty of Versailles. On October 2 he suffered a stroke in Washington and was incapacitated for much of his second term.

Warren Harding died in 1923 of a massive heart attack, though at the time doctors diagnosed his illness as pneumonia, gastritis, food poisoning, and copper poisoning. His successor, Calvin Coolidge, often suffered from debilitating bouts of depression.

Franklin D. Roosevelt was struck with polio in 1921 and never regained the use of his legs. He was never photographed in a wheelchair, and newspapers and radio commentators never mentioned that he could not walk and required 30-pound steel braces on his legs. Camera angles always focused on the upper part of his body. By 1944 Roosevelt was also suffering from hypertension, partial cardiac failure, and acute bronchitis. He died in 1945 of a massive cerebral hemorrhage.

Dwight Eisenhower suffered a heart attack in 1955. The following year he had an operation for ileitis, an intestinal problem, and in 1957 he had a minor stroke.

Of the recent Presidents, the one with the worst health was John F. Kennedy. As a child he had numerous illnesses, including scarlet fever, bronchitis, whooping cough, diphtheria, allergies, and asthma. He had a duodenal ulcer, was color-blind in one eye, and later lost his hearing in one ear. He suffered from a bad back throughout his life and almost died from back surgery in 1954. Kennedy wore a back brace, was fitted for an elevated heel on one shoe, and often used crutches. He used a hydraulic lift to enter and exit *Air Force One.* He did not take painkillers but used cortisone to reduce inflammation. He would swim in the White House heated pool twice a day and take three hot baths daily to alleviate his pain. Kennedy also suffered from adrenal insufficiency (later diagnosed as Addison's disease, a progressive deterioration of the adrenal glands that made it difficult for him to fight infections) and had malaria and sciatica. What was thought to be a suntan epitomizing good health was actually the bronzed skin typical of people suffering from Addison's disease. To treat the disease, Kennedy took medication (cortisone, a steroid hormone) while in the White House. There is no evidence that his use of the medication affected his ability to make decisions. There is, however, an ethical issue involved because Kennedy and his doctors denied that he had Addison's disease or was being treated for it.

Lyndon Johnson had a heart attack that almost took his life in 1955 but suffered no serious illness while President. Richard Nixon took his path-breaking trip to China while suffering from phlebitis, a potentially life-threatening inflammation of a vein in his leg. Ronald Reagan underwent surgery after an assassination attempt in 1981, suffering from a collapsed lung and massive blood loss. Only the quick work of surgeons at the George Washington University Medical Center saved his life. In 1984 he had surgery to remove noncancerous polyps from his large intestine, and in 1985 surgeons removed a cancerous growth from his colon.

President George Bush suffered from atrial fibrillation, or rapid heartbeat, and a thyroid problem in 1991. A combination of intestinal flu and medication caused him to pass out during a state visit on a trip to Japan.

Some political scientists who have studied Presidential health issues have recommended that a panel of physicians be appointed to assist the cabinet secretaries and Vice President in making decisions about when to invoke the 25th Amendment in cases when the President appears to be disabled. Other recommendations include upgrading the capacity of the White House doctors to treat Presidents for mental health problems, including stress and depression.

SEE ALSO

Disability, Presidential; Physician to the President; 25th Amendment

FURTHER READING

Gilbert, Robert E. *The Mortal Presidency.* New York: Basic Books, 1992.
Moses, John B., and Wilbur Cross. *Presidential Courage.* New York: Norton, 1980.

Hendricks, Thomas
VICE PRESIDENT

☆ Born: Sept. 7, 1819, Zanesville, Ohio
☆ Political party: Democrat
☆ Education: Hanover College, B.A., 1841
☆ Military service: none
☆ Previous government service: Indiana House of Representatives, 1848–49; U.S. House of Representatives, 1851–55; commissioner, General Land Office, 1855–59; U.S. Senate, 1863–69;

governor of Indiana, 1873–77
☆ *Vice President under Grover Cleveland, 1885*
☆ *Died: Nov. 25, 1885, Indianapolis, Ind.*

AS A SENATOR, Thomas Hendricks opposed vigorous prosecution of the Civil War and the harsh Reconstruction measures that followed. He was one of Andrew Johnson's strongest defenders in the Senate during his impeachment trial. Hendricks also opposed congressional passage of the 13th, 14th, and 15th Amendments, which dealt with, among other things, the abolition of slavery, voting rights for former slaves, and the application of the principle of due process of law to state governments. Though Hendricks was an unsuccessful candidate for the Democratic Presidential nomination in 1868, he was elected governor of Indiana in 1872. He won the Democratic Vice Presidential nomination in 1876 but was defeated as part of the regional compromise that elected Rutherford B. Hayes President.

Finally elected Vice President in 1884 on a ticket with Grover Cleveland, Hendricks died in office less than nine months later, without having performed any duties of his office.

FURTHER READING

Gray, Ralph D., ed. *Gentlemen from Indiana: National Party Candidates, 1836–1940.* Indianapolis: Indiana Historical Society, 1977.

Hidden-hand Presidency

THE "HIDDEN-HAND Presidency" was the term used by Princeton political scientist Fred Greenstein to describe the Presidency of Dwight David Eisenhower. During his term most historians and po-litical scientists viewed Eisenhower as a political amateur who reigned but did not rule. "This man neither liked the game he was engaged in nor had gained much understanding of its rules," argued political scientist Richard Neustadt in 1960.

Once other researchers gained access to Eisenhower's Presidential papers (which had not been available to Neustadt and other earlier scholars), the image of Eisenhower as an amateur in office underwent substantial revision. Greenstein concluded that Eisenhower was actually a sophisticated politician who had honed his grasp of politics while in the army. During World War II he had to smooth over disputes among Allied officers of several nations, and he eventually worked closely with three world statesmen: U.S. President Franklin D. Roosevelt, French Resistance leader Charles de Gaulle, and British prime minister Winston Churchill.

Greenstein argued that Eisenhower played politics the way he played poker: with a "hidden hand" that was much better than his opponents realized. There were five facets to Eisenhower's approach to politics. First, he was a skillful politician who chose not to let others realize that fact. He camouflaged his participation in politics by relying on others to take a partisan role while he himself played the role of "President of all the people." His adversaries would underestimate him as a politician, but the American people would support him for being "above politics." Yet in reality Eisenhower was extensively involved in Republican party politics. Second, Eisenhower often used language that was deliberately ambiguous or spoke in an evasive, noncommittal, or seemingly confused way. This tactic enabled him to avoid taking unpopular positions on controversial issues, but it also led his adversaries to underestimate him. Third,

Dwight Eisenhower (second from right) meets at the White House with Secretary of State John Foster Dulles, British prime minister Winston Churchill, and British foreign secretary Anthony Eden. According to the "hidden hand" theory, Eisenhower was a sophisticated politician able to skillfully negotiate with world leaders.

Eisenhower avoided dealing in personalities. He never attacked anyone else's motives or made statements that would convert his political adversaries into bitter enemies. He often masked his own negative feelings about those with whom he had to work—including leading members of Congress of his own party—in order to stay on friendly terms with them. Maintaining his image as a genial leader also contributed to Eisenhower's popularity. Fourth, Eisenhower had a keen grasp of psychology: he could step into other people's shoes in order to understand how they viewed the world. He always tried to know what his adversaries were thinking before he engaged them in a controversy. And he tried to think of ways to bring them over to his side. Finally, Eisenhower gave his subordinates important assignments but never lost control of policy. He would share credit for success with subordinates but would let them take most of the blame for the failures, disassociating himself from them when necessary to preserve his own position as a statesman in the eyes of the American people.

Critics of the hidden-hand theory observe that sometimes the "hidden hand" seemed so well hidden that no one could detect Eisenhower's leadership. He never transferred his own popularity to his political party, which suffered disastrous defeats in state and congressional elections in 1958 and lost the Presidency by 1960. He exerted no moral leadership on civil rights for African Americans, which was the key domestic issue of the time. His economic policies resulted in slow rates of growth and two severe recessions. He never groomed anyone to succeed him, and Richard Nixon, who was far from his first choice for President, was able to win the Republican nomination in 1960. Nevertheless, the hidden-hand theory of the Presidency is a useful way to analyze any President's behavior, because it prevents us from underestimating the political skills of incumbents who may be deliberately concealing their role in party politics in order to maintain the image of a statesman.

SEE ALSO

Eisenhower, Dwight David

FURTHER READING

Greenstein, Fred. *The Hidden-Hand Presidency: Eisenhower as Leader.* New York: Basic Books, 1982.
Neustadt, Richard. *Presidential Power and the Modern Presidents.* New York: Free Press, 1991.

Hispanic Americans in the executive branch

IN THE 1950s, when Hector P. García began to work for labor and education reform as a community leader, activist, and physician in Texas, he campaigned to eliminate the "No Dogs or Mexicans Allowed" signs in Texan restaurants and the beating of Mexican schoolchildren for speaking Spanish. In 1968 García was appointed by President Lyndon Johnson to the U.S. Commission on Civil Rights, where he continued the struggle for Hispanic rights on a national level.

Dr. Hector P. Garcia, founder of the American G.I. Forum, was the first Mexican American to serve on the U.S. Commission on Civil Rights.

(Until the 1960s, the imposition of poll taxes prevented many Hispanics from registering to vote.) When García received the Presidential Medal of Freedom in 1984 and the Aztec Eagle (posthumously in 1998), the highest honors bestowed by the U.S. and Mexican governments, it was to recognize the achievements of all Hispanic Americans made possible by the untiring work of García.

Such strides in civil and voting rights paved the way for many firsts for Hispanic Americans in the executive branch. Ramona Acosta Bañuelos was sworn in as the first Hispanic treasurer of the United States on December 17, 1971. The Mexico City native Edward Hidalgo was appointed secretary of the U.S. Navy by President Jimmy Carter in 1979. And in 1990 Antonia C. Novella was the first woman and first Hispanic surgeon general of the United States. The Puerto Rican–born doctor had served as deputy director of the National Institute of Child Health and Human Development before President George Bush appointed her as surgeon general.

Since 1988, when Ronald Reagan appointed Lauro F. Cavazos as secretary of education—the first Hispanic cabinet member—Hispanic Americans have had an increasing presence in the cabinet. The Republican congressman from New Mexico, Manuel Lujan, Jr., became the first Hispanic-American secretary of the interior in 1989. Henry G. Cisneros was sworn into office as President Bill Clinton's secretary of housing and urban development on January 22, 1993, and served until 1996. (Cisneros had been a four-term mayor of San Antonio, Texas, from 1981 to 1989, and president of the National League of Cities in 1985.)

Federico F. Peña served as secretary of transportation in Clinton's first term after serving as mayor of Denver, Colorado, from 1983 to 1991. As secretary, he increased travel safety, enacted new standards for airplanes, and signed aviation agreements with more than 40 nations, expanding U.S. markets overseas. He also served for a brief time as Clinton's secretary of energy.

Bill Richardson, ultimately the highest-ranking Hispanic in the Clinton administration, replaced Peña as secretary of energy on August 18, 1998. Richardson had served as U.S. ambassador to the United Nations from 1987 to 1998 after seven terms as a U.S. congressman from New Mexico. Richardson's negotiation of hostage releases in North Korea, Iraq, Cuba, and Sudan led to his three-time nomination for the Nobel Peace Prize.

The number of Hispanics in the United States is projected to reach 41.1 million by 2010 and 52.7 million by 2020. As of 1998, according to government statistics, the percentage representation of Hispanics in the permanent executive branch work force equaled or exceeded their percentage representation in directly comparable civilian work force occupations, in 5 of 22 executive branch independent agencies of more than 500 employees.

Hobart, Garret
VICE PRESIDENT

☆ *Born: June 3, 1844, Long Branch, N.J.*
☆ *Education: Rutgers College, B.A., 1863*
☆ *Military service: none*

☆ *Previous government service: New Jersey Assembly, 1873–75; New Jersey Senate, 1877–82*
☆ *Vice President under William McKinley, 1897–99*
☆ *Died: November 21, 1899, Paterson, N.J.*

GARRET HOBART was named to the Republican National Committee in 1884 after losing an election for U.S. Senator. He was nominated for the Vice Presidency by Republicans in 1896 to represent the East and balance the Republican ticket geographically. He was one of the most effective presiding officers of the U.S. Senate, in large measure because of his experience presiding over the New Jersey Assembly and Senate.

As Vice President, Hobart cast the tiebreaking vote in the Senate against an amendment to the Treaty of Paris (which ended the war with Spain) that would have promised eventual independence to the Philippines. He was considered a close political adviser of President William McKinley, especially in Republican party affairs. Hobart's death in office in 1899 paved the way for Theodore Roosevelt's Vice Presidential nomination in 1900.

SEE ALSO
McKinley, William

FURTHER READING
Leech, Margaret. *In the Days of McKinley.* New York: Harper & Row, 1959.

Honeymoon, Presidential

THE PRESIDENTIAL "honeymoon" is the short period after a President is inaugurated when the opposition party refrains from attack, Congress is in-clined to support some of the President's initiatives, and the President receives high public approval ratings. Within a month or two partisan attacks generally resume and the honeymoon period ends.

President John F. Kennedy extended the concept by calling on the Soviet Union to extend him a honeymoon period as a goodwill gesture. One of the shortest honeymoons on record was that of Gerald Ford, whose pardon of his predecessor, Richard M. Nixon, for all Watergate crimes sparked public outrage and led to a 30-point drop in popularity in public opinion polls after his first month in office.

Hoover, Herbert C.
31ST PRESIDENT

☆ *Born: Aug. 10, 1874, West Branch, Iowa*
☆ *Political party: Republican*
☆ *Education: Stanford University, B.A., 1895*
☆ *Military service: none*
☆ *Previous government service: U.S. food administrator, 1917–19; U.S. secretary of commerce, 1921–29*
☆ *Elected President, 1928; served, 1929–33*
☆ *Subsequent government service: administrator, civilian relief in Europe, 1945–47; chair of two Commissions on the Organization of the Executive Branch of Government, 1947–49, 1953–55*
☆ *Died: Oct. 20, 1964, New York, N.Y.*

HERBERT CLARK HOOVER became President just as the Great Depression put millions of Americans out of work. He had made his reputation as an engineer and business entrepreneur and then had been one of the most effective cabinet secretaries in the administrations of Warren G. Harding and Calvin Coolidge. Yet Hoover made minimal efforts to end the depression because he was convinced that the business cycle would take care of eco-

nomic recovery with minimal intervention and that "prosperity was just around the corner." His failure to provide effective leadership doomed him to a one-term Presidency and gave the Democrats an opportunity to dominate national politics for a generation.

Hoover was the first President born west of the Mississippi River. His father was a blacksmith and his mother a schoolteacher; both died in his childhood, and he grew up in his uncle's house in Oregon. Hoover worked his way through school beginning at age 10. He studied geology and mining engineering at Stanford University, graduating in 1895, and became a supervisor of mining operations in Australia and then in China. He and his wife, Lou, became fluent in Chinese and were active in the relief of foreigners trapped in the Boxer Rebellion. The Hoovers traveled all over the world on business. By 1908 Herbert Hoover was the head of his own engineering and oil exploration company. In 1909 his lectures at Columbia and Stanford Universities were published as *Principles of Mining*, which became a standard textbook.

In 1914 Hoover was asked by the U.S. consul general in London to supervise the evacuation of 120,000 Americans trapped in Europe at the outbreak of World War I. That same year he became chairman of the privately organized Committee for Relief in Belgium, with the mission of preventing famine in that nation. In three years he raised and spent $1 billion for food relief in Europe. When the United States entered the war in 1917, President Woodrow Wilson named him U.S. food administrator. In the next two years Hoover supervised the rationing and conservation of foodstuffs in the United States and the export of food to U.S. and Allied troops. At the end of the war he became the director general of European Relief and Rehabilitation, in charge of U.S. food relief efforts to more

than 20 nations in Europe with a total population of more than 300 million. He supported Wilson's efforts to join the League of Nations. Hoover also found time to collect wartime manuscripts and documents from many nations, which formed the nucleus of the Hoover Library on War, Revolution, and Peace established at Stanford University.

In 1920 Hoover was an unsuccessful contender for the Republican Presidential nomination, due in part to the opposition of fellow Californian Senator Hiram Johnson, who did not forgive Hoover for his support of the League of Nations. Hoover was named secretary of commerce by President Harding in 1921 and was considered the most capable and honest official in the administration. President Coolidge kept him on and he served through 1928. His department tried to improve the productivity of American industry and to promote international trade and the conservation of resources. In 1924 he received 300 votes for Vice President at the Republican convention but did not get the nomination.

In 1928 Hoover was the favorite to win the Republican nomination for President, largely because of his capable handling of relief efforts during a disastrous flood in Mississippi in 1927. He won several primaries over the opposition of

The shantytowns occupied by destitute Americans during the Depression became known as "Hoovervilles." President Hoover believed that local governments, not the federal government, should help the unemployed.

party leaders and was nominated on the second ballot at the national convention. He won a landslide victory over Alfred E. Smith, the first Catholic candidate for President. Hoover's campaign slogan was "a chicken in every pot and a car in every garage." His promise of continued prosperity ensured his election.

At first Hoover tried to modernize government by creating national commissions on conservation and law enforcement and study groups to improve management of Indian affairs, veterans hospitals, and federal prisons. He got Congress to create a new Federal Farm Board, which helped farmers market their products at stable prices. But Hoover's administration was soon preoccupied with the effects of the stock market crash of October 29, 1929, known as Black Tuesday. Following the crash, industrial production plummeted, the gross national product (the total amount of goods and services produced) fell by almost a third, and unemployment soared from 3 to 25 percent by the end of his term.

Hoover responded with a tax cut to stimulate demand for goods and $400 million in public works projects. He also got the Federal Reserve Board to increase the supply of money, which resulted in lower interest rates and enabled corporations to borrow money cheaply for new projects. In 1930 he signed the Smoot-Hawley Tariff, which raised tariff rates and depressed international trade. Though designed to protect U.S. industry, it further weakened the position of American companies by reducing their exports and led to even higher unemployment, especially in the farm sector, because of foreign retaliation against U.S. farm exports.

Democrats won control of the House in 1930 and came close to winning the Senate. By May 1931 the crash of European stock markets and the resultant

depression in Europe made the situation in U.S. industries dependent on foreign trade and investment even worse. Hoover vetoed a bill passed by the Republican Senate to provide $1 billion in veterans' bonuses, an action Democrats seized upon as an indication of his callousness. In 1932 his administration convinced Congress to create and fund the Reconstruction Finance Corporation to lend money to new enterprises, banks, and city and state governments, but Hoover initially balked at the large amounts Congress was willing to appropriate. The nation viewed his efforts as too little, too late. When more than 100,000 unemployed veterans of World War I marched to Washington in 1932 to ask for early payment of their bonuses and other federal assistance, two of the Bonus Marchers were killed in clashes with local police. On July 28, Hoover ordered General Douglas MacArthur to use the army to disperse the marchers. MacArthur went beyond Hoover's orders and sent his troops in to destroy their tent city as well. Hoover had turned the military against the very soldiers who had fought for the flag in 1918.

Hoover's record in international affairs was dismal. The London Naval Treaty of 1930 acceded to the Japanese naval preeminence in the Pacific. In September 1931 the Japanese embarked on a course of aggression by attacking Manchuria, in northern China. Hoover refused to respond with economic sanctions. An attempt to gain U.S. entry to the World Court, the organization that applied international law to disputes between nations, was defeated by the Senate. The European depression made it difficult for Germany to pay World War I reparations to Allied nations or for those nations to pay back their war loans to the United States. Hoover refused to support proposals to cancel some debts, coordinate monetary policy with Europeans, or lower tariffs to stimulate trade. All the European nations except Finland reneged on their debts.

In 1932, although renominated by his party, Hoover was defeated by Democrat Franklin D. Roosevelt. His defeat was the worst suffered by an incumbent President since William Howard Taft's in 1912. In his last months in office, unemployment climbed to more than one-quarter of the work force. Banks failed in record numbers as people panicked and took their money out.

Hoover wrote 30 books after he retired from the White House, including three volumes of memoirs and *The Ordeal of Woodrow Wilson*, a study of Wilson's failure to obtain Senate consent to the Treaty of Versailles. It was the first time one former President had written a book about another former President. During World War II Hoover tried unsuccessfully to organize food relief efforts to nations occupied by Nazi Germany. After the war he served as coordinator of the European Food Program, advised the U.S. government on occupation policies in Germany and Austria, and chaired two Commissions on the Organization of the Executive Branch of Government that made recommendations for greater efficiency. He remained associated with the conservative wing of the Republican party, and he was asked for advice by leading politicians from his party, including Richard Nixon. Hoover died at the age of 90; John Adams was the only President who lived longer.

SEE ALSO

Coolidge, Calvin; Harding, Warren G.; Roosevelt, Franklin D.; Wilson, Woodrow

FURTHER READING

Fausold, Martin. *The Presidency of Herbert C. Hoover.* Lawrence: University Press of Kansas, 1985.
Hoover, Herbert. *Memoirs.* 3 vols. 1951–52. Reprint. New York: Garland, 1979.
Wilson, Joan Hoff. *Herbert Hoover: Forgotten Progressive.* Boston: Little, Brown, 1975.

Humphrey, Hubert H.
VICE PRESIDENT

☆ *Born: May 27, 1911, Wallace, S.D.*
☆ *Political party: Democrat*
☆ *Education: Denver College of Pharmacy, 1932–33; University of Minnesota, B.A., 1939; University of Louisiana, M.A., 1940*
☆ *Military service: none*
☆ *Previous government service: director, War Production Board, 1942; assistant director, War Manpower Commission for Minnesota, 1943; mayor of Minneapolis, 1945–48; U.S. Senate, 1949–61*
☆ *Vice President under Lyndon B. Johnson, 1965–69*
☆ *Died: Jan. 13, 1978, Waverly, Minn.*

HUBERT HUMPHREY, a New Deal Democrat, gained national attention at the Democratic Presidential nominating convention of 1948. He made a fiery speech in favor of a civil rights plank for the Democratic party platform, a proposal that led to the walkout of Southern Democratic delegates and to the formation of a Dixiecrat third party.

Humphrey was elected to the U.S. Senate in 1948. He started as an outsider but was brought into the inner circle of leadership by Senator Lyndon B. Johnson. In 1961 Humphrey became majority whip, the second-ranking position in the Senate. He favored arms control pacts with the Soviet Union, federal aid for education, and national health insurance, and he was instrumental in achieving passage of the Civil Rights Act of 1964. Lyndon Johnson chose Humphrey to be his running mate in 1964, not only for geographic and ideological balance but because he believed Humphrey best to succeed him.

As Vice President, Humphrey not only presided over the Senate but also

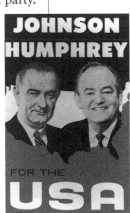

A campaign poster from 1964.

played a role in the development of Johnson's Great Society social programs, often lobbying members of Congress to provide the margin of victory on close votes. He chaired the National Aeronautics and Space Council, the Council on Marine Resources and Engineering, the Council on Native American Opportunity, the Council on Youth Opportunity, and a cabinet-level task force to promote tourism.

Humphrey's influence on foreign policy was small, though he made important trips to Western Europe to discuss military affairs and to the Far East to discuss the Vietnam War. His influence sharply diminished when he began advocating a political settlement of the war. He never went public with his criticisms and remained the chief defender of Johnson's war policies with his public speeches, an activity that caused a break with many of his liberal supporters.

Though Gallup polls after 1965 showed little public support for his quest for the Presidency, Humphrey announced his intention to run after Johnson withdrew his own candidacy in March 1968. Humphrey entered no primaries, so he received less than 2 percent of the primary vote, mostly from write-in ballots. Humphrey still had the support of a majority of the national convention delegates, chosen by state party leaders.

Humphrey won the nomination, but antiwar protesters in the streets of Chicago were involved in violent confrontations with the police, which gave Republican Presidential candidate Richard Nixon an insurmountable lead in public opinion. Even Humphrey's call for a halt to the bombing of North Vietnam, a step opposed by Johnson, could not bring him a victory, though his momentum in the closing days made the race extremely close.

Because Humphrey had won the Democratic nomination despite trailing far behind Eugene McCarthy and Robert Kennedy in primary voting, the Democratic party appointed a commission headed by South Dakota senator George McGovern to reform party rules for the 1972 Presidential nomination.

Humphrey was reelected to the Senate in 1970 but was defeated for the Democratic Presidential nomination in 1972 by George McGovern.

SEE ALSO

Great Society; Johnson, Lyndon B.; Nominating conventions, Presidential; Primaries, Presidential

FURTHER READING

Humphrey, Hubert. *The Education of a Public Man.* Garden City, N.Y.: Doubleday, 1976.
Solberg, Carl. *Hubert Humphrey: A Biography.* New York: Norton, 1984.

Impeachment

IMPEACHMENT IS the procedure for removing a President from office, specified in Article 2, Section 4, of the Constitution. Congress has resorted to the impeachment process in only three cases: President Andrew Johnson was impeached by the House of Representatives but was acquitted by the Senate after a trial in 1868; the House Committee on the Judiciary reported three articles of impeachment against President Richard Nixon in 1974, but he resigned before the full House could vote on them; President Bill Clinton was impeached by the House of Representatives but was acquitted by the Senate after a trial in 1999.

The Constitution provides that the President may be impeached by the House of Representatives. An impeachment is similar to a grand jury indictment, or official accusation, which precedes a criminal trial. A resolution to impeach is introduced on the floor of the House, which refers it to the Judiciary Committee. That committee holds hearings, then takes a formal vote on the articles of impeachment. It reports its findings to the full House, which may drop, amend, approve, or reject the articles by a simple majority vote of those present. A quorum of members—half of the House plus one—is necessary to hold a vote; at present the quorum is 218 members, which means that a minimum of 110 votes is needed to impeach a President.

If the President is impeached, the House then names a manager or a committee of as many as five managers to serve as prosecutors in the Senate trial. The articles of impeachment are signed by the Speaker of the House and conveyed to the Senate by the managers, one of whom reads them aloud to the Senate. They are then transmitted to the President in the form of a subpoena, or demand, to appear for trial.

The chief justice of the United States presides over the trial in the Senate. The President may submit legal briefs (documents containing his defense arguments) and may be represented by legal counsel. He can question witnesses and present evidence on his own behalf. At the end of the trial the Senate votes separately on each article of impeachment. Two-thirds of the senators present are necessary to convict the President and remove him from office. As the voting takes place, the Vice President must be in attendance next to the Senate chamber (in this instance he is not the presiding officer). If the President is convicted, he leaves the chamber and the Vice President enters and takes the oath of office.

Although an impeachment proceeding bears a close similarity to a criminal trial, there are substantial differences. First, the President is not necessarily charged with a criminal offense but with improper conduct in performing the duties of his office. Impeachment is not meant to be a partisan proceeding, nor is it used simply to reflect a lack of confidence in the President's policies or leadership by other branches of government. The Constitutional Convention explicitly rejected attempts to make impeachment overtly political. The delegates rejected proposals to make the President removable on the application of a majority of state governors. They rejected impeachment by a mere majority vote of Congress. They also rejected grounds for impeachment that involved the President's political judgment or vague terms such as "maladministration." They specified instead that the only grounds for impeachment were "Treason, Bribery, or other High Crimes and Misdemeanors." These terms referred to the abuse of power, misapplication of public funds, corruption, criminal conduct, or violating the separation of powers mandated by the Constitution.

A President may also be held responsible for the conduct of his subordinates. He may be charged with a cover-up if he knowingly conceals information regarding a violation of the law or if he fails to remove such officials from office when evidence of their offenses comes to his attention. He may also be charged with failing to see that the laws are faithfully executed, with failing to institute procedures so that officials will act lawfully, or with a conspiracy to see that the laws are violated. A President who testifies falsely in a judicial proceeding may be charged with perjury or obstruction of justice.

The Senate managers of an impeachment may attempt to prove that the President committed a statutory crime, though criminal guilt is not necessary in a case involving abuse of power. If they cannot do so, they may present evidence that the President engaged in a course of

The sergeant at arms of the Senate serves the impeachment summons to President Andrew Johnson.

action or a pattern of behavior that demonstrates "high crimes and misdemeanors." Those seeking a President's impeachment may argue that grounds need not be limited to federal statutes. The Association of the Bar of the City of New York, in assessing grounds for Nixon's impeachment, argued that a President could be removed "for conduct amounting to a gross breach of trust or serious abuse of power" and that these are "not limited to criminal offenses" but refer to acts that undermine the integrity of the government, whether technically criminal or not.

Presidents have several defenses against impeachment. They can argue that impeachment is a criminal trial, in which all the safeguards of the 5th Amendment, which guarantees the due process of law, must apply. And as Nixon put it, "A criminal offense on the part of the President is the requirement for impeachment." The Republicans defending Nixon in 1973 also took this position, although it repudiated their 1868 stand against Andrew Johnson. Presidents may also argue that they cannot be held responsible for the conduct of their subordinates.

Presidents can claim that they believed that their actions were constitutional. If they are charged with failure to execute the laws, they can claim that the laws conflicted with other laws or were themselves unconstitutional. Or they can argue that the alleged offense was a mere technical violation for which impeachment is too severe a penalty. They can argue that the offense was a "low" crime involving personal matters rather than a "high" crime involving abuse of power or violation of the public trust. Or they may claim that the violation of the law was necessary for national security.

Ultimately, the Senate must assess the motives of the President. Did he act in good faith? Was he attempting to usurp or abuse power? Did the ends justify the means? The judgment the senators come to will be political rather than legalistic. The Senate in the Clinton impeachment trial was influenced by public opinion polls, which indicated that Clinton's job approval ratings remained high and that the public, by a 2-to-1 margin, opposed the conviction. Republicans argued that the constitutional law of impeachment was being supplanted by an illegitimate "popular law" nullifying the crimes the President had committed. Democrats argued that the Senate should take into account the judgment of the American people.

Conviction by the Senate does not result in criminal penalties. Punishment is limited to removal from office and disqualification from holding federal office again. If the offense involved a crime, judicial (court) proceedings may be instituted after the President is removed from office.

SEE ALSO

Johnson, Andrew; Clinton, Bill; Nixon, Richard M.; Oath of office; Pardon power; Resignation, Presidential; Watergate investigation

FURTHER READING

Benedict, Michael Les. *The Impeachment and Trial of Andrew Johnson.* New York: Norton, 1973.
Berger, Raoul. *Impeachment: The Constitutional Problems.* 2nd ed. Cambridge: Harvard University Press, 1999.
Black, Charles. *Impeachment.* New Haven: Yale University Press, 1974.
Brant, Irving. *Impeachment.* New York: Knopf, 1972.
Rehnquist, William H., and Cynthia Adams Phillips. *Grand Inquests: The Historic Impeachments of Justice Samuel Chase and President Andrew Johnson.* New York: Quill, 1999.

Trefousse, Hans L. *Impeachment of a President: Andrew Johnson, the Blacks, and Reconstruction.* New York: Fordham University Press, 1999.

Imperial Presidency

"IMPERIAL PRESIDENCY" is the phrase used by some historians and political scientists to refer to the Presidencies of Lyndon B. Johnson and Richard M. Nixon. The notion that the President is above the law and that what he orders is the law, despite conflicting provisions of the Constitution or laws passed by Congress, is the fundamental tenet of the imperial Presidency.

The characteristics of the imperial Presidency are disregard for certain provisions of the Constitution, particularly regarding the power of the Congress to declare war and appropriate funds; excessive reliance by the President on White House aides, rather than the cabinet secretaries; isolation of the President from members of Congress; secrecy in making decisions and the use of executive privilege to prevent congressional or judicial inquiries; and surveillance of political opponents and the use of "dirty tricks" against them, in effect converting politics from a contest into a form of political warfare in which all means are used to defeat the opposition.

Critics of this theory argue that Presidents before and after Lyndon Johnson and Richard Nixon—including Abraham Lincoln, Franklin D. Roosevelt, and Harry Truman—also used their war and budget powers expansively. Johnson and Nixon, the critics maintain, were not the only Presidents to suspend execution of certain constitutional provisions or statutes. Secrecy and the claim of executive privilege have been relied on by several Presidents, including Dwight Eisenhower and John F. Kennedy. Some observers have argued that Presidents Gerald Ford, Jimmy Carter, and Ronald Reagan provide evidence for an "imperiled" rather than "imperial" Presidency. These men, they say, faced excessive congressional oversight, investigation, criticism, micromanagement through legislation, and other congressional checks and balances carried to extremes.

SEE ALSO

Johnson, Lyndon B.; Nixon, Richard M.

FURTHER READING

Schlesinger, Arthur M., Jr. *The Imperial Presidency.* Boston: Houghton Mifflin, 1973.

Impoundment

IMPOUNDMENT IS the power of the President to withhold from federal departments or agencies some or all of the funds appropriated by Congress. The Constitution does not explicitly consider a crucial question about spending powers: Must the President spend the money appropriated by Congress? Or are such appropriations optional, rather than mandatory?

In some instances Congress passes laws permitting or directing the President to withhold funds for programs. The Antideficiency Act of 1950 allows the President to impound funds if a program can be administered more efficiently by spending less. Civil rights laws direct the President to withhold funds from states, counties, cities, and private organizations that discriminate on the basis of race or gender. Faced with budget deficits, Congress sometimes gives the President "across the board" authority to cut all programs by a specified percentage. In all other cases Congress assumes that its appropriations are mandatory.

Some Presidents have claimed that they have a constitutional power of impoundment, which does not require any congressional approval and which permits them to instruct the Treasury to withhold some or all of the funds for programs appropriated by Congress.

Presidents may claim military necessity: President Thomas Jefferson once declined to spend funds appropriated for gunboats on the grounds that the funds would be wasted on inferior ships. President Franklin D. Roosevelt asserted his power as commander in chief during World War II to justify wartime deferrals of nonessential domestic programs. Presidents Harry Truman and John F. Kennedy also cited their powers as commander in chief to justify impounding money designated for weapons.

Richard Nixon was the first President to engage in impoundments on a massive scale. He used no national security rationale because he targeted domestic programs he opposed, such as antipoverty and environmental projects. More than 30 federal lawsuits challenged these impoundments, and all were decided against the President. None of the decisions directly challenged Nixon's assertion that he had a constitutional power of impoundment. Instead, the judges looked at the language of the law requiring that cabinet-level officials spend funds for programs and decided that these laws had not given officials discretion to withhold funding.

Congress also responded negatively to Nixon's impoundments. A 1970 hospital construction bill explicitly forbade impoundments, and that same year a federal highways act was accompanied by a "sense of Congress" resolution that said impoundments were unconstitutional. A foreign aid bill in 1971 contained a provision that no funds could be expended until funds impounded by several departments were released.

By late 1973 Nixon had cut so many pet projects of lawmakers that he had lost the support in Congress of his natural allies, conservative Republicans and Southern Democrats concerned with high levels of federal spending. The backlash against Nixon's actions enabled Congress to pass the Budget and Impoundment Control Act of 1974. Under Title X of that act, the President could defer spending funds to a later year only if the House and the Senate did not disapprove; he could rescind funds—decide not to spend money—that had been appropriated by Congress only by getting it to pass a law to that effect. The law specifically stated that the President had no constitutional power to impound. Since then, most requests to rescind spending have been rejected by Congress, but requests to defer some spending to later years are often accepted.

SEE ALSO

Budget, Presidential; Checks and balances; Executive power; Nixon, Richard M.

FURTHER READING

Fisher, Louis. *Presidential Spending Power.* Princeton, N.J.: Princeton University Press, 1975.

Pfiffner, James. *The President, the Budget, and Congress: Impoundment and the 1974 Budget Act.* Boulder, Colo.: Westview, 1979.

Shuman, Howard E. *Politics and the Budget: The Struggle between the President and the Congress.* Englewood Cliffs, N.J.: Prentice-Hall, 1992.

Inauguration, Presidential

THE INAUGURATION is the ceremony marking the start of a new Presidential term. It consists of the oath of office, an inaugural address, a parade to the White House, and various inaugural balls. The Constitution specifies only the language of the oath that the President must take; it specifies no other inauguration ceremonies.

George Washington's first inauguration was held at Federal Hall in New York City. His second, as well as the inauguration of his successor, John Adams, was held in Philadelphia because the capital had moved there. Thomas Jefferson was the first President to be inaugurated in Washington, D.C. Presidents who assume office upon the death of their predecessor take the oath wherever they are and do not have inaugurations. When Chester Arthur succeeded to the Presidency, he took the oath in New York City; Theodore Roosevelt took the oath in Buffalo, New York; Calvin Coolidge in Plymouth, Vermont; and Lyndon Johnson in Dallas, Texas.

When the inaugural day, January 20, falls on a Sunday, the new President takes the oath in a private ceremony on that day. The public inauguration ceremonies take place on the following Monday, when the oath is repeated. Both Dwight Eisenhower and Ronald Reagan took two oaths.

The inaugural ceremony takes place at the Capitol, not the White House. It is customary for outgoing Presidents to attend the inaugural ceremony and to ride with the incoming President to the Capitol. But John Adams refused to attend Jefferson's inauguration because his son Charles had just died and he wanted to get home. Adams's son John Quincy Adams did not attend Andrew Jackson's inauguration in 1828; Martin Van Buren did not attend William Harrison's; and Andrew Johnson did not attend Ulysses S. Grant's.

Initially, Presidents took the oath and then went indoors to speak to Congress. The first fully outdoor inauguration was held in 1817 for James Monroe, who gave his inaugural address to the public. The first address to be telegraphed to another city was James K. Polk's in 1845. The first photograph of an inauguration was of James Buchanan's in 1857. Benjamin Harrison was the first President to watch the parade from a viewing stand rather than participate in it. Warren Harding was the first President to ride a car to his inauguration in 1921. Four years later,

Grover Cleveland gives his first inaugural address in 1885.

Robert Frost recited his poem "The Gift Outright" at John Kennedy's inauguration in 1961.

Calvin Coolidge's inaugural address was the first to be broadcast on radio. The first to be carried on television was Harry Truman's in 1949.

The Presidential inaugural address sets the tone for the administration. Presidents usually stress national unity and bipartisanship after what is sometimes a divisive and bitter Presidential campaign. Thomas Jefferson, for instance, reassured his political opponents: "We are all Republicans, we are all Federalists." Woodrow Wilson observed, "Here muster, not the forces of party, but the forces of humanity." A President may call for reconciliation, as Abraham Lincoln did in his second inaugural address when he stated his policy toward the defeated Confederacy: "With malice toward none, with charity for all, with firmness in the right as God gives us to see the right, let us strive on to... bind up the nation's wounds." The President may try to banish the doubts and fears that plague the public when his predecessor's policies have failed, as Franklin D. Roosevelt did with his observation that "the only thing we have to fear is fear itself." He may call for change and sacrifice, as John F. Kennedy did when he challenged Americans to "ask not what your country can do for you. Ask what you can do for your country." The newly elected President takes the opportunity to discuss some of the measures he will carry out in office.

The inaugural day ends with the inaugural balls. The first ball was held by Dolley Madison for her husband, James, in 1809. Andrew Jackson, grief-stricken over the death of his wife, Rachel, did not organize a ball. Neither did Woodrow Wilson, Warren Harding, or Calvin Coolidge. Franklin D. Roosevelt held a ball at his first inaugural, but none thereafter. Jimmy Carter organized mere

"parties" to signal a new mood of austerity in Washington and dropped the requirement for formal wear. The Reagan and Bush administrations restored the tradition of the formal inaugural ball, holding several at different locations for Republican supporters.

Several Presidents have thrown the White House open to the public. Andrew Jackson began the tradition, serving an enormous cake. Bill Clinton revived the open-house tradition in 1993.

SEE ALSO
Oath of office

Independent candidates
S E E Third parties

Independent counsel

INDEPENDENT COUNSELS were a post-Watergate attempt to establish a regular means of investigating alleged wrongdoing in the executive branch. Appointed by the Department of Justice or a special panel of judges, an independent counsel could prosecute cases in the federal courts.

The independent counsel replaced the special prosecutor appointed by the attorney general, whose independence was guaranteed only by "guidelines" issued by the attorney general at the time of each appointment, by department regulations. Congress, responding to public lack of confidence in the aftermath of the Watergate crisis, wished to institute a system more independent of the Presidency and attorney general. Instead of leaving the initiative solely to the attorney general, it provided that a majority of either party's membership on the

House or Senate Judiciary Committee could trigger a request for an independent counsel. Instead of leaving the appointment to the discretion of the attorney general, it provided that the appointment of independent counsel would be made by a special three-judge panel of the Court of Appeals for the District of Columbia. In this way Congress sought to restore public confidence in the integrity of prosecutors dealing in matters involving high administration officials.

Title VI of the Ethics in Government Act of 1978 provides for the appointment of an independent counsel to investigate and prosecute the President, Vice President, members of the cabinet, or other political executives appointed by the President if the attorney general receives "specific information" about their possible violation of federal criminal law.

The attorney general conducts a preliminary investigation and then may request the appointment of an independent counsel. The Judiciary Committee of either the Senate or the House may also request the attorney general to conduct a "threshold inquiry," which is a preliminary investigation of allegations of wrongdoing. If the attorney general fails to apply for an independent counsel, he or she must explain the decision to Congress within 30 days.

The independent counsel receives funds from Congress to conduct the investigation and trials. Title VII of the law provides that he or she may not be dismissed by the President or by the attorney general except on grounds of "extraordinary impropriety," thus ensuring the integrity of the investigation.

In 1979 an independent counsel investigated President Jimmy Carter's chief of staff, Hamilton Jordan, on charges that he used cocaine but decided that prosecution was not warranted. President Ronald Reagan's attorney general, Edwin Meese, was subject to two investigations

regarding his efforts to help a friend build an oil pipeline between Iraq and Jordan; he was not indicted. Two former Reagan White House aides, Lyn Nofziger and Michael Deaver, were investigated for lobbying activities within one year after leaving their government positions. An assistant to Samuel Pierce, Reagan's secretary of housing and urban development, was investigated for conflicts of interest involving the award of contracts. Secretary of Labor Ray Donovan was investigated for business activities that had occurred before he joined the Reagan administration. Reagan's secretary of defense, Caspar Weinberger, was indicted in 1992 for giving false statements to Congress about the Iran-Contra affair, in which U.S. arms were sold to Iran and the profits illegally diverted to the Nicaraguan Contras, but he was pardoned by President George Bush in 1992.

The legality of the independent counsel law came under attack from Colonel Oliver North, who was also investigated by the special prosecutor in the Iran-Contra affair. North charged that the appointment of the counsel was a violation of the doctrine of separation of powers (because the prosecutor was appointed by judges and not by the attorney general, a member of the executive branch). The Reagan administration also argued that the statute was unconstitutional because it infringed upon the Presidential removal power. Nevertheless, the Supreme Court upheld the law.

The independent counsel law expired in 1992, and Bill Clinton supported its renewal. The three-judge panel appointed Kenneth Starr to investigate Clinton's Whitewater land dealings. Starr was unable to link Clinton to criminal acts. He referred to the House of Representatives charges that Clinton perjured himself and obstructed justice in court proceedings involving his personal affairs, and the House impeached

Clinton. Because of criticism of how the investigation was handled, with Democrats charging that the prosecution had been overzealous and had denied witnesses their due process rights, Congress in 1999 allowed the independent counsel statute to expire.

SEE ALSO

Appointment power; Ethics, Presidential; Removal power; Watergate investigation

FURTHER READING

Harriger, Katy J. *Independent Justice: The Federal Special Prosecutor in American Politics.* Lawrence: University Press of Kansas, 1991.

Jackson, Andrew

7TH PRESIDENT

☆ Born: Mar. 15, 1767, Waxhaw settlement, S.C.

☆ Political party: Democrat

☆ Education: read law in Salisbury, N.C., 1784–87

☆ Military service: Waxhaw settlement militia, 1780; Tennessee militia, 1802–14; U.S. Army, 1814–18

☆ Previous government service: public prosecutor, Mero District, Tenn., 1787; Tennessee Constitutional Convention, 1796; U.S. House of Representatives, 1796–97; U.S. Senate, 1797–98; Superior Court justice and member of the Tennessee Supreme Court, 1799–1804; territorial governor of Florida, 1821; U.S. Senate, 1823–25

☆ Elected President, 1828; served, 1829–37

☆ Died: June 8, 1845, near Nashville, Tenn.

ANDREW JACKSON was born on the Carolina frontier, the only American President born of immigrant parents. He brought the ways of the West to American politics, revitalizing and democratizing it, and carrying with him a whole generation of men who owed their careers to him. He created the Democratic party, the longest-lasting political party in American history, and he was the dominant political figure between Jefferson and Lincoln.

Jackson's father died just before he was born, soon after arriving from Ireland, and his mother and two brothers died during the Revolutionary War. Jackson entered the war as an orderly, was captured by the British in 1780, and suffered a scar from a saber injury delivered by one of his guards. Jackson read law in North Carolina and became a frontier gambler, lawyer, land speculator, and cotton and tobacco farmer at Hunter's Hill, his plantation near Nashville, Tennessee. He married Rachel Donelson Robards, the daughter of one of the founders of Nashville, worked as a lawyer in debt collection cases, and was closely allied politically with large landowners and local bankers. Jackson helped to draft the state constitution in 1795, served at the state constitutional convention in 1796, and was sent to the U.S. House the following year and then the Senate in 1797, serving one year. He served on the Tennessee Supreme Court from 1799 to 1804 but resigned to devote himself to business. Several reverses forced him to sell Hunter's Hill and move to a smaller plantation, the Hermitage. He bred, raised, and raced horses successfully. In a duel on May 30, 1806, Jackson shot and killed Charles Dickinson for making unflattering remarks about Jackson's wife; one of Dickinson's bullets remained in his chest. In 1813 Jackson was shot in a hotel brawl with Thomas Hart Benton and Jesse Benton, two brothers who dominated politics in Missouri, and the bullet was not removed until 1832.

Jackson took command of the Tennessee state militia during the War of 1812. Fighting the Creek Indians, who were allied with the British, he won the Battle of Horseshoe Bend in Alabama in March 1814. This victory ended the

Creek War, forcing the tribe to cede more than 23 million acres to the United States. In May he was commissioned a major general of the regular army. He then captured Pensacola, Florida, and defeated the British at the Battle of New Orleans in 1815. The British suffered more than 2,000 dead, including their commanding general; American losses totaled 8 killed and 13 wounded. These military victories made Jackson, known as Sharp Knife to the Indians and Old Hickory to the Americans, a national figure.

After the war Jackson fought other Indian tribes, defeating the Chickasaw, the Choctaw, and the Cherokee. In 1818 he commanded troops in the Seminole Wars in Georgia. He invaded Spanish Florida and executed two British subjects who had stirred up an Indian revolt, causing a diplomatic furor. Jackson defeated an attempt by the House of Representatives to censure him. After the United States acquired Florida from Spain, President James Monroe appointed him the first territorial governor.

Jackson was elected to the Senate in 1823, occupying a seat next to Thomas Hart Benton, the man who had nearly killed him in 1813. The two soon became political allies, and Jackson began campaigning for the Presidency. In the election of 1824 he received the most popular and electoral votes of any candidate in the four-person race but not enough to win election. In the contingency election—held because no candidate received a majority of electoral college votes—the House of Representatives chose John Quincy Adams over Jackson and William Crawford. As Speaker of the House, Henry Clay had controlled the key House votes that elected Adams. Adams then named Clay secretary of state, an appointment that led Jackson's followers to charge that a "corrupt bargain" had been made. Jackson resigned

from the Senate in 1825 to organize his next run for the Presidency.

By 1828 the number of voters had almost quadrupled, and in every state except South Carolina electors were chosen directly by the voters, not by the state legislatures. Jackson and Martin Van Buren organized state parties to mobilize and turn out this large

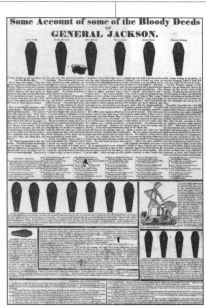

electorate. The huge turnout in what was the first fully democratic election in the United States gave Jackson an overwhelming popular and electoral college vote over his opponent, John Quincy Adams, who ran on the National Republican ticket. But tragedy marred his victory: between his election and inauguration his wife, Rachel, died.

Jackson's accession to power in Washington was akin to a political, social, and economic revolution. By his clothing, his speech, and his manners, Jackson was a "man of the people" with little in common with the Virginia or Massachusetts aristocrats who had previously sat in the White House. He was a military man with little Washington experience, a man with almost no formal education, and the first "outsider" to win the White House. Jackson had swept away the party-less Era of Good Feelings and soon created a new political party, the Democrats, with a strong southern and western base among frontiersmen, small farmers, and workers.

Early in his term Jackson dismissed about one-tenth of the officeholders in Washington and replaced them with his followers. Jackson embraced the principle of rotation in office, in which

The coffins on this handbill reinforce the horror of the "bloody deeds of General Jackson." Andrew Jackson's popularity as a war hero, however, eventually helped him win the Presidency.

government officials are appointed on the basis of political ties, rather than a permanent civil service with lifetime appointments.

Jackson soon became embroiled in traditional Washington society. Peggy O'Neale, the daughter of a saloonkeeper, married Jackson's secretary of war, John Eaton, and was ostracized by other cabinet wives, who claimed she had been having an adulterous affair with Eaton prior to their marriage. Rumors about Mrs. Eaton were spread by the wife of Vice President John C. Calhoun. Jackson took Peggy Eaton's side against the leaders of Washington society. He began to rely on a "kitchen cabinet" of political advisers rather than his cabinet secretaries. Later, his disagreement with Calhoun over the Tariff of Abominations of 1828 led to an open split between them. In the spring of 1831 Jackson forced out the three members of the cabinet who would not accept Peggy Eaton. He established the principle, new in American government, that the cabinet secretaries serve at the pleasure of the President and are subordinate to his will.

Jackson took on the Second Bank of the United States, a private corporation created as the linchpin of national economic policy-making. The national government held one-fifth of the bank's stock and kept its deposits there, and the bank's notes were legal tender (currency). On July 10, 1832, Jackson vetoed a bill passed by Congress that would have rechartered the bank, which was due to expire in 1836, attacking it as a law "to make the rich richer and the potent more powerful." Congress was unable to override his veto.

Jackson made the veto a major issue in his 1832 reelection campaign. He identified the bank with "special privileges" that the government had given to local bankers affiliated with the national bank. He argued that government should remain neutral among financial institutions. The appeal made Jackson seem like a representative of the common man against the wealthy and privileged, though Jackson had not explicitly called for class conflict.

With Martin Van Buren on his ticket, Jackson won an overwhelming victory over Henry Clay. He claimed he had a mandate to destroy the bank. He ordered his secretary of the Treasury, William Duane, to remove Treasury deposits from that bank and place them in state banks that were affiliated with his new party. When Duane refused, Jackson fired him, appointed his attorney general, Roger Taney, to his place, and had the deposits removed. Jackson's opponents in Congress organized a new political party, the Whigs, to oppose his policies and his exercise of Presidential power. The bank went out of existence in 1836. By the end of Jackson's term, the national debt had been entirely paid and the government was running a surplus that Jackson's successor, Van Buren, distributed to the states.

Jackson took personal charge of Indian policy. In 1830 he got Congress to pass a law authorizing him to create new Indian lands west of the Mississippi River and to transport Indians there. He then negotiated with Indian tribes, forcing the Chickasaw, the Choctaw, and

The Trail of Tears, painted by Robert Lindneux in 1840. Jackson's forced removal of eastern Indian tribes to western areas caused great suffering among the Indians, many of whom died during the journey.

the Creek to move west. In 1832 he encouraged Georgia to violate an 1831 Supreme Court ruling, *Cherokee Nation v. Georgia,* that was supposed to prevent Georgia from taking over Cherokee lands, and that tribe was removed forcibly after Jackson left office. Many Indians died along the "trail of tears" during these removals.

As the first President whose election rested on a truly popular base, Jackson translated electoral support directly into Presidential power. When Jackson vetoed a bill rechartering the Second Bank on the grounds that it was unconstitutional (even though the Supreme Court, in the case of *McCulloch* v. *Maryland,* had already ruled that the bank was constitutional), Jackson asserted his authority to make his own decisions about the constitutionality of laws. In firing Duane, he asserted the power of a President to remove cabinet-level officials whose appointments had been approved by the Senate, even though the Constitution makes no mention of a removal power for the President and many senators thought that such removals would require the concurrence of the Senate as well. The Senate responded by rejecting Jackson's nominations for governors on the bank board and his nomination of Taney as associate justice of the Supreme Court. It also censured Jackson, adopting Henry Clay's resolution that "the President, in the late Executive proceedings in relation to the public revenue, has assumed upon himself authority and power not conferred by the Constitution and laws, but in derogation of both." Jackson protested this resolution, and in 1836 it was expunged by the Senate.

Jackson also used Presidential power in a nullification controversy. In November 1832, with Vice President Calhoun's support, South Carolina passed a resolution nullifying, or preventing enforcement of, the high tariffs of 1828 and 1832 within the state. In December, Jackson responded with a proclamation to the people of South Carolina warning them against nullification or secession and reminding them of the supremacy of the national government and its law. He warned the citizens who were preparing to defend South Carolina militarily that "disunion by armed force is treason." Calhoun resigned his office in protest over these tariffs and Jackson's strong stance. In March 1833 Jackson gained from Congress a "Force Bill" giving him the power to use federal force to ensure compliance with the tariff as well as a reduction in the high rates designed to defuse the crisis. After Jackson sent warships to Charleston Harbor, South Carolina backed down, withdrawing its nullification of the tariff on Jackson's birthday. The state tried to save face by passing a new bill nullifying Jackson's Force Bill, however.

The struggle between Jackson and Calhoun epitomized the strains that would eventually tear the Union apart. At a dinner in Washington in 1830 Jackson had given a famous toast: "Our federal Union—it must be preserved." But Vice President Calhoun had responded, "The Union—next to our liberty, most dear." The question of national supremacy would remain an open issue until the end of the Civil War.

After leaving the White House, Jackson retired to the Hermitage, where he lived in poor health until his death on June 8, 1845.

SEE ALSO

FURTHER READING

Ellis, Richard. *The Union at Risk: Jacksonian Democracy, States' Rights, and the Nullification Crisis.* New York: Oxford, 1989.
Remini, Robert V. *Andrew Jackson.* 3 vols. New York: Harper & Row, 1970–84.
Schlesinger, Arthur M., Jr. *The Age of Jackson.* Boston: Little, Brown, 1945.

Jefferson, Thomas

3RD PRESIDENT

☆ *Born: Apr. 13, 1743, Goochland (now Albemarle) County, Va.*
☆ *Political party: Democratic-Republican*
☆ *Education: College of William and Mary, B.A., 1762*
☆ *Military service: none*
☆ *Previous government service: Virginia House of Burgesses, 1769–75; Second Continental Congress, 1775; committee that drafted Declaration of Independence, 1776; Virginia House of Delegates, 1776–78; governor of Virginia, 1779–81; Continental Congress, 1783–84; minister to France, 1785–89; U.S. secretary of state, 1790–93; Vice President, 1797–1801*
☆ *Elected President, 1800; served, 1801–9*
☆ *Subsequent public service: rector, University of Virginia, 1819–26*
☆ *Died: July 4, 1826, Monticello, Va.*

THOMAS JEFFERSON is considered by many to be the most intelligent man ever to occupy the White House. He was a scientist, architect, landscaper, lawyer, inventor, violinist, and philosopher (serving between 1797 and 1815 as president of the American Philosophical Society), as well as the founder and leader of the Democratic-Republican political party. At a White House reception for Nobel Prize winners, John F. Kennedy said he was hosting "probably the greatest concentration of talent and genius in this house except for perhaps those times when Thomas Jefferson ate alone."

Jefferson was born at Shadwell, his father's 10,000-acre plantation near Charlottesville, Virginia. After graduating from college, he read law for five years and was admitted to the bar in 1767. Five years later he had obtained 5,000 acres for a plantation to secure his financial independence. As a member of the Virginia Committee of Correspondence in 1774, he wrote a defense of American independence called "A Summary View of the Rights of British America," which argued that the British Parliament, elected by 150,000 British voters, had no right to control the legislatures or courts of millions of Americans, no right to prevent Americans from prohibiting the slave trade, no right to quarter British soldiers in American homes, and no right to use American taxes to support British troops in the colonies. Virginia's Williamsburg Convention could not accept all the principles and did not officially endorse the document, but it established Jefferson as one of the preeminent political theorists of the Revolution. In 1775, in response to prime minister Lord North's proposals to compromise with the colonies, Jefferson wrote "Causes for Taking Up Arms," which inspired revolutionary sentiment and rejected the British offer. At the Continental Congress in 1776 he was chosen to write the Declaration of Independence, and with only a few changes his draft became the document signed on July 4, 1776.

Jefferson returned from Philadelphia in September 1776, was elected to the Virginia legislature, and set to work organizing a legal code for its new state government. He wrote the Statute of Virginia for Religious Freedom, which ended the status of the Episcopal church as the state's established religion and affirmed the principle of separation of church and state. He also wrote a new penal code and much of the state constitution. His bill to prohibit the importation of slaves into Virginia was passed in 1778.

In 1779 Jefferson was elected governor, but he proved an ineffective wartime leader. British troops under General Charles Cornwallis occupied the capital at Richmond, and Jefferson himself, shortly after leaving office in 1781, was

Jefferson invented this folding desk and used it to draft the Declaration of Independence.

Jefferson designed Monticello, his home in Virginia, in a classic Italian style.

almost captured by a British raiding party at his Monticello estate.

He then published *Notes on the State of Virginia*, which described the social and political life of his state. In 1783, after his wife's death, he returned to Congress, where he worked on a committee to consider the peace treaty with Great Britain and another to establish territorial government for the Northwest Territories ceded by the British; his proposals were later embodied in the Northwest Ordinance of 1787. Though Congress initially refused to include his ban on slavery in the territories when it considered his proposal in 1784, it did ban slavery in these territories in 1787. Between 1785 and 1789 Jefferson served as minister to France, so he did not participate in the Constitutional Convention of 1787. He supported adoption of the U.S. Constitution but urged the addition of a Bill of Rights.

Jefferson joined the administration of George Washington in 1790 as secretary of state. He soon became involved in a bitter rivalry with Secretary of the Treasury Alexander Hamilton over foreign policy. Hamilton favored a pro-British "neutrality" in the Franco-British wars,

while Jefferson favored strict neutrality and took a pro-French position. Hamilton favored creation of a national bank; Jefferson argued that the bank exceeded the powers of the national government and favored northern interests. At the end of 1793, after writing a report recommending closer ties to France, Jefferson resigned from the cabinet and, with James Madison, began to organize the Democratic Societies. These associations later became a political party in opposition to the Federalist faction then in power.

In 1796 Jefferson ran for President against Federalist John Adams. Jefferson received the second-highest total in the electoral college vote, and in accordance with the procedures then used, he assumed the Vice Presidency. When the Federalists passed the Alien and Sedition Acts of 1798, which made it a criminal offense to criticize the government, Jefferson opposed the tendency of the Federalists "to silence, by force and not by reason," the complaints and criticisms of the people. In response, he drafted the Kentucky Resolves, in which he argued that an unconstitutional act passed by the national government, in this case violating 1st Amendment freedoms of speech and press, may be nullified by state governments.

In the election of 1800 Jefferson and his running mate, Aaron Burr, each received the same number of votes in the electoral college (the electoral votes at that time did not distinguish between President and Vice President). Jefferson was chosen President in the contingency election held by the House of Representatives. This was the first election in the United States in which power was transferred from one party to another. It was also the first election in which the electoral college voting had been organized by parties: all but one elector voted for his party's nominees.

Jefferson was the first President to be inaugurated in the new capital, Washington, D.C. He rode to his inauguration on his own horse rather than in a carriage, and after taking the oath of office reassured his political opponents with the conciliatory words, "We are all Republicans, we are all Federalists." With the motto "That government is best which governs least," Jefferson began to overturn many of the Federalist policies. He abolished new federal judgeships that the Federalists had created in 1801; trimmed back the Treasury Department's attempts to direct the national economy; eliminated domestic taxes (especially on whiskey); turned domestic matters back to the states; and reduced the national debt. He modernized the navy but cut back on the army, though he did establish the military academy at West Point. He arranged for the purchase of the Louisiana Territory from Napoleon Bonaparte for $15 million, which doubled the area of the United States. Although the Constitution makes no mention of acquiring territory (referring only to admission of new states to the Union), Jefferson downplayed the constitutional issues to complete the transaction.

Jefferson authorized Meriwether Lewis and William Clark to organize an expedition to map and report on the vast expanse of land. Congress then established a military government for the territory, which was gradually organized into 13 states. Jefferson was also successful when he used the navy against the pasha of Tripoli and the Barbary pirates; within four years their threat to U.S. shipping was diminished after a series of American naval victories. Jefferson did have to pay $60,000 to secure the release of American prisoners of war, however.

With the nation peaceful and prosperous, in 1804 Jefferson crushed his Federalist opponent, Charles Cotesworth Pinckney, to win reelection to a second term. Jefferson then tried to remove Federalist Supreme Court justice Samuel Chase but could not secure the necessary two-thirds vote in the Senate, a result that confirmed the independence of the judiciary from political interference.

In foreign affairs Jefferson suffered setbacks. Napoleon refused to sell East or West Florida. Great Britain and France began to interfere with U.S. shipping. The Embargo Act of 1807, which forbade all foreign trade, meant hundreds of American ships sat and rotted in ports while sailors were idle and merchants lost their markets. The act was widely criticized and was repealed by Congress near the end of Jefferson's administration. Congress replaced it with the Non-Intercourse Act of 1809, a law that restored American trade to all nations except England and France, which would have to declare their respect for American shipping to restore trade. Jefferson's poor handling of maritime policy eroded his support within his own party. Though five state legislatures passed resolutions requesting that he run for a third term, Jefferson declined.

After retiring from office, Jefferson returned to Monticello and remained there for the rest of his life. The government purchased his magnificent library after the War of 1812 to form the nucleus of the second Library of Congress (the British having burned the first). Jefferson was responsible for the chartering of the University of Virginia in 1819. He designed the campus and its buildings and served as the first rector of the university. He also designed the state capitol building. Jefferson died on July 4, 1826, just a few hours before his great rival and friend John Adams, on the 50th anniversary of the signing of the Declaration of Independence.

SEE ALSO

Adams, John; Burr, Aaron; Electoral college; Madison, James; 12th Amendment; Washington, George

FURTHER READING

Cunningham, Noble E., Jr. *In Pursuit of Reason: The Life of Thomas Jefferson.* Baton Rouge: Louisiana State University Press, 1987.

Cunningham, Noble E., Jr. *The Process of Government Under Jefferson.* Princeton, N.J.: Princeton University Press, 1978.

Ellis, Joseph J. *American Sphinx: The Character of Thomas Jefferson.* New York: Knopf, 1997.

Koch, Adrienne. *Jefferson and Madison: The Great Collaboration.* New York: Oxford, 1969.

McDonald, Forrest. *The Presidency of Thomas Jefferson.* Lawrence: University Press of Kansas, 1997.

Peterson, Merrill D. *Thomas Jefferson and the New Nation.* New York: Oxford, 1970.

Johnson, Andrew

17TH PRESIDENT

☆ Born: Dec. 29, 1808, Raleigh, N.C.
☆ Political party: Democrat; elected Vice President as Unionist
☆ Education: no formal education
☆ Military service: military governor of Tennessee, 1862–64
☆ Previous government service: alderman, Greeneville, Tenn., 1829–30; mayor of Greeneville, 1831–35; Tennessee State Constitutional Convention, 1834; Tennessee House of Representatives, 1835–37, 1839–41; Tennessee Senate, 1841–43; U.S. House of Representatives, 1843–53; governor of Tennessee, 1853–57; U.S. Senate, 1857–62; Vice President, 1865
☆ Succeeded to Presidency, 1865; served, 1865–69
☆ Subsequent government service: U.S. Senate, 1875
☆ Died: July 31, 1875, Carter Station, Tenn.

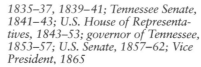

ANDREW JOHNSON was a Southern Democrat elected on the Unionist ticket with President Abraham Lincoln in 1864. His Southern sympathies and conciliatory Reconstruction policies caused him to flout the Reconstruction Acts passed by Congress, and he became the first and so far the only President to be impeached by the House of Representatives and tried by the Senate. This conflict with Congress weakened the Presidency for the remainder of the century.

Johnson's father was a laborer and his mother a barmaid. His father died when he was three, and his mother barely survived by sewing and taking in laundry. She could not afford to send him to school, and Johnson became a tailor's apprentice at 14. He and his brother opened their own tailor shop in Carthage, North Carolina; then, at 18, he opened his own shop in Greeneville, Tennessee. He married the next year and his wife, Eliza, taught him how to read, write, and count. He learned how to speak in public by participating in a debating society at a nearby college.

Johnson became active in local politics, identifying with poor whites and denouncing the rich planters and financiers. As governor of Tennessee, he supported free public education. He also supported slavery (and actually owned several slaves himself) and attacked abolitionists. But he broke with his party while he was in the Senate to support homesteading on western lands (providing 160 acres for each settler who worked the land for five years), eventually getting the Homestead Act passed by Congress in 1862.

Johnson ran for the Democratic nomination for President in 1860, but was never in real contention. He supported Democrat John C. Breckinridge over Lincoln in the election.

When the Civil War came, Johnson denounced the secessionists, and by June 1861 he was the only Southern senator to remain in his seat and refuse to join the Confederacy. He sponsored a resolution in the Senate declaring that the aim of the war was reunion and not the emancipation of slaves.

President Lincoln appointed Johnson military governor of Tennessee in 1862, and he managed to end rebellion in the state by 1864. Johnson was an obvious choice for the Vice Presidential nomination, running as a Democrat with the Republican Lincoln on a coalition Unionist ticket. Only 42 days into his second term Lincoln was shot, and Johnson succeeded to the Presidency on April 15, 1865.

Johnson began his Presidency by issuing a proclamation of amnesty on May 29, 1865, to all citizens in the states that had seceded except for certain civil and military officers and citizens with property worth more than $20,000; he appointed provisional civil governors in the Southern states; he reestablished state governments on lenient terms (requiring merely that they ratify the 13th Amendment, which abolished slavery and absolved the U.S. government from paying Confederate debts); and he issued pardons to 14,000 Southern officers who applied, including General Robert E. Lee. Johnson refused to confiscate the property of former rebels. He left questions of voting rights to the states and did nothing when the new state governments instituted "black codes" that deprived former

slaves of the right to vote, serve on juries, testify in lawsuits, or possess firearms (and in many states banned them from occupations other than farming). In 1866 he vetoed a civil rights bill that would have extended citizenship and legal protection to the former slaves and denounced the proposed 14th Amendment, which would have accomplished the same thing. On August 20, 1866, Johnson announced that the "insurrection" was over and that "peace, order, tranquility and civil authority now exist in and throughout the whole of the United States."

Radical Republicans in Congress fought Johnson and pushed stiffer Reconstruction measures on the South. When Congress reconvened in December 1865, it refused to seat Southern congressional delegations, thus preventing the South from obtaining a majority in Congress. In April 1866 Congress developed its own plans for Reconstruction, which would guarantee blacks the right to vote but take it away from former Confederate soldiers. In June Congress passed the 14th Amendment, guaranteeing black voting rights and due process of law. All the Southern states except Tennessee refused to ratify it, and Congress refused to lift its ban on their representation in the

Andrew Johnson's tailor shop in Greeneville, Tennessee, which he opened at age 18. Johnson began his political career by championing the cause of poor whites and denouncing the rich.

Johnson, depicted as a king in this cartoon by Thomas Nast, ultimately faced an impeachment trial for defying a law passed by Congress.

national legislature. In July Congress extended the life of the Freedmen's Bureau, the agency to protect freed slaves, over Johnson's veto.

To defeat the radical Republicans, Johnson organized a National Union Movement of Democrats and conservative Republicans to try to elect supporters of his Reconstruction policies in the 1866 elections. He campaigned across the Midwest for his candidates and policies. The result was that voters chose radical Republicans over the Democrats favored by Johnson, and the new Congress had a veto-proof Republican majority determined to bend the President to its will.

On March 2, 1867, Congress passed the first Reconstruction act: it divided the South into five military districts, with Freedmen's Bureau officials and military tribunals protecting the rights of blacks. The military would create a new list of voters in each state, who would, in turn, organize state constitutional conventions. The military governors could purge civil officials and state legislators whom they viewed as "disloyal." An army of occupation, 20,000 strong, enforced military rule. Johnson vetoed this Reconstruction law, which was then passed over his veto, and thereafter did as little as possible to enforce it. He began removing Republican officeholders from the executive branch and replacing them with Democrats, and he encouraged Southern states to vote against ratification of the 14th Amendment.

To prevent Johnson from interfering with congressional policies, Congress passed the Tenure of Office Act on March 2, 1867. Johnson vetoed this law, but Congress passed it over his veto. It prevented Johnson from dismissing

cabinet secretaries or other high-level officials until the Senate had consented to their successors, thus giving the final word on dismissals to the Senate. It also passed a law preventing Johnson from dismissing the commander of the army without Senate consent and requiring the President to issue his military orders through the general of the army, Ulysses S. Grant.

To test the law, Johnson asked for the resignation of Secretary of War Edwin M. Stanton and then suspended him when he refused to resign. On January 13, 1868, the Senate refused to concur in Stanton's suspension. Disregarding the Tenure of Office Act, Johnson fired Stanton on February 21. Three days later the House of Representatives impeached Johnson for "high crimes and misdemeanors." The articles of impeachment concentrated on this violation of the law but added that Johnson's conduct toward Congress had involved "disgrace, ridicule, hatred, contempt and reproach." It did not include the charge by one member, George S. Boutwell, that Johnson himself was part of the plot to murder Lincoln. The Senate acquitted Johnson on May 16, 1868. The vote was 35 for conviction and 19 for acquittal, one vote short of the two-thirds majority necessary for conviction. Seven Republicans voted to dismiss the charges. The acquittal was unpopular, and all five of these senators who sought reelection were defeated.

Why did the Senate acquit Johnson? A few Republicans who favored the nomination of Ulysses S. Grant in 1868 voted to acquit because if Johnson had been removed, the president pro tempore of the Senate, Benjamin Wade, would have become President. That would have made it likely that Wade would have secured the Republican party's next Presidential nomination over Grant. Johnson agreed, even before the vote, to end his defiance of the Senate and nominate General John M. Schofield—a military man who would follow the Reconstruction policy of the Congress—to become the new secretary of war. In effect, Johnson gave up the powers and influence of his office as the price of maintaining his place in office.

In spite of the domestic turmoil and impeachment crisis, in foreign affairs the Johnson administration was quite successful. Most of the credit rests with Secretary of State William Seward, who had a free hand to enforce the Monroe Doctrine, warning European powers not to interfere in the Western Hemisphere. In 1863 the French emperor Napoleon III had put Maximilian on the throne as emperor of Mexico. At the end of the Civil War, U.S. pressure forced the French to pull their troops out of Mexico and abandon Maximilian, who soon fell victim to a Mexican firing squad. The Johnson administration tamped down a crisis with Great Britain by enforcing neutrality laws, which prohibited U.S. citizens from using military force against other nations, against the Irish-American Fenians who made several armed forays into Canada in an attempt to annex Canadian territory. Civil War claims against Great Britain for building Confederate naval vessels that sank Union ships were sent to arbitration. In another foreign policy triumph, Secretary Seward negotiated a treaty to purchase Alaska from Russia for $7.2 million. Though at the time it was ridiculed as "Johnson's Polar Bear Garden" and "Seward's Folly," the purchase of Alaska turned out to be a great bargain. But Seward was unable to get Senate consent to acquire the Virgin Islands, Hawaii, Cuba, Puerto Rico, Greenland, or Iceland.

Andrew Johnson left office embittered, riding out of the capital without even speaking to his successor on Inauguration Day. He was defeated in a House election in 1872. When he returned to the Senate in 1875, only 13 of the 35 senators who had voted for his impeachment remained. One of them, Oliver P. Morton of Indiana, shook his hand in a gesture of reconciliation. Three months later, on vacation at his daughter's home in Tennessee, Johnson collapsed from a stroke. He requested that he be buried with a copy of the Constitution as a pillow and the Stars and Stripes for his shroud.

SEE ALSO
Grant, Ulysses S.; Impeachment; Lincoln, Abraham; Removal power

FURTHER READING
Benedict, Michael Les. *The Impeachment and Trial of Andrew Johnson.* New York: Norton, 1973.
McKitrick, Eric L. *Andrew Johnson and Reconstruction.* New York: Oxford, 1988.
Sefton, James. *Andrew Johnson and the Uses of Constitutional Power.* Boston: Little, Brown, 1980.

Johnson, Lyndon B.
36TH PRESIDENT

☆ *Born: Aug. 27, 1908, near Stonewall, Tex.*
☆ *Political party: Democrat*
☆ *Education: Southwest Texas State Teachers College, B.S., 1930; Georgetown Law School, 1934*
☆ *Military service: U.S. Navy, 1942*
☆ *Previous government service: aide to U.S. Representative Richard Kleberg, 1932–34; Texas director, National Youth Administration, 1935–37; U.S. House of Representatives, 1938–49; U.S. Senate, 1949–61; Senate minority leader, 1953–55; Senate majority leader, 1955–61; Vice President, 1961–63*
☆ *Succeeded to Presidency, 1963; served, 1963–69*
☆ *Died: Jan. 22, 1973, Johnson City, Tex.*

LYNDON BAINES JOHNSON assumed the Presidency after the assassination of John F. Kennedy. He won passage of his

Lyndon Johnson signs the Civil Rights Act of 1964. In the second row of the audience, visible just behind LBJ, is Martin Luther King, Jr.

Great Society domestic programs and was elected President in one of the greatest landslides in American history. He escalated U.S. involvement in Vietnam, eventually sending more than 500,000 troops to fight. Mounting casualties in an unwinnable war led to his withdrawal from the race for a second elected term in 1968.

Johnson grew up in Johnson City, Texas, which was named for his grandfather. After high school he went to California for a year, then returned home and worked on a road gang. After graduating from Southwest Texas State Teachers College he taught at a high school in Houston and in 1932 worked for Richard Kleberg, a member of the House of Representatives. In 1935 he became Texas director of the National Youth Administration, a New Deal agency, and began building a campaign organization for his political career. Meanwhile, Johnson's wife bought an Austin radio station and gradually accumulated a large fortune that made the family financially secure.

Johnson was elected to Congress in a special election in 1937 as a New Deal Democrat, and remained in the

House until 1949. In 1941 he was defeated in a special election for the U.S. Senate. He was the first member of Congress to go into active duty during World War II, winning a Silver Star for gallantry in action when his plane was fired upon in the South Pacific. In July 1942 President Franklin D. Roosevelt ordered all legislators in active service to report back to Congress, and Johnson returned to the House.

In 1948, after winning a runoff Democratic senatorial primary against Texas governor Coke Stevenson by only 87 votes out of a million cast, Johnson won the general election against his Republican opponent by a 2-to-1 margin. Because of the likelihood that some of his votes in the primary were obtained fraudulently, he became known to his enemies as "landslide Lyndon."

Johnson quickly moved up the ladder in the Senate. He became the Democratic party whip in 1951, chaired the Preparedness Committee, which investigated government contracts during the Korean War, was elected minority leader in 1953, and ran the Senate as majority leader after the 1954 election returned it to Democratic control. He instituted the Johnson Rule, giving every Democratic senator, no matter how junior, at least one good committee assignment. He secured passage of the Civil Rights Acts of 1957 and 1960. In doing so, Johnson became identified as a westerner rather than a southerner in order to advance his Presidential ambitions—no southern officeholder had been elected President for more than a century.

In 1960 Johnson ran for the Democratic Presidential nomination but lost to

Senator John F. Kennedy on the first ballot by a 2-to-1 margin. When Kennedy offered Johnson the Vice Presidency, he accepted, to the astonishment of many of Kennedy's aides. Johnson helped Kennedy win several southern and western states that were decisive in the Democratic victory. As Vice President, Johnson headed the space council, which decided to put the headquarters for manned space flight in Houston, Texas. He also chaired the President's Committee on Equal Employment Opportunity and the Peace Corps Advisory Council.

On November 22, 1963, John Kennedy was assassinated in Dallas, Texas. Johnson had been in the President's motorcade, and he took the oath of office on *Air Force One,* which flew the new President, along with Jacqueline Kennedy and her slain husband, back to Washington. "All that I have I would have given gladly not to be standing here today," Johnson told the grief-stricken nation when he addressed a joint session of Congress. "Let us continue," he told the nation, announcing that he would keep Kennedy's cabinet and top aides.

Johnson continued with Kennedy's domestic programs, expanding them and labeling them the Great Society. He won passage of the Civil Rights Act of 1964, which ended racial discrimination in public accommodations, and passage of a set of programs to reduce poverty, which led to the creation of the Office of Economic Opportunity in 1964.

In the summer of 1964, Johnson was nominated by the Democrats by acclamation. He crushed his Republican opponent, conservative Barry Goldwater, winning more than 61 percent of the popular vote. Johnson swept a large number of liberal Democrats into Congress and used his party majority to win passage of his Great Society programs. In the next two years Congress passed a federal aid to education act, health care reimbursement programs for the aged and the poor, new urban programs (including the Department of Urban Affairs), a tax cut that sparked economic growth, and a foreign trade bill that spurred U.S. exports. In 1967 Congress approved a new Department of Transportation.

Perhaps the most significant law Johnson won from Congress was the Voting Rights Act of 1965, a measure to protect the voting rights of blacks in the South; it tripled the number of black registered voters within three years, and within a decade changed the Democratic party from a party of white conservative segregationists into a biracial coalition of moderates.

In foreign affairs Johnson concentrated on U.S. involvement in Vietnam. In August 1964, after reports of attacks on U.S. naval vessels in the Gulf of Tonkin, he asked Congress for a resolution authorizing him to take all necessary measures to protect the armed forces. Soon thereafter Johnson escalated U.S. involvement, first by ordering the bombing of North Vietnam in the winter of 1965, then by ordering U.S. troops into combat in the spring. U.S. troops in Vietnam increased to 100,000 by the fall, and more than half a million by the end of 1966.

Democrats suffered large losses in the midterm elections of 1966 because of antiwar sentiment, though they retained majorities in both the House and Senate. Antiwar sentiment in the United States led to demonstrations against the war on college campuses and in Washington. With

Protesters denounce the war in Vietnam. In part because of Johnson's war policies, the 1968 election went to the Republicans.

no end to the war in sight and American casualties growing rapidly, Johnson's popularity slid. By late 1966 his ability to get Congress to pass his programs had diminished.

Johnson made progress in arms control talks with the Soviet Union, though in January 1967 he signed the Outer Space Treaty with Soviet premier Aleksei Kosygin, which banned placement of nuclear weapons in earth orbit, on the moon or other planets, or in deep space. In 1968 the United States became a party to the Nuclear Nonproliferation Treaty, which prohibited the transfer of nuclear weapons to other nations and prohibited assistance to nonnuclear nations in the making or acquisition of nuclear arms.

In January 1968 the North Vietnamese launched the Tet Offensive in Saigon and other cities. Americans watched television images of the American embassy under siege, and public opposition to the war increased. In March Johnson barely defeated an antiwar Democratic challenger, Eugene McCarthy, in the New Hampshire primary. Knowing that with the Democrats so divided his renomination would be worthless, Johnson withdrew from the race on March 31. He also announced a reduction in the bombings of North Vietnam in an attempt to seek peace. But the war continued with no letup on the ground, and American casualties passed the 40,000 mark. Johnson helped his Vice President, Hubert Humphrey, secure the Democratic nomination, but his war policies hurt Humphrey, who lost the election to Richard Nixon.

In giving up his office after one elected term, Johnson followed the pattern set by other Vice Presidents who took office after the death of an incumbent. Although Theodore Roosevelt, Calvin Coolidge, and Harry Truman were subsequently elected in their own

right, none of them ran immediately for a second elected term. In January 1969, an exhausted and emotionally spent Johnson retired to his ranch near Johnson City, Texas. He worked on his memoirs and helped organize his Presidential library at the University of Texas in Austin. He died of a heart attack on his beloved ranch, just one day before the Paris Peace Accord, which ended U.S. involvement in the Vietnam War, was concluded.

SEE ALSO

Gulf of Tonkin Resolution; Humphrey, Hubert H.; Kennedy, John F.; Nixon, Richard M.

FURTHER READING

Califano, Joseph. *The Triumph and Tragedy of Lyndon Johnson: The White House Years.* New York: Simon & Schuster, 1991.
Dallek, Robert. *Flawed Giant: Lyndon B. Johnson, 1960–1973.* New York: Oxford, 1998.
Dallek, Robert. *Lone Star Rising.* New York: Oxford, 1991.
Evans, Rowland, and Robert Novak. *Lyndon B. Johnson: The Exercise of Power.* New York: New American Library, 1966.
Goodwin, Doris Kearns. *Lyndon Johnson and the American Dream.* New York: Harper & Row, 1976.
Johnson, Lyndon. *Vantage Point: Perspectives of the Presidency.* New York: Holt, Rinehart & Winston, 1971.

Johnson, Richard M.

VICE PRESIDENT

☆ Born: Oct. 17, 1780, Beargrass (Louisville), Ky.

☆ Political party: Democrat

☆ Education: studied law at Transylvania University, 1800–1801

☆ Military service: Kentucky Rifle Regiment, 1812–13

☆ Previous government service: Kentucky House of Representatives, 1805–6; U.S. House of Representatives, 1807–12, 1814–19, 1830–36; U.S. Senate, 1820–29

☆ Vice President under Martin Van Buren, 1837–41

☆ *Subsequent government service: Kentucky House of Representatives, 1841–42*
☆ *Died: Nov. 19, 1850, Frankfort, Ky.*

RICHARD JOHNSON was the only Vice President ever chosen by the U.S. Senate in a contingency election. He served in the War of 1812 as colonel of a Kentucky rifle regiment and claimed to have killed the Indian chief Tecumseh at the Battle of the Thames in 1813, a feat for which he received a sash from Congress. While a member of Congress, Richard Johnson pressed President James Madison to declare war against Great Britain. He became Andrew Jackson's key political lieutenant in Congress and helped the President break the social isolation of Peggy Eaton, the wife of the secretary of war who was accused of adultery, in Washington society. He was rewarded in 1836 when Jackson advised Martin Van Buren, the Democratic Presidential nominee, to put Johnson on the ticket as his running mate.

The Democratic national convention had little enthusiasm for Johnson, fearing that his reputation for running a saloon in Louisville and his relationship with an African-American slave woman would hurt the ticket. Virginia announced that it would not support the Vice Presidential nominee in the election. The Whigs ran William Harrison, known as the Hero of Tippecanoe, for President, and the Democrats countered with a song that went, "Rumpsey Dumpsey, rumpsey dumpsey, Colonel Johnson killed Tecumseh!" With Virginia supporting William Smith and Maryland, South Carolina, Georgia, and Tennessee supporting John Tyler, the electoral college did not give Johnson a majority vote. He received 147 electoral votes, missing a majority by one vote, while his running mate, Van Buren, won the Presidency handily with 170. The Senate, in accordance with the 12th Amendment, chose the Vice President. It had to choose between the top two vote-getters, Johnson and Whig candidate Francis Granger. On the first vote the Senate elected Johnson, 33 to 16.

Johnson played no significant role in Van Buren's administration. The Democrats refused to renominate him in 1840 and, in fact, made no nomination for Vice President. Nevertheless, Johnson received 48 electoral college votes for Vice President—almost half of those coming from his old enemy Virginia—but the Whig ticket won the election.

In 1841 Johnson returned to Kentucky to serve in the legislature. In 1844 he made a tour of northern states, hoping in vain to drum up support for a run for the Presidency, but he received few votes at the Democratic convention.

SEE ALSO

Electoral college; 12th Amendment

FURTHER READING

Meyer, Leland W. *The Life and Times of Colonel Richard M. Johnson of Kentucky.* New York: Columbia University Press, 1932.

Kennedy, Jacqueline

FIRST LADY

☆ *Born: July 28, 1929, Southampton, N.Y.*
☆ *Wife of John F. Kennedy, 35th President*
☆ *Died: May 19, 1994, New York, N.Y.*

JACKIE BOUVIER came from a wealthy, socially prominent family and was educated in private schools. She attended Vassar College and graduated from George Washington University in 1951. She became a photographer and columnist for the *Washington Times-Herald* until she married Senator John F. Kennedy in 1953. They had two children (another died in infancy), Caroline and John, Jr. As First Lady, Jackie Kennedy

Jacqueline Kennedy stands with her husband as he makes his acceptance speech in Hyannisport, Massachusetts, after winning the 1960 election.

became an international celebrity. Her beauty and her sense of fashion set the style for the New Frontier, for the capital, and for much of the nation. Her husband once said admiringly, "I am the man who accompanied Jacqueline Kennedy to Paris." She busied herself in a project to renovate and restore several of the public rooms of the White House with authentic period antiques. In February 1962 she showed off the results of her work in a televised tour of the White House. The program, and her efforts at restoration, received widespread acclaim. She took several trips abroad with her husband and one trip by herself to India, which were widely covered by the news media. She accompanied her husband to Dallas, Texas, and was with him on November 22, 1963, when he was assassinated. The films of her reaching over her husband's body to pull a Secret Service officer into the limousine, then standing with Lyndon Johnson as he took the oath of office on *Air Force One,* and finally accompanying her husband's remains from the plane when it landed in Washington, with blood still on her dress, are images that remain indelibly part of the national consciousness.

Jackie Kennedy emerged from seclusion after the assassination to be romantically linked with several of the wealthiest men in the world. She married Greek shipping magnate Aristotle Onassis in 1968. In 1975, after his death, she became a book editor for a New York publishing house.

SEE ALSO

First Lady; Kennedy, John F.; White House

FURTHER READING

Birmingham, Stephen. *Jacqueline Bouvier Kennedy Onassis.* New York: Grosset & Dunlap, 1978.
Gallagher, Mary B. *My Life with Jacqueline Kennedy.* New York: David McKay, 1969.
Kelley, Kitty. *Jackie Oh!* Secaucus, N.J.: Lyle Stuart, 1978.

Kennedy, John F.

35TH PRESIDENT

☆ *Born: May 29, 1917, Brookline, Mass.*
☆ *Political party: Democrat*
☆ *Education: Harvard College, A.B., 1940; Stanford University Business School, 1940*
☆ *Military service: U.S. Navy, 1941–45*
☆ *Previous government service: U.S. House of Representatives, 1949–53; U.S. Senate, 1953–60*
☆ *Elected President, 1960; served, 1961–63*
☆ *Died: Nov. 22, 1963, Dallas, Tex.*

JOHN FITZGERALD KENNEDY was the youngest person ever elected President and the first Catholic to serve as the nation's chief executive. His Presidency continued the New Deal and Fair Deal domestic programs of Franklin D. Roosevelt and Harry S. Truman and attempted to maintain a position of world leadership for the United States. He died in office before the promise of his Presidency could be fulfilled.

Kennedy was the second son of Rose Fitzgerald Kennedy and Joseph P. Kennedy. His father was a financier and former chairman of the Securities and Exchange Commission who was active in the Democratic party. John Kennedy was voted "most likely to succeed" at the Choate School. After serving for a time as secretary to his father, who in 1937 had been appointed ambassador to Great Britain by President Franklin D. Roosevelt, Kennedy graduated from

Harvard in 1940. His senior thesis, "Appeasement at Munich," a study of the British appeasement of Adolf Hitler, was awarded high honors. It was published that same year under the title *Why England Slept,* becoming a best-seller.

Kennedy enlisted in the navy in October 1941, and on August 2, 1943, his PT Boat 109 was sunk by a Japanese destroyer. Two of the crew died, but Kennedy helped to rescue his 10 surviving crew members and was awarded the U.S. Navy and Marine Corps medal and a Purple Heart for injury. He returned home a hero, though a naval inquiry into the sinking indicated poor seamanship and command on Kennedy's part.

In 1945 Kennedy was discharged from the navy, worked briefly as a reporter for the Hearst newspapers, and the following year won election to the House of Representatives from a district in Boston. He was reelected twice and in 1952 defeated incumbent Republican Henry Cabot Lodge, Jr., for a Senate seat. Kennedy's accomplishments in Congress were minimal. He had one of the worst attendance records, which may have been due to his having Addison's disease, which required daily implantation of a steroid compound in his thighs.

Kennedy had a spinal operation in 1954, and while recuperating he wrote *Profiles in Courage,* a series of biographies of American politicians who had gone against public opinion to do what they believed was right. It was published in 1955 and won a Pulitzer Prize for biography the following year. In 1956 Kennedy campaigned for the Vice Presidential slot on the Democratic ticket, but the convention nominated Estes Kefauver instead. Later, Kennedy would say that losing that contest was the best thing that could have happened to him, because the Democratic ticket went down to a crushing defeat. Kennedy was

reelected to the Senate by a large margin and began organizing a campaign for the next Presidential nomination.

In 1960 Kennedy defeated Hubert Humphrey and several others in the Democratic field in seven primary contests: in West Virginia his victory demonstrated that an overwhelmingly Protestant state would vote for a Catholic candidate. He was nominated by the Democratic convention on the first ballot, defeating Senate majority leader Lyndon Johnson handily. He then offered Johnson the second spot on the ticket, and to the surprise of many of Kennedy's advisers, Johnson accepted. Kennedy's July 15 acceptance speech offered Americans a "New Frontier" and promised "to get America moving again."

In the November election Kennedy and Johnson won a majority of electoral college votes against Republican nominee Richard M. Nixon and his running mate, Henry Cabot Lodge, but they received less than half the popular vote. At age 43, Kennedy was the youngest man ever elected President (though Theodore Roosevelt had been a year younger when he succeeded to the office).

"Ask not what your country can do for you," Kennedy said in his inaugural address, "ask what you can do for your country." He challenged youthful idealists to join the Peace Corps, which he

To minimize the pain from a wartime back injury, John Kennedy frequently sat in a rocking chair in the Oval Office.

created by executive order a few weeks later, to help with the development of other nations. He got Congress to create an Alliance for Progress in Latin America to provide foreign aid in the Western Hemisphere. He created an arms control agency to pursue arms limitations talks with the Soviet Union. He challenged the nation to put a man on the moon by the end of the decade, a feat accomplished in 1969, right on schedule.

Kennedy's New Frontier legislative program was designed to get the U.S. economy moving again after the recession and slow growth of the years under Dwight Eisenhower. It emphasized an investment tax credit and other tax breaks for business. His proposed social programs were extensions of the New Deal: federal aid to education, medical care for the elderly, urban mass transit, a new Department of Urban Affairs, and regional development for Appalachia. Much of this legislation was stalled in Congress by a coalition of Republicans and conservative Southern Democrats, though Congress did pass an increase in the minimum wage, higher Social Security benefits, and a public housing bill. It also passed a trade expansion act that significantly increased U.S. exports and opened up foreign markets.

Kennedy's refusal to provide for aid to parochial (church-run) schools in his federal aid to education bill doomed its chances. In 1962 Kennedy sent federal troops to Mississippi to ensure that James Meredith, an African-American student, could enroll at the University of Mississippi and attend classes without harassment. In 1963 he used federal troops in Alabama to enforce federal court desegregation orders. But Kennedy delayed introducing civil rights legislation until late spring 1963. On August 28, 1963, a March on Washington for Peace and Justice, which attracted more than 200,000 people, convinced

Kennedy to push Congress harder for comprehensive civil rights laws. In a televised speech Kennedy identified with the marchers, saying that the grandchildren of the slaves freed by Lincoln "are not yet freed from the bonds of injustice … and this nation, for all its hopes and all its boasts, will not be fully free until all its citizens are free."

Kennedy's foreign policy emphasized militant anticommunism. In his inaugural address he laid down a gauntlet to communists: "Let every nation know, whether it wishes us well or ill, that we shall pay any price, bear any burden, meet any hardship, support any friend, oppose any foe to assure the survival and the success of liberty."

On April 17, 1961, an operation sponsored by the Central Intelligence Agency (CIA) against Cuban communist leader Fidel Castro began: 1,500 Cuban exiles landed in Cuba at the Bay of Pigs, hoping to spark an uprising. They were surrounded and defeated by the Cuban army. At the last minute Kennedy refused to provide them with air cover for their operation in order to avoid overt U.S. involvement. Kennedy accepted full responsibility for the fiasco, however, noting that "victory has a hundred fathers, but defeat is an orphan." The 1,100 prisoners held by Castro were ransomed by the United States for $53 million in food and medical supplies.

After East Germany constructed the Berlin Wall to seal off the communist side of the city from the West in August 1961, Kennedy traveled to Berlin to show solidarity with its citizens. He proclaimed in German, "Ich bin ein Berliner" (I am a Berliner). In October 1962 Kennedy found out that the Soviet Union had shipped offensive missiles and bombers to Cuba; after quarantining the island with U.S. naval forces, he insisted that the Soviets remove their offensive forces, and after a tense standoff they did so. In

Robert and Edward Kennedy escort their sister-in-law Jacqueline at John Kennedy's burial at Arlington National Cemetery.

August 1963 Kennedy and Soviet leader Nikita Khrushchev signed the Limited Test Ban Treaty, which banned nuclear testing in the atmosphere, outer space, and the oceans. Only underground testing, which presented no risk of radioactive fallout, would be permitted.

Kennedy ordered U.S. military advisers and trainers to South Vietnam, 18,000 in all, to prop up a pro-American government against attempts by communist guerrillas to undermine it. But he also decided to allow South Vietnamese military units to overthrow President Ngo Dinh Diem and install a new military leader. Although Kennedy hoped the new regime would improve the situation, the November 1, 1963, coup began a prolonged period of instability in South Vietnam that all but ensured that U.S. troops would be needed for the war.

On November 22, 1963, while visiting Dallas, Texas, to help unify the feuding state Democrats, John Kennedy was shot and killed by two bullets fired from the Book Depository building while riding in a motorcade through the center of town. Texas governor John Connally was wounded. Lee Harvey Oswald, the suspected assassin, was taken into custody by Dallas police, but two days later he was killed by Dallas nightclub owner Jack Ruby while being transferred from his cell to an office for questioning. A national commission headed by Chief Justice Earl Warren concluded that Oswald, acting alone, had shot the President in the rear of the head with a rifle and that Oswald had been mentally ill.

The conclusions of the Warren Commission remain controversial. The House Select Committee on Assassinations argued in 1979 that there were at least three shots fired rather than two. Others believe that Kennedy was killed by a bullet, fired from a nearby grassy knoll, that entered the front of his head; that theory would point to a conspiracy rather than a lone assassin. But the House panel's final conclusion was that Oswald had fired all three shots, two of which hit Kennedy and one missed. Nevertheless, conspiracy theories continue to capture the public imagination, and the answer to the question "Who killed Kennedy?" remains unclear to many Americans.

The Kennedy era was brief. It began the transition from an era of confrontation to an era of negotiation in the cold war. Kennedy was the first President born in the 20th century: his youth, vigor, and style under pressure created a "Camelot on the Potomac" for a generation of Americans who came of age during World War II and the first years of the cold war.

SEE ALSO

Assassinations, Presidential; Cuban Missile Crisis; Debates, Presidential; Health, Presidential; Johnson, Lyndon B.; Kennedy, Jacqueline; Monroe Doctrine; New Frontier; Nixon, Richard M.; Primaries, Presidential

FURTHER READING

Bradley, Benjamin. *Conversations with Kennedy.* New York: Norton, 1975.
Parmet, Herbert. *J.F.K.: The Presidency of John F. Kennedy.* New York: Dial, 1983.
Schlesinger, Arthur M., Jr. *A Thousand Days: John F. Kennedy in the White House.* Boston: Houghton Mifflin, 1965.

King, William
VICE PRESIDENT

☆ *Born: Apr. 7, 1786, Sampson County, N.C.*
☆ *Political party: Democrat*
☆ *Education: University of North Carolina, B.A., 1803*
☆ *Military service: none*
☆ *Previous government service: North Carolina House of Commons, 1808–10; U.S. House of Representatives, 1810–16; secretary of legation, U.S. mission to Russia, 1816–18; U.S. Senate, 1818–44, 1848–52; president pro tempore of the Senate, 1850–52; minister to France, 1844–46*
☆ *Vice President under Franklin Pierce, 1853*
☆ *Died: Apr. 18, 1853, Cahaba, Ala.*

AS A DEMOCRATIC party leader in the Senate, William King represented southern regional interests, and he received votes for Vice President at several Democratic conventions. At the 1852 convention he supported James Buchanan, but when Franklin Pierce was nominated, the second spot went to King to unify the party. King was elected but was dying of tuberculosis. He went to Cuba to seek a cure, and Congress passed a law that allowed him to take the oath of office there on March 4, 1853. He returned to his plantation in Alabama and died a few weeks later. He never set foot in Washington or performed any official duties during his brief term.

Kitchen cabinet

THE KITCHEN cabinet is the name given to Presidential advisers who do not hold high public office but who wield great influence in the White House. President Andrew Jackson, upset because his cabinet secretaries did not rein in their wives during the Peggy Eaton affair (in which the wife of the secretary of war was accused of a prior adulterous act), relied on two newspaper editors and three minor officials in the Treasury Department instead of convening cabinet meetings. His political enemies accused him of using a "kitchen cabinet" instead of the real one.

This cartoon satirizes Andrew Jackson's kitchen cabinet. The cart symbolizes the government, which is driven by a figure made of teapots, a soup pot, and a bellows, among other items.

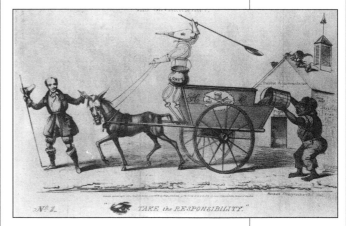

Earlier, Thomas Jefferson had been accused of forming an "invisible cabinet" that dealt in "backstairs influence" at the White House. Later, Theodore Roosevelt had a "tennis cabinet" and Warren Harding a "poker cabinet" of advisers. Harry Truman was criticized for relying on his Missouri Gang, and he struck back at critics by claiming to have organized his own kitchen cabinet, which included a secretary for inflation, secretary of reaction, secretary for columnists, and secretary of semantics. President Ronald Reagan invited a group of California business entrepreneurs who had been active in funding his campaigns to serve as informal advisers, but after some bad publicity the White House staff got Reagan to distance himself from them.

SEE ALSO

Brains Trust; Cabinet; Jackson, Andrew

FURTHER READING

Safire, William. *Safire's Political Dictionary.* New York: Ballantine, 1978.

Libraries, Presidential

PRESIDENTIAL LIBRARIES preserve Presidential papers and documents; acquire books, films, and videotapes about Presidents; conduct oral history interviews with members of Presidential administrations; sponsor research conferences; and provide scholars with access to Presidential documents.

The White House papers and documents of all Presidents from George Washington through Warren Harding are located in the manuscript division of the Library of Congress in Washington, D.C. All Presidents beginning with Herbert Hoover have donated their White House papers to separate Presidential libraries. The libraries are built with private funds. The Presidential Libraries Act of 1955

provided that the National Archives and the National Park Service would maintain the libraries and grounds and would fund professional archivists to take care of and catalog all Presidential papers. These libraries are supervised by their own governing boards and library staffs. The Presidential Libraries Act of 1986 provided that George Bush and his successors would have to use private funds to operate as well as build their Presidential libraries.

The Richard M. Nixon Library is an entirely private operation that receives no public funding and does not contain any original Presidential documents. According to the terms of the Presidential Recordings and Materials Preservation Act of 1974 and subsequent laws, Nixon's original papers and tapes are stored in a warehouse controlled by the National Archives.

Presidential libraries opened prior to 1978 are subject to restrictions imposed by each individual President on the use of his White House papers. The Presidential Records Act of 1978 divides materials for all Presidents elected after 1980 into two categories: Presidential papers and personal papers. The personal papers are those that "do not relate to or have an effect upon the carrying out of the constitutional, statutory, or other official or ceremonial duties of the President," such as a personal diary or personal correspondence. Presidents may put whatever restrictions they wish on their personal papers.

In the category of Presidential papers, former Presidents can restrict national security information and personnel files for up to 12 years; all other types of Presidential papers must be open within 5 years. Individuals such as cabinet secretaries or White House aides who donate materials (including oral histories) to Presidential libraries may place their own restrictions on use.

SEE ALSO

Ex-Presidency; Appendix 3: Presidential Historic Sites and Libraries

FURTHER READING

Berman, Larry. "Presidential Libraries: How Not to Be a Stranger in a Strange Land." In *Studying the Presidency*, edited by George C. Edwards and Stephen J. Wayne. Knoxville: University of Tennessee Press, 1983.

Kumar, Martha Joynt. "Presidential Libraries: Gold Mine, Booby Trap, or Both?" In *Studying the Presidency*, edited by George C. Edwards and Stephen J. Wayne. Knoxville: University of Tennessee Press, 1983.

Schick, Frank S. *Records of the Presidency: Presidential Papers and Libraries from Washington to Reagan.* Phoenix, Ariz.: Oryx, 1989.

Lincoln, Abraham

16TH PRESIDENT

☆ *Born: Feb. 12, 1809, near Hodgenville, Ky.*
☆ *Political party: Whig (in Congress); Republican*
☆ *Education: sporadic schooling in lower grades*
☆ *Military service: Illinois volunteer regiment, 1832*
☆ *Previous government service: postmaster, New Salem, Ill., 1833–36; Illinois General Assembly, 1834–41; U.S. House of Representatives, 1847–49*
☆ *Elected President, 1860; served, 1861–65*
☆ *Died: Apr. 15, 1865, Washington, D.C.*

USING MILITARY force to defeat the Southern secessionists and win the Civil War, Abraham Lincoln acted in accordance with his oath of office to preserve the Union. In doing so, he used emergency powers that no previous President had exercised. His twin policies, emancipation of slaves and reconciliation of North and South, were his greatest legacies to a war-torn nation.

Lincoln was born in a log cabin in Kentucky. He was the first President born outside the original 13 states that formed the Union. When he was seven, his family moved to another log cabin in Indiana, where his father cleared and farmed 160 acres. His mother died when he was nine and his father married Sarah Bush Johnston, whose three children moved into the log cabin with Lincoln and his sister, Sarah. After his farm chores young Abe educated himself by lantern light, borrowing books from neighbors and nearby towns. He grew to his full size of six feet, four inches and gained a reputation not only as a scholar but also as a wrestler and axeman.

At age 22 Lincoln struck out on his own and settled in New Salem, Illinois. He worked as a storekeeper and was a captain in a campaign against the Black Hawk Indians, but he saw no action and his store failed. He then worked as a surveyor and postmaster. He lost a contest for the state legislature in 1832 ("The only time I have ever been beaten by the people," he later said), but he was elected two years later on the Whig ticket. He also studied law and was admitted to the bar in 1836. Lincoln became a successful lawyer in Springfield, and his clients included the Illinois Central Railroad and other corporations. In 1839 he met Mary Todd, and they married in 1842.

Lincoln entered national politics in 1846, when he was elected as a Whig to the U.S. House of Representatives. He introduced a bill to end slavery in the nation's capital, but it was never brought to a vote. His support for the Wilmot Proviso (a bill to outlaw slavery in territories acquired from Mexico), his opposition to the Mexican-American War (he voted for a resolution in Congress that described it as "a war unconstitutionally and unjustly begun by the President"), and his campaigning for Zachary Taylor in the election of 1848 were unpopular

Lincoln visits General George McClellan and other Union officers in 1862, after the Battle of Antietam.

positions in Illinois, and he declined to seek reelection.

In various speeches in 1854, Lincoln opposed the Kansas-Nebraska Bill sponsored by Senator Stephen A. Douglas. The bill provided for a popular vote on the question of slavery in each of the territories. In two debates with Douglas, Lincoln argued that the Missouri Compromise of 1820, which forbade slavery north of Missouri's southern boundary, should be retained. He argued that only in free states could poor white workers improve their circumstances, because there they would not be competing against slave labor.

Lincoln failed in a bid to obtain a Senate seat in 1855, but the following year he helped organize the Republican party and nearly won its Vice Presidential nomination. In 1858 Lincoln challenged Douglas for his Senate seat. "A house divided against itself cannot stand," he told the Illinois Republican party convention in his acceptance speech, adding, "I believe this Government cannot endure permanently half slave and half free." In a second series of Lincoln-Douglas debates held around the state, Lincoln hammered at Douglas for ignoring the moral dimension of the slavery question, calling slavery a "moral, social and political evil." Lincoln lost the election but gained a national reputation.

In February 1860 Lincoln delivered an antislavery speech in New York City and was applauded by his audience and by New York newspapers, which made him a contender for the Republican Presidential nomination. In May, he won the nomination by defeating the favorite, William H. Seward, on the third ballot, after his campaign managers promised cabinet positions to politicians from Ohio, Indiana, and Pennsylvania.

The Whigs nominated John Bell, the Northern Democrats nominated Stephen A. Douglas, and the Southern Democrats bolted from their party to nominate John C. Breckinridge. Lincoln, along with Vice Presidential nominee Hannibal Hamlin, was elected with a 39.8 percent plurality of the popular vote but a large majority in the electoral college. He said farewell to his friends in Springfield and took a train east. Because of a plot against his life, he left his train in Philadelphia and arrived without notice in Washington, D.C., on February 23, 1861. By that time seven states of the lower South had already left the Union, and a peace convention in

Lincoln with his son Thomas (Tad) four days before he was fatally shot in April 1865.

Richmond, Virginia, was trying to forge a compromise under the auspices of former President John Tyler. Lincoln gave the delegates to the convention no encouragement, however.

Lincoln took the oath of office on March 4, 1861. "We must not be enemies," he pleaded with Southern leaders in his inaugural address. He reminded them that no state had a right to leave the Union "upon its own mere motion" and warned that he had taken an oath of office to enforce federal laws. "In your hands, my dissatisfied fellow-countrymen, and not in mine, is the momentous issue of civil war." He rejected the Crittenden Compromise, which would have permitted slavery in the Western states below the Mason-Dixon line. Lincoln would allow slavery to continue where it already was but would not hear of extending it across the lower states to the West.

After his inauguration Lincoln informed the governor of South Carolina that he would resupply the federal garrison at Fort Sumter in Charleston Harbor with ammunition, food, and medicine, but would send no reinforcements or weapons. On April 12, 1861, the South Carolina government responded by opening fire on Fort Sumter, and two days later its commander surrendered.

Congress was not in session, and Lincoln did not call it into emergency session. Instead, relying on his own Presidential powers, on April 15 he proclaimed a blockade of Southern ports, called on the states for 75,000 volunteers to join the army and enforce federal laws, suspended the privilege of the writ of habeas corpus (so that he could arrest and hold people without taking them to court), rounded up thousands of Confederate sympathizers in the border states, and spent funds from the U.S. Treasury without obtaining congressional appropriations. Then, on July 4, Lincoln called Congress into session and informed the legislators of what he had done. Within the month Congress retroactively ratified his actions.

For several years the war went badly for the North. In July the First Battle at Bull Run in Virginia was a defeat for Union forces, with more than 3,500 dead and wounded. A campaign to capture Richmond bogged down. The South won victories at Fredericksburg and at the Second Battle of Bull Run. The Union instituted a draft to replace troops fallen in battle. In New York City draft riots showed strong antiwar sentiment among many Northerners. But eventually the war effort succeeded. In 1862 Union forces led by generals Ulysses S. Grant and Don C. Buell began to win victories along the Mississippi River, and Admiral David Farragut captured New Orleans. On January 1, 1863, Lincoln issued a Proclamation of Emancipation that freed slaves in states in secession. As Union forces advanced into enemy territory, former slaves became a decisive source of manpower for the Union forces.

In 1863 the fortunes of war turned toward the North. On July 3, Union forces defeated more than 90,000 troops led by Robert E. Lee at Gettysburg, Pennsylvania. The following day Grant divided the Confederacy with the capture of Vicksburg, Mississippi. President Lincoln named him commander of the Union armies early in 1864, and he faced off against Lee in Virginia, taking huge losses but steadily moving forward. Meanwhile, General William Tecumseh Sherman began a successful march from Tennessee into Georgia, eventually seizing and burning Atlanta.

The election of 1864 would decide whether or not the war would continue. Lincoln received the Republican nomination and chose the military governor of Tennessee, Andrew Johnson, a Democrat, to run with him on a coalition Unionist ticket. Democrats challenged Lincoln's exertion of Presidential power, called for a halt to hostilities and the return of slave-holding states to the Union, and nominated General George B. McClellan, whom Lincoln had relieved of command. Successes in the field, especially the capture of the last port on the Gulf of Mexico at Mobile Bay by Admiral Farragut, led many voters to believe the war would soon be over. Lincoln won 55 percent of the popular vote and almost all the electoral votes in the election.

Lincoln's second inaugural address stressed a policy of reconciliation toward the South: "With malice toward none, with charity for all, with firmness in the right as God gives us to see the right, let us strive on to finish the work we are in, to bind up the nation's wounds, to care for him who shall have borne the battle and for his widow and his orphan—to do all which may achieve and cherish a just and lasting peace among ourselves and with all nations." In 1864 he had vetoed the Wade-Davis Reconstruction bill passed by Congress because he opposed its harsh terms. Louisiana, Arkansas, Tennessee, and Virginia reestablished state governments and petitioned Congress for recognition but were denied. On April 11, two days after Robert E. Lee surrendered his army to Grant,

Lincoln again called for the former Confederate states to be readmitted to the Union on lenient terms.

On the evening of April 14, while attending a performance of *Our American Cousin* at Ford's Theatre in Washington, Lincoln was shot by John Wilkes Booth, an actor and Southern sympathizer, and died the next morning. As his body was taken back to Springfield, mourners lined the 1,700-mile route to pay their respects to the Great Emancipator.

SEE ALSO

Amnesty, Presidential; Assassinations, Presidential; Buchanan, James; Emancipation Proclamations; Gettysburg Address; Grant, Ulysses S.; Hamlin, Hannibal; Johnson, Andrew; War powers

FURTHER READING

Current, Richard N. *The Lincoln Nobody Knows*. Westport, Conn.: Greenwood, 1980.
Donald, David Herbert. *Lincoln Reconsidered*. New York: Vintage, 1961.
Kunhardt, Philip B., Jr., et al. *Lincoln: An Illustrated Biography*. New York: Knopf, 1992.
McPherson, James M. *Abraham Lincoln and the Second American Revolution*. New York: Oxford, 1991.
Neely, Mark E. *The Abraham Lincoln Encyclopedia*. New York: McGraw-Hill, 1982.

Madison, Dolley

FIRST LADY

☆ Born: May 20, 1768, Guilford County, N.C.
☆ Wife of James Madison, 4th President
☆ Died: July 12, 1849, Washington, D.C.

BORN DOROTHEA PAYNE, Dolley (also spelled Dolly) Madison grew up on a plantation in Virginia. In 1783 her father freed his slaves, sold his plantation, and started a factory in Philadelphia. Dolley Payne was married to John Todd, a Philadelphia lawyer, in 1789.

Four years later Todd and their new-born son died of yellow fever. Dolley and her oldest son survived.

Dolley remained in Philadelphia. After a four-month courtship, she married James Madison in 1794. He was 17 years older than his bride, but they maintained a close and loving relationship for 42 years. While James Madison was shy and industrious, Dolley was outgoing and loved to entertain. She was noted for her beautiful gowns and elaborate makeup and hairstyling.

When Thomas Jefferson appointed Madison his secretary of state in 1801, the couple moved from Madison's Virginia plantation to Washington, D.C., where Dolley soon became the center of the Jefferson administration's social life. Both Jefferson and Aaron Burr were widowers, and Dolley was asked, as the wife of the senior department secretary, to preside over Presidential dinners and receptions. Her friendship with President Jefferson made her an unofficial First Lady in his administration. In 1809, when her husband became President, Dolley Madison simply continued with her duties as Washington's hostess.

Dolley Madison insisted on formal etiquette at all state functions. Beginning in May 1809 she held an informal Wednesday evening "salon" that was open not only to Washington officials but also to the general public. In August 1814, during the War of 1812, British troops captured the capital and burned many of its buildings. Dolley Madison managed to safeguard historical paintings, the White House silver, velvet curtains, a clock, and important state papers from the White House before fleeing to Virginia. After the British withdrew, the Madisons returned to Washington, where they lived in the Octagon House, which was loaned to them by the French government, until the White House could be rebuilt.

After Madison's retirement from the Presidency, the couple lived for 20 years at their plantation, Montpelier. After her husband's death in 1836, Dolley returned to Washington, where she lived for 13 years until her death.

SEE ALSO
First Lady; Madison, James

FURTHER READING
Dean, Elizabeth L. *Dolly Madison: The Nation's Hostess*. Boston: Lothrop, Lee & Shepard, 1928.

Madison, James
4TH PRESIDENT

☆ *Born: Mar. 16, 1751, Port Conway, Va.*
☆ *Political party: Democratic-Republican*
☆ *Education: College of New Jersey (Princeton), B.A., 1771*
☆ *Military service: none*
☆ *Previous government service: Committee of Safety, 1774; Virginia Constitutional Convention, 1776; Virginia House of Delegates, 1777, 1784–86; Virginia Governor's Council, 1778–80; Continental Congress, 1779–83; Annapolis Convention, 1786; federal Constitutional Convention, 1787; Virginia constitutional ratifying convention, 1788; U.S. House of Representatives, 1789–97; U.S. secretary of state, 1801–9*
☆ *Elected President, 1808; served, 1809–17*
☆ *Subsequent public service: Virginia Constitutional Convention, 1829; rector, University of Virginia, 1826–36*
☆ *Died: June 28, 1836, Montpelier, Va.*

JAMES MADISON is known as the "father of the Constitution" because he played a major role at the Constitutional Convention of 1787. He drafted the Virginia Plan, with which the convention began its work, and he was instrumental in adding to the powers of Congress and the Presidency and in providing for a system of checks and balances among

the branches of government. His own Presidency, however, was beset with difficulties, largely because of the workings of the checks and balances he had helped to create.

Madison grew up on his affluent family's plantation, Montpelier. Educated at the College of New Jersey, he then studied law and became a member of Orange County's Committee of Safety in 1774, at the start of the Revolution. At Virginia's constitutional convention of 1776 he fought for a clause protecting freedom of religion. He served in the Governor's Council for most of the remainder of the war. In the 1780s, as a member of the Continental Congress under the Articles of Confederation, he advocated strengthening its powers (particularly the power of taxation) to provide more effective government. In 1785, in the Virginia House of Delegates, he fought successfully for separation of church and state. With Alexander Hamilton he helped to organize the Annapolis Convention of 1786, a meeting of five states that proposed stronger powers for the national government in interstate commerce, and the Constitutional Convention in Philadelphia in 1787.

At that convention Madison helped put together the key compromises that kept the convention going, though the delegates rejected a number of his proposals, including a council of state to share executive power, a congressional veto on state laws, a Senate share in the Presidential power to pardon, a Supreme Court power to impeach the President, and a Supreme Court share in the Presidential veto power. Madison also unsuccessfully opposed any extension of the slave trade, which the convention decided to protect until 1808. Madison later published his notes on the convention debates, which are today the primary source for historians studying the convention.

Madison teamed up with Hamilton and John Jay to write *The Federalist Papers,* a set of essays defending the Constitution against attack by its critics and calling for its ratification. Madison wrote under the pen name Publius. He led the pro-Constitution faction at the Virginia ratifying convention, opposing the Anti-Federalists led by Patrick Henry and James Monroe.

Although Madison was passed over by the Virginia legislature for election to the U.S. Senate, in 1788 he defeated James Monroe in the first elections held for the House of Representatives. As a member of the first Congress, Madison fulfilled a campaign pledge by proposing a Bill of Rights to protect civil liberties from actions of the national government. He also drafted legislation that organized the departments of Foreign Affairs, War, and the Treasury. He soon opposed the financial program of the first Treasury secretary, Alexander Hamilton, particularly the protective tariff (a tax on imported goods), as well as Washington's Proclamation of Neutrality, which kept the United States out of a war between Great Britain and France. Together with Thomas Jefferson, Madison organized an opposition faction that later became the Democratic-Republican party, and they attracted to it most of the Anti-Federalists of the 1780s.

During the undeclared naval war with France in 1798 the Federalist Congress passed the Alien and Sedition Acts, which made it a crime to publish criticism of government war policies. In response, in 1798 Madison and Jefferson wrote the Kentucky and Virginia Resolutions, which stated that the Alien and Sedition Acts were unconstitutional and which implied that the states need not enforce them. This was a reversal of Madison's strong "nationalist" position of the 1780s, when he wanted national law to be supreme over state laws.

The British burned Washington in 1814. The Capitol, the President's House, and other public buildings were ruined.

After Jefferson was elected President in 1800, Madison became his secretary of state. He defended the Louisiana Purchase and supported Jefferson's decision to ask Congress to pass an Embargo Act, which would ban trade with European nations while they were at war. His negotiations with Spain to acquire Florida were unsuccessful.

In 1808 the Republican congressional caucus nominated Madison for the Presidency. He defeated his Federalist opponent, Charles Cotesworth Pinckney, 122 electoral votes to 47.

Foreign policy preoccupied the Madison Presidency; the President acted as his own secretary of state until the appointment of James Monroe in 1811 to replace the incompetent Robert Smith. In 1809 Congress repealed Jefferson's Embargo Act, which forbade carrying foreign goods on American ships, and replaced it with the Non-Intercourse Act, which banned all trade with England and France until those countries ceased interfering with U.S. shipping. Madison declared that trade with Great Britain would be permitted but soon found that assurances that U.S. ships would be left alone were not honored by the British government. Madison issued a nonintercourse proclamation against Great Britain in November 1810. Congress then passed a bill that ended all restrictions on U.S. trade with Europe. It promised, however, that if the British would cease harassing American ships, the United States would bar trade with its enemy France, and if the French would cease harassment, the United States would bar trade with Great Britain. French emperor Napoleon promised freedom of the seas to U.S. ships, and Madison issued a nonintercourse proclamation against the British. Then Napoleon betrayed Madison by issuing new decrees against U.S. shipping, forcing the President to admit to Congress that his policy had failed.

The "war hawks" in Congress urged Madison to declare war against Great Britain, and they pressed for an invasion of Canada. Although the nation was unprepared for war and large parts of New England opposed it, on June 1, 1812, Madison bowed to the war hawks in his party and sent a secret message to Congress asking for a declaration of war. Not everyone approved of war, and the declaration carried in the House by 79 to 49 and in the Senate by only 19 to 13. Madison signed the declaration on June 18, 1812. He had already been unanimously renominated by the Republican caucus, and in the general election he defeated DeWitt Clinton.

The War of 1812 was a disaster. A U.S. invasion of Canada failed, and much of the Northwest Territory, including the key outpost at Detroit, was retaken by the British. By 1813 the British navy had bottled up U.S. naval vessels and blockaded the American coast. After defeating Napoleon in Europe, the British were able to transfer 14 new regiments to the war effort in the United States. They marched into Washington, D.C., on August 24, 1814, and burned the Capitol, the President's House, and other public buildings in retaliation for a U.S. raid on Toronto the year before. When Madison returned to the capital, he took up residence in the Octagon House, near the ruined President's House. Congress reassembled in the old patents and post office building next to the ruined Capitol Building. Disgruntled Federalists met in Hartford, Connecticut, in December 1814 to demand that Madison end the war. Republicans claimed that Federalists at the meeting, known as the Hartford Convention, were plotting to secede from the Union.

But the news was not all bad. Heroic resistance by the defenders of Fort McHenry prevented the British from capturing Baltimore and inspired Francis Scott Key, who was imprisoned on a British ship attacking the fort, to write "The Star-Spangled Banner." The British suffered major defeats in northern New York State and Mobile, Alabama. Then Andrew Jackson won the Battle of New Orleans. Even before that battle, the British and U.S. peace negotiators had signed the Treaty of Ghent (though news had not yet reached the United States), and Madison urged the Senate to consent to it. The United States failed to gain any of its war aims and was lucky to keep all its territory intact. But Americans had not conceded any rights to a greater power and had demonstrated their willingness to fight for freedom of the seas.

At the end of the war Madison turned to domestic matters. He called for a larger military, a protective tariff, a system of roads and canals, and a national university. Congress authorized a stronger military establishment and passed the first protective tariff in U.S. history but did not act on the bill for a university—something Madison had tried to put in the Constitution in 1787. He also won congressional approval to charter the Second Bank of the United States.

Madison retired to his plantation at Montpelier in 1817. He participated in the Virginia Constitutional Convention of 1829, organized his notes of the federal convention of 1787 for publication, and was rector of the University of Virginia from 1826 until his death in 1836.

SEE ALSO

Creation of the Presidency; Jefferson, Thomas; Madison, Dolley; Monroe, James; Washington, George

FURTHER READING

Brant, Irving. *James Madison.* Indianapolis: Bobbs-Merrill, 1961.
Ketcham, Ralph. *James Madison: A Biography.* Charlottesville: University of Virginia Press, 1990.
Rakove, Jack N. *James Madison and the Creation of the American Republic.* Glenview, Ill.: Scott, Foresman, 1990.
Rutland, Robert A. *James Madison: The Founding Father.* New York: Macmillan, 1987.

Marine Band, U.S.

THE MARINE Band, known as "the President's own," is a unit of the U.S. Marine Corps. It is assigned to play at the White House on ceremonial occasions, such as the arrival of a foreign head of state, state dinners, and cultural events. The director of the Marine Band serves as the musical adviser to the President in organizing the music for ceremonial occasions.

Established on July 11, 1798, by President John Adams, the band is the

The U.S. Marine Band and its director, John Philip Sousa, pose for a formal portrait in 1891.

oldest musical organization in the U.S. armed forces and the oldest continuous unit of the Marine Corps. It has played at every Presidential inauguration since Thomas Jefferson's in 1801 and at every inaugural ball since James Madison's in 1809. The first dancing at the White House occurred in 1828, during the Presidency of John Quincy Adams, to the music of the Marine Band.

The band achieved its greatest prominence after 1880 when John Philip Sousa assumed the position of musical director and transformed it into the best band in the nation. Its concerts in Washington, D.C., became cultural events when it premiered Sousa's new marches, such as "Semper Fidelis" and "The Washington Post" march, which inspired a dance craze in the United States and Europe. In 1891 Sousa took the band on its first national tour, and since then the band has made such tours every fall except during wartime. The Marine Band's recordings of Sousa marches were some of the first ever made for Thomas Edison's phonograph.

Today the band or its individual performers play more than 600 times each year. In 1990 it made an 18-day concert tour of the Soviet Union as part of a historic Soviet-American Armed Forces Band Exchange designed to promote better understanding between the two nations.

SEE ALSO

"Hail to the Chief"; "Ruffles and Flourishes"

FURTHER READING

Kirk, Elise. *Music at the White House.* Urbana: University of Illinois Press, 1986.

Marshall, Thomas R.

VICE PRESIDENT

☆ *Born: Mar. 14, 1854, North Manchester, Ind.*
☆ *Political party: Democrat*

☆ *Education: Wabash College, 1873; read law, 1874–75*
☆ *Previous government service: governor of Indiana, 1909–10*
☆ *Vice President under Woodrow Wilson, 1913–21*
☆ *Subsequent government service: U.S. Coal Commission, 1922–23*
☆ *Died: June 1, 1925, Washington, D.C.*

THOMAS MARSHALL was a lawyer active in Democratic party campaigns, and he served one term as governor of Indiana. He was a favorite-son candidate for President in 1912, and after switching his delegation to Woodrow Wilson he was rewarded with the Vice Presidential nomination. He served for two terms, the first Vice President to do so in nearly a century. He presided over the Senate with fairness and over the cabinet when Wilson was in Paris negotiating the Treaty of Versailles after World War I. Marshall told the secretaries that he was presiding "informally and personally" and not seeking "to exercise any official duty or function." At first opposed to U.S. entry into World War I, Marshall loyally supported Wilson's decision to intervene as well as the Treaty of Versailles. He opposed the woman suffrage amendment in the postwar period. He offered a definitive word on the Vice Presidency when he quipped: "There were two brothers. One ran away to sea,

Vice President Thomas Marshall draws draft numbers in 1918.

the other was elected Vice President, and nothing was ever heard from either of them again." Marshall is also remembered as the man who said, "What this country needs is a good five cent cigar." Marshall had Presidential ambitions of his own, but Wilson successfully blocked him. After his Vice Presidency, Marshall served on the U.S. Coal Commission.

SEE ALSO

Wilson, Woodrow

FURTHER READING

Marshall, Thomas. *Recollections of Thomas R. Marshall, Vice President and Hoosier Philosopher.* Indianapolis: Bobbs-Merrill, 1925.
Thomas, Charles M. *Thomas Riley Marshall: Hoosier Statesman.* Oxford, Ohio: Mississippi Valley Press, 1939.

McKinley, William

25TH PRESIDENT

☆ *Born: Jan. 29, 1843, Niles, Ohio*
☆ *Political party: Republican*
☆ *Education: Allegheny College, 1860; Albany Law School, 1866*
☆ *Military service: 23rd Ohio Volunteer Infantry, 1861–65*
☆ *Previous government service: prosecuting attorney, Stark County, Ohio, 1870–71; U.S. House of Representatives, 1877–85, 1887–91; governor of Ohio, 1892–96*
☆ *Elected President, 1896; served, 1897–1901*
☆ *Died: Sept. 14, 1901, Buffalo, N.Y.*

WILLIAM McKINLEY protected the interests of big business while doing little to alleviate the social problems caused by industrialization. McKinley's victory in the Spanish-American War made the United States into a world power and transformed the Presidency into an office of world leadership.

McKinley grew up in a small town in Ohio. During the Civil War he enlisted in the 23rd Ohio Volunteer Infantry, serving as an aide to Colonel Rutherford B. Hayes. He was promoted to major for bravery in the Battle of Fisher's Hill.

After the war McKinley studied law. He was elected prosecuting attorney of Stark County in 1869 but was defeated for reelection two years later. In 1876 he was elected to the U.S. House of Representatives, where he gained a reputation for supporting high tariffs. His grandfather and father were iron manufacturers, which may explain why he championed business interests as chair of the Committee on Ways and Means. But the high rates of the McKinley Tariff Act of 1890 were so unpopular with the voters that he was defeated in the next election. He then organized two successful campaigns for governor of Ohio with the help of Mark Hanna, a Cleveland businessman and political fundraiser.

In 1896 the Republican convention nominated McKinley for President on the first ballot, and Hanna organized his successful campaign. McKinley sat on his front porch in Canton, Ohio, and greeted 750,000 visitors from 30 states while his Democratic opponent, William Jennings Bryan, frantically traveled 18,000 miles by rail. Hanna organized a pro-tariff, pro-business coalition for McKinley, who won by a healthy margin in the electoral college.

McKinley presided over a period of industrial expansion. He supported the record-high Dingley Tariff of 1897. Soon he had to turn his attention to foreign affairs. Spain was trying to put down a rebellion in its Cuban province that had begun in 1895. The Spanish commander, known as Butcher Weyler, put Cuban civilians into concentration camps and American opinion swung solidly behind the rebellion. The sinking of the U.S.S. *Maine* in Havana Harbor on February 15, 1898, with the loss of 260 lives, fanned the war fever in the United States. On March 1, the U.S. Naval

The White House telegraph room during the Spanish-American War. Maps on the wall show the location of military units.

Court of Inquiry sent its findings to Washington—results that implicated Spain (though the U.S. Navy much later, in 1976, agreed with the results of the Spanish investigation that claimed that the explosion was an accident). McKinley tried to prevent war by winning some concessions from Spain, including the closing of the concentration camps and an armistice with the Cuban rebels. But two days after the Spanish made those concessions, McKinley finally bowed to public opinion and asked Congress for a declaration of war. On April 19 Congress passed a joint resolution authorizing U.S. intervention to win Cuban independence from Spain.

With Admiral George Dewey's destruction of the Spanish Pacific fleet in Manila, the Philippines, on May 1, 1898, the United States became a world power with global influence. Three days later, Congress approved a long-standing resolution of annexation for the Hawaiian Islands. According to the terms of the Treaty of Paris with Spain in December 1898, the United States became a colonial power, occupying Cuba (temporarily), Puerto Rico, and Guam and gaining Wake Island and Samoa in 1899.

McKinley then won a series of victories in Congress for his foreign policy. He got Senate consent for the Treaty of Paris in spite of the opposition of House Speaker Thomas Reed and the Anti-Imperialist League, an American organization opposed to the acquisition of colonies. McKinley's tariff reciprocity policies, designed to encourage free trade in selected markets—trade under low or no tariffs—were accepted by Congress even though they contradicted traditional Republican support for protectionist tariffs. He won passage of the Spooner Amendment, which allowed him to institute military government in the Philippines, and the Platt Amendment, which permitted U.S. intervention in Cuban affairs.

In his annual message to Congress in 1899, McKinley denied the claim of the Philippine leader Emilio Aguinaldo that Admiral Dewey had promised independence to the islands in return for local help against the Spanish. The McKinley administration was determined to keep the islands. To do so, it put down a bloody rebellion of Philippine patriots that lasted three years and employed 120,000 U.S. soldiers.

In 1900 the McKinley administration (along with Japan and several Western nations) intervened in China with 2,500 troops to put down the Boxer Rebellion against Westerners in Beijing. The United States received a payment of $25 million from China for damages suffered but returned $18 million so that Chinese students could study in the United States. McKinley also intervened twice in Nicaragua to protect lives and property.

McKinley's Vice President, Garret Hobart, died in office in 1899, and McKinley accepted Theodore Roosevelt as the choice of the Republican convention to be his running mate in 1900. Mark Hanna opposed the nomination. "Don't you realize there's only one life between this madman and the Presidency?" he asked convention delegates. McKinley's margin over William Jennings Bryan improved in their 1900 rematch, and he became the first President since Ulysses S. Grant to win a second consecutive term.

McKinley was shot by Leon Czolgosz, an anarchist, at the Pan-American Exposition in Buffalo, New York, on September 6, 1901, and died of his wounds eight days later. Hanna and the Republican party would now have to deal with Teddy Roosevelt and his progressive policies.

SEE ALSO

Hobart, Garret; Roosevelt, Theodore; Treaty powers

FURTHER READING

Gould, Lewis L. *The Presidency of William McKinley.* Lawrence: Regents Press of Kansas, 1980.
Leech, Margaret. *In the Days of McKinley.* New York: Harper, 1959.
Morgan, H. Wayne. *William McKinley and His America.* Syracuse, N.Y.: Syracuse University Press, 1963.

Messages, Presidential

ARTICLE 2, Section 3, of the Constitution provides that the President shall "from time to time give to the Congress information of the State of the Union and recommend to their consideration such measures as he shall judge necessary and expedient."

Between 1801 and 1911 Presidents from Thomas Jefferson through William Howard Taft transmitted an annual message to Congress at the opening of each session. It included reports from all the departments of government. President James Monroe used his 1823 message to announce the Monroe Doctrine as a matter of U.S. foreign policy. Lincoln used his messages to discuss the military situation in the Civil War. Theodore Roosevelt used his messages to educate the American people about child labor and the protection of the environment. William Howard Taft called for reforms in the federal budget process.

Woodrow Wilson revived the practice of George Washington and John Adams of speaking to a joint session of Congress, rather than sending an annual written message. Since 1945 this speech has been known as the State of the Union address.

Presidents may also send messages to Congress while it is in session. These have included Andrew Jackson's messages to the Senate during the controversies over the Bank of the United States, James Buchanan's 1860 messages to Congress about the impending secession of Southern states; Abraham Lincoln's Civil War messages; Franklin D. Roosevelt's messages on legislation proposed for recovery from the Great Depression; and Harry Truman's message proposing a Fair Deal for postwar economic conversion to civilian industries.

The Constitution also requires the President to send Congress a message outlining his reasons for vetoing legislation. Sometimes, Presidents send Congress messages that explain their understanding of the law when they sign bills.

Other Presidential messages required by law include the ones that accompany the Budget of the United States and the Economic Report of the President. Both are delivered each January as Congress begins its new session.

SEE ALSO

Budget, Presidential; Council of Economic Advisers; Fair Deal; Monroe Doctrine; New Deal; Veto power

Modern Presidency

THE MODERN Presidency is the term used by historians and political scientists

to describe the Presidential office since the early 1930s. The characteristics of the modern Presidency, as developed by Franklin D. Roosevelt and consolidated by Harry Truman, Dwight Eisenhower, and John F. Kennedy, are as follows: increased constitutional powers in foreign affairs and national security; use of the White House Office and the Executive Office of the President to supervise the bureaucracy; greater willingness to use the powers of the office to deal with economic and social problems; greater attempts to win passage of the Presidential legislative agenda; and greater ability to dominate public opinion by using radio and television.

SEE ALSO

Eisenhower, Dwight David; Kennedy, John F.; Roosevelt, Franklin D.; Truman, Harry S.

FURTHER READING

Greenstein, Fred I., ed. *Leadership in the Modern Presidency*. Cambridge: Harvard University Press, 1988.

Mondale, Walter F.

VICE PRESIDENT

☆ *Born: Jan. 5, 1928, Ceylon, Minn.*
☆ *Political party: Democrat*
☆ *Education: University of Minnesota, B.A., 1951; LL.B., 1956*
☆ *Military service: U.S. Army, 1951–53*
☆ *Previous government service: attorney general of Minnesota, 1960–64; U.S. Senate, 1964–77*
☆ *Vice President under Jimmy Carter, 1977–81*

WALTER ("FRITZ") Mondale rose through the ranks of the Minnesota Democratic Farmer Labor party (DFL), which is affiliated with the national Democratic party. The DFL supports small business owners, farmers, and union workers and is part of the liberal wing of the Democratic party.

Mondale was appointed attorney general of Minnesota in 1960, then appointed to the U.S. Senate in 1964 to fill the unexpired term of Hubert Humphrey. He was elected to the Senate in 1966 and reelected in 1972.

Throughout Mondale's career in state politics and the Senate, he was an effective advocate for liberal programs. In 1976 he was mentioned as a possible Presidential candidate but decided, in his words, that he did not have the "fire in the belly" to run for the Presidency. As a northern liberal and Washington insider, he was a perfect balance on the 1976 ticket to southern moderate and Washington outsider Jimmy Carter.

As Vice President, Mondale presided over the Senate, and during a debate on an energy bill made a number of important rulings that made it easier to shut off a filibuster. But his real influence was felt in the White House itself. He worked closely with Carter, who gave Mondale a White House office right next to his own, let him attend any high-level meetings he wished, and had a private lunch with him at least once a week.

Carter named Mondale a senior adviser, with concurrent authority over the entire White House staff. Key staffers such as Chief of Staff Hamilton Jordan and Press Secretary Jody Powell publicly termed themselves his subordinates.

Mondale headed several Vice Presidential task forces assigned to develop new programs for the administration, including a group dealing with long-range goals. He was a principal legislative tactician in dealings with Congress and an adviser on economic policy. He even helped Carter choose many of his cabinet secretaries.

Carter described his relationship with Mondale this way: "I see Fritz four to five hours a day. There is not a single aspect of my own responsibilities in which Fritz is not intimately associated.

Walter Mondale (right) and Jimmy Carter had a private lunch together at least once a week.

He is the only person that I have with both the substantive knowledge and political stature to whom I can turn over a major assignment."

Mondale did not always succeed in pushing Carter in a liberal direction. He strongly supported a proposed tax rebate, but Carter withdrew his proposal when it appeared it would be defeated. Mondale favored higher minimum wages and higher government payments to farmers for surplus crops—positions Carter did not adopt. Mondale was more successful in national security matters, as when he convinced Carter to cancel the B-1 bomber project.

Mondale was part of an informal group that Carter used to keep in contact with the "network"—the campaign workers who would be needed for the reelection effort of 1980—and he helped Carter defeat the strong challenge of Senator Edward Kennedy for the Democratic Presidential nomination in 1980.

"I have been closer to a President than maybe any Vice President in history," Mondale concluded at the end of his term. He might have added that he also played a major part in the transformation of the Vice Presidency from a ceremonial and constitutional position to one with important functions within the executive branch.

SEE ALSO
Vice President

FURTHER READING

Gillon, Steven M. *The Democrat's Dilemma: Walter F. Mondale and the Liberal Legacy.* New York: Columbia University Press, 1992.
Lewis, Finlay. *Mondale: Portrait of an American Politician.* Rev. ed. New York: Harper & Row, 1984.
Mondale, Walter. *The Accountability of Power.* New York: David McKay, 1975.

Monroe Doctrine

IN HIS annual message to Congress on December 2, 1823, President James Monroe stated, "The American continents, by the free and independent condition which they have assumed, are henceforth not to be considered as subjects for future colonization by any European power."

Monroe was responding to Russian claims to the Oregon Territory and to an attempt by the Russian-American Trading Company to exclude U.S. ships from the waters near its trading post in Spanish California. In October 1823 Russian czar Alexander I sent a letter to his allies in the Holy Alliance—France, Spain, and Austria—in which he observed that newly independent Latin American nations had set up republics contrary to the European "political system." He called for allied European governments to join in overthrowing those republics and replacing them with monarchies. Monroe warned in his message, "We could not view any interposition for the purpose of oppressing them or controlling in any other manner their destiny, by any European power" as other than an unfriendly act. Monroe added, "It is impossible that the allied powers should extend their political system to any portion of either continent without endangering our peace and happiness."

With his hand on the globe, James Monroe formulates the Monroe Doctrine with his advisers.

Monroe based the right of the United States to protest against European intervention upon the practice of the United States to keep out of all entangling alliances in Europe. He disclaimed any intention of interfering in Latin American internal affairs, and he pledged not to interfere with existing colonies or dependencies of any European power.

Monroe decided to make his statements after strong pressure from Secretary of State John Quincy Adams. In 1822 the United States had recognized several Latin American states and exchanged ministers with them. In 1823 the restored Spanish monarch Ferdinand VII called for an international conference to consider the claims to independence made by these states. On August 20, 1823, the British foreign minister, George Canning, proposed to Richard Rush, the U.S. minister in London, that the United States and Great Britain join in a declaration that the two nations were opposed to intervention in American affairs by European powers. President Monroe at first agreed to Canning's proposal, with the strong endorsement of former Presidents Thomas Jefferson and James Madison, but Adams proposed that the United States issue its own declaration. He had a strong influence on Monroe's eventual decision and the language of his message to Congress.

The Monroe Doctrine, combined with the support of the British navy, put an end to all plans for intervention in Latin America by European powers. By 1824 the United States negotiated with Russia a treaty by which Russia withdrew any territorial claims on the Oregon Territory, and in 1867 the U.S. acquisition of Alaska ended Russian colonization in North America.

The French fared no better: although they successfully intervened in Argentina in 1840, their attempt to establish a sphere of influence in Mexico met with failure. During the U.S. Civil War, French troops established the Austrian Maximilian as emperor of Mexico. The United States protested, and after the Civil War ended 50,000 U.S. troops were posted near the Mexican border, and Mexican troops loyal to the Mexican rebel Benito Juárez pressured the French to withdraw. Maximilian was killed by a Mexican firing squad at Querétaro in 1867.

The Monroe Doctrine was extended in 1905 by Secretary of State Richard Olney, who asserted that existing European colonies in the Americas were "unnatural and inexpedient," that "the United States is practically the sovereign on this continent, and its fiat is law upon the subjects to which it confines its interposition." He further argued that to disregard the Monroe Doctrine would be a violation of international law, that it would require arbitration between European colonies and Latin American nations, and that refusal to adhere to the Monroe Doctrine would be grounds for war. The Roosevelt Corollary, named for President Theodore Roosevelt, stated that the United States would not permit other nations to collect debts in this hemisphere but would do what it could to collect them itself.

The Olney and Roosevelt corollaries were highly unpopular in Latin America. They were eventually revoked by the

State Department in 1928 in a memorandum that stated that the United States would no longer take military action on behalf of other nations to collect debts owed by Latin American nations. President Franklin D. Roosevelt instituted a Good Neighbor Policy. By the Montevideo Treaty of 1933 and the Buenos Aires Protocol of 1936, the United States renounced the right of intervention in Latin American affairs.

During World War II the Monroe Doctrine was "pan-Americanized" so that all nations in the hemisphere would participate. The Latin nations and the United States met in Panama in 1939 to sign the "Resolution on the Transfer of Sovereignty of Geographic Regions of the Americas Held by Non-American States," a long title for a simple agreement to prevent European possessions from falling into the hands of the Axis nations—Germany, Italy, and Japan. During the cold war the United States intervened in Latin American affairs to reduce what it perceived to be communist influence in the hemisphere. In 1954 President Dwight Eisenhower ordered the Central Intelligence Agency (CIA) to back Colonel Castillo Armas in an invasion to eliminate the leftist government of Guatemala headed by Jacobo Arbenz. After Fidel Castro established a pro-Soviet regime in Cuba in 1959, Soviet military advisers, combat troops, airplanes, and offensive missiles were brought to the island. President John F. Kennedy used the Monroe Doctrine during the Cuban Missile Crisis of 1962 as one of the justifications for imposing a quarantine on that nation until the Soviet Union removed its offensive weapons from Cuba. On October 23, 1962, the Organization of American States gave the United States a mandate to use force if necessary in compelling their removal.

SEE ALSO

Adams, John Quincy; Cuban Missile Crisis; Kennedy, John F.; Monroe, James

FURTHER READING

May, Ernest R. *The Making of the Monroe Doctrine.* Cambridge: Harvard University Press, 1975.

Perkins, Dexter. *Hands Off: A History of the Monroe Doctrine.* Rev. ed. Boston: Little, Brown, 1963.

Monroe, James

5TH PRESIDENT

☆ *Born: Apr. 28, 1758, Westmoreland County, Va.*
☆ *Political party: Democratic-Republican*
☆ *Education: College of William and Mary, 1774–76*
☆ *Military service: 3rd Virginia Infantry, 1776–80*
☆ *Previous government service: Virginia House of Delegates, 1782, 1787, 1810; Virginia Governor's Council, 1781–83; Continental Congress, 1783–86; Annapolis Convention, 1786; Virginia constitutional ratifying convention, 1788; U.S. Senate, 1790–94; minister to France, 1794–97; governor of Virginia, 1799–1802, 1811; minister to Great Britain, 1803–7; U.S. secretary of state, 1811–17; U.S. secretary of war, 1814–15*
☆ *Elected President, 1816; served, 1817–25*
☆ *Subsequent public service: Virginia Constitutional Convention, 1829; regent, University of Virginia, 1826–31*
☆ *Died: July 4, 1831, New York, N.Y.*

JAMES MONROE was a brilliant secretary of state whose Presidency restored peace and prosperity in the aftermath of the War of 1812. Monroe was born into a family without much money, but relatives helped him attend the College of William and Mary. He left after two years to fight with the 3rd Virginia Infantry under General George Washington during the Revolutionary War. He fought in several battles and was wounded while leading a charge at the Battle of Trenton. In 1780 he left the military and studied law

This painting in the Capitol depicts the Louisiana Purchase negotiations. Monroe (center) was appointed by President Thomas Jefferson to buy New Orleans from France, but he was able to secure the entire Louisiana Territory.

under Thomas Jefferson, who was at that time governor of Virginia. In 1782 he served in the Virginia Governor's Council, then in the Congress under the Articles of Confederation from 1783 to 1786. Although he opposed ratifying the new U.S. Constitution, Monroe soon took part in national politics. He was defeated by James Madison for a seat in the House of Representatives in 1788, but two years later was selected by the Virginia legislature for a seat in the U.S. Senate, where he opposed the Federalist economic programs of Alexander Hamilton.

President George Washington appointed Monroe to be U.S. minister to France. He refused to defend the Jay Treaty with Great Britain to the French government, believing the terms to favor British interests against the French, and Washington recalled him. He published a defense of his conduct and an attack on the Federalist foreign policy in a book, *A View of the Conduct of the Executive in the Foreign Affairs of the United States* (1797). He then served three terms as governor of Virginia.

In 1803 President Jefferson appointed Monroe to a mission to France to purchase New Orleans. Finding that the Emperor Napoleon wished to sell even more land, Monroe exceeded his instructions and negotiated a treaty to purchase the entire Louisiana Territory.

The following year, however, he failed in an attempt to negotiate the purchase of Florida from Spain. In 1806 he negotiated a commercial treaty with Great Britain that seemed so favorable to the British that President Jefferson refused to submit it to the Senate. In response, Monroe entered the Presidential contest in an attempt to defeat Jefferson's protégé, James Madison. But in a replay of their 1788 contest, Madison defeated Monroe once again, this time for the Democratic-Republican caucus nomination.

In spite of their political rivalry, Madison appointed Monroe secretary of state in 1811. Simultaneously appointed secretary of war just after the British sacking of the capital in 1814, Monroe prevented an outright British victory, and he oversaw a favorable peace treaty that ended the War of 1812. By a narrow margin the Democratic-Republican congressional caucus nominated him for the Presidency in 1816. He handily won the general election against Federalist candidate Rufus King.

Because the Capitol had been burned to the ground by the British, Monroe's inauguration took place at the Brick Capitol, a temporary meeting hall for Congress. The Monroes could not move into the President's House, soon to be known as the White House, for six months, and Congress could not use the Capitol again until 1819.

Monroe's two terms saw the disappearance of the Federalist party and the brief establishment of a "no party" period known as the Era of Good Feelings. Sectional conflicts among the North, South, and West took the place of party competition. Monroe was reelected in 1820 by a 231-to-1 vote in the electoral college. The one dissenting vote was cast by William Plumer, an elector from New Hampshire, who wished to reserve the honor of a unanimous vote for Washington alone.

Monroe appointed an exceptional cabinet: John Quincy Adams as secretary of state, John C. Calhoun as secretary of war, William Crawford as secretary of the Treasury, and William Wirt as attorney general—all men of Presidential stature. The cabinet met 180 times during Monroe's two terms, and most decisions were made by consensus.

In domestic affairs Monroe reduced taxes and paid off much of the public debt. He signed the Missouri Compromise of 1820, which forbade slavery in the Louisiana Territory above the southern boundary of Missouri, in spite of his doubts that Congress had the constitutional power to exclude slavery from any part of the Union. The compromise preserved sectional peace. Monroe vetoed the Cumberland Road Bill in 1822 because he did not think it was constitutional for the national government to charge tolls for national roads. The following year, however, he submitted his own public works program for construction of roads and canals, to be funded by the national government out of general revenues.

Monroe's major accomplishments were in foreign affairs. In 1818 the United States settled its fishing disputes with Canada, which involved the right of Americans to fish off the coast of Labrador. By the Adams-Onis Treaty (1819) the United States acquired Florida from Spain and all Spanish claims to the Oregon Territory were granted instead to the United States. The United States recognized the newly independent nations of Latin America, and the Monroe Doctrine established the principles that European states were neither to colonize in the New World nor interfere with the governments there. Monroe's only significant failure involved the Senate, which refused to consent to a treaty with Great Britain that would have allowed navies of both nations to put an end to the illegal trade in African slaves.

Monroe retired in 1825 to Oak Hill, his Virginia plantation. He was the last of the "Virginia dynasty" to occupy the White House. Monroe acted as a regent of the University of Virginia and presided over the Virginia state constitutional convention in 1829. He died on a visit to New York City on July 4, 1831.

SEE ALSO

Congressional caucus; Jefferson, Thomas; Madison, James; Monroe Doctrine; Washington, George

FURTHER READING

Ammon, Harry. *James Monroe: The Quest for National Identity.* New York: McGraw-Hill, 1971.
Dangerfield, George. *The Era of Good Feelings.* New York: Harcourt, Brace, 1952.

Morton, Levi

VICE PRESIDENT

☆ *Born: May 16, 1824, Shoreham, Vt.*
☆ *Political party: Republican*
☆ *Education: no formal education*
☆ *Military service: none*
☆ *Previous government service: U.S. House of Representatives, 1879–81; minister to France, 1881–85*
☆ *Vice President under Benjamin Harrison, 1889–93*
☆ *Subsequent government service: governor of New York, 1895–96*
☆ *Died: May 16, 1920, Rhinebeck, N.Y.*

LEVI MORTON was successful as a financier, establishing the large Wall Street banking firm of L. P. Morton and Company. In the 1870s the firm, by then known as Morton, Bliss and Co., helped refinance the national debt. Morton moved into politics and was elected to the U.S. House of Representatives in 1878. Three years later, President James

Garfield appointed him U.S. minister to France.

Morton was nominated for Vice President on the Republican ticket in 1888 to provide geographic balance and access to the administration for Wall Street. As Benjamin Harrison's Vice President, Morton was an advocate of civil service reforms and good-government practices designed to reduce fraud and corruption. These measures were supported by much of the business community.

After the Democrats took back the White House in 1893 Morton served one term as governor of New York. He then returned to Wall Street and founded another financial company, retiring from business in 1909.

SEE ALSO
Harrison, Benjamin

National security adviser

THE NATIONAL security adviser (NSA) serves as the principal adviser to the President on national security matters, supervises the staff of the National Security Council (NSC), and organizes the meetings of the NSC. The NSA prepares initial drafts of National Security Decision Directives (NSDD) for NSC consideration and monitors the implementation of national security decisions made by the President. Appointed by the President without Senate consent, the NSA is a White House aide with no statutory powers or duties and is not a member of the National Security Council.

The NSA may play several different roles in Presidential decision making. President Dwight Eisenhower used Robert Cutler, his special assistant for national security affairs, as a "custodian-manager" to see that all options were being considered, especially for long-range planning. Cutler also had to ensure that the elaborate staffing method Eisenhower put in place (with 76 aides to the National Security Council) was operating smoothly.

President John F. Kennedy used McGeorge Bundy as one of his key advisers and policymakers. Bundy was less concerned with process and paperwork than with policy advocacy, especially in short-term crisis management. Similarly, Lyndon Johnson used Walt Rostow as a policy advocate for escalating the Vietnam War and as a defender of that policy before Congress.

President Richard Nixon relied on Henry Kissinger as his principal adviser in foreign policy and national security, sent him on a top secret diplomatic mission to the People's Republic of China, and entrusted him with negotiating arms control agreements with the Soviet Union. Kissinger used the NSC staff to dominate interdepartmental committees concerned with arms control negotiations with the Soviets and with defense budgeting.

President Jimmy Carter used Zbigniew Brzezinski to formulate his foreign policy goals and as a counterweight to his secretary of state, Cyrus Vance, making him the first national security adviser with cabinet rank. Brzezinski presided over NSC committees dealing with intelligence, arms control, and crisis management.

During Ronald Reagan's administration, two advisers with a military background, marine colonel Robert McFarlane and navy admiral John Poindexter, took operational control of policy when they oversaw the sale of arms to Iran

Henry Kissinger (right) served as Richard Nixon's national security adviser. Kissinger used his diplomatic skills to improve relations with China and the Soviet Union.

and the transfer of some of the profits to the Contra resistance movement in Nicaragua. Instead of developing policy proposals for the President and the NSC, the NSA and the Political-Military Affairs Directorate of the NSC developed policies and implemented them on their own.

In the aftermath of the Iran-Contra affair, President Reagan appointed Frank Carlucci and then Colin Powell as NSA. They implemented the recommendations of the Tower Commission, the panel appointed by Reagan to investigate the affair. They dissolved the Political-Military Affairs Directorate, making the NSA accountable to all members of the NSC; allowed all departments to present policy options to the President; and served as impartial custodians of the national security advisory process.

SEE ALSO

Commander in chief; Cuban Missile Crisis; Decision making, Presidential; National Security Council; Secretary of state

FURTHER READING

Brzezinski, Zbigniew. *Power and Principle.* New York: Farrar, Straus & Giroux, 1983.
Kissinger, Henry. *White House Years.* Boston: Little, Brown, 1979.

National Security Council

THE NATIONAL Security Council (NSC) is the unit of the Executive Office of the President that assists the President in making and executing national security decisions. It was established by the National Security Act of 1947, according to which it consisted of the President, who chaired its meetings, the secretary of state, the secretary of defense, and the service secretaries of the army, navy, and air force. The director of Cen-

tral Intelligence was not a member but would serve as an adviser.

In 1949 Congress amended the law to change the composition of the council: the three service secretaries were dropped and the Vice President was added. The chair of the Joint Chiefs of Staff became an adviser to the council and attended its meetings. The President might "from time to time" designate other officials to sit on the council or attend its meetings, and 20 or more officials have often been invited. The NSC has a staff of 40 or more aides, supervised by the assistant to the President for national security.

The NSC has no powers of its own, takes no votes, and makes no decisions. Presidential decisions made after NSC deliberations are embodied in National Security Decision Directives and are implemented by the executive departments of the federal government.

The NSC staff monitors national security communications in the Situation Room, located in the White House basement, and in a Crisis Management Center located in the Executive Office Building (equipped with computers and projection facilities for the display of information). These communications include State Department instructions to U.S. embassies and missions, Defense Department messages to military commands, and Joint Chiefs of Staff orders to the regional military commanders in chief. Data from the Pentagon's National Military Command Center in Colorado Springs, Colorado, can be simultaneously displayed in the Situation Room.

Although Presidents Harry Truman and Dwight Eisenhower convened the NSC frequently, most Presidents rely on very small meetings with their key

John McCone, director of the CIA, arrives at the White House for a National Security Council meeting to discuss the Cuban Missile Crisis.

national security advisers much more than on meetings of the council itself. President Kennedy used the Ex Comm, a smaller "executive committee" of the national security officials, to deliberate in situations such as the Berlin Crisis and the Cuban Missile Crisis. Lyndon Johnson relied on his Tuesday lunch with the secretaries of war and defense, the director of Central Intelligence, chair of the Joint Chiefs, and his national security adviser, to plan strategy for the war in Vietnam. Richard Nixon worked closely with Henry Kissinger, his national security adviser, on improving relations with the People's Republic of China and the Soviet Union, and sometimes they were referred to as the "two-man band." Jimmy Carter held Friday breakfasts with his Vice President, the secretaries of state and defense, and his national security adviser to deal with the Iran hostage crisis and relations with the Soviets. Ronald Reagan used the National Security Planning Group, consisting of the members of the NSC, the director of Central Intelligence, the national security adviser, and three top White House political aides. Reagan was the first President to include political advisers in national security decision making.

SEE ALSO

Cuban Missile Crisis; Decision making, Presidential; Director of Central Intelligence; National security adviser; Secretary of defense; Secretary of state

FURTHER READING

Report of the President's Special Review Board [Tower Commission]. Washington, D.C.: Government Printing Office, 1987.

New Deal

THE NEW DEAL was the term used by Franklin D. Roosevelt to describe his domestic program. "I pledge to you,"

Roosevelt told the Democratic national convention in Chicago in his 1932 acceptance speech, "I pledge myself, to a new deal for the American people." According to speech writers Raymond Moley and Samuel Rosenman, both of whom used the term in drafts of the speech, neither they nor Roosevelt had any idea that the phrase, designed simply as campaign rhetoric, would become so significant. The term had been used earlier at the convention, when John McDuffie of Alabama nominated John Nance Garner for Vice President with the words, "There is a demand for a new deal in the management of the affairs of the American people."

The phrase may have been borrowed from the British campaign of David Lloyd George, who ran for prime minister in 1919 with the slogan "A New Deal for Everyone." American reformers had also used the phrase, including Senator Carl Schurz of Missouri in 1871, Woodrow Wilson in his campaign for New Jersey governor in 1910, and Senator Robert La Follette of Wisconsin in 1912.

The New Deal involved three activities: First, Roosevelt had to restore confidence in the banking system and end the panicked withdrawals of funds that threatened thousands of banks. Then he had to stabilize prices in order to encourage businesses and farmers to resume production. Finally, he had to provide new federal assistance to those he described in his second inaugural address as the third of the nation that was "ill-housed, ill-clad, ill-nourished."

Roosevelt's efforts began on March 6, 1933, when he proclaimed a bank holiday and called Congress into special session. In the hundred days of that session, from March 9 through June 15, Congress passed Roosevelt's program: the Emergency Banking Act, the Agricultural Adjustment Act, and the National Industrial Recovery Act, as well as the bills

The American Guide Series was one of many cultural projects sponsored by the Works Progress Administration.

Mary McLeod Bethune was the director of the Division of Negro Affairs for the National Youth Administration during the New Deal era.

creating the Tennessee Valley Authority (which built dams and power stations to provide power in a six-state region), the Home Owners Loan Corporation (which made mortgage loans to encourage home owning), and the Federal Emergency Relief Administration (which provided funds to the jobless). Roosevelt also took the United States off the gold standard to prevent a run on government gold reserves by people worried about the value of the currency.

Later New Deal laws created public housing for workers, unemployment insurance, and Social Security benefits (pensions) for workers when they retired. Other laws made federal grants to states to provide welfare for needy families with children and established a legal framework for organizing labor unions and for collective bargaining with management (to discourage companies from breaking strikes by employing nonunion labor or intimidating workers from joining unions). New Deal legislation also created public service jobs for the unemployed, including the Civilian Conservation Corps for youths and the Works Progress Administration, which sponsored environmental and cultural public works projects. Other new government agencies included the Federal Communications Commission (which regulated radio broadcasting and telephone companies), the Securities and Exchange Commission (which regulated stock markets to ensure fair trading practices), the National Labor Relations Board (which ensured the rights of workers to unionize and

bargain collectively with management), the Federal Housing Administration (which constructed public housing), and the Rural Electrification Administration (which brought electric lines to rural areas that had never had power before).

SEE ALSO

Brains Trust; Roosevelt, Franklin D.

FURTHER READING

Dubofsky, Melvyn, and Stephen Burwood, eds. *The New Deal.* New York: Garland, 1990.
Eden, Robert, ed. *The New Deal and Its Legacy.* Westport, Conn.: Greenwood, 1989.
Louchheim, Katie, ed. *The Making of the New Deal.* Cambridge: Harvard University Press, 1983.
McElvaine, Robert S. *The Depression and New Deal: A History in Documents.* New York: Oxford, 1999.

New Freedom

THE NEW FREEDOM was the term used by Woodrow Wilson in the 1912 Presidential campaign to describe his domestic program. Wilson believed that "private monopoly is indefensible and intolerable" and that national government should break up such large concentrations of corporate wealth. This view distinguished him clearly from his two opponents. Wilson claimed that President William Howard Taft stood for the interests of big business and that ex-President Theodore Roosevelt's New Nationalism program to regulate big business would prove unworkable.

Wilson also argued for lower tariffs (taxes on imported goods) to benefit consumers. He called for reform of the banking system to ensure stability in the money supply and end financial panics as well as to provide more credit (lending money), especially to small businesses.

Congress approved most of the New Freedom program in 1913 and 1914, including the Underwood Tariff Act, which cut tariffs by about 25 percent; the Federal Reserve Act, which established the Federal Reserve Board to regulate the banks and the money supply; the Clayton Anti-Trust Act, which made it more difficult to establish a monopoly in an industry; and the Federal Trade Commission Act, which prevented business practices that unfairly restrained trade. Later in his administration Wilson got Congress to pass laws to aid merchant seamen in dealing with shipowners, to provide an eight-hour day for railroad workers, and to help farmers repay their loans. Congress passed his proposal to ban child labor but the law was declared unconstitutional by the Supreme Court.

SEE ALSO
Wilson, Woodrow

FURTHER READING
Wilson, Woodrow. *The New Freedom.* 1913. Reprint. Englewood Cliffs, N.J.: Prentice-Hall, 1961.

New Frontier

THE NEW FRONTIER was the term used by John F. Kennedy to describe the challenges facing the United States. In his acceptance speech for the Democratic nomination for President in 1960, Kennedy said, "We stand today on the edge of a new frontier—the frontier of the 1960s, a frontier of unknown opportunities and paths." He added, "The new frontier of which I speak is not a set of promises—it is a set of challenges. It sums up not what I intend to offer the American people, but what I intend to ask of them."

Kennedy's speech was drafted by his speech writer, Theodore Sorensen. The term *New Frontier* had previously been used in 1934 as the title of a book written by Secretary of Agriculture Henry A. Wallace, in 1936 speeches by Presidential candidate Alf Landon, and in a 1959 speech by historian Arthur Schlesinger, Jr.

The term *New Frontiersmen* refers to the kind of appointees Kennedy brought into government: relatives such as Robert F. Kennedy and Sargent Shriver; academics such as Schlesinger; and Democratic party liberals such as Adlai Stevenson and Chester Bowles. New Frontiersmen joined Kennedy in touch football and other active sports, and several were noted for their wit and style.

Many of the Kennedy administration programs are referred to as New Frontier measures. These include the Peace Corps, the Alliance for Progress in Latin America, a trade expansion act, an increase in the minimum wage, a federal housing act, and an Area Redevelopment Act to benefit depressed rural areas. Kennedy suffered defeats on many bills, however, including federal aid to education, creation of the Department of Urban Affairs, medical insurance for the elderly, and urban mass transit. Most of the unfinished New Frontier agenda was passed by Congress during the Presidency of Lyndon Johnson.

SEE ALSO
Kennedy, John F.

FURTHER READING
Sorensen, Theodore. *Kennedy.* New York: Harper & Row, 1965.

News conferences

NEWS CONFERENCES are official meetings between the President and journalists that are reported in newspapers and on television and radio.

Theodore Roosevelt was the first President to invite reporters into the

Ronald Reagan, known as the "Great Communicator," takes reporters' questions at a news conference in 1986.

White House, providing the press with a room in the newly constructed executive office wing. He hired a press secretary to give news releases to reporters. Roosevelt also talked to reporters himself but only off the record. William Howard Taft discontinued the practice of meeting with reporters and had as little to do with them as possible.

Formal news conferences were begun by Woodrow Wilson, who met with reporters once or twice a week for more than two years. He canceled these meetings in 1915, citing "national security" reasons after the sinking of the *Lusitania* by Germany, but that was only an excuse. Wilson was fed up with reporters asking him personal questions about his family.

Warren Harding, a former newspaper publisher, played cards and golf with White House reporters. He held news conferences twice a week and opened them to all accredited reporters. He invented the title "White House spokesman" to allow the press to quote the President without direct attribution to him. Calvin Coolidge held conferences with reporters, but they could not quote the President or attribute anything to him; consequently there was no "news" in the conference. Herbert Hoover required

that questions be submitted one day in advance, and during the Depression he suggested that reporters submit their stories to the White House for "clearance." He held meetings with publishers to complain about their White House reporters and excluded reporters whose stories were critical of him from attending the conferences.

News conferences were used extensively by Franklin Roosevelt, who allowed 20 or so reporters to crowd into the Oval Office twice each week. He eliminated the practice of submitting questions in advance and enjoyed sparring and joking with the reporters. After his first session, they applauded Roosevelt's performance. Harry Truman was more formal, holding news conferences in the State Department's Indian Treaty Room (in what is now the Old Executive Office Building). He stood at a podium looking down at the reporters; he required them to identify themselves before asking questions; and he reduced the sessions to one a week. He also allowed radio stations to broadcast taped excerpts, making news conferences public events.

Dwight Eisenhower filmed conferences for television news and allowed reporters to quote him directly. For the first time, Eisenhower also permitted reporters to transcribe questions and answers, and the *New York Times* began to print them. Five days after his inauguration, John Kennedy decided to move his news conferences from the White House to an auditorium in the new State Department building that could seat more than 400 reporters. He also permitted live television coverage. The most recent innovation came from Gerald Ford, who allowed reporters to ask follow-up questions after the President responded to the first inquiry.

A news conference typically begins with a brief statement by the President. The reporters then raise their hands and the President recognizes them, often by name. The first questioners are usually the representatives of the wire services, followed by correspondents for the national television or radio networks, and then by other reporters. The conference ends when the senior wire service correspondent says, "Thank you, Mr. President."

Presidents need not hold news conferences. Coolidge held more than 100 every year; Franklin Roosevelt held them weekly, but Kennedy held them only every other month. Lyndon Johnson was so apprehensive about appearing on television without a prepared speech that he delayed holding a televised conference until February 29, 1964, nearly three months after he had succeeded to the office. He held few conferences during the Vietnam War after reporters accused him of a "credibility gap."

Richard Nixon also held few news conferences; in his first he told reporters that he would not discuss serious issues in "off-the-cuff responses." Sometimes he engaged in hostile exchanges with reporters, most notably CBS News correspondent Dan Rather. He refused to hold conferences during the last months of the Watergate crisis. Jimmy Carter held 59 conferences but very few during the Iran hostage crisis because he did not want to report on his lack of progress in freeing the hostages. Ronald Reagan, the "Great Communicator," held only 27 during his first term and held none through most of the Iran-Contra affair.

SEE ALSO
Press secretary

FURTHER READING
Cater, Douglas. *The Fourth Branch of Government.* New York: Vintage, 1959.
French, Blaire A. *The Presidential Press Conference: Its History and Role in the American Political System.* Washington, D.C.: University Press of America, 1982.
Smith, Carolyn. *Presidential Press Conferences.* Westport, Conn.: Praeger, 1990.

Nixon, Richard M.
37TH PRESIDENT

☆ Born: Jan. 9, 1913, Yorba Linda, Calif.
☆ Political party: Republican
☆ Education: Whittier College, B.A., 1934; Duke University Law School, LL.B., 1937
☆ Military service: U.S. Navy, 1942–46
☆ Previous government service: U.S. House of Representatives, 1947–51; U.S. Senate, 1951–53; Vice President, 1953–61
☆ Elected President, 1968; served, 1969–74; resigned, 1974
☆ Died: Apr. 22, 1994, New York, N.Y.

RICHARD NIXON was the only President ever to resign his office and only the second (the other was Andrew Johnson, and later, Bill Clinton) ever to be involved in impeachment proceedings in the House of Representatives. Some historians called him an "imperial" President because he relied excessively on Presidential powers and failed to collaborate with Congress. Although he ended U.S. involvement in the Vietnam War and won diplomatic agreements with the Soviet Union and China, his misuses of power destroyed his Presidency.

Nixon's parents ran a lemon grove and a grocery store, and Richard worked for them before and after school. He graduated second in his class from Whittier College and third in his class from Duke University Law School, then practiced law in Whittier. He met Thelma ("Pat") Ryan at a dramatic society and married her in 1940. At the start of World War II Nixon worked for the Office of Price Administration, implementing rationing of automobile tires. He joined the navy and served as an operations officer for an air transport squadron flying in the South Pacific, then as a lawyer negotiating contracts, until his discharge in 1946 with the rank of lieutenant commander.

Just as Nixon was leaving the navy, a group of prominent Republicans in Whittier began looking for a prospective candidate, preferably a young veteran, to run for Congress against the liberal Democratic incumbent Jerry Voorhis. Nixon was offered the nomination, and he defeated Voorhis in a series of debates, charging his opponent with accepting the support of pro-communist labor unions. While in Congress, Nixon served on the House Un-American Activities Committee and was instrumental in the investigation of State Department official Alger Hiss, who had been charged by Whittaker Chambers, a senior editor of *Time* magazine, with being a member of a communist spy ring during World War II. Hiss was later convicted of perjury (lying under oath) and sentenced to five years in prison for denying to the committee that he had ever met Chambers.

Nixon's work on the committee gained him a national reputation as a hard-line anticommunist. He also served on the House Committee on Education and Labor, which wrote the pro-business Taft-Hartley Act. He strongly supported Harry Truman's proposal for the Marshall Plan for European reconstruction after World War II. Nixon ran for the Senate in 1950, defeating liberal Democrat Helen Gahagan Douglas by insinuating that her voting record was "pink" (pro-communist) and referring to her as the "pink lady." He became the youngest Republican in the U.S. Senate.

In 1952 Nixon convinced members of the California delegation to the Republican convention to support Dwight Eisenhower's candidacy rather than Robert Taft or favorite son Earl Warren. Eisenhower then chose Nixon to run with him. Newspapers charged that while Nixon was a senator, he accepted $18,000 from supporters to defray his personal expenses. Eisenhower insisted that Nixon make a full and public explanation. Nixon made a nationwide television broadcast on September 23, 1952, in which he defended his actions and won over the public when he insisted that whatever else might happen, he would never return one gift—a dog that his children had named Checkers. The overwhelmingly positive response to his "Checkers speech" convinced Eisenhower to keep Nixon on the ticket, and they were elected by a large margin. Nixon was the youngest person ever to be elected Vice President.

Nixon worked tirelessly to elect Republican candidates to Congress and state offices. When Eisenhower was ill, he presided with great discretion over 19 meetings of the cabinet and 26 meetings of the National Security Council. He made numerous trips abroad and was the target of violent anti-U.S. demonstrations in several Latin American nations

A campaign banner from 1968.

Richard Nixon dines with Chinese premier Chou En-Lai at a banquet in Beijing in February 1972.

in 1958. He debated Soviet premier Nikita Khrushchev at the American National Exposition in Moscow in 1959, reinforcing his anticommunist image with the American television audience.

Nixon was the odds-on favorite to win the Republican Presidential nomination in 1960. He won the primaries without opposition but then faced a last-minute bid by New York governor Nelson Rockefeller. With Eisenhower's endorsement, Nixon fended off Rockefeller, then compromised with him on a Republican party platform that implicitly criticized the performance of the Eisenhower administration. This agreement alienated Eisenhower, who did little campaigning for the ticket.

Nixon engaged in four Presidential debates with Democratic candidate John F. Kennedy, and a majority of television viewers thought that he lost the first one badly. With the economy in a recession, Nixon lost several key states, and vote fraud may have played a part in his losses in Illinois and Texas. Nixon lost the election but refused to contest the results.

In 1962 Nixon ran for governor of California but was defeated by incumbent governor Edmund G. Brown, Jr. He held a press conference after the election

in which he attacked the media for bias and insisted, "You won't have Nixon to kick around anymore." He moved to New York City and practiced law with the newly renamed firm of Nixon, Mudge, Rose, Guthrie, Alexander and Mitchell. But Nixon had not retired from politics: he campaigned effectively for Republican congressional candidates in the 1966 midterm elections.

In 1968 Nixon again won the Republican nomination, defeating George Romney, Nelson Rockefeller, and Ronald Reagan. With the Democratic party split between hawks who supported Hubert Humphrey and antiwar activists who favored Eugene McCarthy and Robert Kennedy (assassinated in June after winning the California primary), Nixon entered the general election well ahead of Humphrey. But the race tightened up after his opponent endorsed a halt to the bombing of Vietnam. In a three-person race (the other candidate was southerner George Wallace, running on a segregationist platform of the American Independent party), Nixon won only 43.4 percent of the popular vote, defeating Humphrey by less than 1 percent.

Nixon was only the fifth Presidential candidate to win the office after a prior defeat (the others were Thomas Jefferson, Andrew Jackson, William Henry Harrison, and Grover Cleveland), and the only one to win against a new opponent rather than against the candidate who had previously defeated him. He was also the first former Vice President since Martin Van Buren in 1836 to be elected to the Presidency without first having succeeded to the position after the death of a President.

"I shall consecrate my office," Nixon pledged in his inaugural address, "to the cause of peace among nations." He announced a policy to "Vietnamize" the war in Vietnam and remove most of the 500,000 U.S. ground combat forces. Soon U.S. combat casualties were sharply reduced. In 1970 he invaded neighboring Cambodia in pursuit of Vietnamese communist forces, an action that led to widespread protests and demonstrations in the United States. By 1972 almost all U.S. forces had been removed from South Vietnam, and on January 27, 1973, after a Christmas bombing campaign against North Vietnam, the United States came to an agreement with the North Vietnamese: a cease-fire was proclaimed, U.S. prisoners of war were returned, and U.S. military involvement in the Vietnam War ended. Air force bombing continued against the communists in Cambodia, however, until Congress overrode a Nixon veto and ordered a halt to the bombing by August 15, 1973. Then Congress passed the War Powers Resolution of 1973, also over Nixon's veto, which provided that Congress must approve of any military action by a President within 60 days or the forces must be withdrawn.

Although Nixon had made his career as a staunch anticommunist, in 1971 he reversed his long-standing opposition to seating communist China in the United Nations. Then, in February 1972, he became the first President to visit the People's Republic of China. He established low-level diplomatic relations with that nation, naming George Bush to head a "mission" to Beijing, though without formal recognition of its government. In May 1972 Nixon made a trip to the Soviet Union and completed a significant arms control agreement involving limitations on intercontinental ballistic missiles. On May 28 he made a televised speech to the people of the Soviet Union, reassuring them that the United States did not have aggressive intentions against them. This summit conference ushered in a period of détente, or relaxation of tensions, between the two superpowers. Numerous other agreements in science, space, technology, and trade were also signed over the next two years.

In domestic affairs Nixon was checked by Congress and the courts. He opposed busing to overcome racial imbalance in public schools. Instead, he proposed $2 billion in funding to bring inner-city schools up to par with those in more affluent communities, but Congress refused to consider his proposal. He nominated two conservative southerners to the Supreme Court, Clement Haynesworth and G. Harrold Carswell, neither of whom was accepted by the Democrat-dominated Senate. He tried to eliminate many of Lyndon Johnson's Great Society programs, including the Office of Economic Opportunity, which ran the War on Poverty, and he impounded funds for many programs. But he was blocked from implementing his plans by the Democratic Congress and federal court orders requiring him to spend impounded funds.

Although Nixon positioned himself as a conservative, spending for many social welfare programs, including Social Security, Medicare, and Medicaid, increased greatly during his tenure. A national system of food stamps costing billions of dollars was developed as part of the welfare system. Nixon proposed, and Congress accepted, a reallocation of government funds to state and local governments. This plan replaced many grants for specific programs with broader "bloc" grants, giving states more flexibility. He also won passage of a revenue-sharing measure that provided $5 billion annually from the national Treasury to state and local governments. However, Congress refused to pass his program for "family allowances" to replace welfare, an idea that would have significantly increased social welfare spending.

Although Nixon was a free-market Republican, opposed to much government regulation of the economy, for the first time in U.S. history he presided over the use of wage and price controls in peacetime (from 1971 to 1973) in order to check inflation. He also proposed large increases in spending for the environment and created the Council on Environmental Quality. An Arab oil embargo against the United States, imposed during the Yom Kippur War involving Israel and Syria and Egypt in 1973, led Nixon to impose new regulations on energy producers and users. Nixon proposed Project Independence, a plan to make the United States economy energy-independent of Arab oil producers within a decade. Nixon vetoed a Democratic bill that would have regulated energy prices, preferring to rely in part on higher oil prices as an incentive for U.S. oil producers to increase domestic production.

Nixon won a landslide reelection victory in 1972 over his Democratic opponent, Senator George McGovern of South Dakota. This election set the pattern for the next two decades in all elections except 1976: liberal Democrats were trounced by conservative Republicans who won southern states on the basis of "backlash" politics. But Republicans continued to be a minority in both Congress

Demonstrators rally in front of the White House during the Watergate scandal to call for Nixon's impeachment.

and in state governments—part of the pattern of "split government."

Early in Nixon's second term, it was revealed that operatives working for the Committee to Re-Elect the President had burglarized the Democratic National Committee headquarters in the Watergate office complex in 1972. The scandal gradually enveloped many senior White House aides and three cabinet secretaries, and as it came closer to the President his popularity dropped.

On October 10, 1973, Vice President Spiro T. Agnew resigned as part of a plea bargain in a court case involving bribes paid to him by Maryland construction contractors before and during his tenure as Vice President. Congress approved Nixon's nomination of House minority leader Gerald Ford to fill the vacancy.

In 1974 the House Judiciary Committee began an inquiry into the Watergate scandal to determine if Nixon should be impeached. Late in July the Supreme Court issued a ruling requiring Nixon to turn over evidence in criminal trials of his aides, in spite of his claim that it was his executive privilege to keep information about Presidential decisions from the courts. The tape recordings Nixon made of conversations in the Oval Office indicated that he had participated in a cover-up of the Watergate burglary.

Nixon resigned his office on August 9, 1974, shortly after the House committee voted to recommend three articles of impeachment to the full House. He was succeeded by Vice President Gerald Ford, who on September 8, 1974, issued Nixon a "full, free and absolute pardon" for all crimes committed during his Presidency. Nixon accepted the pardon, admitting "mistakes" in the way he had handled Watergate, but made no admission that he was guilty of any crimes.

In retirement Nixon moved to an affluent community in New Jersey, completed his memoirs, *RN*, and wrote many books on foreign policy. He gradually assumed a role as a senior foreign policy adviser to Republican Presidents.

Richard Nixon died of a stroke at the age of 81.

SEE ALSO

Agnew, Spiro T.; Amnesty, Presidential; Debates, Presidential; Eisenhower, Dwight David; Executive privilege; Ex-Presidency; Ford, Gerald R.; Humphrey, Hubert H.; Impeachment; Imperial Presidency; Kennedy, John F.; Pardon power; Succession to the Presidency; War powers; War Powers Resolution; Watergate investigation

FURTHER READING

Ambrose, Stephen. *Nixon.* 2 vols. New York: Simon & Schuster, 1987.
Morris, Roger. *Richard Milhous Nixon.* New York: Henry Holt, 1990.
Nixon, Richard. *RN: The Memoirs of Richard Nixon.* 2 vols. New York: Warner, 1978.
Parmet, Herbert. *Richard Nixon and His America.* Boston: Little, Brown, 1990.
Pious, Richard M. *Richard Nixon: A Political Life.* Englewood Cliffs, N.J.: Silver Burdett, 1992.

Nominating conventions, Presidential

EVERY FOUR years, delegates from state political parties meet to nominate their party candidate for President of the United States. Conventions replaced the congressional caucus, in which the senators and representatives would nominate a candidate, which was discredited after the election of 1824.

The Anti-Masons held the first national convention in September 1830 to organize themselves as a political party. They aimed to stop what they believed was a plot by the Masonic order (a fraternal group) to seize political power. They decided to hold a Presidential nominating convention on September 26, 1831, and nominated William Wirt of Maryland, who then confessed that he had once been a member of the Masons. The convention stood by its nomination. The second convention was held by the National Republican party on December 12, 1831; it nominated Henry Clay.

The Democratic party held its first convention at the saloon in the Baltimore Athenaeum in May 1832. It accepted President Andrew Jackson's request that it nominate Martin Van Buren for Vice President. Since Jackson was already President, the convention did not actually nominate him but passed a resolution that concurred in the "nominations" he had received "in various parts of the Union" by Democratic state parties. The Democrats also passed a rule requiring nominees to win the votes of two-thirds of the delegates—a rule that was not discarded in favor of a simple majority vote until 1936. The two-thirds rule gave the South a "veto" over Democratic nominees and led to nominations of several northern Democrats with southern sympathies, such as James Buchanan, just prior to the Civil War. It also contributed to convention deadlocks; the 1924 Democratic convention endured 103 rounds of balloting.

From the 1830s through the 1960s state delegations were chosen and controlled by state party leaders. "Less than one hundred men in any convention really dictate what occurs," explained Bronx, New York, Democratic party boss Ed Flynn in 1948. The unit rule required all delegates in a state to vote the way the majority of the delegates wished, ensuring boss control of a unified state delegation. "What the party wants," British commentator Lord Bryce observed, "is not a good President but a good candidate," one who would distribute the spoils of victory, appointments and government contracts, to the bosses and their party followers. Although major-party candidates did not appear at their party's convention until Franklin Roosevelt flew to Chicago to claim his nomination in 1932, their managers bargained with the bosses who controlled state delegations over future Presidential appointments and other political favors.

"I authorize no bargains and will be bound by none," Abraham Lincoln telegraphed his managers in 1860. "Damn Lincoln," his zealous managers responded. They won Indiana's support for Lincoln by offering Caleb Smith the post of secretary of the interior; took Pennsylvania by giving Simon Cameron the War Department; and made New York's Salmon Chase secretary of the Treasury to seal their victory. Lincoln fretted over the public reaction to these deals: "What will they think of their honest Abe when he appoints Simon Cameron?" Similarly, Woodrow Wilson publicly rejected deal making to win the 1912 Democratic nomination. Yet his campaign managers dealt away cabinet positions and the Vice Presidency to gain Wilson his victory on the 46th ballot, a strategy also used by Franklin Roosevelt in his 1932 nominating battle.

In 1968 the boss-dominated convention system lost its legitimacy. Although voters in Democratic party primaries overwhelmingly chose antiwar contenders Robert Kennedy and Eugene McCarthy,

the bosses at the Chicago convention chose Vice President Hubert Humphrey to be the party's Presidential nominee—even though Humphrey had not entered the primaries. After the Democratic election defeat, a party reform commission recommended changes in party rules that would take control of the selection of convention delegates away from state parties and give it to the party voters. The Republicans soon followed suit.

Since the 1970s the 4,288 Democratic and 2,209 Republican delegates have been selected by the party voters in primaries or open caucuses. In the Democratic party, a candidate receives a share of convention delegates proportional to the percentage of votes he or she has won in the primary. The Republican party uses a winner-take-all procedure in which the candidate with the most votes wins an entire state delegation. In either event, the candidates, not the party bosses, control the state delegations once the voters have given them their specified share through the primary voting. The candidate for President who wins the majority of the delegates dominates the convention.

"The rise of the primaries has made it inevitable that the nomination is settled before the convention begins," noted New York senator Daniel Moynihan, adding, "The convention does not decide and it does not debate." Nevertheless, delegates decide on the content of the party platform and determine changes in party rules for the next nominating convention.

Delegates from both parties are generally better educated and more affluent than the rank-and-file members of the parties. Most Republican delegates call themselves conservatives, while Democratic delegates are almost evenly split between liberals and moderates. Democratic delegates usually take positions more liberal than the party

rank-and-file members or all voters, whereas Republicans are more conservative, especially on issues such as abortion, prayer in the schools, gun control, and gay rights.

Democratic party rules require that half the delegates be women; the Republicans do not have such a rule, but more than two-fifths of their delegates in 1992 were women. Since the 1970s the Democrats have had more Catholic, Jewish, and African-American representation at their convention than the Republicans.

Convention delegates are experienced in elective politics: more than two-thirds at most conventions have held public or party office, and more than half have attended previous conventions. Democratic rules provide for a category of superdelegates: most Democratic members of the House and Senate are added automatically to their state delegation. They may vote for whomever

they wish, though they invariably vote according to the preferences of the majority of the delegates at the convention, adding to the front-runner's advantage.

Modern conventions usually last four days, with most of the proceedings organized by the contender who has won the primaries. The first evening's proceedings are devoted to speeches and films introducing the candidate and party to television viewers and to "housekeeping" business—accepting the credentials of the delegates, dealing with challenges to delegates, and adopting convention rules. The second day is devoted to discussion of the party platform, which is adopted that evening. Platforms do not bind candidates, but once in office most Presidents implement the large majority of platform pledges.

The third evening is devoted to nominating speeches for the Presidential candidate, followed by the vote for the

Posters supporting the nomination of Jimmy Carter flood the floor at the 1980 Democratic national convention in New York.

candidate. The victorious candidate then addresses the convention and a nation-wide television audience either that evening or the following evening. On the fourth evening the Vice President is nominated and makes an acceptance speech.

Prime-time convention coverage in 1968 by the three networks consisted of 90 hours; by 1992 it was down to less than 30. In 1984 the networks dropped gavel-to-gavel coverage in the evening and by 1992 their prime-time coverage averaged 1 to 2 hours per day. The networks reduced coverage because viewership had diminished.

If the country knows who will be nominated before the first ballot is even cast, what then is the point of holding a convention? "Our activists and leaders still need to meet with each other," Georgia Republican representative Newt Gingrich points out, to confer about "their beliefs and about the future." The public can watch television summaries of the proceedings on the networks or gavel-to-gavel coverage on C-SPAN. Conventions provide an opportunity for newspapers and magazines to comment on the direction being taken by the candidate and party.

Television coverage of the nominating and acceptance speeches is an important part of the campaign: the acceptance speech can win the confidence of the nation or destroy the campaign even before it starts. Barry Goldwater self-destructed at the Republican convention in 1964 when he told his conservative supporters that "extremism in the defense of liberty is no vice." Walter Mondale's candor at the Democratic convention held in 1984—"Taxes will go up, and anyone who says they won't is not telling the truth"—provided the Republicans with campaign ammunition.

Candidates who avoid these traps usually benefit from a "convention bounce," rising in the polls after favor-able television coverage. According to *New York Times*/CBS polls, in 1992 Bill Clinton jumped an incredible 24 points, taking a 56-to-31 percent lead over George Bush. Just after the Republican convention, Bush bounced back, cutting Clinton's lead substantially.

A party convention sets the stage not only for the general election but also for the next nomination. It gives party leaders across the nation a chance to see potential candidates in action: holding receptions, giving interviews, making speeches, and participating in platform fights. The news media may even poll delegates about their choices for the next election, establishing the field of contenders, though this technique must be taken with a grain of salt. In 1988 Bill Clinton's dull speech led pundits to dismiss him as a serious Presidential contender, yet he won the 1992 nomination.

SEE ALSO

Congressional caucus; Humphrey, Hubert H.; Jackson, Andrew; Lincoln, Abraham; Mondale, Walter F.; Roosevelt, Franklin D.; Van Buren, Martin; Wilson, Woodrow

FURTHER READING

Ceaser, James. *Presidential Selection.* Princeton, N.J.: Princeton University Press, 1979.
Chase, James S. *Emergence of the Presidential Nominating Convention, 1789–1832.* Urbana: University of Illinois Press, 1973.
Davis, James. *National Conventions in an Age of Party Reform.* Westport, Conn.: Greenwood, 1983.

Oath of office

THE CONSTITUTION (Article 2, Section 1) provides that before assuming office the President must take the following oath or affirmation: "I do solemnly swear (or affirm) that I will faithfully execute the office of President of the United States, and will, to the best of my ability,

William McKinley takes the oath of office in 1901.

preserve, protect and defend the Constitution of the United States."

George Washington added the words "so help me God" at the first inauguration, a practice followed by all his successors. He took the oath with his left hand on a Bible and his right hand raised toward heaven. Although the Constitution does not require that the oath be taken on a Bible, most other Presidents have done so. The Bible is always opened to a passage, and no two Presidents have chosen the same one. Franklin Pierce was the only President to affirm rather than swear his oath.

Usually, the President takes the oath in the public inaugural ceremony. However, when the Presidential term begins on a Sunday, it is the custom to delay the inauguration until Monday. In that case the President takes the oath of office privately at noon on Sunday and repeats it at the inauguration the next day.

The Constitution does not specify who administers the oath. At George Washington's inauguration the oath was administered by the chief justice of New York State, Robert R. Livingston, because the Supreme Court had not yet

been appointed. Since the inauguration of John Adams, it has been the custom for the oath to be administered by the chief justice of the United States at all regular inaugurations.

However, federal judges, magistrates, state judges, and even a notary public have administered oaths when Vice Presidents assumed the Presidency after the sudden death of the incumbent. Only three of nine men who succeeded to the Presidency because of death or resignation took their oath from the chief justice of the United States.

Some Presidents have argued that the oath confers a responsibility on the President not otherwise mentioned in the Constitution to cease the "faithful execution of the law" if he believes such a law to be unconstitutional. Andrew Jackson, in his message to Congress vetoing the Second Bank of the United States, argued that he had a right to refuse to enforce laws or judicial decisions if he did not believe them to be constitutional. He claimed that this duty was required by his oath of office. President Abraham Lincoln justified his use of emergency powers during the Civil

War by referring to his oath to "preserve, protect, and defend the Constitution." President Andrew Johnson, during his impeachment trial, also argued that the President need not execute laws he deemed unconstitutional.

SEE ALSO
Inauguration, Presidential

Office of Administration

THE OFFICE of Administration is the unit of the Executive Office of the President that handles housekeeping functions for the White House Office, including payroll and accounting, central purchasing, and the law and general reference libraries. Its Reference Center, with access to government and commercial computer databases, provides the President and White House staff with background research under deadline pressures.

The office trains White House aides in the use of computers and has equipped more than 1,100 White House staffers and members of the Executive Office of the President with personal computers. Its OASIS system software provides electronic mail, calendar and time management software, and access to wire services and databases using modems, and it allows staffers to fax documents from their computers. It does not store documents centrally, nor does it handle classified and top secret information.

In the early 1990s the system was organized around three minicomputers in the data center named Chip, Dale, and Opus, with backup memory units named Bugs and Daffy. The OASIS network is connected to *Air Force One,* the President's airplane, via satellite. All White House computers with the exception of the one used personally by the President are networked so that information can move rapidly throughout the White House Office. Because much of the system was installed in 1988, the Clinton administration replaced most of it with an advanced network of workstations and laptop computers in the first months of 1993.

SEE ALSO
Executive Office of the President; White House Office

FURTHER READING
Sullivan, Nick. "The Ultimate Home Office: The White House." *Home Office Computing,* February 1992, 44–45.

Office of Congressional Relations

ALSO KNOWN as the Congressional Liaison Office or Legislative Affairs Office, the Office of Congressional Relations (OCR) is a unit of the White House Office that assists the President in communicating with members of Congress about legislation. It also handles congressional mail and requests for information addressed to the White

Postmaster General James Farley (right) served as Franklin Roosevelt's liaison to Congress. Here, Farley holds a press conference.

House. Its offices are in the West Wing of the White House; on Capitol Hill staffers operate out of the Vice President's suite on the Senate side and the office of the leader of the President's party on the House side.

Prior to World War II, White House liaison with Congress was handled by cabinet- and subcabinet-level officials, especially those who had served in Congress. Woodrow Wilson instituted the Common Council Club, a group of 30 subcabinet officials (including Assistant Secretary of the Navy Franklin D. Roosevelt) to round up support on Capitol Hill. Roosevelt used his postmaster general, James Farley, and he reserved the position of assistant secretary of commerce for an official in charge of congressional liaison.

During World War II the War Department performed liaison for the Roosevelt administration, with more than 200 officers assigned to its Legislation and Liaison Division. The Bureau of the Budget's Legislative Reference Division also lobbied in Congress. After the war the newly created Department of Defense established an assistant secretary for congressional liaison, the Department of State named an assistant secretary for congressional relations, and between 1949 and 1963 the other departments followed suit, assigning more than 500 officials to these units.

Departmental liaison offices were supervised by White House aides. Dwight Eisenhower created the first such formal unit in the White House Office. John F. Kennedy retained the unit. Richard Nixon, who named the office the Office of Congressional Relations, organized it into Senate and House divisions. President Jimmy Carter also relied on Vice President Walter Mondale, a former senator. Presidents George Bush and Bill Clinton used Vice Presidents Dan Quayle and Albert Gore in the same capacity.

SEE ALSO
Executive Office of the President

FURTHER READING
Bond, Jon R., and Richard Fleisher, eds. Polarized Politics: *Congress and the President in a Partisan Era.* Washington, D.C.: Congressional Quarterly, 2000.
Fisher, Louis. *Constitutional Conflicts Between Congress and the President.* 4th ed. rev. Lawrence: University Press of Kansas, 1997.
Hersman, Rebecca K. C. *Friends and Foes: How Congress and the President Really Make Foreign Policy.* Washington, D.C.: Brookings Institution, 2000.
Huitt, Ralph K. "White House Channels to the Hill." In *Congress against the President,* edited by Harvey C. Mansfield, Sr. New York: Academy of Political Science, 1975.
Manley, John. "Presidential Power and White House Lobbying." *Political Science Quarterly* 93, no. 2 (Summer 1978): 255–75.
Pyle, Christopher H., and Richard M. Pious, eds. *The President, Congress, and the Constitution: Power and Legitimacy in American Politics.* New York: Free Press, 1984.

Office of Government Ethics

THE OFFICE of Government Ethics oversees ethical standards for the White House Office, the Executive Office of the President, and for the executive branch departments. It was created by the Ethics in Government Act of 1978. The director is appointed by the President with the advice and consent of the Senate for a five-year term. Every two years the director submits to Congress a report about implementation of ethics laws.

The Office of Government Ethics develops rules and regulations regarding standards of conduct, identification of conflicts of interest, and financial disclosure in consultation with the attorney general and the Office of Personnel Management. They are officially promulgated by the President, and the Office of Government Ethics then supervises compliance by providing government officials with advisory letters and formal advisory opinions that deal with their particular situations.

SEE ALSO

Ethics, Presidential; Executive Office of the President; White House Office

FURTHER READING

Eastland, Terry. *Energy in the Executive: The Case for the Strong Presidency.* New York: Free Press, 1992.

Office of Management and Budget

THE OFFICE of Management and Budget (OMB) prepares the Budget of the United States, which constitutes the President's annual budget request to Congress. It was created as the Bureau of the Budget (BOB) by the Budget and Accounting Act of 1921. Originally located in the Treasury Department, the BOB was moved to the Executive Office of the President in 1939 and renamed the Office of Management and Budget in 1970.

The OMB has 500 or so professional staff members. Its Budget Division prepares the Budget of the United States and drafts of the President's annual budget message. It also reviews and revises the congressional testimony of department secretaries when they request funds from the appropriations committees. Once Congress has appropriated funds, the OMB controls the rate of spending by departments through a system of quarterly allotments. It can also recommend to the President that he defer spending to future years or even rescind scheduled spending—both actions that require ultimate approval by Congress. It can order the reprogramming of funds (transferring money from one activity to another) within an agency or across agency lines.

The OMB's Management Division suggests to department secretaries ways for the departments to be run more efficiently. Its Division of Federal Procurement Policy recommends ways of cutting purchasing costs. Its Legislative Division performs a legislative clearance function: it reviews all requests by departments to Congress for new legislation and decides if such requests should become "part of the President's program" (bills that the President personally endorses), "in accordance with the program of the President" (merely acceptable to the White House), or should be blocked as "not in accord with the program of the President." It reviews all legislation passed by Congress within five days and advises the President on whether these "enrolled bills" should be signed or vetoed. Finally, the OMB Division of Information and Regulatory Affairs reviews all regulations proposed by departments to see if they are consistent with the President's policies and should go into effect, a system known as regulatory clearance.

Until the 1970s the Bureau of the Budget was committed to the concept of "neutral competence." This meant that its career civil servants would provide expert advice to a succession of Presidents from both parties and would work dispassionately for the President's goals, whether liberal or conservative. The BOB's first director, Charles Dawes, established the rule that "the Budget Bureau must be impartial, impersonal, and nonpolitical."

President Richard Nixon preferred a partisan and political operation. He reorganized the BOB into the Office of Management and Budget. He installed the OMB director in the West Wing of the White House with other senior political advisers. Political appointees, called program associate directors, were placed over career civil servants to make the agency more responsive to Presidential politics. A majority of the division managers and their top-ranking aides soon left, reducing the OMB's expertise. Presidents Gerald Ford, Jimmy Carter, Ronald Reagan, and George Bush all appointed key political advisers as OMB directors, reducing to some extent the competence of the agency in forecasting expenditures and consequently reducing its influence with Congress as well.

SEE ALSO

Budget, Presidential; Executive Office of the President; Impoundment

FURTHER READING

Berman, Larry. *The Office of Management and Budget, 1921–1979.* Princeton, N.J.: Princeton University Press, 1979.

Mosher, Frederic C. *A Tale of Two Agencies: A Comparative Analysis of the General Accounting Office and the Office of Management and Budget.* Baton Rouge: Louisiana State University Press, 1984.

Tomkin, Shelley Lynne. *Inside OMB: Politics and Process in the President's Budget Office.* Armonk, N.Y.: M. E. Sharpe, 1998.

Office of Science and Technology Policy

THE OFFICE of Science and Technology Policy (OSTP) is a unit of the Executive Office of the President whose director serves as the principal scientific adviser to the President. The office was established by the National Science and Technology Policy, Organization, and Priorities Act of 1976 to advise the President on scientific and technological matters; evaluate the scale, quality, and effectiveness of national government policies in science and technology; and advise the President on proposed funding for scientific research and development. The agency also prepares reports on science and

technology that are mandated by Congress. The agency coordinates its work with the Office of Management and Budget and helps prepare those parts of the federal budget that deal with science and technology, such as the space program.

The director of the Office of Science and Technology Policy chairs the cabinet-level Federal Coordinating Council for Science, Engineering, and Technology, which uses task forces of government officials to recommend policies to promote more effective planning for federal scientific, engineering, and technology programs that affect more than a single federal agency or department.

The President's Council of Advisers on Science and Technology is a group of nongovernment scientists who provide the President with independent advice so that he is not entirely reliant on the director of the OSTP in formulating policy.

SEE ALSO

Decision making, Presidential; Executive Office of the President; Office of Management and Budget

FURTHER READING

Technology and Economic Performance: Organizing the Executive Branch for a Stronger National Technology Base. New York: Carnegie Commission on Science, Technology, and Government, 1991.

The Office of Science and Technology Policy makes recommendations to the President about funding for scientific research at American universities.

Office of U.S. Trade Representative

THE OFFICE of U.S. Trade Representative is a unit of the Executive Office of the President that develops the United States's policies on international trade. Created by an executive order of President John F. Kennedy in 1963, the office is headed by the U.S. trade representative, a cabinet-level officer with the rank of ambassador, who reports directly to the President.

The U.S. trade representative is the chief representative of the United States for all activities concerning the General Agreement on Tariffs and Trade (GATT), an international agreement subscribed to by most nations, including negotiations on future GATT tariff adjustments. The trade representative negotiates with the Organization for Economic Cooperation and Development (OECD), a 24-nation organization of advanced industrial nations, when the OECD takes up trade and agricultural commodity issues. The trade representative also serves as a member of the boards of directors of the Export-Import Bank (which makes low-cost loans to foreign purchasers) and the Overseas Private Investment Corporation (which insures overseas private investments) and serves on the National Advisory Council for International Monetary and Financial Policy.

The Omnibus Trade and Competitiveness Act of 1988 gave the trade representative authority to implement sanctions against foreign nations that have not abided by the principles of free trade stated in international trade agreements with the United States. The threat of sanctions provides the trade representative with a negotiating tool that is used for "managed trade" agreements with nations that export more to the United States than they import from this country.

SEE ALSO

Executive Office of the President

FURTHER READING

Tyson, Ann Scott. "U.S. Ambassador Hides Steel Behind Silk Scarves." *Christian Science Monitor,* Apr. 30, 1999, p. 1.

Oval Office

THE OVAL OFFICE is the informal name for the President's office in the West Wing of the White House. The original Oval Office was located in the center of the West Wing when it was constructed in 1909. The office was moved to the southeast corner of the West Wing in 1934, during the Presidency of Franklin D. Roosevelt, when the wing was renovated. It opens onto the Rose Garden and faces the rear lawn.

The Presidential office is oval in shape. Its exterior wall holds a large bay window with steel sash frames and

Lyndon Johnson at work in the Oval Office.

bulletproof glass panes. The bay window allows the office to be flooded with southern sun through much of the day. The ceiling is decorated with a medallion of the Presidential seal. The United States and Presidential flags are located behind the President's desk. Near the fireplace is a seating area for casual conversation.

The name Oval Office came into general use during Richard Nixon's administration. It is also used by reporters as a substitute for the name of the President, as in "the Oval Office has decided…" The White House Historical Association began referring to the Oval Office rather than the President's Office in 1973.

SEE ALSO
White House

Pardon power

THE CONSTITUTION (Article 2, Section 2) grants the President the power to reprieve and pardon individuals who have committed crimes or other offenses against the United States. A reprieve is a temporary postponement of a court's sentence, designed to give the President time to consider a request for a pardon or a reduction of the sentence. A pardon stops any further criminal judicial process from proceeding and, in effect, makes a "new person" of the offender. Amnesty is a pardon granted to a class of offenders. In the case *Ex parte Garland* (1867) the Supreme Court said of a pardon that "in the eye of the law the offender is as innocent as if he had never committed the offense." A pardon restores to the offender all civil and political rights.

The framers of the Constitution gave the President the pardon power to prevent miscarriages of justice and also to provide the President with a way to end treasonous activities such as rebellion.

The President may not use the pardon power to overrule the impeachment process. Indeed, if the President used a pardon to prevent the execution of the laws, that would constitute an impeachable offense, according to Chief Justice William Howard Taft in *Ex parte Grossman* (1925). Any conditions that a President attaches to a pardon issued to an individual are subject to review by the Supreme Court. In two cases, *Ex parte Garland* and *Klein* v. *United States* (1872), the Supreme Court ruled that the pardon power could not be regulated by congressional legislation, leaving the judiciary itself as the only check on the pardon power.

Pardons are administered by the Department of Justice. The attorney general provides the President with recommendations about pardons. The attorney general, in turn, relies on the department's Office of Pardon Attorney.

After Thomas Jefferson assumed the Presidency in 1801, he pardoned members of the Democratic Societies, most of them his political supporters, who had been convicted of violating the Alien and Sedition Acts of 1798. At the end of the Civil War, President Andrew Johnson proclaimed amnesty for most Confederate soldiers and pardoned Jefferson Davis, President of the Confederate States of America. He also pardoned Dr. Samuel Mudd, the doctor who set John Wilkes Booth's broken leg after Booth assassinated Abraham Lincoln. In 1921 President Warren G. Harding issued a pardon to labor organizer and Socialist party leader Eugene V. Debs for antiwar organizing with only one condition: Debs had to travel to Washington and meet Harding in person to receive his pardon. In 1971 President Richard Nixon commuted the prison

Socialist leader Eugene Debs was pardoned by Warren Harding on Christmas Day 1921 after he had served 2½ years in prison for obstructing the draft during World War I.

Gerald Ford appears before the House Judiciary Committee to answer questions about his pardon of Richard Nixon.

term of a former president of the Teamsters Union, Jimmy Hoffa, on condition that Hoffa take no further part in union activities.

The most unpopular pardon was issued by Gerald Ford to his predecessor, Richard Nixon, in 1974 for all offenses against the United States that he had committed "or may have committed or taken part in." These offenses involved the obstruction of justice in the Watergate scandal of 1972, because of which Nixon resigned his office. Ford's public approval rating nose-dived from 71 to 49 percent within a week after he issued the pardon. His press secretary resigned in protest, and the pardon probably cost Ford the Presidential election of 1976. He appeared before the House Judiciary Committee to answer questions about the pardon, claiming "there never was at any time any agreement whatsoever concerning a pardon to Mr. Nixon if he were to resign and I were to become President." Ford insisted that he had issued the pardon to Nixon to end "the long national nightmare" of Watergate. By a 55-to-24 vote, the Senate passed a resolution opposing pardons for other Watergate conspirators.

President Ronald Reagan did not offer pardons to any of those accused of violating federal laws in the Iran-Contra affair, but near the end of his term President George Bush pardoned six participants, including Caspar Weinberger, former defense secretary. Some critics charged that President Bush had pardoned Weinberger in order to prevent testimony or the introduction of evidence at the trial that might have implicated Bush directly in the cover-up. The independent counsel for Iran-Contra prosecutions, Lawrence Walsh, condemned the Presidential pardon, charging that "the Iran-Contra cover-up, which has continued for more than six years, has now been completed."

SEE ALSO

Amnesty, Presidential; Bush, George; Ford, Gerald R.; Nixon, Richard M.; Reagan, Ronald; Watergate investigation

FURTHER READING

Adler, David Gray. "The President's Pardon Power." In *Inventing the American Presidency*, edited by Thomas Cronin. Lawrence: University Press of Kansas, 1989.

Patronage, Presidential

PRESIDENTIAL PATRONAGE is the giving of appointments or other considerations to members of Congress and state political party leaders to increase the President's influence with them. Initially, there were few Presidential appointments, and President George Washington named his revolutionary war colleagues to these posts. Thomas Jefferson used appointments to build up the new state parties. "No duty the President had to perform was so trying as to put the right man in the right place," he observed.

Andrew Jackson established the principle of "rotation in office," by which he meant that when a new party took over the White House, the President would appoint new officeholders in the bureaucracy, not just the cabinet. These appointments were designed to build up the Democratic party that Jackson had created. Senator William Marcy of New York, in a speech delivered to the Senate in January 1832, observed that the Jacksonians "see nothing wrong in the rule that to the victors belong the spoils of the enemy." Postal routes and postmasterships were awarded to local politicians in Jackson's party. The collectors of the ports, collectors of fees, Indian agents, and other federal officials were usually well connected to state parties or Jackson's congressional supporters.

This cartoon by Thomas Nast supports civil service reform to prevent government officials from giving jobs to their political supporters.

Abraham Lincoln relied on patronage to secure passage of the 13th Amendment, which outlawed slavery. Benjamin Harrison and William McKinley used patronage to pass tariffs, and McKinley used it to assure Senate approval of the Treaty of Paris. William Howard Taft denied patronage to members of his party who refused to support his legislative program, which infuriated them and led to a split within the Republican party.

No President can afford to ignore the patronage demands of his party. Postmaster General Albert Burleson advised President Woodrow Wilson that "these little offices mean a great deal to the Senators and Representatives in Congress. . . . If they are turned down, they will hate you and will not vote for anything you want." Franklin Roosevelt used patronage to win support for crucial military preparedness legislation prior to the attack at Pearl Harbor.

President Dwight Eisenhower acted as if he were above the pettiness of party politics, but actually he was very much involved. He came out of a cabinet meeting one day and wrote in his diary, "Everything seems to have been patronage this morning." Lyndon Johnson used patronage to cement a relationship with the opposition party. By taking care of the patronage requests made by Senate minority leader Everett Dirksen, Johnson won crucial Republican votes for his Civil Rights Act of 1964 and his Voting Rights Act of 1965.

SEE ALSO
Appointment power

FURTHER READING
Wilson, Woodrow. *Congressional Government.* New York: Meridian, 1956.

Perks, Presidential

PRESIDENTS RECEIVE perks that entitle them to special extensions of power. Certain luxuries, such as the fully staffed White House residence, Camp David retreat, *Air Force One,* and Presidential helicopters and limousines, are provided as much to symbolize Presidential power as to facilitate the conduct of official business. In addition to their salaries, Presidents receive generous expense accounts to pay for official entertaining and travel, and they retire with a pension and a government-funded office and staff. Former Presidents and their spouses are also entitled to Secret Service protection. Recent Presidents have all established Presidential libraries to house their papers and to commemorate the accomplishments of their administrations. Although con-

The John F. Kennedy Library and Museum, in Boston, is the nation's official monument to President Kennedy.

structed with private money, the libraries are maintained by the federal government under the jurisdiction of the National Archives and Records Administration.

Physician to the President

FROM GEORGE Washington's administration through Andrew Jackson's, Presidents used their own doctors, who brought in specialists when necessary. Jackson and many of his successors, especially after the Civil War, relied on military physicians, who provided care to the First Family without charge.

In modern times Presidents have used a combination of private and military doctors. The President's personal doctor and several military assistants and nurses form the White House Medical Unit. Their facilities include a medical suite in the White House itself and facilities in the Executive Office Building, where there is also a dental suite.

The President has medical checkups and is treated for illness at Walter Reed Army Hospital or Bethesda Naval Medical Center. When the President travels, a doctor is part of his entourage and an emergency medical unit is available at all times. A blood supply for the President is always available at a local hospital, and an ambulance is often stationed near the most convenient exit from the place where the President is staying.

SEE ALSO

Disability, Presidential; Health, Presidential; Succession to the Presidency

FURTHER READING

Gilbert, Robert E. *The Mortal Presidency.* New York: Basic Books, 1992.

Wiegele, Thomas C. "Presidential Physicians and Presidential Health Care." *Presidential Studies Quarterly* 20 (Winter 1990): 71–89.

Pierce, Franklin
14TH PRESIDENT

☆ *Born: Nov. 23, 1804, Hillsborough, N.H.*
☆ *Political party: Democrat*
☆ *Education: Bowdoin College, B.A., 1824*
☆ *Military service: New Hampshire Volunteers, 1846–48*
☆ *Previous government service: New Hampshire House of Representatives, 1829–33; U.S. House of Representatives, 1834–36; U.S. Senate, 1837–42; U.S. attorney for New Hampshire, 1842–46*
☆ *Elected President, 1852; served, 1853–57*
☆ *Died: Oct. 8, 1869, Concord, N.H.*

FRANKLIN PIERCE's Presidency was marked by family tragedy. Two months before Pierce assumed office, his son Benjamin was killed in a railroad accident. Mrs. Pierce did not attend her husband's inauguration, and she secluded herself in the White House for two years. She wore black mourning clothes each day and refused to take part in Washington life. Distracted by his wife's grief, Pierce was an ineffectual leader in domestic and foreign affairs.

Franklin Pierce was the son of Benjamin Pierce, a revolutionary war hero who was twice elected governor of New Hampshire. Franklin attended Bowdoin College, where he became friendly with Nathaniel Hawthorne, who later wrote his biography. At age 23 he became a lawyer and began his own spectacular rise in state Democratic politics, becoming speaker of the state legislature at age 26. He then served several terms in Congress, where he strongly

supported the policies of President Andrew Jackson, especially the veto of the national bank. He became a U.S. senator at age 36. Pierce served in the Mexican-American War as a brigadier general of volunteers from his state under the overall command of General Winfield Scott and was injured at the Battle of Contreras when he fell off his horse. He returned to his New Hampshire law practice at the end of the war.

Pierce was a dark-horse contender for the Democratic nomination in 1852. The convention deadlocked between leading candidates James Buchanan and Lewis Cass, and Pierce was the convention's compromise choice on the 49th ballot. He defeated General Scott, who had won the Whig nomination, by a large margin, in a campaign that emphasized sectional unity. His sweep of states (he lost just four) was the greatest landslide since the election of James Monroe. It began the disintegration of the Whig party. At age 48, Pierce had capped his political career by becoming the youngest President up to that time.

Pierce tried to give the South a major role in his administration by appointing Jefferson Davis from Mississippi as his secretary of war and a coalition of Southern planters and Northern financiers to his cabinet, none of whom wished to push the abolitionist cause. Pierce and the cabinet agreed on most issues: he made not a single change of personnel during his entire term.

Pierce used federal law enforcement to implement the Fugitive Slave Act, which required federal and state officials to assist slave owners in recovering slaves who had fled to free states in the North. He encouraged the construction of transcontinental railroads to bind the nation together, and the Gadsden Purchase from Mexico (for $10 million) was made with a new southern rail link in mind. In 1854 Pierce signed the Kansas-Nebraska Act, establishing new territorial governments and ending the Missouri Compromise. It provided that when the Kansas and Nebraska territories applied for statehood, their citizens would determine whether or not the state would be free or slave. Soon Kansas was in flames as pro-slavery "border ruffians" and fiery abolitionists such as John Brown fought over its future.

Pierce blundered in foreign affairs. He believed that territorial expansion might be a way to unite North and South. In his inaugural address he hinted at his goal of annexing Cuba, and he even had his Vice President take his inaugural oath on that island. Pierce instructed the U.S. ministers to Spain, Great Britain, and France to meet in Ostend, Belgium, to prepare recommendations about the possible purchase of Cuba from Spain. Their memorandum to Pierce, known as the Ostend Manifesto, proposed to offer the Spanish up to $110 million, but it advocated an invasion to seize the island if the Spanish refused to sell. The secret dispatch was leaked to Whig newspapers, causing great embarrassment to the administration and aborting diplomatic efforts for the sale.

Pierce was more successful in opening Japan to foreign trade through the expedition of Commodore Matthew Perry in 1853. In 1856 Pierce recognized

Franklin Pierce and Senator Stephen Douglas are shown forcing a black man down the throat of an antislavery settler from Kansas. The cartoon blames Pierce and the Democrats for the bloody fighting in Kansas after the Kansas-Nebraska Act was passed.

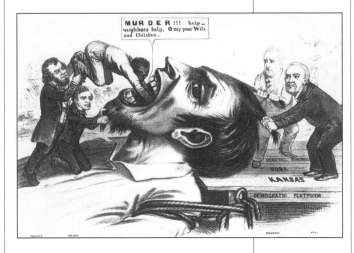

A portrait of Commodore Matthew Perry by a Japanese artist. Pierce sent Perry to Japan in 1853 to establish trade relations.

a dictatorship in Nicaragua established by William Walker, an American who had taken over that nation by force and had begun to introduce slavery as a prelude to having Nicaragua apply for admission to the Union as a slave state. Although an expansionist, Pierce rejected Hawaii's application to join the Union, though he agreed to a request by King Kamehameha to place the islands under U.S. protection from European powers seeking conquest or trade concessions.

Because of his domestic and foreign policy blunders, Pierce was ignored at the Democratic convention of 1856, and he returned to Concord, New Hampshire. During the Civil War he gained local notoriety by opposing the policies of the Republican party and claiming that the Emancipation Proclamation was unconstitutional.

SEE ALSO
Buchanan, James

FURTHER READING
Gara, Larry. *The Presidency of Franklin Pierce.* Lawrence: University Press of Kansas, 1991.
Nichols, Roy Franklin. *Franklin Pierce: Young Hickory of the Granite Hills.* Philadelphia: University of Pennsylvania Press, 1958.

Pocket veto

THE POCKET veto is the power of the President to veto a bill sent to him within the 10-day period prior to congressional adjournment, without any possibility of a congressional override. The Constitution (Article 1, Section 7) provides that if Congress passes a bill and sends it to the President, he has 10 days in which to veto the bill and return it with his objections. But if Congress adjourns within that 10-day period, the President cannot return the bill with a

veto message and any bill that has already been sent to the President is automatically vetoed unless he decides to sign it into law. The end-of-session pocket veto (named for the practice of putting the bill in the President's pocket until Congress adjourns) cannot be overridden by a two-thirds vote of each chamber; it is irreversible. The President sends no message to Congress indicating his objections to the measure, nor does he return the bill to either chamber for further action. A new bill must be introduced and go through the entire legislative process.

In the *Pocket Veto Case* (1929), the Supreme Court decided that "adjournment" meant not only end-of-session adjournments but could also mean recesses, or district work periods, within a congressional session. The key issue was not whether Congress intended to return but whether its absence prevented return of the bill within the designated 10-day period.

Presidents have sometimes abused the pocket veto. They have killed measures when Congress adjourned or recessed for short periods, even when Congress intended to return within 10 days and could easily have received the President's regular veto message. Both Presidents Richard Nixon and Gerald Ford used the pocket veto during interim adjournments of a few days during a session of Congress—Nixon to kill a health care bill and Ford to veto vocational rehabilitation, farm labor, and wildlife refuge measures. Congress responded to this misuse of the pocket veto by designating officers in each chamber to receive veto messages from the President, thereby attempting to retain the ordinary veto system. In the 1970s Senate leaders began the practice of waiting until Congress returned from short recesses before sending bills it had passed to the White House in order to avoid the entire issue.

In 1974 the U.S. Court of Appeals for Washington, D.C., ruling in *Kennedy v. Sampson,* barred the President's use of the pocket veto during short congressional recesses, provided an officer was appointed by Congress to receive an ordinary Presidential veto message.

SEE ALSO

Checks and balances; Veto power

FURTHER READING

U.S. Congress. Senate. Committee on the Judiciary. Subcommittee on Separation of Powers. *Constitutionality of the President's Pocket Veto Power.* 92nd Cong., 1st sess., 1971.

Vose, Clement. "The Memorandum Pocket Veto." *Journal of Politics* 26, no. 2 (May 1964): 397–405.

Polk, James K.
11TH PRESIDENT

☆ *Born: Nov. 2, 1795, Mecklenburg County, N.C.*
☆ *Political party: Democrat*
☆ *Education: University of North Carolina, B.A., 1818*
☆ *Military service: none*
☆ *Previous government service: Tennessee House of Representatives, 1823–25; U.S. House of Representatives, 1825–39; Speaker of the House, 1835–39; governor of Tennessee, 1839–40*
☆ *Elected President, 1844; served, 1845–49*
☆ *Died: June 15, 1849, Nashville, Tenn.*

JAMES K. POLK was a Jacksonian Democrat whose expansionist policies led to the Mexican-American War and the acquisition of vast territories in the Southwest. He was the first President to decline to seek a second term.

Polk was born on a small farm on the North Carolina frontier. His father became a large landowner in Tennessee and Polk was able to attend college. Two years after graduating he began to practice law in Columbia, Tennessee.

Polk began his political career by serving with Andrew Jackson in the Tennessee legislature, and later he was the leading spokesman in Congress for the Jackson administration, serving as majority leader of the Democrats and chair of the powerful Ways and Means Committee. He was elected Speaker in 1835. He helped to secure the repeal of the Second Bank of the United States, earning the name Young Hickory because of his support for the President, Old Hickory. In 1839 he won election as governor of Tennessee but was defeated in the 1841 and 1843 elections.

Polk made a political comeback in Presidential politics in 1844. He favored the annexation of the independent nation of Texas and negotiations with Great Britain to acquire territory in the Northwest, which later became known as the Oregon Territory. He received Jackson's support over John Tyler, who opposed annexing Texas. Polk was the Democratic party's first dark horse, or unknown nominee, winning in a sectional compromise on the ninth ballot. The word was sent from Baltimore to the capital by telegraph—the first use by a political party of Samuel F. B. Morse's new invention—and the recipients thought the machine was not working because it seemed so improbable that Polk was the nominee.

In the Presidential election Polk's rival, Whig candidate Henry Clay, exclaimed, "Who is James K. Polk?" The Democrats took up the question as a defiant campaign slogan, and in a fierce campaign Polk defeated Clay, receiving 49.6 percent of the popular vote to Clay's 48.1. At age 49 he was the youngest person yet to serve as President.

Polk's Presidency was distinguished by its expansionist policies. Polk claimed it was the "manifest destiny" of the nation to expand from the Atlantic to the Pacific. He added more territory to the

Union than any President except Thomas Jefferson. His quiet diplomacy secured an 1846 boundary agreement with Great Britain that settled the northern borders of the United States along the 49th parallel; the United States and Britain each gave up about half their claims. His policy was more warlike in the Southwest. Even before Polk's inauguration, his predecessor, John Tyler, claimed that the election was a mandate to annex Texas, and he supported a joint resolution of Congress to start the procedure. Texas entered the Union in December 1845, which caused Mexico to sever diplomatic relations with the United States. Polk's attempts to buy California and disputed Texas territory from Mexico for $25 million were rebuffed: the Mexicans would not permit U.S. envoys to present their proposal. In late 1845 Polk ordered 3,000 U.S. troops under the command of Zachary Taylor into a disputed border area between the Rio Grande and Rio Nueces in the state of Texas.

On May 9, 1846, Polk laid before his cabinet a proposal for a declaration of war, on the grounds that Mexico had refused to receive his envoy and had refused to pay damage claims for losses of U.S. lives and property. Just that evening, word reached the capital that there had been a skirmish between Mexican and U.S. forces that had resulted in death or injury to 16 U.S. soldiers. Polk had Congress declare war on May 13, 1846, saying that Mexican forces had "invaded our territory and shed American blood upon the American soil." In fact, the events occurred in disputed territory after U.S. forces trained their cannons on the town square of Matamoros.

The war was a military success: General Winfield Scott captured Mexico City on September 14, 1847, while Colonel Stephen Kearny took control of New Mexico and California. The Treaty of Guadalupe Hidalgo, signed February

At the "American Hotel," citizens read news of the Mexican-American War. Polk went to war to expand the boundaries of the nation and won control of California and New Mexico.

2, 1848, ended the war. The United States took possession of the Mexican provinces of Upper California and New Mexico, and the two countries established a border at the Rio Grande in Texas. Polk agreed to pay Mexico $15 million for the territories and also to pay $3,250,000 in claims made by U.S. citizens against Mexico. Nevertheless, the treaty was unpopular with abolitionists in the North, who saw it as a way to extend slavery. Ulysses S. Grant, who served in the war, called it "one of the most unjust ever waged by a stronger against a weaker nation." Abraham Lincoln, a Whig member of Congress at the time, devoted his first speech in the House of Representatives to criticizing Polk's decision, saying that Mexico "was in no way molesting or menacing the United States." Needless to say, the Mexicans have never forgotten Polk for taking away half their nation. In 1848 Polk's effort to buy Cuba for $100 million was rejected by Spain.

In domestic policy, Polk secured passage of the Walker Tariff Act of 1846, which reduced tariffs, or taxes on imported products, and thus fulfilled a campaign promise popular in the South and among farmers. He later blocked the Whig programs of high tariffs, federally funded internal improvements, and a national bank, which the Whigs proposed when they took control of Congress in the midterm elections of 1846. Polk also vetoed measures to use federal funds to improve rivers and harbors.

Polk alienated the antislavery faction of his party with his Mexican policy. He opposed the Wilmot Proviso, a congressional measure intended to bar slavery from the territories newly conquered from Mexico but that failed to pass. His own idea to extend the Missouri Compromise line west and bar slavery below the 36th parallel was ignored. Congress was unable to pass laws governing the new territories because of the slavery issue. Polk was exhausted from his efforts to hold his party together and fend off the Whig majority in Congress, and decided not to seek a second term. His last message to Congress spoke of an "abundance of gold" in California, setting off the gold rush of 1849. Polk died during a cholera epidemic shortly after leaving office.

SEE ALSO

Jackson, Andrew; Tyler, John; Van Buren, Martin

FURTHER READING

Bergeron, Paul H. *The Presidency of James K. Polk.* Lawrence: University Press of Kansas, 1987.
Sellers, Charles Greer. *James K. Polk, Continentalist, 1843–1846.* Princeton, N.J.: Princeton University Press, 1966.

Polls, Presidential

SEE Public opinion, Presidents, and the media

Postmodern Presidency

THE POSTMODERN Presidency is a term used by some political scientists to describe the Presidential office since Jimmy Carter's administration of the late 1970s. They argue that the White House does not have the fiscal or political resources necessary to meet the President's international responsibilities. In large measure this is because of the increased relative economic strength of other industrial nations, which prevents the United States from dominating international trade and finance, and the lack of American public support for foreign aid and other international commitments.

To succeed in the White House, the President must operate in a world of increasing international interdependency rather than U.S. superiority. The President must cooperate with other nations rather than act unilaterally; he must understand the limits of U.S. economic, diplomatic, and military power and keep U.S. commitments in balance; he must obtain support in the international community for U.S. goals from other world leaders and international organizations such as the United Nations, the North Atlantic Treaty Organization, and the Group of Seven Industrialized Nations.

According to Richard Rose, a political scientist at the University of Strathclyde, Scotland, postmodern Presidents can be classified as follows: world leaders who have a strong influence on policy and have the support of the international community; vulnerable Presidents who have great policy influence but are opposed by much of the international community; isolated Presidents who have support from around the world but face opposition within the United States; and failing Presidents who have neither foreign nor domestic support.

Presidents may, during the course of their terms, fit into more than one of these categories. George Bush was a *world leader* during the Persian Gulf War because he forged an international coalition at the United Nations that voted to use force if necessary to repel Iraqi

Ronald Reagan (fourth from right) meets with other world leaders at the 1983 Summit of Industrialized Nations in Williamsburg, Virginia. The concept of the postmodern Presidency recognizes that the United States cannot isolate itself from other nations.

aggression. Members of the coalition then contributed money and armed forces to the effort. He was also a world leader in his efforts to ensure the safety of relief workers delivering food to the starving people of Somalia.

In contrast, Jimmy Carter was an *isolated President* when he tried to promote a policy of energy independence. He was unable to win public or congressional support for his initiatives and was also opposed by many foreign nations. His failure to impose serious conservation measures contributed to continued U.S. dependence on foreign oil.

Ronald Reagan was a *vulnerable President* in much of his foreign policy. He had considerable support within the United States for increased defense expenditures and development of the Star Wars antimissile system, but he lacked support from many allies for these policies. Reagan was a *global failure* in his policy of trying to overthrow the Sandinista regime in Nicaragua. His funding of the Contra opposition violated the law and was not supported by a majority of the American people.

SEE ALSO

Bush, George; Carter, Jimmy; Reagan, Ronald

FURTHER READING

Rose, Richard. *The Postmodern President.* 2nd ed. Chatham, N.J.: Chatham House, 1991.

President's Council on Physical Fitness and Sports

THE PRESIDENT's Council on Physical Fitness and Sports (PCPFS) is an advisory council, part of the Executive Office of the President, that promotes and encourages the development of physical fitness and sports programs in American life. The PCPFS was created by executive order by President Dwight Eisenhower in 1956 and was first chaired by Vice President Richard Nixon.

The PCPFS encourages schools, business and industry, government, recreation agencies, and sports organizations to increase support for activities that promote physical fitness. It has established local Councils on Physical Fitness and Sports; a Presidential Sports Award Program to encourage fitness through regular participation in sports;

the Healthy American Fitness Leader Awards, in cooperation with private industry; and the President's Challenge, a physical fitness awards program for children in the fourth through sixth grades. Each year the PCPFS recognizes outstanding school physical fitness programs in each state with special awards. Selected schools serve as demonstration sites for teacher education programs and foreign visitors. By Presidential proclamation, each May is National Physical Fitness and Sports Month, and the council prepares radio and television announcements and public service information on physical fitness during that month. It also sponsors an annual "running and fitness week" in cooperation with the American Running and Fitness Association. The PCPFS has also sponsored programs for the estimated one in six children who are "physically underdeveloped." It encourages schools to identify these children and establish programs designed specifically to improve their physical fitness and sports performance.

Twenty private citizens serve on the council. Members have included such sports celebrities as bodybuilder Arnold Schwarzenegger, basketball star Earvin ("Magic") Johnson, Olympic gold medal runner Jackie Joyner-Kersee, and tennis stars Chris Evert and Pam Shriver. They are appointed by the President and report to the President and the secretary of the Department of Health and Human Services. A full-time staff of eight carries out the programs of the council.

Actor and former body-builder Arnold Schwarzenegger served as chairman of the President's Council on Physical Fitness and Sports.

Press conferences

SEE News conferences

Press secretary

THE PRESS secretary, who is also director of the White House Press Office, is the Presidential assistant in charge of relations with the media. The title was first used in the Hoover administration.

The press secretary is the only official who "speaks for the President" to the press. The press secretary holds one or two daily briefings for correspondents in the West Terrace briefing room of the White House, during which correspondents are briefed about appointments, the President's daily schedule, upcoming travel plans, and Presidential messages and speeches. (This information is also summarized in daily news releases distributed to White House reporters.) Then the press secretary takes questions.

The Press Office issues credentials, or permission to attend White House news conferences, to about 1,500 journalists and provides office space in the West Terrace for 30 White House correspondents. Its Office of Public Liaison also provides services to newspapers and television stations across the country, including interviews with officials using the White House television studios. It prepares a "press plan" for all Presidential domestic and overseas trips to encourage favorable media coverage. It makes travel arrangements for as many as 300 reporters on major Presidential trips.

The press secretary organizes the President's news conferences and prepares briefing books for the President to study before the conference. The secretary helps the President prepare. After the conference the secretary issues corrections of any Presidential misstatements.

Pierre Salinger was one of the most successful press secretaries. A member of John Kennedy's inner circle of political advisers, he also had good rapport with the Washington press corps. Unlike many of the tall and athletic New Frontiersmen, Salinger was short, overweight, and decidedly unathletic. He joked about himself and about everyone else, but he was a consummate professional when it came to helping reporters meet their deadlines with reliable and interesting stories. He quickly became one of the most popular figures in Washington and one of the most adept at getting good press for his boss.

Press secretaries, usually former reporters, frequently have conflicts with other senior Presidential aides, often because they are not given advance notice of important Presidential decisions and then are accused by their former colleagues of deception. Press Secretary Jerry terHorst resigned from Gerald Ford's administration because he was not told in advance about Richard Nixon's pardon.

Press secretaries are often accused of trying to manipulate the media by "managing" the news. In 1985, at a summit with Soviet president Mikhail Gorbachev, Larry Speakes was concerned that President Ronald Reagan receive favorable press coverage. He made up some Presidential statements. Many months later, he admitted what he had done and apologized. But the damage had been done: in the future no one could be sure that a Presidential quote passed on by the press secretary had actually been said by the President. In recent years the person in charge of relations with the media has taken the title

Press Secretary Pierre Salinger briefs reporters during the Cuban Missile Crisis in 1962.

"director of communications," and the director's assistant is known as the press secretary.

SEE ALSO
Public opinion, Presidents, and the media; White House Office

FURTHER READING
Nelson, W. Dale. *Who Speaks for the President? The White House Press Secretary from Cleveland to Clinton.* Syracuse, N.Y.: Syracuse University Press, 1998.
Nessen, Ron. *It Sure Looks Different on the Inside.* Chicago: Playboy Press, 1978.
Powell, Jody. *The Other Side of the Story.* New York: Morrow, 1984.
Speakes, Larry. *Speaking Out: Inside the Reagan White House.* New York: Scribners, 1988.
Stephanopoulos, George. *All Too Human: A Political Education.* Boston: Back Bay, 2000.

Primaries, Presidential

PRESIDENTIAL PRIMARIES are contests held by state political parties to determine the composition of state delegations to the national nominating conventions. State election laws establish the rules for primaries: in *closed primaries* only voters registered in the state party may vote; in *open primaries* independents may also vote; in *crossover primaries* voters from any party as well as independents may participate. Turnouts in primaries are low. Through the 1970s, approximately 11 percent of the eligible voters participated; since then, the percentage has almost doubled, to 21 percent.

The first Presidential primary was held in Florida, which in 1904 created a "preference" primary that did not bind its state's convention delegates. In 1905 Governor Robert M. La Follette of Wisconsin won passage of the first state law creating a delegate-selection primary in time for the 1908 conventions. That same year Oregon adopted a "first ballot" primary that bound the state delegation to vote for the winner of the primary on the first convention ballot. North Dakota, Nebraska, Wisconsin, and New Jersey followed suit.

By 1912 a dozen states had established primaries, including California, Illinois, Maryland, Massachusetts, Michigan, and South Dakota, but many were "preference" primaries, in which voters could not only choose delegates but also express a preference for their party's nomination. Sometimes this could lead to confusing results. In Massachusetts, for instance, the state's voters selected a slate of Theodore Roosevelt supporters to go to the convention but expressed their "preference" for William Howard Taft. Ex-President Roosevelt, after losing the Republican nomination and deciding to run on the Progressive party ticket, called for a national primary that would end such anomalies and allow voters in each party to choose the Presidential nominee without the need for a convention.

As of 1916, 20 states held primaries, and President Woodrow Wilson also endorsed the idea of a national primary. But the pendulum swung in the other direction: in the 1920s, because of high costs and low voter participation, eight states dropped primaries and returned to the caucus system. Until the 1970s, between 12 and 17 states used the primary system, while the remainder used the caucus system.

Candidates could lose a majority of primaries—or not enter them—and still win their party's Presidential nomination. The list includes Woodrow Wilson and William Howard Taft in 1912, Warren Harding in 1920; Herbert Hoover in 1932; Thomas Dewey in 1948; Dwight Eisenhower in 1952; and Hubert Humphrey in 1968. Conversely, winning primaries did not ensure a contender of winning the Presidential nomination. In 1912 Theodore Roosevelt won every primary but was defeated for the Republican nomination by incumbent President William Howard Taft, primarily because Taft controlled patronage vital to state parties. In 1948 Harold Stassen won three early Republican primaries but could not derail the candidacy of Thomas Dewey.

Entering primaries enabled candidates to dispel doubts about their electability and gain the support of political bosses who controlled a majority of the convention delegates. In 1960 John F. Kennedy won primaries in Wisconsin and West Virginia, demonstrating that a Catholic could do well with Protestant voters. In 1968 Richard Nixon won enough primaries to dispel his "loser" reputation.

By 1968 primaries were held in 17 states, accounting for 37.5 percent of the Democratic and 34.3 percent of the Republican convention delegates. That year, Hubert Humphrey won the Democratic nomination without having entered a single Democratic primary. To rank-and-file Democrats, many of whom had voted for Humphrey's rivals Eugene McCarthy and Robert Kennedy, the system seemed undemocratic.

Democrats, stung by their defeat in the 1968 Presidential election, organized the Commission on Party Structure and Delegate Selection, known as the McGovern-Fraser Commission. As a result of its recommendations, six more states adopted the primary system by 1972, and another eight by 1976. There were 35 Presidential primaries by 1980 and 38 by 1992. Republican state parties followed suit.

Today, in any given election between two-thirds and three-quarters of each party's convention delegates are chosen in primaries. Even more significant, party rules require that the preferences of the voters be translated directly into election

FURTHER READING

Cook, Rhodes. *United States Presidential Primary Elections, 1968–1996: A Handbook of Election Statistics.* Washington, D.C.: Congressional Quarterly, 2000.

Davis, James W. *Presidential Primaries: Road to the White House.* Westport, Conn.: Greenwood, 1980.

Ranney, Austin. *Curing the Mischiefs of Faction: Party Reform in America.* Berkeley: University of California Press, 1975.

Shafer, Byron E. *Quiet Revolution: The Struggle for the Democratic Party and the Shaping of Post-Reform Politics.* New York: Russell Sage Foundation, 1983.

New Hampshire is always the first state to hold Presidential primaries, and Dixville Notch is traditionally the first town to report its results.

of delegates. Gone are the "preference" primaries that had no effect on the composition of the state delegation.

A string of primary victories now translates into large numbers of convention delegates committed to a candidate. Primary winners also get momentum; they receive more campaign contributions and favorable media exposure, and they rise in the public opinion polls. In 1976 Jimmy Carter went from less than 1 percent support in the polls to more than 30 percent on the basis of his victory in the New Hampshire primary.

Contenders who do poorly in early primaries find that their contributions dry up and Treasury funding for their campaign is cut off. The early primaries winnow the field down to two or three serious contenders. Then a regional grouping (such as Super Tuesday in the South, on which day six or more states hold primaries) or primaries in large states such as New York may propel one of the contenders far to the front. Since 1972, any front-runner who has emerged from the primary season with more than 41 percent of the delegates has been nominated.

SEE ALSO

Carter, Jimmy; Caucuses, Presidential nominating; Election campaigns, Presidential; Kennedy, John F.; Nixon, Richard M.; Nominating conventions, Presidential; Wilson, Woodrow

Public opinion, Presidents, and the media

IN MODERN times, Presidents have frequently found it in their interest to appeal directly to the public for support on issues. The framers of the Constitution, however, did not expect Presidents to appeal to the public or to be popular figures. They were concerned that Presidents might become "hard" demagogues, by dividing the people along class or territorial lines, or "soft" demagogues, flattering the voters in order to mislead them. The system of indirect election by the electoral college was, in part, a safeguard against a President's appealing to the people or holding himself directly accountable to the electorate.

In the 19th century, Presidents were not expected to make such appeals, and one of the articles of impeachment against President Andrew Johnson involved the charge that he had made speeches in an attempt to gain public support for his Reconstruction policies. Presidents were not expected to show up at their party's national convention to accept the nomination, nor were they expected to campaign for office. They did not give a State of the Union address to Congress but sent a detailed written message instead. They did not make political or policy speeches but stuck to vague platitudes of "civic republicanism" when addressing audiences. They had no direct dealings with the press.

The first President to depart from these practices was Theodore Roosevelt, who used the Presidency as a bully pulpit in furthering his Square Deal program and who met regularly with reporters. Woodrow Wilson revived Thomas Jefferson's practice of delivering an annual address to Congress, and he held press conferences. Wilson sent messages to Congress outlining his New Freedom legislative program, and he made three speeches and held conferences to get his ideas before the public and gain support for his program. Wilson believed that Presidential rhetoric was appropriate and did not have to be demagogic, or inflammatory, provided that it attempted to educate the public rather than simply manipulate it and provided it was for the public interest rather than partisan political advantage.

Franklin Roosevelt was the first President to use public opinion polls, taking advantage of polls already being conducted by the Department of Agriculture about support for the New Deal. He also used private pollsters under contract to the Democratic National Committee. To influence public opinion in favor of the New Deal, he used radio "fireside chats," provided movie theaters with newsreel footage of New Deal programs, and had government agencies send press releases about his programs to newspapers. He created public information offices in New Deal agencies and coordinated them through the White House Press Office.

Modern Presidents use their State of the Union addresses and special messages to Congress as media events to present their position to television audiences. Their communications directors' press secretaries provide the media with briefings and with the White House "spin" on, or interpretation of, events.

Presidents make televised addresses during crises, obtaining free time from the major networks. Occasionally, a request for free time will be rejected if it seems too partisan. Presidents are reluctant to bump popular prime-time programs, and the White House limits speeches so as not to jade its audience. Presidents also rely on pseudo-events, events staged simply for media coverage. President Ronald Reagan visited schools, where he read from Shakespeare's plays to dramatize his theme that "back to basics" was more important than more federal financial aid. Presidents Jimmy Carter and Bill Clinton held "town meetings" to discuss issues with concerned citizens.

The White House relies on pollsters to conduct public opinion surveys whose results help shape their programs. President Reagan received nightly "tracking" polls that indicated shifts in opinion on issues and support for the President.

Most Presidents have been poor media performers, ill at ease in front of cameras and the press, including Presidents Lyndon Johnson, Richard Nixon, Gerald Ford, Jimmy Carter, and George Bush. Many Presidential speeches that try to sway public opinion are unsuccessful. President Ford's speech unveiling his economic program, complete with a WIN button (standing for "Whip Inflation Now"), became a national joke. The more President Carter appealed for support for his energy program, the lower his approval ratings fell. One study by political scientists of 56 public issues showed that on only a few did Presidents sway public opinion, and then only when they were popular; otherwise, their efforts often made things worse.

At best, Presidents draw attention to problems and get the media and the public to focus on them. Sometimes they do so by their speeches and messages and sometimes by making decisions that set events in motion. But rarely do they persuade the American public; more likely, they activate opinions that already were present.

Presidents who have high public approval ratings are much more likely to hold press conferences, give speeches on issues, and pressure Congress to pass ambitious legislative programs. Popular Presidents have some persuasive ability in dealing with the public and with Congress. A popular President usually gets more support from members of his party than an unpopular President, especially on veto override votes. The proportion of Presidential requests in Congress that pass often varies directly with Presidential popularity. According to some political scientists, with every percentage point increase in public support, there is an increase in the probability that his bills will pass Congress. Unpopular Presidents are less likely to propose major new initiatives and are more likely to face restrictions on their powers by Congress. The unpopular Presidents are more likely to veto bills but are also more likely to have them overridden by Congress.

Unpopular Presidents may face renomination challenges in an election year. Such challenges caused Presidents Harry Truman and Lyndon Johnson to withdraw from the race. Presidents who win such challenges are likely to lose in the general election, the fate that befell Presidents Ford, Carter, and Bush. An unpopular President may bequeath problems to his party: every 10-point decline in the President's approval rating results, on average, in a 4-point drop in the percentage of the popular vote his party will obtain in the next Presidential election. An unpopular President drives voters away from identifying with his party; a succession of popular Presidents brings voters into the party.

SEE ALSO

Fireside chat; Messages, Presidential; News conferences; Press secretary; Reagan, Ronald; Roosevelt, Franklin D.; Roosevelt, Theodore; Speech writers; State of the Union address

FURTHER READING

Brody, Richard A. *Assessing the President: The Media, Elite Opinion, and Public Support.* Stanford, Calif.: Stanford University Press, 1992.

Edwards, George, III. *The Public Presidency: The Pursuit of Popular Support.* New York: St. Martin's, 1983.

Kernell, Samuel. *Going Public: New Strategies of Presidential Leadership.* 3rd ed. Washington, D.C.: Congressional Quarterly, 1997.

Page, Benjamin, and Robert Shapiro. *The Rational Public.* Chicago: University of Chicago Press, 1991.

Ponder, Stephen. *Managing the Press: Origins of the Media Presidency, 1897–1933.* New York: St. Martin's, 1999.

Rubin, Richard. *Press, Party, and Presidency.* New York: Norton, 1978.

Quayle, J. Danforth

VICE PRESIDENT

☆ *Born: Feb. 4, 1947, Indianapolis, Ind.*

☆ *Political party: Republican*

☆ *Education: DePauw University, B.S., 1969; Indiana University Law School, J.D., 1974*

☆ *Military service: Indiana National Guard, 1969–75*

☆ *Previous government service: chief investigator, Consumer Protection Division, Office of Indiana Attorney General, 1970–71; administrative assistant to governor of Indiana, 1971–73; director, Inheritance Tax Division, Indiana Department of Treasury, 1973–74; U.S. House of Representatives, 1977–81; U.S. Senate, 1981–89*

☆ *Vice President under George Bush, 1989–93*

DAN QUAYLE left public life to work in his family's newspaper business as

215

REAGAN, RONALD

associate publisher of the *Huntington Herald-Press* from 1974 to 1976. He returned to politics when he was elected to the U.S. House of Representatives in 1976, serving two terms. He was twice elected to the U.S. Senate from Indiana by large margins.

George Bush astonished his party and the nation by choosing Dan Quayle to be his running mate in 1988. Quayle had not been considered one of the leaders of the Senate, but his strongly conservative voting record helped Bush to solidify his base with the dominant wing of the Republican party. Press coverage was overwhelmingly negative throughout his tenure in office. Though Quayle had some accomplishments in the Senate (such as passage of an important job training bill), media coverage made it seem as if he were an intellectual lightweight.

As Vice President Quayle gathered a staff of experienced conservative intellectuals who helped him stake out his own policy positions, he lobbied with his former colleagues in the Senate for Bush's domestic program. As chair of the National Aeronautics and Space Council, he oversaw a major study on the effectiveness of the space program and was an advocate of a manned lunar landing on Mars. As chair of the White House Council on Competitiveness, he promoted deregulation of business. He also implemented a "privatization" policy whereby cities and counties might sell airports and other facilities built with federal funds to the private sector. He was considered a strong supporter of Israel and was a strong proponent of military action against Iraq after it invaded Kuwait in 1990.

Quayle played a highly visible role in the 1992 Presidential campaign, attempting to shore up the Republican party's conservative base by campaigning against "the cultural elites" of the United States. He claimed that journalists,

professors, abortion rights activists, and Hollywood television and music producers did not share the values of mainstream Americans. He attacked the television character Murphy Brown for having a child out of wedlock and thereby weakening "family values."

A majority of the American public disapproved of Quayle's divisive campaign style; in the summer of 1992 national public opinion polls put his popularity at around 20 percent, and 60 percent of the public wanted Bush to choose another running mate. His failure to spell *potato* correctly at a spelling bee (he spelled it *potatoe*) prompted the comedian Jay Leno to quip, "Maybe he should stop watching 'Murphy Brown' and start watching 'Sesame Street.'"

SEE ALSO

Bush, George

FURTHER READING

Broder, David S., and Bob Woodward. *The Man Who Would Be President: Dan Quayle.* New York: Simon & Schuster, 1992.
Fenno, Richard. *The Making of a Senator: Dan Quayle.* Washington, D.C.: Congressional Quarterly, 1989.
Rosenthal, Andrew. "Quayle's Moment." *New York Times Magazine,* July 5, 1992.

Reagan, Ronald
40TH PRESIDENT

☆ *Born: Feb. 6, 1911, Tampico, Ill.*
☆ *Political party: Republican*
☆ *Education: Eureka College, B.A., 1932*
☆ *Military service: U.S. Army Air Force, 1942–45*
☆ *Previous government service: governor of California, 1967–74*
☆ *Elected President, 1980; served, 1981–89*

RONALD WILSON REAGAN was the first actor to be elected President. He was also the oldest man ever elected and the first to have been divorced. Reagan brought conservatives to power in the Republican party and in the nation. His economic program of tax and spending cuts led to a boom between 1982 and 1987 that stimulated economic growth, but it also led to high federal budget deficits and the conversion of the United States from the largest creditor to the largest debtor in the world. His popularity declined during the Iran-Contra crisis but returned to high levels as he left office. The most popular President since Dwight Eisenhower, he was the first since Franklin Roosevelt to serve two or more full terms and hand over the office to a member of his own party.

Reagan's father worked in a shoe store and for the Works Progress Administration during the New Deal, and his mother was a store clerk. Reagan was a popular football player in high school and won election as student government president. At Eureka College he also played football, participated in student government, and joined the drama society.

After graduating from college in 1932 with a major in economics, he began his career as a radio sports announcer in Iowa. In 1937 he became a contract motion picture actor for Warner Brothers, starring in such movies as *Knute Rockne —All American, King's Row,* and *Bedtime for Bonzo.* He married actress Jane Wyman in 1940; they had two children (one adopted), then divorced in 1948.

During World War II, Reagan served as a captain in the army, making films for the military. He was elected president of the Screen Actors Guild in 1947 and served through 1952, devoting much of his time to combating the influence of communists in the union. He was active in Democratic politics, supporting Harry Truman for President in 1948 and Helen Gahagan Douglas against Richard Nixon in the California senatorial contest of 1950. In 1952 he

married Nancy Davis, a contract actress at MGM, and they had two children. Between 1954 and 1962 he was the host of the television show *General Electric Theater.* In 1959 Reagan again led the Screen Actors Guild, this time in a strike that gave actors a share in television profits from their movies.

Reagan became more conservative in the 1950s and supported the Presidential candidacies of Eisenhower in 1952 and 1956 and Nixon in 1960. He switched his voter registration to the Republican party in 1962. In October 1964 Reagan gave a televised speech for Barry Goldwater, the Republican candidate for President. After Goldwater's defeat, Reagan became one of the leading conservative spokesmen.

Reagan was twice elected governor of California, in 1966 and 1970, but for six of his eight years in office he had to work with a Democratic legislature. He cut the welfare rolls, instituted the Medi-Cal program to pay medical bills for the poor, increased income taxes in order to eliminate a projected budget deficit (but later gave rebates when the government ran a surplus), and managed to lower property taxes. He took a strong stance against student demonstrators protesting the Vietnam War who closed down many campuses of the state university system, and he more than doubled funding for California's public colleges and universities.

Reagan was a dark-horse candidate for the Republican Presidential nomination in 1968, but Nixon won the nomination on the first ballot. Reagan declined to run for a third gubernatorial term and challenged President Gerald Ford for the Republican nomination in 1976. Reagan lost the nomination by a slim margin. His followers did influence the Republican party platform, which repudiated much of Ford's foreign policy

A poster for the 1957 movie Hellcats of the Navy, *which starred Ronald Reagan and Nancy Davis. They were married five years earlier.*

of détente, or accommodation, with the Soviet Union.

In 1980 Reagan ran again for the Republican nomination, defeating George Bush handily. Reagan attempted to get ex-President Ford to join the ticket, but Ford insisted on a "co-Presidency" arrangement in which he would share responsibility for policy-making. Reagan then chose Bush to complete the ticket.

With interest rates close to 20 percent, inflation around 12 percent, and unemployment near 10 percent, the voters responded by giving Reagan a landslide victory over President Jimmy Carter and independent candidate John Anderson. Reagan's coattails brought in a Republican-controlled Senate, though the House remained strongly Democratic.

Reagan's inaugural address emphasized economic recovery and putting all Americans back to work. He called for fewer government regulations and lower taxes. Reagan's first State of the Union address offered a four-point program of reduced expenditures, tax cuts, lessened government regulation, and policies to reduce inflation.

Reagan had a "hands off" management style that involved setting overall priorities but then delegating to others the work of translating these into specific policies. He often seemed lackadaisical in his duties: "It's true that hard work never killed anybody, but why take the chance?" he would joke.

Reagan was known as the Great Communicator. No President in the 20th century, with the possible exception of Teddy and Franklin Roosevelt, could match his ability as a speech maker. He presented his arguments to the American people in the form of stories. He used concrete examples involving real people rather than abstract principles to make his points. And often the public responded to his down-to-earth analogies. The Democrats had no one who could match him, and often the President would bypass Congress and appeal directly to the people to support his conservative policies.

Eventually, Reagan's inattention to details and disinterest in economic theory would catch up with him. His budget and tax numbers never did add up. A few of his subordinates were involved in conflicts of interest that led to embarrassing investigations. In his second term, his national security advisers took advantage of his management style to launch illegal operations, then covered up their involvement by lying to Congress.

On March 30, 1981, Reagan was shot outside a hotel in Washington, D.C., by John W. Hinckley, Jr., in an attempted assassination. The President lost a great deal of blood and at one point was near death, but the bullet had not hit any vital organs and he soon recovered. His popularity soared, which helped him deal with Congress in promoting his plan, popularly known as Reaganomics. Much of what Reagan asked for was passed by Congress in June. But instead of promoting prosperity, Reaganomics took the nation into a steep recession, a time of decline in the gross national product and an increase in unemployment. As joblessness increased, Reagan's popularity plummeted, down to the levels of Nixon during the Watergate scandal.

In foreign affairs Reagan took a confrontational line with the Soviets, referring to the U.S.S.R. as the "evil empire." He announced plans to equip NATO forces in Europe with new medium-range Pershing nuclear-tipped missiles. He asked for funds to deploy a new generation of intercontinental MX missiles. He reversed President Jimmy Carter's decision to cancel the B-1 bomber and ordered development of the radar-evading Stealth bombers and fighters. He increased the size of the navy to

A campaign poster from 1980.

Ronald Reagan (right) and Soviet leader Mikhail Gorbachev sign a treaty in 1987 to gradually eliminate medium- and short-range missiles in Europe.

600 surface ships and ordered new submarines and aircraft carriers. He announced a Strategic Defense Initiative program of antimissile weapons to defend against Soviet attack, which his critics promptly dubbed Star Wars. Over five years he increased the annual level of defense spending from $200 billion to $300 billion.

Reagan equipped the government of El Salvador in its fight against leftist guerrillas and also supported the Contra rebels in their struggle against the Sandinista government of Nicaragua. He provided covert funding for anticommunist rebels in Afghanistan. He ordered the invasion of Grenada in October 1983, ostensibly to protect American medical students during disorders between two factions of the Marxist government; this action led to the replacement of the leftist government with leaders backed by the United States. Reagan also used U.S. Marines as part of an international peacekeeping force in Lebanon but withdrew the forces several months after guerrillas blew up the marine barracks, killing 241 marines in October 1983.

The economy started to revive in 1983 and with it Reagan's standing in the polls. Reagan was almost unanimously renominated in 1984 for the Presidency. He handily defeated the Democratic nominee, former Vice President Walter Mondale.

In Reagan's second term the economy continued to expand, resulting in millions of new jobs, record corporate profits, and lower inflation. Reagan adhered to the supply-side theory of economics, concentrating on stimulating the supply of goods and services. He felt that lower tax rates on producers would stimulate the economy and produce greater tax revenues, which could shrink the deficit. But the result of tax cuts turned out to be massive budget deficits: in the Reagan years the total national debt rose from $1 trillion (accumulated through 190 years of U.S. history) to $3 trillion. Moreover, the nation had entered the Reagan years with a surplus in its accounts with foreign nations but began to run large trade deficits and became a debtor nation for the first time since before World War I. The stock market rose dramatically, then dropped sharply on October 19, 1987; the Dow Jones average (of stock prices) lost a third of its value in a few days. Deregulation of financial institutions led to a savings and loan scandal, in which bank officials used poor judgment in making loans and some then engaged in criminal behavior to cover up their losses. The eventual bailout by the national government to keep the financial system stable would cost taxpayers at least $150 billion. The Tax Reform Act of 1986 reduced personal income tax rates, contributing to a great accumulation of wealth for those in the top 10 percent of the population. But the bottom fifth of the population was paying a higher percentage of their income in taxes at the end of the decade than at the beginning because of increases in Social Security taxes.

The Reagan years were marked by an increase in economic inequality, as the rich got richer much faster than others benefited. Young adults with children actually found their incomes decreasing through the decade. The percentage of Americans in poverty increased during the decade from 12 to 15 percent. Meanwhile, Reagan had won cuts in various social welfare programs for the poor: job training, Medicaid, food stamps, and welfare. Although the total amount spent on these programs increased, individuals often found their allotments cut.

During the Reagan years Republican appointments to the Supreme Court and lower federal courts gave conservatives much more influence than they had enjoyed before. Reagan appointed Supreme Court justices Sandra Day O'Connor, the first woman on the high court, and conservative law professor Antonin Scalia. The Senate rejected two of Reagan's other Supreme Court nominees, Court of Appeals judges Robert Bork and Douglas Ginsburg, but Reagan managed to gain confirmation of another federal judge, Anthony Kennedy. Reagan also promoted Associate Justice William Rehnquist to chief justice upon the retirement of Warren Burger.

In foreign affairs the defense buildup brought the Soviets to the negotiating table in a position of weakness. In 1987 the United States and the Soviet Union signed the Intermediate-Range Nuclear Forces Treaty, which provided for gradual dismantling of all Soviet and U.S.

Ronald Reagan (left) and Chief Justice Warren Burger with Sandra Day O'Connor after she was sworn in as a Supreme Court justice in 1981.

medium- and short-range missiles in Europe. Another Reagan success occurred in the Middle East: the President deterred Libya from organizing international terrorist forces when he ordered a bombing raid on Libya in 1986 in retaliation for a bombing on a disco in West Germany frequented by U.S. troops. That bombing killed 37 people, including the daughter of Libyan leader Mu'ammar Qaddafi. In 1987 Reagan used the navy to convoy Kuwaiti ships in the Persian Gulf and prevent the Iranian navy from imposing a blockade on oil tankers.

Reagan committed a major foreign policy blunder, however, that nearly destroyed his Presidency. He agreed to sell arms to Iran in a secret attempt to bolster moderates in that nation's government who were willing to free Western hostages. Some of the profits from the sales were then transferred to the Contra rebels to help fund their battle against the Nicaraguan government. The funding violated the Boland Amendment, a law passed by Congress that had cut off U.S. government funds to the Contras.

The arms sales and fund transfers were disclosed in the fall of 1986, just after the Democrats regained control of the Senate in the congressional elections. The Democrats then organized a full-scale investigation of the Iran-Contra affair. For months Reagan seemed preoccupied with the crisis and his government was paralyzed. His national security adviser, members of the NSC staff, several top White House aides, and his chief of staff resigned. There was no evidence linking Reagan directly to the transfer of funds to the Contras, but the Tower Commission, appointed by the President to study the incident, determined that national security affairs in the White House had been mismanaged. The President implemented most of the reforms in procedures suggested by the commission.

In retirement Reagan worked at his

ranch near Santa Barbara, California, gave occasional speeches, and wrote his memoirs until he was incapable of doing so because of Alzheimer's disease.

SEE ALSO

Budget, Presidential; Bush, George; Carter, Jimmy; Ford, Gerald R.; War Powers Resolution

FURTHER READING

Boyer, Paul, ed. *Reagan As President: Contemporary Views of the Man, His Politics, and His Policies.* Chicago: Ivan R. Dee, 1990.

Cannon, Lou. *President Reagan: The Role of a Lifetime.* New York: Simon & Schuster, 1991.

D'Souza, Dinesh. *Ronald Reagan: How an Ordinary Man Became an Extraordinary Leader.* New York: Free Press, 1997.

Johnson, Haynes. *Sleepwalking through History: America in the Reagan Years.* New York: Norton, 1991.

Muir, William Ker, Jr., and Robert B. Hawkins. *The Bully Pulpit: The Presidential Leadership of Ronald Reagan.* San Francisco: Institute for Contemporary Studies Press, 1992.

Thompson, Kenneth W., ed. *Leadership in the Reagan Presidency: Seven Intimate Perspectives.* Lanham, Md.: Madison Books, 1992.

Removal of the President

SEE Impeachment

Removal power

ARTICLE 2 of the Constitution, which gives the President the power to appoint government officials, does not explicitly provide the President with the power to remove officials. In *Federalist Paper* No. 77, one of a series of newspaper articles written in 1788 in support of the Constitution, Alexander Hamilton argued that the Senate's power of "advice and con-

sent" to Presidential nominations also extended to removals unless Congress legislated otherwise. But James Madison, in the 1789 congressional debates over a removal clause in the law creating the Department of Foreign Affairs, argued for an unrestricted Presidential removal power. When Congress created the War and Treasury departments, it followed Madison's argument and acknowledged the removal power of the President.

George Washington secured the resignation of Edmund Randolph as secretary of state in 1795. An intercepted letter implied that Randolph would pursue a pro-French policy in exchange for a bribe; when Washington showed the letter to Randolph, he promptly submitted his resignation. All told, Washington removed 17 officials whose appointments had been approved by the Senate.

John Adams was the first President to remove a cabinet secretary without the formality of a resignation. Incensed at Secretary of State Timothy Pickering's interference with his French policy and his failure to support Adams's nomination of his son-in-law for adjutant general, Adams wrote to Pickering asking for his resignation. When Pickering did not respond, Adams fired him with an abrupt written notice. Adams also removed 20 other civil officers.

President Thomas Jefferson fired John Adams's son-in-law, Colonel William Smith, surveyor of the Port of New York. Smith had taken part in a plot against Spanish possessions in South America, a violation of U.S. law. Jefferson removed a total of 109 officers. James Madison fired his secretary of state, Robert Smith, for incompetence, claiming that whatever talents Smith had, he did not "possess those adapted to his station." Madison also obtained the resignation under pressure of General John Armstrong as secretary of war after Armstrong failed to prepare the capital against the arrival of British troops during the War of 1812 and the city was sacked.

For the most part the removals by Presidents through the 1820s involved wrongdoing in office, not partisan politics. In 1820 Congress had little problem with Presidential removals: it passed a Tenure of Office Act specifying fixed four-year terms for officers handling funds but made them removable at the pleasure of the President.

Controversy erupted in the administration of Andrew Jackson, who established the principle of rotation in office on partisan grounds. Jackson's removal of his political enemies was abrupt, arbitrary, and unrestrained by law. But in all nonpolitical cases involving employees, it was Jackson's common practice to provide them with notice and the elements of due process, similar to a fair trial, and to discharge them only after a complete investigation of allegations.

Jackson was the first President to claim the power to remove cabinet officials simply for disagreeing with Presidential policy, if they did not follow his orders. By law, the Treasury secretary had the responsibility of depositing the funds of the United States in such banks as he saw fit. Jackson asked Secretary of the Treasury William J. Duane to remove the funds from the Bank of the United States and deposit them in state banks. Duane declined to do so, arguing, "Congress confers discretionary power." Jackson responded, "A secretary, sir, is merely an executive agent, a subordinate." When Duane defied Jackson's orders, he was fired.

The opposition Whigs argued against an unrestricted Presidential right of removal. Henry Clay offered a Senate resolution in 1834 stating, "The Constitution of the United States does not vest in the President the power to remove, at his pleasure, officers under the Government of the United States, whose officers have been established by law." Instead, Congress would legislate the length of their service. Clay further proposed a law requiring that the power of removal be exercised only "in concurrence with the Senate," but Jackson used his influence to defeat this and other similar proposals.

The Whig-dominated Senate did manage to pass a Resolution of Censure against Jackson, who sent a "Response" claiming that he possessed the right of "removing those officers who are to aid [him] in the execution of the laws." The Whigs put in their 1836 platform the notion that Congress possessed sole removal power. One of their Presidential nominees, William Henry Harrison, pledged never to remove a Treasury secretary without approval of Congress.

During the Civil War, Congress established the office of comptroller of the currency, specifying a five-year term and authorizing his removal only with the consent of the Senate. In 1864 Congress passed a statute requiring the President to submit to Congress the reasons for removal of consular clerks in the Department of State. An 1865 law gave military officers dismissed by the President the right to apply for a trial.

In the aftermath of the Civil War, Congress passed two measures to protect its Reconstruction policies from President Andrew Johnson, who wished to pursue policies favorable to the Southern states. The Command of the Army Act, passed on March 2, 1867, provided that "the General of the Army shall not be removed, suspended, or relieved from command, or assigned to duty elsewhere than at said headquarters, except at his own request, without the previous approval of the Senate." The Tenure of Office Act, passed the same day, provided that "every person holding any civil office to which he has been appointed by and with the advice and consent of the Senate...shall be entitled to hold such office until a successor shall have been in like manner appointed and duly qualified." During a Senate recess the President could suspend an official for reason of misconduct in office, criminal activity, incapacity, or legal disqualification, but he would be restored to his office if the Senate refused to endorse the President's action. Both acts were passed over Johnson's veto.

After Congress adjourned, Johnson asked Secretary of War Edwin Stanton to resign. When Stanton refused, in August 1867, the President, seemingly acting in accordance with the laws, suspended him and authorized General Ulysses S. Grant to act as secretary of war. Johnson had outmaneuvered Congress, using a provision in the law that permitted him to suspend a department secretary until the Senate reconvened. But when the Senate did so, it reinstated Stanton. Now Johnson acted for the first time in apparent violation of the Tenure of Office Act. He removed Stanton while the Senate was in session and appointed General Lorenzo Thomas secretary of war. The House then voted articles of impeachment against Johnson.

At his Senate trial Johnson argued that the Tenure of Office Act was unconstitutional. He also argued that even if the act were constitutional, his removal of Stanton did not violate it. Stanton had been appointed by Lincoln; Johnson argued that the law could not prevent a President from removing an official nominated by his predecessor but covered only those nominations he himself had made. Johnson was tried in the Senate and escaped removal by just one vote, and Stanton surrendered his office. Congress did not repeal the last provisions of the law until 1887.

In the landmark 1926 Supreme Court case *Myers* v. *United States,* Chief Justice William Howard Taft recognized the removal power as a Presidential

Edwin Stanton, secretary of war under Abraham Lincoln, was removed by Andrew Johnson in violation of the Tenure of Office Act.

power and struck down all congressional efforts to pass legislation about the Presidential removal power.

In *Humphrey's Executor* v. *United States* (1935), the Court retreated somewhat from the *Myers* case. It distinguished between officials doing executive tasks and those engaged in "quasi-legislative" and "quasi-judicial" ones. Quasi-judicial officials, such as commissioners of regulatory agencies like the Federal Trade Commission, could be insulated from the Presidential removal power by legislation. Moreover, in *Wiener* v. *United States* (1958) the Supreme Court held that Presidential removal power did not extend to such officials even when Congress has not protected them by law.

The courts and Congress have also protected special prosecutors and independent counsels who investigate high-level scandals involving the Presidency, such as the special prosecutor in the Watergate investigation. President Richard Nixon ordered Attorney General Elliott Richardson to dismiss Archibald Cox for pursuing the inquiry further than Nixon wished. Richardson, who had given the Senate his word that he would not do so except for "extraordinary improprieties on his [Cox's] part" and who had issued regulations protecting

Cox, promptly resigned. The deputy attorney general, William Ruckelshaus, was ordered to fire Cox, and when he refused, Nixon fired him, too. Finally, Solicitor General Robert Bork, who had become acting attorney general, fired Cox.

In *Nader* v. *Bork* (1973) a district court agreed that Cox had been illegally removed from office because the removal violated the department's regulations regarding the special prosecutor. Subsequently, the Ethics in Government Act of 1978 prohibited the removal of an independent counsel (or special prosecutor) except for extraordinary impropriety, physical disability, mental incapacity, or "any other condition that substantially impairs the performance of such special prosecutor's duties."

SEE ALSO

Appointment power; Censure, resolutions of; Executive branch; Executive power; Impeachment; Independent counsel; Jackson, Andrew; Johnson, Andrew

FURTHER READING

Corwin, Edward S. *The President's Removal Power under the Constitution.* New York: National Municipal League, 1927.
Fisher, Louis. *Constitutional Conflicts between President and Congress.* Princeton, N.J.: Princeton University Press, 1985.

Resignation, Presidential

THE CONSTITUTION (Article 2, Section 1) specifies that if the President resigns, the office of President "devolves on," or transfers to, the Vice President. The 25th Amendment states that in case of resignation, the Vice President "shall become President."

The mechanisms for a Presidential resignation are as follows: The President signs a letter, addressed to the secretary

of state, specifying the time at which resignation from the office becomes effective. The Vice President is notified by the secretary of state and takes the oath of office at the designated time.

Only one President has ever resigned. Richard Nixon resigned at noon on August 9, 1974, to avoid impeachment by the House of Representatives for high crimes and misdemeanors for his involvement in the Watergate scandal. He was succeeded by Gerald Ford, who took the oath in a ceremony at the Capitol.

SEE ALSO

Ford, Gerald R.; Nixon, Richard M.; Secretary of state; Succession to the Presidency; Watergate scandal

Richard Nixon bids farewell to the White House staff in 1974. Nixon is the only President to have resigned from office.

Rockefeller, Nelson
VICE PRESIDENT

☆ *Born: July 8, 1908, Bar Harbor, Maine*
☆ *Political party: Republican*
☆ *Education: Dartmouth College, B.A., 1930*
☆ *Military service: none*
☆ *Previous government service: director, Office of Inter-American Affairs, U.S. Department of State, 1940–44; assistant secretary of state for Latin American Affairs, 1944–45; chair, Advisory Board on International*

*Development, 1950–51; chair,
Advisory Committee on Government
Organization, 1953–58; undersecretary
of health, education, and welfare,
1953–54; special assistant to the
President for foreign affairs, 1954–55;
governor of New York, 1959–73*
☆ *Vice President under Gerald R.
Ford, 1975–77*
☆ *Died: Jan. 26, 1979, New York, N.Y.*

NELSON ROCKEFELLER was the second Vice President to be nominated by a
President and confirmed by Congress
under the 25th Amendment. The son of
one of the richest men in the United
States, John D. Rockefeller, founder of
Standard Oil, Nelson Rockefeller devoted
most of his career to government service.
He held executive appointments under
Presidents Franklin Roosevelt, Harry
Truman, and Dwight Eisenhower, and
he served as one of Eisenhower's principal foreign policy advisers on arms control in the mid-1950s.

Rockefeller first won elective office
in 1958, when he defeated Averell Harriman to become governor of New York.
Reelected three times, he was responsible for building a huge state office complex in Albany, constructing the New
York State thruway system, and establishing the State University of New York
as one of the largest university systems
in the nation.

Rockefeller tried for the Republican
Presidential nomination in 1960 but
withdrew before the Republican convention in a deal with front-runner Richard
Nixon that led to the liberalization of
the party's platform on civil rights and
foreign policy. In 1964 he led the liberal
wing of the Republican party and again
tried for the nomination but was defeated by the conservative Barry Goldwater
after a bruising primary season. In 1968
he lost a third nomination bid, again
to Nixon.

On August 20, 1975, President
Gerald Ford used the provisions of the
25th Amendment to fill the vacancy in
the Vice Presidency (caused by Ford's
succession to the Presidency after Nixon's resignation). Ford nominated Rockefeller for Vice President. To do so, he
had to override the wishes of conservatives who preferred George Bush. Four
months later, after lengthy hearings, the
Senate and House both consented to
Rockefeller.

As presiding officer of the Senate,
Rockefeller played a major role in weakening the tradition of unlimited debate.
He made several rulings that closed off
debate by a three-fifths vote instead of
the customary two-thirds. Rockefeller
became one of Ford's key domestic
advisers. He had a weekly lunch with the
President and unlimited access to him.
Ford accepted Rockefeller's proposal for
a government corporation to develop
energy self-sufficiency for the nation but
opposed his suggestion that the national
government help New York City with-
stand a fiscal crisis. Ford incorporated 6
of Rockefeller's 19 suggestions for
domestic policy in his 1976 State of the
Union address. Rockefeller developed
these proposals by serving as chair of the
Domestic Council. He also chaired a
number of Presidential commissions,
such as the National Commission on
Productivity and Work Quality and the
National Commission on Water Quality,
and he was a member of the Commission on the Organization of Government
and the Conduct of Foreign Policy. He
conducted a major review of the Central
Intelligence Agency. But he admitted to
the Senate, when presiding over it for
the last time, that "these past two years,
in all candor, cannot be said to have
sorely tried either my talents or my
stamina."

Rockefeller helped Ford secure renomination in 1976 against a determined

challenge by Ronald Reagan. He delivered the New York delegation to Ford at the convention and later helped raise large sums of money for Ford's campaign. But Ford felt he could not afford to have Rockefeller run for Vice President because he would risk losing the nomination to the conservative Reagan. Rockefeller voluntarily withdrew from the ticket before the nominating season began and retired from public service at the end of his term.

SEE ALSO

Ford, Gerald R.; Nixon, Richard M.; 25th Amendment

FURTHER READING

Benjamin, Gerald, and T. Norman Hurd, eds. *Rockefeller in Retrospect.* Albany, N.Y.: Rockefeller Institute of Government, 1984.
Kramer, Michael, and Sam Roberts. *I Never Wanted to Be Vice President of Anything.* New York: Basic Books, 1976.
Turner, Michael. *The Vice President as Policy Maker: Rockefeller in the Ford White House.* Westport, Conn.: Greenwood, 1982.

Roosevelt, Eleanor

FIRST LADY

☆ *Born: Oct. 11, 1884, New York, N.Y.*
☆ *Wife of Franklin D. Roosevelt, 32nd President*
☆ *Died: Nov. 7, 1962, New York, N.Y.*

ELEANOR ROOSEVELT was a leader of the liberal wing of the Democratic party and the wife of Franklin D. Roosevelt, the 32nd President. Her parents died during her childhood, and she was raised by her grandmother and educated in England. In 1905 she married her fifth cousin (once removed) Franklin Delano Roosevelt. At her wedding she was given away by her uncle, President Theodore Roosevelt.

Eleanor Roosevelt helped her husband in the early stages of his political career, acting as his confidante and adviser. They had six children, one of whom died in infancy. She cared for her husband after he became ill with polio and while he was convalescing at Warm Springs, Georgia. Then she embarked on her own career as a teacher at the Todhunter School in New York City. She fought against racial segregation in the South and headed the women's platform committee at the 1924 Democratic national convention, which proposed many liberal programs later adopted by her husband in the 1930s.

Eleanor Roosevelt became active in her own right in trade union causes. She worked with her husband in his successful campaign for the New York governorship in 1928. When she became First Lady in 1933, she strongly lobbied her husband to adopt liberal causes.

In 1933 Eleanor Roosevelt became the first First Lady to hold a press conference so that women reporters, then barred from the regular Presidential news conferences, could be accommodated. She broadcast a regular 15-minute radio program in which she commented on politics. She wrote a syndicated newspaper column, "My Day," which concentrated on women's issues until 1939 and then on public affairs in general, and in

Eleanor Roosevelt visits a Works Progress Administration project in Iowa that converted a city dump into a waterfront park.

1941 she began writing a column, "If you ask me," for the *Ladies' Home Journal.* She resigned in 1939 from the Daughters of the American Revolution because the organization refused to allow the African-American opera singer Marian Anderson to give a concert in Washington's Constitution Hall. She took many trips across the country during the Depression to see how New Deal recovery programs were working, serving as her husband's "eyes and ears." During World War II she traveled as her husband's emissary to raise troop morale on three fronts.

In 1945 President Harry Truman named Eleanor Roosevelt a U.S. delegate to the United Nations. She played a major role in securing UN adoption of the Universal Declaration of Human Rights in 1948, although the U.S. Senate refused its consent. She left her post in 1952. But she remained active in Democratic politics, working for liberal candidates and causes, especially those involving civil rights and liberties, and her endorsements were highly sought after and often crucial in New York State and national elections. In 1961 President John F. Kennedy reappointed her to the U.S. delegation to the UN, where she served until her death.

SEE ALSO

New Deal; Roosevelt, Franklin D.

FURTHER READING

Cook, Blanche Wiesen. *Eleanor Roosevelt, 1884–1933.* New York: Viking, 1992.
Cook, Blanche Wiesen. *Eleanor Roosevelt: The Defining Years, 1933–1938.* New York: Viking, 1999.
Lash, Joseph P. *Eleanor and Franklin.* New York: Norton, 1971.
Roosevelt, Eleanor. *The Autobiography of Eleanor Roosevelt.* New York: Harper, 1961.
Roosevelt, Eleanor. *On My Own.* New York: Harper, 1958.
Roosevelt, Eleanor. *This I Remember.* 1949. Reprint. Westport, Conn.: Greenwood, 1975.

Roosevelt, Franklin D.

32ND PRESIDENT

☆ Born: Jan. 30, 1882, Hyde Park, N.Y.
☆ Political party: Democrat
☆ Education: Harvard College, A.B., 1903; Columbia University Law School, 1904–7
☆ Military service: none
☆ Previous government service: New York Senate, 1911–13; assistant secretary of the navy, 1913–20; governor of New York, 1929–33
☆ Elected President, 1932; served, 1933–45
☆ Died: Apr. 12, 1945, Warm Springs, Ga.

FRANKLIN DELANO ROOSEVELT was President during the Great Depression and World War II. He demonstrated the power of the modern Presidency to restore public confidence and win speedy passage of recovery legislation. In spite of considerable isolationist sentiment in Congress, he provided aid to Great Britain and the Soviet Union that prevented their defeat at the hands of Adolf Hitler, and after U.S. entry into World War II he led the Allied coalition to victory over Germany. Roosevelt created the New Deal coalition within the Democratic party, which dominated national politics through the 1960s.

Roosevelt was descended from a wealthy family of Dutch settlers and was a fifth cousin of President Theodore Roosevelt. He was educated by private tutors, then at the elite Groton School and at Harvard College, where he studied history and became editor of the student newspaper, the Harvard *Crimson.* He studied law at Columbia University but did not graduate. He married his fifth cousin Eleanor Roosevelt, passed the bar, and began to practice law in New York City in 1908.

In 1910 Roosevelt won election to the state senate from rural Duchess

County (a seat that no Democrat had won since the Civil War). He was appointed assistant secretary of the navy in 1913 by Woodrow Wilson and served until 1920. That year he won the Democratic Vice Presidential nomination and campaigned strenuously for the League of Nations and Treaty of Versailles, but he was defeated. The following year, while vacationing at his family retreat on Campobello Island in Canada, he came down with polio. For the rest of his life he was paralyzed below the waist, though he went through arduous rehabilitation at a spa in Warm Springs, Georgia. In 1927 Roosevelt founded the Warm Springs Foundation to treat other victims of polio.

Although he used a wheelchair and was weighed down with heavy leg braces, Roosevelt remained an important figure in New York Democratic politics. He attended his party's national conventions in 1924 and 1928, both times giving nominating speeches for the "Happy Warrior," Al Smith. Although Smith was crushed in 1928, in part because he was a Roman Catholic, Roosevelt spoke out against religious intolerance and won the governorship of New York.

As governor, Roosevelt lowered taxes and electric rates and created a state power authority, state parks, and state highways. In 1930, in the midst of the Depression, he created the first state public relief agency and the first system of unemployment insurance. He was reelected by the greatest landslide ever received by a New York gubernatorial candidate.

In 1932 Roosevelt won the Democratic nomination for President, becoming the first person ever to win a Presidential nomination after being defeated in a Vice Presidential election. He flew to Chicago and became the first Presidential nominee in U.S. history to deliver his acceptance speech in person. "I pledge you, I pledge myself," he told the delegates, "to a New Deal for the American people." He defeated Herbert Hoover by a landslide. Riding his political coattails, the Democrats increased their majorities in the House and Senate.

Roosevelt's 1932 election and the three that followed brought into power the New Deal coalition: white Protestant southerners, northern Jews and Catholics, blacks, labor union members, and small farmers. That coalition would convert the Democrats into the majority party, dominate the Presidential elections (with only two exceptions) through the 1960s, and control most of the Congresses into the 1990s.

Roosevelt continued Woodrow Wilson's transformation of the Democratic party from its Jeffersonian and Jacksonian traditions of states' rights and limited governmental regulation to an emphasis on national economic regulation and social welfare programs for the poor, the unemployed, the sick, and the elderly.

As Roosevelt took his oath of office, there were millions unemployed, farmers and home owners had seen their land or homes foreclosed, industrial production was sinking, and thousands of banks had been closed by state governors to prevent

In this cartoon, Franklin Roosevelt faces criticism about his New Deal programs from Wendell Willkie, who ran against Roosevelt in the 1940 election.

a run on their deposits. "Let me assert my firm belief that the only thing we have to fear is fear itself," Roosevelt told the American people in his inaugural address, "nameless, unreasoning, unjustified terror which paralyzes needed efforts to convert retreat into advance." He took measures to end that fear. He declared a bank holiday to end the run on deposits, then got Congress to pass an emergency banking bill to regulate banks. Only those that were declared solvent were allowed to reopen. By executive order he took the nation off the gold standard to protect dwindling Treasury reserves from people who wanted to exchange dollars for gold, which they thought would be more valuable in hard times. The bank panic was over.

Roosevelt began his administration with the "hundred days" of emergency

The Civilian Conservation Corps hired young men to plant trees, construct reservoirs, and do other conservation work.

legislation. Banking deposits were guaranteed by the Federal Deposit Insurance Corporation, restoring depositor confidence. An Economy Act permitted the President to cut federal employees' salaries and veterans' pensions. The Federal Emergency Relief Administration gave states funds to provide public works jobs to the unemployed, and the Civilian Conservation Corps gave work to young people. The Home Owners Loan Corporation helped home owners avoid foreclosures. The Farm Credit Administration provided funds for farmers in the growing season; the Farm Mortgage Refinancing Act provided them with loans to make mortgage payments; and the Agricultural Adjustment Administration helped stabilize farm prices by limiting production and establishing marketing quotas. The National Industrial Recovery Act allowed industrial producers to stabilize prices and restore production. The Tennessee Valley Authority built

30 dams that provided cheap power for farms and industry and better agricultural techniques to parts of seven states in the poverty-stricken Tennessee Valley. The Works Progress Administration funded artists and writers and photographers to undertake public cultural projects such as painting murals in government buildings.

Roosevelt continued his recovery program by creating more New Deal agencies, such as the Securities and Exchange Commission to regulate financial markets, the Federal Communications Commission to regulate telephone and radio (and later television), and the National Industrial Relations Board to regulate labor-management relations. He got the national government involved in public housing, rural electrification, public service jobs, unemployment insurance, and old-age pensions.

Although Roosevelt did not lift the nation out of the Depression, his active and energetic leadership and his ability to restore public confidence helped alleviate the worst suffering. In 1936 he won a landslide victory against Republican Alf Landon, winning a greater percentage of the popular vote than in 1932.

In Roosevelt's second inaugural address he pledged to relieve the poverty of "one third of a nation ill-housed, ill-clad, ill-nourished." To do so, he moved against the Supreme Court, which had declared several recovery laws unconstitutional. Roosevelt proposed to "pack" the court with an additional appointee for every justice over the age of 70—giving him six new appointments. Members of Congress, even those from his own party, were reluctant to see Roosevelt dominate the court.

Roosevelt's court-packing plan was defeated in Congress in 1937. He would later appoint enough justices to secure a firm liberal majority on the court. But after the court-packing fight, a conservative coalition of Southern Democrats and Republicans in Congress blocked most of Roosevelt's New Deal proposals.

Roosevelt maintained strict neutrality in European affairs until the summer of 1939. But after a trip to the United States by the British king and queen, he recommended that Congress amend the neutrality laws to allow nations that might go to war with the Axis powers (Germany, Italy, and Japan) the right to buy supplies from the United States. After Germany invaded Poland on September 1, 1939, Roosevelt initiated a "cash and carry" policy to arm the British. The British paid cash and carried the goods away in their own ships.

In the summer of 1940 Roosevelt began a national preparedness program, had Congress give him authority to draft troops, and raised the ceiling on the national debt. In September, using an executive order to bypass the Senate's advice and consent power over treaties, Roosevelt concluded a "destroyer deal" with Great Britain: in return for providing the British with 50 old destroyers useful for submarine warfare, the United States received the use of British military bases in the Caribbean.

Because of the ominous international situation, Roosevelt broke with tradition and accepted a unanimous third nomination for President. He promised the American people, "Your sons will not fight in a foreign war," and he defeated Republican Wendell Willkie. In his State of the Union address in 1941, he put forth his vision of a postwar world when he enunciated the Four Freedoms: freedom of speech and expression; freedom for every person to worship God in his own way; freedom from want; and freedom from fear.

In 1941 Congress passed the Lend-Lease Act, which provided military assistance to Great Britain and the Soviet Union. The United States, in the Presi-

dent's words, became the "arsenal of democracy" against the Axis dictatorships. Although Roosevelt gave "shoot on sight" orders to the navy against German submarines in the North Atlantic in 1941, landed U.S. troops in Iceland, closed Italian and German consulates, and froze Japanese assets in the United States, he did not ask Congress for a declaration of war because most Americans opposed it. In August 1941 Roosevelt met with British prime minister Winston Churchill to draft the Atlantic Charter, an eight-point plan on common principles of a democratic postwar world. The following month the U.S. Navy began to convoy British merchant ships carrying lend-lease supplies.

The Japanese attacks on Pearl Harbor (in the Hawaiian Islands), on the Philippines, and on Guam, which all took place on December 7, 1941, led Roosevelt to ask Congress to declare war not only on Japan but on Germany and Italy as well. Early in 1942 a coalition of 26 nations subscribed to the Atlantic Charter. Following Roosevelt's suggestions, these nations called themselves the United Nations. In 1943 Roosevelt and Churchill called for an unconditional Axis surrender.

In June 1944 Allied troops under the command of General Dwight D. Eisenhower launched the Normandy

Roosevelt (center) meets with Soviet premier Joseph Stalin (left) and British prime minister Winston Churchill in Teheran to discuss war strategy.

invasion in France. With the war going successfully, Roosevelt received a fourth Democratic nomination and defeated Republican challenger Thomas E. Dewey.

In February 1945 Roosevelt traveled to Yalta in the Soviet Union to discuss plans for peace with Churchill and Soviet dictator Joseph Stalin. Stalin and Churchill discussed spheres of influence for their nations, parts of Europe and the Middle East where they would have dominant political and economic influence. Roosevelt, in poor health, was not in a position to argue forcefully against them and in favor of the U.S. position of open markets and equal access for all the great powers. This led some critics to claim that Roosevelt had "sold out" the nations of eastern Europe to Stalin. While resting at Warm Springs, Georgia, in preparation for the San Francisco conference that was to create the United Nations, Roosevelt died of a cerebral hemorrhage on April 12, 1945.

SEE ALSO

Brains Trust; Court-packing plan; Executive Office of the President; Garner, John Nance; Hoover, Herbert C.; Modern Presidency; New Deal; Roosevelt, Eleanor; Term of office; Truman, Harry S.; Two-term tradition; Wallace, Henry; White House Office

FURTHER READING

Burns, James MacGregor. *The Lion and the Fox*. New York: Harcourt Brace, 1956.
Dallek, Robert. *Franklin Roosevelt and American Foreign Policy, 1932–1945*. New York: Oxford, 1979.
Davis, Kenneth Sydney. *FDR: Into the Storm, 1937–1940: A History*. New York: Random House, 1993.
Leuchtenburg, William E. *Franklin D. Roosevelt and the New Deal*. New York: Harper & Row, 1963.

Roosevelt, Theodore

26TH PRESIDENT

☆ *Born: Oct. 27, 1858, New York, N.Y.*
☆ *Political party: Republican*
☆ *Education: Harvard College, A.B.,*
1880; Columbia University School of Law, 1881
☆ *Military service: 1st U.S. Volunteer Cavalry, 1898*
☆ *Previous government service: New York State Assembly, 1881–84; U.S. Civil Service commissioner, 1889–95; president, New York City Board of Police Commissioners, 1895–96; assistant secretary of the navy, 1897–98; governor of New York, 1899–1901; Vice President, 1901*
☆ *Succeeded to Presidency, 1901; served, 1901–9*
☆ *Died: Jan. 6, 1919, Oyster Bay, N.Y.*

THEODORE ("TEDDY") Roosevelt was the youngest person ever to serve as President of the United States and the first Vice President who succeeded to the Presidency to win election in his own right. He used the powers of the Presidency to the hilt, especially in foreign affairs, and he was the first President to act as the leader of a world power. His motto was "Speak softly and carry a big stick," yet in spite of his militaristic attitudes, the nation remained at peace. Not a single member of the armed forces died in combat during his term—almost a unique accomplishment among U.S. Presidents.

Roosevelt was afflicted with asthma as a boy but built himself up with exercise. He graduated from Harvard and attended law school briefly. In the New York Assembly he strayed frequently from the Republican party to take an independent position. He wrote several popular histories, beginning with *The Naval War of 1812*. When his wife Alice Lee died in childbirth in 1884 (on the same day he learned of the death of his mother), he went out West to a ranch in the Dakota Territory to recover from his grief.

Roosevelt returned to the East to run for mayor of New York City in 1886, but he finished third and went back to the ranch with his new wife, his childhood friend Edith Carow. There he wrote biographies of Senator Thomas Hart Benton and Gouverneur Morris (an influential delegate to the federal Constitutional Convention), and the two volumes of *The Winning of the West*. In 1889 he returned east again and was named to the U.S. Civil Service Commission by President Benjamin Harrison. He transferred thousands of patronage jobs to the merit system. In 1895 he became president of the New York City Board of Police Commissioners.

When President William McKinley took office in 1897, he named Roosevelt assistant secretary of the navy. Roosevelt promoted ship construction and deployed much of the fleet in the Far East, where Admiral George Dewey was able to secure Manila Bay and win control of the Philippines at the beginning of the Spanish-American War. Roosevelt himself organized the 1st U.S. Volunteer Cavalry, known as the Rough Riders. As their commander, he led them into battle at Kettle Hill near Santiago de Cuba, which newspaper accounts called the "charge up San Juan Hill."

Roosevelt's battlefield exploits, recounted in his book *The Rough Riders* (1899), won him the governorship of New York. His reform program so upset party leaders that they arranged for him to receive the Vice Presidential nomination in 1900. Roosevelt was so bored with the inactivity of the Vice Presidency that he seriously considered finishing law school. But six months after his inauguration, on September 14, 1901, President William McKinley died of an assassin's bullet and Roosevelt took the Presidential oath.

At 42, Roosevelt was the youngest person ever to assume the office. He pledged to continue McKinley's policies but soon demonstrated his reformist and independent streak, much to the chagrin of the Republican leaders who had put him on the ticket. He developed the "stewardship" theory of the Presidency: the chief executive could and should take all measures necessary for the welfare of the American people, even if they were not specifically mentioned in the Constitution.

Roosevelt instituted more than 30 court cases against corporations, charging them with violations of antitrust laws—conspiring to control markets or fix prices. He insisted that coal mine owners negotiate with their miners. This was the first time that a President had acted as a neutral umpire in a dispute between management and labor. In 1902 he secured passage of the Newlands Reclamation Act, which funded irrigation projects in the West. He increased the acreage of national parks and forests fivefold, much of it by executive orders creating five national parks. He also established the first federal bird reservation and 50 bird sanctuaries to protect endangered species. For the first time, a President focused public attention on conservation and the environment, and he got Congress to establish the U.S. Forest Service. In 1903 Congress created the Department of Commerce and Labor. To head it, Roosevelt nominated the first Jewish cabinet secretary, Oscar Straus.

In foreign affairs Roosevelt presided over the expansion of American naval power, sending the Great White Fleet on a tour around the world from 1907 to 1909 to demonstrate the power of the United States to other nations. He insisted that the United States be the dominant naval power in the Pacific. When the government of Colombia refused to ratify an agreement that would allow the United States to begin construction of a canal across the isthmus of Panama (then a Colombian province), Roosevelt encouraged revolutionists to declare Panama independent and used the navy to

A Teddy Roosevelt Rough Rider doll.

prevent Colombian warships from quelling the revolt. Soon, he concluded an agreement with the new nation, granting the United States a zone in which to construct a canal. In 1904 the President announced the Roosevelt Corollary to the Monroe Doctrine, which, in effect, made the United States the "policeman" in the Western Hemisphere.

In 1904 Roosevelt was unanimously nominated for President by the Republican party and won election in his own right by defeating Democrat Alton B. Parker. He declared that he viewed his first three years in the White House as a full first term, and that, therefore, his second term would be his last.

Roosevelt continued his activist foreign policies. He took full control of the finances of the Dominican Republic in 1905 in order to pay its debts to U.S. and European creditors. When the Senate balked at consenting to a commercial treaty with the Dominican Republic because southern senators considered it harmful to southern sugar growers, Roosevelt implemented its terms by calling it an executive agreement, which did not require Senate consent. That same year Roosevelt mediated an end to the Russo-Japanese War at the Portsmouth Conference, receiving the 1906 Nobel Peace Prize for his efforts. He donated his $40,000 prize to a foundation for promoting better labor-management relations.

With solid Republican majorities in both chambers of Congress, in 1906 Roosevelt won passage of three important laws: the Pure Food and Drug Act and the Meat Inspection Act, which established new safety standards for consumers, and the Hepburn Railroad Act, which strengthened the enforcement power of the Interstate Commerce Commission over railroads.

In 1908 Roosevelt honored his two-term pledge and helped secure the Republican Presidential nomination for his protégé William Howard Taft. The two men eventually broke over Taft's conservative policies, and in 1910 Roosevelt went on a nationwide speaking tour, promoting a program of New Nationalism. To Roosevelt, the issue was simple: the Republican party should be the "party of the plain people," not "the party of privilege and of special interests." He called for government regulation of corporations and natural resources, a minimum wage, and limitations on the length of the workday.

In 1912 Taft defeated Roosevelt for the Republican nomination. Roosevelt's followers then organized a new party, the Progressive party, and nominated him. Roosevelt told them he felt "as strong as a bull moose," and the press then dubbed it the Bull Moose party. His platform emphasized democratization of U.S. politics; its proposals included the reversal of judicial decisions by popular vote, direct election of U.S. senators, woman suffrage, and referenda (direct popular votes) on legislation.

With Republican voters split between the regular Taft and the insurgent Roosevelt, Democrat Woodrow Wilson won the White House. Toward the end of his life, Roosevelt attempted unsuccessfully to get Wilson to offer him a commission so he could lead a new group of volunteers to fight in World War I. He died in 1919, shortly after the war's end.

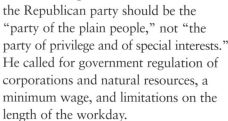

Roosevelt poses with John Muir, the founder of the Sierra Club, in Yosemite National Park in 1903. Roosevelt set up five national parks and set aside 148 million acres for national forests.

SEE ALSO
Executive agreements; McKinley, William; Monroe Doctrine; Taft, William Howard; Two-term tradition; Wilson, Woodrow

FURTHER READING
Cooper, John Milton, Jr. *The Warrior and the Priest: Woodrow Wilson and Theodore Roosevelt.* Cambridge: Harvard University Press, 1983.
Gould, Lewis L. *The Presidency of Theodore Roosevelt.* Lawrence: University Press of Kansas, 1991.
Harbaugh, William H. *Power and Responsibility: The Life and Times of Theodore Roosevelt.* New York: Oxford, 1975.
McCullough, David. *Mornings on Horseback.* New York: Simon & Schuster, 1981.
Morris, Edmund. *The Rise of Theodore Roosevelt.* New York: Coward, McCann & Geoghegan, 1979.

"Ruffles and Flourishes"

"RUFFLES AND FLOURISHES" is the trumpet fanfare that traditionally heralds the arrival of a head of state. When it announces the President, it is followed by the playing of "Hail to the Chief." The "ruffles" (short drumrolls) and the "flourishes" (a bugle call) are generally played four times.

SEE ALSO
"Hail to the Chief"; Marine Band, U.S.

Running mate

SEE Ticket

Salary, Presidential

THE CONSTITUTION (Article 2, Section 1) provides that the salary of the President is set by Congress, which may neither raise nor lower it during his term. In 1789 Congress fixed the salary at $25,000 per year. It was raised to $50,000 in 1873 and to $75,000 in 1909. From 1949 to 1968 it was $100,000, from 1969 to 2000 it was $200,000, and in 2000 it was increased to $250,000. The salary is subject to federal income tax.

Since 1949, Presidents have also received an expense account of $50,000, which in 1951 was made subject to federal income tax. In 1906 Congress authorized $25,000 annually for traveling expenses, a sum that it increased to $40,000 in 1948 and $100,000 in 1969. That year the President was also given a $12,000 entertainment allowance.

Since 1978, Congress has provided the President with an annual appropriation of $1 million in discretionary funds, which may be used for personnel and services needed for the national interest.

SEE ALSO
Ex-Presidency; White House Office

Salute to the President

ACCORDING TO military tradition, as a head of state, a President or ex-President is entitled to a 21-gun salute. The same salute is given to presidents of other republics or to monarchs of foreign nations. Heads of foreign governments, such as prime ministers, are entitled to 18-gun salutes. To commemorate the independence of the United States, the 21-gun salute is often fired in the following sequence: 1-7-7-6.

Seal, Presidential

THE PRESIDENTIAL seal is the symbol of the Presidential office. To ensure the authenticity of a document, the seal appears on any Presidential order or commission to federal office and on any document published in the President's name. Representations of the Presidential seal appear on *Air Force One* and *Marine One* and are placed on lecterns at which the President speaks.

The seal consists of a coat of arms encircled by 50 stars representing the states of the Union and the words "Seal of the President of the United States."

The coat of arms consists of a shield placed upon the breast of an American eagle. In its right talon the eagle holds an olive branch, symbolizing peace; in its left talon it holds a bundle of 13 gray arrows, representing the original colonies. Its beak grasps a gray scroll inscribed with the Latin words *E Pluribus Unum* ("Out of many, one"). Behind and above the eagle is a radiating glory (rays of light that emanate from a single point), on which appears an arc of 13 gray cloud puffs and a constellation of 13 gray five-pointed stars. This coat of arms is almost identical to the Great Seal of the United States.

The eagle on the coat of arms faced left, toward the gray arrows, until President Harry Truman ordered that it face right, looking toward the olive branch of peace.

SEE ALSO
Flag, Presidential

Secretary of defense

THE SECRETARY of defense is the administrator of the Department of Defense and the principal civilian adviser to the President on military matters.

Secretary of Defense Dick Cheney (right) and General Colin Powell appear before the House Armed Services Committee to discuss the proposed defense budget in 1992.

The secretary serves as a member of the President's "inner cabinet" of advisers and, by law, as a member of the National Security Council. With the chair of the Joint Chiefs of Staff, the secretary participates in the formulation of military strategy, reviews recommendations of the Pentagon's weapons acquisition committees, and recommends new weapons systems to the President. The secretary has the primary responsibility for preparing the military budget and defending it before military subcommittees of the House and Senate Appropriations Committees. He serves as the principal spokesperson for the administration when testifying before the House and Senate Armed Services Committees.

The President issues military orders to the secretary of defense, who transmits them through the Joint Chiefs of Staff to the military commands of the service branches. Each command operates under the supervision of CINCs, the commanders in chief of operational forces. Each CINC reports to the Joint Chiefs, who, in turn, report to the secretary of defense and the President. A Presidential decision to move troops, to engage enemy forces, or to use nuclear weapons is always transmitted through the secretary of defense, who may lawfully countermand the Presidential orders if there is reason to believe that the President is not physically or mentally competent to make the decision.

SEE ALSO

Cabinet; National Security Council

Secretary of state

THE SECRETARY of state is the administrator of the Department of State and the principal spokesperson for the President on U.S. foreign policy. The secretary serves as a member of the President's "inner cabinet" of advisers and, by law, as a member of the National Security Council. The secretary has the primary responsibility for preparing the budget for foreign affairs programs, including diplomatic missions, foreign aid to developing nations, and contributions to multinational organizations such as the World Bank, the Inter-American Development Bank, and the International Monetary Fund. The secretary defends foreign affairs programs before subcommittees of the House and Senate Appropriations Committees and is the principal spokesperson for the administration before the House Foreign Affairs Committee and Senate Foreign Relations Committee. The President may also assign the secretary to communicate foreign policy to foreign heads of state or to serve as the principal U.S. diplomat at international conferences.

As head of the first department of government established in 1789, the secretary is first in line to succeed to the Presidency in the event there is no Vice President, Speaker of the House, or president pro tempore of the Senate to assume the office. A Presidential resignation is submitted to the secretary of state.

Though some secretaries are highly influential advisers and policymakers, others have merely administered the State Department. Thomas Jefferson, the first secretary of state, resigned from George Washington's cabinet because his pro-French policies were not adopted. For the first two decades of the 19th century, each secretary of state was an influential shaper of foreign policy, and each became the next President: James Madison, James Monroe, and John Quincy Adams. Daniel Webster ran U.S. foreign policy when President John Tyler and the Whig Congress remained stalemated in domestic matters. William Seward wrote a memorandum to Abraham Lincoln in which he offered to run foreign policy, but Lincoln wrote back that as President he would retain final responsibility; Seward's main accomplishment was buying Alaska from Russia. Franklin Roosevelt used Presidential assistants to implement his policies, bypassing his secretary of state, Cordell Hull. President Harry Truman, by contrast, relied heavily on George Marshall, who proposed the Marshall Plan for economic recovery in Western Europe after World War II, and Dean Acheson. Acheson was the architect of the U.S. policies of collective security—making alliances to confront aggressor nations—and containment of communist aggression.

Dwight Eisenhower's secretary of state, John Foster Dulles, initiated the policy of "brinkmanship," which involved pushing a situation to the brink by threatening to use the armed forces (including nuclear weapons) to prevent communist regimes from expanding their influence. Dean Rusk served in the administrations of John F. Kennedy and Lyndon Johnson; he was preoccupied with resisting communist aggression in Southeast Asia, and he defended the Johnson administration against charges that it was not willing to negotiate a peace with North Vietnam.

Richard Nixon's secretary of state, William Rogers, was overshadowed by National Security Adviser Henry Kissinger: his one major initiative, the Rogers Plan for Mideast Peace, went nowhere. Eventually he was succeeded by Kissinger, who as secretary of state engaged in successful "shuttle diplomacy" between Jerusalem and Cairo to bring about a disengagement of opposing forces in the Sinai Peninsula after the Yom Kippur War of 1973. Cyrus Vance, Jimmy Carter's secretary of state, resigned as a matter of honor after Carter ordered a U.S. raid to free diplomats held hostage by Iran; Vance had been kept in the dark about the raid and had not been able to keep his promise to the Senate to brief it in advance of any military action.

Ronald Reagan's first secretary of state, Alexander Haig, suggested to the President that he be the "vicar" of U.S. foreign policy, but Reagan never gave him full responsibility, and Haig was involved in conflicts with Vice President George Bush and National Security Adviser Richard Allen. He offered to resign so many times that eventually Reagan accepted. Secretary George

Shultz opposed Reagan's plan to sell arms to Iran and was frozen out of policy-making. But after the Iran-Contra scandal erupted, Shultz became the dominant figure in the Reagan administration because he had the confidence of Congress. George Bush's secretary of state was his close political adviser and campaign manager, James Baker. The two dominated foreign policy in much the way Nixon and Kissinger had done, though Baker failed to convince Iraq to pull out of Kuwait and his Middle East Peace Conference failed to achieve an agreement between Israel and the Arab states.

Madeleine Albright was the first woman to be appointed secretary of state, and Bill Clinton nominated her in part to make history. She was neither a close political adviser nor a national security official he relied upon prior to her appointment. Clinton assigned Albright highly public roles in dealing with Congress, particularly the chairman of the Senate Foreign Relations Committee, Jesse Helms, with whom she developed some rapport that was helpful in providing the State Department with

Secretary of State William Seward sits to left of the globe in this painting commemorating Seward's purchase of Alaska from Russia.

funding. Albright had a tendency to substitute bombastic and inflated rhetoric for quiet diplomacy, and often she had little to show for her efforts. Her most constructive work involved the negotiations between Israel and the Palestinians as the two sides worked to develop a framework for a peace agreement.

SEE ALSO

Cabinet; Decision making, Presidential; National security adviser; National Security Council

FURTHER READING

Acheson, Dean. *Present at the Creation.* New York: Norton, 1969.
Chace, James. *Acheson: The Secretary of State Who Created the American World.* New York: Simon & Schuster, 1998.
Haig, Alexander. *Caveat.* New York: Macmillan, 1984.
Kissinger, Henry. *White House Years.* Boston: Little, Brown, 1979.
Shultz, George. *Turning Point.* New York: Macmillan, 1993.

Secret Service, U.S.

THE U.S. SECRET Service is a unit of the Department of the Treasury that is responsible for ensuring the safety of the President and Vice President and their families, the President-elect and Vice President–elect and their families, major Presidential and Vice Presidential candidates and their families, and former Presidents and their families. The Secret Service also protects visiting heads of foreign states or governments and other foreign visitors to the United States when designated to do so by the President.

The director of the Secret Service is chosen by the secretary of the Treasury from the ranks of service personnel. The 1,800 special enforcement agents are trained in hand-to-hand combat, firearms, emergency medicine, safe and evasive driving, surveillance, and field investiga-tion at the Federal Law Enforcement Facility in Brunswick, Georgia, and the service's school in Beltsville, Maryland.

The Secret Service Office of Investi-gations has jurisdiction over federal crimes involving currency, counterfeiting, fraudulent electronic transfers of funds, and other financial crimes.

The Secret Service's Office of Protec-tive Operations provides security at the White House and other Presidential offices, at the official residence of the Vice President in the District of Colum-bia, and at foreign diplomatic missions in Washington, D.C., and throughout the United States.

The White House Detail is assigned to the President. It protects the President in the Oval Office (a button enables him to summon agents at any time) and on trips within the United States and abroad. It arranges for all security and coordinates efforts of the Federal Bureau of Investigation and local law enforce-ment agencies in the area a President visits, making sure that all areas are safe and secure. It ensures that no surveil-lance devices are in use in the White House or any place the President visits.

The Office of Protective Research conducts background checks on individ-uals who have made threats against the President or other people protected by the Secret Service. It keeps tabs on more than 50,000 individuals who are viewed as potential threats to the President. Some 400 people on the "watch list" are placed under surveillance when the Pres-ident is in their vicinity.

The White House is guarded by 500 Uniformed Division officers of the Secret Service, who patrol the outer and middle perimeters. The inner perimeter and the mansion itself are secured by more than 100 agents in civilian clothes from the Presidential Protective Detail. The Tech-nical Security Division guards against surveillance and bugging of the White

Secret Service agents rush to the aid of Press Secretary James Brady (right) and a police officer in the 1981 assassination attempt on Ronald Reagan. The suspect is being held in the background.

House, and agents screen all visitors to the White House for weapons. All packages entering the White House are examined. Each year about 250 mentally disturbed people and 400 visitors carrying guns are apprehended as they enter the White House on guided tours.

The Secret Service was established during the Civil War, when the Union Army organized a group of agents under the command of Colonel L. C. Baker for counterintelligence (finding Confederate spies) and detection of counterfeit currency. Some of the agents were transferred to the Treasury Department in July 1865. In the 1870s the Secret Service investigated crimes against blacks in the South committed by the Ku Klux Klan, a white supremacist group. In 1898 President William McKinley ordered it to gather military and foreign intelligence during the Spanish-American War, and it also did such work during World War I. After the war its intelligence roles were taken over by the Federal Bureau of Investigation and military intelligence agencies.

In 1901, after the assassination of President McKinley, his successor, Theodore Roosevelt, ordered the Secret

Service to protect the President. Beginning with two agents, the protective detail expanded to 40 agents by 1940. Congress authorized the Secret Service to protect the President in 1906, the President-elect in 1908, and the Vice President in 1962. Retired Presidents, widows of Presidents, and their minor children came under protection in 1965. (Widows lose protection if they remarry.) In 1971 foreign heads of state and other individuals designated by the President, such as Presidential candidates, and in 1976 candidates' wives, were included. The Uniformed Division was transferred from the District of Columbia Police by President Warren Harding in 1922 and was made a part of the Secret Service in 1930.

SEE ALSO

Assassinations, Presidential

FURTHER READING

Jeffreys-Jones, Rhodri. *American Espionage: From Secret Service to CIA.* New York: Free Press, 1977.

Matusky, Gregory, and John P. Hayes. *U.S. Secret Service.* New York: Chelsea House, 1988.

McCarthy, Dennis V. N. *Protecting the President: The Inside Story of a Secret Service Agent.* New York: Morrow, 1985.

Melanson, Philip. *The Politics of Protection: The U.S. Secret Service in the Terrorist Age.* New York: Praeger, 1984.

Sequoia

SEE Yacht, Presidential

Sherman, James

VICE PRESIDENT

☆ *Born: Oct. 24, 1855, Utica, N.Y.*
☆ *Political party: Republican*
☆ *Education: Hamilton College, B.A., 1878*
☆ *Military service: none*
☆ *Previous government service: mayor of Utica, 1885; U.S. House of Representatives, 1887–91, 1893–1909*

AS A REPUBLICAN, James ("Sunny Jim") Sherman pulled a major upset in overwhelmingly Democratic Utica, New York, to become its mayor in 1884. A member of the U.S. House of Representatives for 20 years, he chaired the Indian Affairs Committee and served on the Rules Committee. He was a close ally of the powerful Speakers Thomas Reed and Joseph Cannon.

When William Howard Taft of Ohio was nominated for President in 1908, Sherman was chosen to represent eastern Republican interests and balance the ticket. He did next to nothing as Vice President. When President Taft asked him to help pass a Republican bill in Congress, Sherman replied that "acting as a messenger boy is not part of the duties of a Vice President." He was renominated for Vice President by the Republicans in 1912 but died while campaigning in his native Utica. The Republican National Committee replaced him on the ticket with Columbia University president Nicholas Murray Butler.

Special Prosecutor

SEE Independent counsel

Speech writers

THE WHITE HOUSE employs a staff of aides who draft Presidential speeches, messages to Congress, proclamations, executive orders, greetings to White House visitors, eulogies, opening statements at news conferences, and other public statements and documents.

Each President has used speech writers differently. They may write first drafts for the President to polish, or provide phrases and slogans, or translate complicated policy proposals into language for a mass audience. Some speech writers are influential assistants to the President who offer policy suggestions and may influence White House decision making. Others are wordsmiths with no policy influence.

The speech-writing office is part of the White House Office. It works with the White House Research Unit, which checks the facts contained in any Presidential statement, especially quotations, dates, statistics, and historical references.

Presidents have relied on speech writers since George Washington received help from Thomas Jefferson, James Madison, and Alexander Hamilton on his state papers and farewell address. Andrew Jackson's veto messages to Congress were drafted by his attorney general. Abraham Lincoln wrote his own speeches and documents, including the Gettysburg Address and Emancipation Proclamation. Woodrow Wilson, who had written books and articles as a professor, also wrote his own speeches. Franklin Roosevelt used several speech

Ronald Reagan meets with White House speech writer Peggy Noonan.

writers, including playwright Robert Sherwood. Dwight Eisenhower used journalist Emmet Hughes. Most of John F. Kennedy's speeches were drafted by his counsel, Theodore Sorensen; other Kennedy speech writers included historian Arthur M. Schlesinger, Jr., Ambassador to India John Kenneth Galbraith, and White House aide Richard Goodwin. Ronald Reagan relied heavily on Peggy Noonan, one of the first women speech writers in the White House.

Some speech writers have gone on to distinguished careers. Jack Valenti, an aide to Lyndon Johnson, became president of the Motion Picture Association of America. One of Richard Nixon's speech writers, William Safire, became a columnist for the *New York Times;* another, Pat Buchanan, became a talk-show commentator and contender for the Republican Presidential nomination in 1992 and 1996. Two of Jimmy Carter's speech writers, James Fallows and Hendrik Hertzberg, went on to become influential writers and magazine editors.

Several Presidential speech writers have written important memoirs about the Presidencies in which they served. These include Robert Sherwood (*Roosevelt and Hopkins*), Samuel Rosenman (*The Roosevelt I Knew*), Emmet Hughes (*Ordeal of Power,* which is about his years with Eisenhower), Theodore Sorensen (*Kennedy*), Arthur M. Schlesinger, Jr. (*A Thousand Days*), and William Safire (*Before the Fall*).

SEE ALSO

Fireside chat; Gettysburg Address; Messages, Presidential; News conferences; State of the Union address; Washington's Farewell Address; White House Office

FURTHER READING

Noonan, Peggy. *What I Saw at the Revolution.* New York: Random House, 1990.
Tulis, Jeffrey. *The Rhetorical Presidency.* Princeton, N.J.: Princeton University Press, 1987.

Spoils

SEE Patronage, Presidential

Square Deal

THE SQUARE Deal was the term used by Theodore Roosevelt in his campaigns against financial trusts, business interests that controlled markets or restrained trade, and the domination of the U.S. economy by the "predatory rich." "We demand that big business give people a square deal," he insisted on a nationwide tour in 1901 to rally public support for proposed legislation to regulate corporations. In his 1904 election campaign Roosevelt used the term to describe his domestic program, promising, "I shall see to it that every man has a square deal, no more and no less."

Roosevelt's Square Deal promised a "balance" between the claims of management and labor, producers and consumers. He was not against large corporations per se, and he had no intention of eliminating large accumulations of private wealth. Rather, he intended to act against their tendency to use the powers of national and state governments against labor and consumers. He called for the creation of a new cabinet department of Commerce and Industries, which would be able to regulate industries engaged in interstate commerce. Instead, in 1903 Congress created a Department of Commerce and Labor but did not give it the regulatory powers proposed by the President.

Roosevelt then turned to the courts to reduce excessive corporate power in the marketplace. His most famous lawsuit was filed in 1902 against the Northern Securities Company, a creation of

Theodore Roosevelt stalks "bad trusts" and keeps "good trusts" on a leash. Roosevelt proposed government regulations for business to prevent the exploitation of the labor force and consumers.

the financier J. P. Morgan. Along with E. H. Harriman and James J. Hill, Morgan had combined several railroads into the company in an effort to obtain a monopoly on rail transport in the Midwest and Far West. The Supreme Court upheld Roosevelt in 1904 and dissolved the merger. Roosevelt also filed suits against Standard Oil and tobacco and meat trusts for violations of the Sherman Anti-Trust Act.

In 1906 Roosevelt consolidated his Square Deal with several legislative victories. Congress passed the Meat Inspection Act, the Pure Food and Drug Act, and the Hepburn Railroad Act, which regulated industries and prevented trusts from fixing prices or providing consumers with unsafe products.

SEE ALSO
Roosevelt, Theodore

FURTHER READING
Hofstadter, Richard. "The Conservative as Progressive." In *The American Political Tradition.* New York: Knopf, 1948.
Mowry, George W. *Theodore Roosevelt and the Progressive Movement.* Madison: University of Wisconsin Press, 1946.

State of the Union address

THE STATE of the Union address is the speech the President makes to a joint session of Congress at the beginning of the legislative session. This address is in accordance with Article 2, Section 3, of the Constitution, which provides that the President shall "from time to time give to Congress information of the State of the Union." Since 1945 the speech has been known as the State of the Union address, although it is not called by that name in the Constitution.

Presidents George Washington and John Adams addressed Congress in person at the beginning of each session, usually arriving in elegant coaches drawn by white horses and attended by riders in fancy livery. The ostentatious display offended Thomas Jefferson, who ended the practice and sent a message to Congress by his private secretary in 1801.

President Woodrow Wilson revived the earlier custom in 1913 when he addressed Congress in person. Calling for quick passage of a banking bill, he also found it an "urgent necessity" for Congress to pass bills on agriculture, railroads, and mine safety. Wilson's discussion of Presidential priorities deeply offended many constitutional lawyers, who believed that the President should leave national priorities to Congress. Wilson also addressed Congress in person on a tariff act, reminding the lawmakers that he was "a person, not a mere department of government, hailing Congress from some isolated island of jealous power... a human being trying to cooperate with other human beings in a common service."

All Presidents since Wilson have continued his practice of addressing Congress in person to build support for their programs. The first message to be broadcast on the radio was delivered by Calvin Coolidge in 1923. It aided his attempt to secure the Republican nomination for President the following year. Franklin Roosevelt announced much of his New Deal program in his State of the Union addresses, which were also broadcast on radio. Harry Truman presented his entire Fair Deal program of civil rights, housing, and medical care in his addresses.

Woodrow Wilson addresses Congress in 1918. Wilson was the first President since John Adams to give the State of the Union address in person, rather than send a written message.

President Dwight Eisenhower's 1953 State of the Union address was the first to be televised. By the 1960s the address was switched to prime-time viewing hours in the evening to attract the maximum audience. Richard Nixon not only gave a State of the Union address but followed it up in 1971 with a State of the World address outlining his vision of U.S. foreign policy. No President since has given two such speeches to Congress.

Preparation of the State of the Union address takes months and is itself part of the process of government decision making about public policy. The President asks department secretaries and outside experts for ideas about new programs. Cabinet councils and Presidential advisory agencies help the President sift through these ideas and determine priorities. The President then calls on speech writers and political advisers in the White House Office to help prepare drafts of the speech.

Determining what goes into the President's speech is the first step in the struggle to turn ideas into new government programs. As Nixon's speech writer Bryce Harlow put it, each cabinet secretary was "demanding that more space

be given to their problems, to which I had to respond that the President says he wants this document kept shorter than a two-hour speech." A few weeks before the speech is to be delivered, the White House may leak parts of it to reporters as a "trial balloon." If public reaction, as gauged by the President's pollsters, is favorable, the proposals will remain in the President's speech, but controversial items might be dropped.

SEE ALSO

Messages, Presidential; Washington's Farewell Address

FURTHER READING

Hinckley, Barbara. *The Symbolic Presidency.* New York: Routledge, Chapman & Hall, 1990.
Tulis, Jeffrey. *The Rhetorical Presidency.* Princeton, N.J.: Princeton University Press, 1987.

Steel seizure

IN 1952, PRESIDENT Harry Truman seized steel mills across the United States and put them under federal government control during a labor dispute in order to guarantee steel production during the Korean War. The seizure was overturned by the Supreme Court in the case of *Youngstown Sheet and Tube* v. *Sawyer* (1952), one of the few times in U.S. history that a Presidential executive order has been ruled unconstitutional.

During the Korean War wages and prices were regulated by government agencies according to legislation passed by Congress. In 1952 the labor unions were negotiating with the steel companies for an industrywide settlement. The Wage Stabilization Board recommendations for higher wages were accepted by labor but rejected by management. The Office of Price Stability would have permitted price increases only if they were much lower than those desired by industry. With talks at an impasse, the unions went on strike.

Truman felt that he could not let the strike continue when defense industries depended on steel production. The President considered applying the Defense Production Act of 1950 to end the strike, but neither management nor labor was willing to apply its arbitration provisions. Under the Selective Service Act of 1948 the President could seize factories if orders were not being fulfilled. But the government would have to place direct orders with steel plants, the process would take time, and the Defense Department was pressing for immediate action.

Truman could also have applied the Taft-Hartley Act of 1947, which regulated peacetime labor-management relations. Under Title II, National Emergency Provisions, of the act, the President could appoint a board of inquiry to determine the facts and obtain a federal court injunction for a 60-day "cooling off" period. Fifteen days later, the National Labor Relations Board would conduct a secret vote of workers on the last employer offer. If the strike still could not be settled, the President could ask Congress for a law ending the strike. Truman did not wish to use this law: wildcat strikes might imperil production, and there was no assurance that the courts would grant the injunction or that Congress would impose a settlement if all else failed. Moreover, the President had vetoed the Taft-Hartley bill in 1947 as anti-labor, and it was opposed by the Democratic party and his labor allies. If he invoked that law, he would lose face.

Truman decided to seize the mills based on his constitutional authority as President and commander in chief. (Woodrow Wilson in World War I and Franklin Roosevelt in World War II had both seized defense plants to ensure that war production authorized by Congress was maintained.) Truman issued Executive Order 10340, which directed his secretary of commerce "to take possession of and operate the plants and facilities of certain steel companies." Truman delivered a speech to the American people justifying the seizures, but a rebuttal by the president of one of the seized companies was more effective: 43 percent of the public opposed Truman.

The steel companies sued the secretary of commerce. In June the Supreme Court issued its decision. Only three justices of the Supreme Court were impressed with the President's argument that he had constitutional authority to seize the mills. Six justices, in several opinions, ruled against the President. Each emphasized that Congress had legislated the procedures it wished to be used in strike situations. Congress had specifically rejected the possibility of Presidential seizure when it passed the Taft-Hartley Act. The Supreme Court forced Truman to return the mills to the owners, because, in Justice Robert Jackson's words, he had taken his constitutional powers as commander in chief and had "turned inward, not because of rebellion, but because of a lawful economic struggle between industry and labor." Such a struggle could not be resolved unilaterally by the President, the Court ruled, but must follow the laws passed by Congress. The strike lasted seven weeks after the mills were returned to the owners and then was settled.

SEE ALSO

Commander in chief; Executive orders; Truman, Harry S.

FURTHER READING

Marcus, Maeva. *Truman and the Steel Seizure Case.* New York: Columbia University Press, 1977.

Stevenson, Adlai

VICE PRESIDENT

☆ Born: Oct. 25, 1835, Christian
    County, Ky.
☆ Political party: Democrat
☆ Education: Illinois Wesleyan
    University, 1854; Centre College,
    1855–57; read law, 1858
☆ Military service: none
☆ Previous government service: master
    in chancery in Illinois, 1860–64;
    Illinois state's attorney, 1865–69;
    U.S. House of Representatives,
    1875–77, 1879–81; first assistant
    postmaster general, 1885–89
☆ Vice President under Grover
    Cleveland, 1893–97
☆ Subsequent government service: mone-
    tary commission to Europe, 1897
☆ Died: June 14, 1914, Chicago, Ill.

ACTIVE IN Democratic politics, Adlai
Stevenson campaigned for Stephen A.
Douglas against Abraham Lincoln in the
1858 Senate contest. He was appointed
master in chancery (state judge) in Illinois
in 1860 and served through 1864. He
was first assistant postmaster general in
Grover Cleveland's first administration,
and "Adlai's Axe" chopped down 40,000
Republican postmasters. Because of his
actions, the Republican-controlled Senate
blocked his nomination for the Supreme
Court in 1889. After obtaining the support of the Illinois delegation for Cleveland at the Democratic convention in
1892, he was rewarded with the Vice
Presidential nomination, and for the next
four years he presided over the Senate that
had blocked him from the Supreme Court.

After leaving office, Stevenson
served on a monetary commission to
Europe in 1897. He ran for Vice President in 1900 on William Jennings
Bryan's losing ticket and was defeated in
the race for governor of Illinois in 1908.

Stevenson's grandson, Adlai E.
Stevenson II, unsuccessfully ran for President twice on the Democratic ticket, in
1952 and 1956. His great-grandson,
Adlai E. Stevenson III, served as a U.S.
senator from Illinois from 1970 to 1980.

FURTHER READING

Schlup, Leonard. "The American Chame-
leon: Adlai E. Stevenson and the Quest
for the Vice Presidency in Gilded Age Politics." *Presidential Studies Quarterly* 21
(Summer 1991): 511–29.

Succession to the Presidency

IF THE PRESIDENT is removed from
office because he has been impeached
and convicted of a crime, or if he dies,
resigns, or cannot discharge the powers
and duties of the office, the Constitution
(Article 2, Section 1) provides that "the
same shall devolve [settle] on the Vice
President," who completes the remainder
of his predecessor's term. There are no
provisions for a special election. It is not
clear from the text whether the words
"the same" refer to the office of President
or simply to the "powers and duties" of
the office, which would make the Vice
President, upon taking over, the "acting
President." William Henry Harrison died
in 1841, becoming the first President to
die in office. His Vice President, John
Tyler, took the oath of office as President
and refused to be considered acting President, thus settling the issue. The first
clause of the 25th Amendment, adopted
in 1967, confirms Tyler's position. It
states clearly, "In case of the removal of
the President from office or of his death
or resignation, the Vice President shall
become President."

If there are vacancies for both
President and Vice President, the same
section of the Constitution provides that
Congress shall determine "what officer

shall then act as President, and such officer shall act accordingly." The language seems to indicate that the person assumes the powers of the office but is acting President. In 1792 Congress passed the first succession law, providing that the president pro tempore of the Senate would be next in line, then the Speaker of the House, until an interim election was held. In 1886 Congress changed the order of succession, starting with cabinet officers in the order in which their departments had been created, and dropped any provision for an interim election.

The most recent law, passed in 1947, provides that the Speaker of the House is next in line, followed by the president pro tempore of the Senate and then the cabinet secretaries, in the order in which their departments were founded, starting with the secretary of state. The acting President would serve "until the expiration of the then current Presidential term," an explicit rejection of the idea of an interim election.

SEE ALSO

Cabinet; Disability, Presidential; Health, Presidential; 25th Amendment; Vice President

FURTHER READING

Silva, Ruth. *Presidential Succession.* Ann Arbor: University of Michigan Press, 1951.
Sindler, Allen. *Unchosen Presidents.* Berkeley: University of California Press, 1976.

After John Kennedy's assassination in Dallas, Lyndon Johnson is sworn in as President aboard Air Force One. He is flanked by his wife, Lady Bird (left) and Jacqueline Kennedy, widow of the slain President.

Taft, William Howard

27TH PRESIDENT

☆ Born: Sept. 15, 1857, Cincinnati, Ohio
☆ Political party: Republican
☆ Education: Yale College, B.A., 1878; Cincinnati Law School, LL.B., 1880
☆ Military service: none
☆ Previous government service: assistant prosecuting attorney, Hamilton County, Ohio, 1881–82; collector of internal revenue for Cincinnati, 1882–83; assistant county solicitor, Hamilton County, 1885–87; justice, Superior Court of Cincinnati, 1887–90; U.S. solicitor general, 1890–92; presiding judge, 6th Circuit Court of Appeals, 1892–1900; president, Philippine Commission, 1900–1901; civil governor of the Philippines, 1901–4; U.S. secretary of war, 1904–8
☆ Elected President, 1908; served, 1909–13
☆ Subsequent government service: joint chairman, National War Labor Board, 1917–18; chief justice of the United States, 1921–30
☆ Died: Mar. 8, 1930, Washington, D.C.

WILLIAM HOWARD TAFT viewed the President as "chief magistrate" of the nation—someone who would hear the arguments of lower officials and then make his decision—not as a national leader who would use public opinion to lead the nation in his own direction. Taft argued that Presidential power was limited by the express language of the Constitution and that the President could not use the "general welfare" clause of its preamble to extend his powers further to meet the needs of the people (as his predecessor Theodore Roosevelt had argued). When Taft broke with the former President over conservation policies, he opened a split in the Republican party that guaranteed his defeat for a second term.

Taft was born into a staunch Republican family. His grandfather had been a judge in New England, and his

father, Alphonso Taft, had been secretary of war and attorney general in President Ulysses S. Grant's administration and minister to Russia and Austria during Chester Arthur's Presidency. Taft graduated from Yale second in his class, attended law school in Cincinnati, practiced law briefly, and then spent much of his career as a judge. His highest ambition was to serve on the Supreme Court. In a sense his Presidency was a detour to his lifelong goal, one he accepted because of the urging of his brothers and his wife.

After serving for many years as a state and federal judge, and as solicitor general in the U.S. Justice Department, Taft was tapped by President William McKinley in 1900 to serve as president of the U.S. Philippine Commission, set up to administer the islands the United States had won from Spain in the Spanish-American War. Taft believed that the "little brown brothers" on the islands were not ready for self-rule, so he organized a civil government to replace U.S. military rule and was named the first civil governor of the Philippines the following year. While he was working to pacify the island, he twice declined offers of a Supreme Court appointment from Theodore Roosevelt.

In 1904 Taft became Roosevelt's secretary of war. He met secretly with Count Katsura of Japan on July 29, 1905, to discuss a proposed Japanese protectorate (control over politics and the economy) in Korea once the Russo-Japanese War was concluded. Taft's acquiescence paved the way for the success of the Portsmouth Peace Conference that ended the war. In 1906 Taft helped prevent a potential rebellion in Cuba against a U.S.-supported regime. The United States imposed a provisional government under the terms of the Platt Amendment, which permitted U.S. intervention in Cuban affairs.

William Howard Taft (center) at the dedication of the Pan American Union Building in Washington, D.C.

Roosevelt designated Taft his successor, and he easily won the Republican nomination of 1908. Taft defeated the Democratic nominee, William Jennings Bryan, though in the heat of the campaign he had to leave his front porch in Cincinnati and campaign vigorously in the Midwest—the first time in U.S. history that both major-party candidates actively campaigned among the people for votes.

When Taft was inaugurated, it was the first time since 1837 that a President had successfully transferred power to his preferred successor. But Taft soon disappointed Roosevelt with his inability to provide effective leadership. He held as few press conferences as he could and was unable to rally public opinion behind him. While Roosevelt spent a year in Africa hunting big game, Taft allied himself with Republican conservatives and signed the Payne-Aldrich Tariff, which made only minor cuts in the high taxes on imports that had been set in 1897 by the Dingley Tariff Act. By accepting a high tariff he alienated himself from the progressive wing of the party.

Not all Taft's policies were conservative, however. The tariff act contained the first federal tax on corporate profits. Taft enforced the Sherman Anti-Trust Act to a greater extent than the "trust buster" Roosevelt had, winning lawsuits against the Standard Oil Company of New Jersey, American Tobacco Company, Du Pont de Nemours, and the American Sugar Refining Company. He limited the workday of federal employees to eight hours and created a commission to consider workmen's compensation legislation, which would provide money to injured workers. He proposed an amendment to the Constitution that would permit a personal income tax.

Taft called for a new budget process in which the President would have the primary responsibility for formulating an executive budget, but Congress ignored his requests. He got Congress to approve a new department of labor, enlarge the national park system, and create a bureau of mines. Congress extended the jurisdiction of the Interstate Commerce Commission to cover telephones, telegraph lines, underwater cable lines, and radio. A new campaign finance law proposed by Taft required candidates for Congress to make public their campaign expenditures.

In foreign policy Taft won arbitration treaties with Great Britain and France to provide for peaceful resolution of disputes, but these were blocked by the Senate. He barely got Senate approval for a trade agreement with Canada, and the Canadian parliament defeated it. The President instituted a foreign policy of "dollar diplomacy," which he defined as "substituting dollars for bullets" in an attempt to increase U.S. trade and influence abroad. The government worked with commercial banks to dominate the finances of Caribbean and Central American governments: it ran their customs houses (which collected duties on imported goods), helped establish local banks, floated loans for development, and secured contracts and markets for U.S. businesses.

Taft abandoned dollar diplomacy for more forceful intervention when he landed 2,500 marines in Nicaragua to take control of the country, and he also sent troops into Honduras, Cuba, and China to end threats to U.S. property. "Peaceful Bill" did keep U.S. troops out of Mexico during a revolution that erupted in 1910. Taft upset foreign nations by signing a 1912 law that exempted U.S. shipping companies from paying tolls for use of the Panama Canal. This law seemed to violate the Hay-Pauncefote Treaty, which established that all nations would pay the same tolls; Taft construed it to mean all nations except the United States. The law was repealed in 1913 after Taft left office.

Theodore Roosevelt split with his protégé in 1910 after Taft fired Gifford Pinchot, chief of the Division of Forestry and a defender of Roosevelt's conservation policies. Taft sided with his secretary of the interior, Richard Ballinger, who had opened for sale a tract of public land in Alaska that Roosevelt had previously designated not for sale. (Within a year, after a public outcry, Ballinger was forced to resign and the sale was canceled.)

In the fall of 1910 ex-President Theodore Roosevelt made a nationwide tour to 20 cities, where he articulated a progressive program of government regulation known as the New Nationalism. Meanwhile, Congress passed a series of bills providing for low tariffs on wool, cotton, and other goods, which Taft vetoed, further reducing his popularity in the Middle West. In the 1910 midterm elections Democrats won the House of Representatives and increased their Senate seats from 32 to 42; Republican Senate seats dropped from 59 to 49.

By February 1912, Roosevelt was openly campaigning for the Republican Presidential nomination, reversing his pledge not to seek a third term by claiming he had meant he would not seek three consecutive terms. Taft became the first sitting President to campaign for his own renomination. Roosevelt defeated him in most of the 15 Presidential primaries, even in Ohio. But Taft managed to secure the Republican nomination in 1912, in part through his control of southern delegations that consisted primarily of black officeholders dependent on his patronage and in part through the support of big-city political machines, or organizations. Roosevelt contested these "Taft delegations" with his own supporters. But the Republican National Committee, controlled by Taft, seated 235 of the southerners who favored him, awarding only 20 to the Roosevelt delegates and ensuring Taft's victory. Roosevelt then ran as a third-party candidate.

It was a bitter campaign. Taft called Roosevelt an egotist and a demagogue; Roosevelt called Taft a weakling and a fathead with the brains of a guinea pig. With the Republican vote split, Democrat Woodrow Wilson won the election. Taft ran a poor third, winning only the eight electoral college votes of Utah and Vermont. Republicans remained in a minority in the House, lost control of the Senate, and lost a majority of state governments. After four years of Taft his party was divided and in shambles. "I am glad to be going," he said as he left office. "This is the lonesomest place in the world."

After leaving the White House, Taft taught constitutional law at Yale Law School and was elected president of the American Bar Association. He served on the National War Labor Board during World War I. Finally, in 1921, he achieved his goal in life: President Warren Harding appointed him to the Supreme Court. As chief justice, Taft's most notable achievements were eliminating a large backlog of cases by gaining passage of the Judge's Act, which gave the court more discretion in deciding which cases to hear. In 1926, he wrote the majority opinion in *Myers* v. *United States,* which held that the President had a constitutional power to remove officials whose appointment had been consented to by the Senate.

The Tafts, like the Adamses and the Kennedys, are an American political dynasty. Taft's son, Robert Alphonso Taft, became a U.S. senator from Ohio in 1939. Known as Mr. Republican, he was one of the most influential Republican senators ever to serve. He was a contender for the Republican Presidential nomination in 1940, 1948, and 1952 but was never nominated. His son, Robert Taft, Jr., served as majority leader of the Ohio House of Representatives, as a U.S. representative in the 1960s, and as a senator from 1970 to 1976.

SEE ALSO

Removal power; Roosevelt, Theodore; Wilson, Woodrow

FURTHER READING

Coletta, Paolo E. *The Presidency of William Howard Taft.* Lawrence: University Press of Kansas, 1973.
Manners, William. *TR and Will: A Friendship That Split the Republican Party.* New York: Harcourt, Brace & World, 1969.
Taft, William Howard. *Our Chief Magistrate and His Powers.* New York: Columbia University Press, 1916.

Taylor, Zachary

12TH PRESIDENT

☆ *Born: Nov. 24, 1784, Orange County, Va.*
☆ *Political party: Whig*
☆ *Education: tutored through elementary grades*
☆ *Military service: Kentucky Militia, 1806; U.S. Army, 1808–49*
☆ *Previous civilian government service: none*
☆ *Elected President, 1848; served, 1849–50*
☆ *Died: July 9, 1850, Washington, D.C.*

ZACHARY TAYLOR was the second and last Whig to be elected President of the United States, and like his predecessor William Henry Harrison, he did not complete his term of office. Taylor had spent his whole life as a career military officer, on garrison duty in frontier posts and in the thick of battle against Indians in Florida and during the Mexican-American War. He was the first President without experience in elective or appointive office, though not the last. Taylor had never even cast a vote in a Presidential election before being elected to the office.

Taylor was born in Virginia but grew up on a large farm on the Kentucky frontier. He was tutored but never went to school. He entered the army with a commission as a lieutenant, which his cousin, Secretary of State James Madison, obtained for him. He was promoted to major for his defense of Fort Harrison, Indiana, against attacks by the Indian chief Tecumseh.

As a colonel, he defeated the Black Hawk Indians in 1832, and he later defeated the Seminole Indians in 1837, rising to the rank of general after the Battle of Lake Okeechobee. In February 1847, Taylor defeated the Mexican general Santa Anna at the Battle of Buena Vista.

The Whigs nominated Taylor in 1848 for the same reason they had nominated Harrison: he was a war hero. Taylor was also a southerner and a slaveholder (in 1841 he had bought a Mississippi plantation with many slaves) who would attract support in the South from a party with little popular following there. He won the Whig nomination on the fourth ballot over Henry Clay, Daniel Webster, and Winfield Scott. Helped by a split in the Democratic party, with Martin Van Buren running on a Free-Soil ticket and Lewis Cass running as a regular Democrat, Taylor was elected with fewer popular votes than Cass and Van Buren combined. However, his solid electoral college majority, in part due to electoral votes from four southern

General Zachary Taylor watches his troops defeat the Mexican forces at the Battle of Buena Vista in 1847.

states, proved the soundness of the Whigs' "southern strategy."

Taylor took little role in policy-making, leaving it to Whig congressional leaders in accordance with the party's view that Presidents should preside but not attempt to govern. After the California gold rush of 1849, Taylor ordered the state's military governor to hold elections in the territory. Ironically, those elections resulted in a state constitutional convention that wrote a state constitution outlawing slavery. The new state government began to function in 1850 and sought admission to the Union, strongly backed by Taylor.

Taylor wanted California, New Mexico, and Utah all to be admitted to the Union. This proposal caused him to split with Whig congressional leaders, who were more mindful of southern opposition to the admission of "free" states that would outlaw slavery and end the balance in the Union of 15 slave and 15 free states. Taylor took a strong stand against the southerners in Congress who threatened secession if California entered the Union as a free state, and he threatened senators from Georgia that he would crush any attempt at secession. Taylor was opposed to the Compromise of 1850, proposed by Henry Clay, that resolved the issue. The compromise, consisting of five separate laws, admitted California as a free state and abolished the slave trade in the nation's capital but balanced these measures with a stringent new law for the return of runaway slaves and the organization of Utah and New Mexico state governments without any determination about slavery. Taylor referred to this compromise as the "Omnibus Bill" and probably would have vetoed the measures had he lived.

Taylor's most significant achievement in foreign affairs was the negotiation of the Clayton-Bulwer Treaty (1850) with Great Britain, which provided that any canal built in Central America would be under joint Anglo-American control. This defused a crisis that might have led to hostilities that neither nation wanted.

Taylor died in office on July 9, 1850, of acute gastroenteritis and was succeeded by Millard Fillmore.

SEE ALSO
Fillmore, Millard

FURTHER READING
Bauer, Jack K. *Zachary Taylor: Soldier, Planter, Statesman of the Old Southwest.* Baton Rouge: Louisiana State University Press, 1985.
Smith, Elbert B. *The Presidencies of Zachary Taylor and Millard Fillmore.* Lawrence: University Press of Kansas, 1988.

Tenure of Office Act

SEE Removal power

Term of office

ACCORDING TO Article 2, Section 1, of the Constitution, the President serves a fixed four-year term. At the Constitutional Convention in 1787, the Virginia Plan with which the delegates began their work left blank the number of years the executive would serve but provided that the executive would be "ineligible a second time." Then the committee of the whole, by a 5-to-4 vote, provided that the President would serve a seven-year term and be ineligible for reelection, rejecting an alternative idea for a three-year term with two reelections permitted. A later proposal by Alexander Hamilton to elect a "Supreme Governour" for a lifetime term was also rejected. Finally, the Committee on Postponed Matters decided on a provision for a four-year term, coupled with

This postcard celebrates Grover Cleveland's return to the White House in 1892. He was the only President elected to two nonconsecutive terms.

eligibility for re-election to an unlimited number of terms.

Until the election of 1936, Congress set the inaugural date for March 4. A lame-duck session of the previously elected Congress lasted from the November election through the following March and often included many defeated members of Congress. The lame-duck Congress was entitled to choose the President and Vice President in case of a deadlock in the electoral college. The Congress elected with the President did not meet until 14 months after the election—unless the President called it into special session.

In 1933, when the 20th Amendment was ratified, this set the Presidential inaugural date for January 20, which shortened substantially the time between election and inauguration. Franklin D. Roosevelt was the first President to be inaugurated under the new system, beginning his second term on January 20, 1937.

The 20th Amendment also provided that the newly elected Congress would meet on January 3 following the election, even before the President assumed office, thus shortening the lame-duck period of the previous Congress. Usually, the outgoing Congress has adjourned prior to the November election and does not come back into session. The new Congress chooses the President and Vice President in case of a deadlock in the electoral college.

The 22nd Amendment, ratified in 1951, provides that no person may be elected President more than twice.

SEE ALSO

Electoral college; Succession to the Presidency; 22nd Amendment; Two-term tradition

Third parties

EARLY IN the history of the United States, two dominant parties emerged and became entrenched as the Democrats and the Republicans. Third parties have frequently risen to challenge their dominance, focusing on issues that the two major parties either ignored or suppressed. Sometimes a third party can supplant one of the major parties, as the Republican party did in the 1850s when it replaced the Whigs by opposing the spread of slavery into the western territories. More often, the major parties absorb the new ideas put forward by the third parties, which eventually disband.

The Tertium Quids, the nation's first third party, was formed in 1801 after John Randolph, the chairman of the House Ways and Means Committee, broke with President Thomas Jefferson on the issue of states' rights. This political group dissolved once Jefferson maneuvered Randolph out of office, but it did set an example for the possibilities of organized dissent through multiparty politics.

Third parties have traditionally formed to strengthen certain groups' support for or opposition to the general direction of American politics. The American Party (or Know-Nothings, as they were commonly called) enjoyed a short-lived success in the 1850s by opposing immigration. The Know-Nothings won offices nationwide in the 1854 elections, due in large part to a growing xenophobia, but they were

The American Party, or Know-Nothings, used scripts such as this one in the mid-19th century to avoid accepting Roman Catholics, foreigners, or their sympathizers as party members.

soon absorbed into the broader-based Republican party.

Third-party candidates have often run in Presidential elections. The Populist party, formed to aid beleaguered farmers, ran a strong third in the 1892 Presidential election. As the Socialist party candidate, Eugene V. Debs made four unsuccessful bids for president from 1900 to 1912. Despite their losses, the Populists and Socialists inspired the Democrats and Republicans to adopt many of the reforms they advocated, including a progressive income tax and federal banking and business regulation.

In 1912 former President Theodore Roosevelt broke from the Republican party and ran for President as the Progressive (or Bull Moose) party candidate. Running on a strong reform platform that included woman suffrage, an end to child labor, and greater federal regulation of the economy, Roosevelt ran second in the race, beating Republican President William Howard Taft but losing to the Democrat, Woodrow Wilson.

Third-party candidates seek to affect the outcome of elections by disrupting voter loyalties to the major parties. In 1948 Southern Democrats walked out of the Democratic convention after it adopted a civil rights plank. The States Rights (or Dixiecrat) party ran South Carolina governor Strom Thurmond for President. Meanwhile, former Vice President Henry Wallace also broke with the Democratic party and ran for President as the Progressive

party candidate. Despite these defections, President Harry S. Truman held the core of the Democratic party together and scored an upset victory for reelection. Similarly, in 1968 and 1972, Alabama governor George Wallace campaigned as the American party candidate for President in order to oppose the Democratic party's support for civil rights legislation. Wallace captured a large portion of the southern vote with his anti-Washington platform.

Believing that the two-party system had become less flexible due to the growing importance of outside interest groups and multimillion-dollar campaigns, third-party candidates ran increasingly strong challenges in several elections toward the end of the 20th century. In 1980 Illinois representative John Anderson left the Republicans and ran as an Independent for President, hoping to carve a constituency out of the disenchanted. Attempting to bring people on the outside of the two-party system together by representing a variety of interests, Anderson won 7 percent of the national vote. His effort was a precursor of the Reform party, founded by wealthy businessman H. Ross Perot.

Perot ran for President on the Reform ticket in both 1992 and 1996. In 1992 he received 13 percent of the vote, making the difference that enabled Democrat Bill Clinton to unseat the Republican President George Bush. Despite winning more than 19 million votes—a record for any third party—Perot received no votes in the electoral college. This constitutional system, by which voters choose electors equal to the number of senators and representatives in their state and which requires a candidate to win a majority of electors to win the Presidency, has continued to force parties to remain national coalitions rather than splintered regional or issue groups. Third parties serve as a testing ground for new issues, and as a banner under which disaffected voters can rally, but their failure to gain ground in the electoral college usually sends their issues and their voters back into the two major parties.

Ticket

A TICKET consists of candidates for different offices who appear on an election ballot under the same party symbol and who run as a team. Prior to the election of 1804, tickets were informal because all candidates ran for Presidential electoral votes; the runner-up became Vice President. The 12th Amendment, which took effect that year, called for separate electoral votes for President and Vice President. That year, for the first time, there were distinct candidates for the two positions, and Thomas Jefferson and George Clinton were the winning ticket.

In 1840 Martin Van Buren ran for President with different Vice Presidential candidates on his ticket in each state. That was because the Democratic national convention had resolved not to endorse any one candidate for the Vice Presidency and to leave it instead to state parties to "nominate" their own Vice Presidential candidates to appear on the ballot with Van Buren.

Occasionally, a party has nominated a Vice Presidential candidate from the opposition party. John Tyler ran for Vice President on the Whig ticket in 1840 but was himself a Democrat. In 1864 Republican Abraham Lincoln ran with Democrat Andrew Johnson on the National Unionist ticket to gain votes from Democrats in the border states, such as Tennessee.

Major-party candidates sometimes run simultaneously on minor-party tickets.

In 1868, for example, Ulysses S. Grant and Henry Wilson ran not only as Republicans but also on the National Working Men's party ticket. Their opponents, Horace Greeley and Benjamin Brown, ran not only as Democrats but also as Liberal Republicans and as candidates of the Liberal Republican Party of Colored Men. In 1896 William Jennings Bryan received the nomination of both the Democratic and the Populist parties, and in 1900 Bryan and Adlai Stevenson received the Democratic and Silver Republican nominations.

Of the 52 Presidential elections held between 1789 and 1992, only 7 resulted in the reelection of a President and the incumbent Vice President. The only Presidents who kept their running mates for a second term were George Washington, James Monroe, Woodrow Wilson, Franklin Roosevelt, Dwight Eisenhower, Richard Nixon, and Ronald Reagan.

Tompkins, Daniel
VICE PRESIDENT

☆ *Born: June 21, 1774, Fox Meadows, N.Y.*
☆ *Political party: Democratic-Republican*
☆ *Education: Columbia College, B.A., 1795*
☆ *Military service: New York State Militia, 1812–14*
☆ *Previous government service: New York State Constitutional Convention, 1801; New York State Assembly, 1803–4; U.S. House of Representatives, 1805; associate justice, New York Court of Appeals, 1805–7; governor of New York, 1807–17*
☆ *Vice President under James Monroe, 1817–25*
☆ *Died: June 11, 1825, Tompkinsville, N.Y.*

DANIEL TOMPKINS was considered for several appointments, including secretary of state, during James Madison's Presidency, but his career was confined to

New York State until 1817. During the War of 1812, as governor of New York and commander in chief of the New York State militia and the Third Military District of the United States, Tompkins found it necessary to borrow money to supply his troops. He borrowed much of the money on his own credit. Creditors later seized his personal fortune to repay bills the military had incurred on his signature. At the end of the war Tompkins applied to the Treasury for repayment but his accounts were challenged, leaving him with severe financial problems.

Tompkins was sponsored by New York politicians as a potential Presidential candidate in 1816, but he attracted little support among the Republicans in Congress (the congressional caucus) who would determine the party's choice. James Monroe, who won the Republican nomination, accepted Tompkins as his running mate.

While Vice President, Tompkins tried to clear up his tangled financial affairs. In poor health and drinking heavily, he spent most of his term in New York City. He was defeated for the New York governorship in 1820 but ran for reelection with Monroe and served a second term as Vice President. In 1824, near the end of his second term, Congress finally authorized the Treasury to reimburse him for $95,000 in expenses.

SEE ALSO
Monroe, James

Transitions, Presidential

MANY ACTIVITIES occur prior to and immediately after a new President enters office. Planned transitions occur at the end of a departing President's term and last from the election to shortly after the inauguration. Unplanned transitions

occur almost instantaneously when a President dies or resigns; they take several weeks to complete.

The planned transition involves briefings on the policies of the outgoing administration (especially national security secrets); preparation of the inaugural address and the first message to Congress requesting legislation; preparation of revisions to the budget of the outgoing President; recruitment of personnel to fill the 3,000 political appointments that constitute a Presidential administration; and analysis of each department and agency in order to exert maximum White House influence on its operations.

In an unplanned transition the Vice President takes the Presidential oath of office. He then speaks to the nation about the events that led to his succession, usually by addressing a joint session of Congress.

Only recently have Presidents cooperated with their successors in planning smooth transitions. In 1944 Franklin Roosevelt began the custom of briefing his major-party opponent on national security matters, and in 1952 Truman did the same. Dwight Eisenhower established the custom of providing a personal briefing for his successor (John F. Kennedy), and the two men created the precedent of designating aides to serve as liaisons between the incoming and outgoing administrations.

Outgoing Presidents usually want their successors to endorse their last

Outgoing President William Howard Taft (left) and incoming President Woodrow Wilson ride to the 1913 inauguration.

projects. Herbert Hoover, in the midst of the Great Depression, attempted to get President-elect Franklin Roosevelt to support his proposals for economic recovery. Incoming Presidents generally do not give these endorsements, because they wish to preserve their freedom of action. Consequently, there is often some friction between outgoing and incoming Presidents; it is rare but not unknown for the outgoing President to skip the inauguration ceremonies entirely.

Until the 1960s the expenses involved in the transition were borne by the winning candidate and his party. In 1960 Kennedy and the Democratic National Committee spent $300,000. Congress later passed the Presidential Transition Act of 1963, which provided $900,000 for the "orderly transfer of a President and the inauguration of a new President." Funds were increased to keep up with inflation. The Presidential Transition Effectiveness Act of 1988 provided that in 1992 the newly elected President would receive $3.5 million and the departing President would receive $1.5 million. Under the new law, the President-elect's transition organization would be required to limit private contributions to no more than $5,000 from a single source and to report all such contributions. These limits and disclosure provisions were designed to prevent big-money contributors from buying influence and access in the new administration.

SEE ALSO

Succession to the Presidency

FURTHER READING

Brauer, Carl M. *Presidential Transitions: Eisenhower through Reagan.* New York: Oxford, 1986.

Pfiffner, James P. *The Strategic Presidency: Hitting the Ground Running.* Chicago: Dorsey, 1988.

Pfiffner, James P., and R. Gordon Hoxie. *The Presidency in Transition.* New York: Center for the Study of the Presidency, 1989.

Treaty of Versailles

THE TREATY of Versailles was the agreement negotiated by the victorious Allied nations with the defeated Central Powers to end World War I. The failure of the U.S. Senate to consent to the treaty was a major defeat for President Woodrow Wilson.

The treaty was negotiated at a peace conference held between January and June 1919 at the Palace of Versailles outside of Paris, France. It was attended by 32 nations but dominated by Prime Minister David Lloyd George of Great Britain, Prime Minister Georges Clemenceau of France, Prime Minister Vittorio Orlando of Italy, and President Woodrow Wilson of the United States. Wilson shattered precedent by attending the conference in person rather than naming the secretary of state or a special envoy as chief of the delegation. He was the first U.S. President to go to Europe during his term. Wilson's delegation did not include any leaders of Congress. Instead, Wilson took hundreds of experts to advise him about the peoples and politics of Europe.

Wilson's Fourteen Points program renounced territorial gains for the United States and denounced secret understandings. He called for "open covenants openly arrived at." The other Allies, however, had already come to agreement about the spoils of war, especially German colonies in Africa and the division of the Ottoman Empire in the Middle East.

Signed by the defeated German government in June 1919, the Treaty of Versailles was a vindictive settlement. Germany was forced to accept sole responsibility for the war, pay $56 billion in reparations to the victors, and disarm. The French were allowed to occupy

The peace conference convenes in the ornate palace at Versailles.

German territory for 15 years and to regain the province of Alsace-Lorraine, which Germany had conquered in 1871. Poland was given a corridor to the sea through the German province of Prussia, which cut Germany in two. Altogether, Germany was stripped of 10 percent of its people, one-eighth of its territory, and all its overseas possessions. From the Ottoman Empire the British received mandates, or territories, in Palestine, Trans-Jordan, and Iraq, and the French received Syria and Lebanon. Japan acquired Germany's Pacific islands.

The only victory for Wilson during the negotiations was the inclusion of a League of Nations as part of the treaty. The league would be an assembly of all sovereign nations, pledged to preserve the independence and territorial integrity of each member.

Wilson returned home in June to press for U.S. participation in the League of Nations. Opposition came from German Americans and Italian Americans and from isolationists in the South and West. Wilson had not consulted with the Senate during the negotiations and had not tried to win over the influential

chairman of the Foreign Relations Committee, Republican Henry Cabot Lodge of Massachusetts. Lodge led the fight against the league. He disliked Wilson and believed the United States should retain complete freedom of action in international affairs. Although Lodge was no isolationist, he managed to unite the isolationist wing of his party, known as the Irreconcilables, with his own followers around a series of "fourteen reservations" to the treaty (an echo of Wilson's Fourteen Points). One provided for U.S. withdrawal from the league by concurrent resolution of Congress, a method not subject to Presidential veto. Another provided that the President could not direct troops in a league peacekeeping operation—an attack on the President's power as commander in chief. Still another would have prevented the President from making interim appointments to an international organization when the Senate was in recess.

The most important reservation amended the treaty by stating that the United States would retain complete freedom of action in foreign affairs and that only Congress had the right to commit U.S. forces to military action—not the league or the President.

In September 1919 Wilson embarked on a nationwide speaking tour to rally support for the League of Nations. His tour was exhausting and he collapsed on September 25 in Pueblo, Colorado. He returned to Washington and suffered a stroke on October 2.

On November 19 Democrats in the Senate voted down the treaty with the Lodge reservations; then Lodge's Republican coalition voted down Wilson's version of the treaty. Although more than two-thirds of the Senate favored some sort of league, they were caught between Wilson and Lodge, and no treaty could pass. For the first time, the Senate rejected a peace treaty negotiated by the President. The United States never became a member of the League of Nations. Instead, Congress passed a joint resolution in 1921 officially recognizing an end to hostilities with Germany and other Central Powers.

SEE ALSO

Treaty powers; Wilson, Woodrow

FURTHER READING

Ambrosius, Lloyd E. *Woodrow Wilson and the American Diplomatic Tradition: The Treaty Fight in Perspective.* Cambridge: Cambridge University Press, 1987.
Bailey, Thomas A. *Woodrow Wilson and the Great Betrayal.* Chicago: University of Chicago Press, 1963.
Wilson, Woodrow. *The Hope of the World.* New York: Harper, 1920.

Treaty powers

THE CONSTITUTION provides that the President "shall have the Power, by and with the Advice and Consent of the Senate, to make Treaties, provided two-thirds of the Senators present concur." The framers expected the Senate to play a major role in the treaty-making process. In fact, most drafts at the Constitutional Convention gave the Senate the power to make treaties, and it was not until 10 days before the convention adjourned that the President was given the major role in negotiating treaties.

Does the Senate's advice come only when the President submits a treaty draft to the Senate? Or can the Senate advise the President while he is negotiating the treaty? The language of the Constitution does not divide treaty making into separate stages for negotiation and Senate consent. Rather, the President "makes" the treaty with the advice and consent of the Senate, which seems to imply a role for the Senate in the negotiations.

George Washington set the early precedents. While negotiating an Indian treaty, he suggested that "the business may possibly be referred to their [the Senate's] deliberations in their legislative chamber." Washington met with the Senate on August 22, 1789, to obtain its advice. The senators decided they would not commit themselves to any treaty draft that Washington presented to them that day. Washington had to return two days later in order to obtain their consent, but the experience of consultation soured him. He never again consulted in advance with the Senate in person. When he negotiated the Jay Treaty with Great Britain, he consulted with Senate leaders in writing and submitted the complete treaty to the Senate only after it was completed.

Since Washington's time, practices have varied. Until 1815 it was the custom for Presidents to send a special message to Congress before starting negotiations and again when treaty drafts had been concluded. Since then, some Presidents have consulted informally with congressional leaders before negotiations, as President Chester Arthur did in 1884 on a treaty with the independent islands of Hawaii. Many have given extensive briefings to senators while negotiations were in progress, as Secretary of State Dean Acheson did with key senators about the North Atlantic Treaty Organization treaty of 1949. One senator, Walter George, actually wrote part of the treaty for the administration.

The composition of the negotiating team may help the President secure Senate consent. President Harry Truman used a Republican, John Foster Dulles, as his chief negotiator for the treaty with Japan at the end of World War II to give it bipartisan support. For arms control negotiations some Presidents have given senators an informal "veto" over members of their negotiating teams or allowed senators to send staff members to negotiating sessions as observers. Since 1962 members of Congress have been advisers on trade agreement negotiations, and President Jimmy Carter named 26 senators as "official advisers" to his arms negotiating team at Geneva in 1977 and 1978.

Sometimes, Presidents have even put members of Congress in their negotiating delegations, as William McKinley did when he included three senators in his Treaty of Paris delegation in 1900.

President Woodrow Wilson did not favor this kind of collaboration: he argued that Presidents should negotiate treaties by themselves and then submit them to the Senate. When he negotiated the Treaty of Versailles in 1919, he did not include a single member of the Senate in his delegation, nor did he provide Congress with any information about negotiations. The Senate defeated the treaty. Jimmy Carter almost committed the same error, failing to include senators on his negotiating team or provide them with briefings when he negotiated the Panama Canal Treaty in 1977. To save the treaty in 1979, Carter agreed to amendments negotiated by several senators with the Panamanian government.

The two-thirds provision by which the Senate gives its formal consent has been interpreted since 1953 to mean two-thirds of a quorum (the minimum number of members necessary to transact business). The Senate may amend the treaty before giving its consent, in which case the new language must be accepted by the other nation. The Senate may also express its "reservations" about the language. Such a document is sent to the other nation but does not require its consent.

After the Senate consents to a treaty, the President may ratify it by signifying to the other nation that it is in effect, or he may withhold ratification if he decides not to implement it. He may withhold ratification because circumstances have changed, because he objects to amendments, or because he foresees problems with the other nation's adherence to it.

Between 1789 and 1969, 23 of 195 treaties submitted by the President were defeated by the Senate. These included a treaty to annex Texas in 1844 and Wilson's Treaty of Versailles in 1919. Although most treaties since World War II have been adopted, the Senate has sometimes blocked or amended important Presidential initiatives. These include the heavily amended Panama Canal Treaties of 1979 and the Strategic

Calvin Coolidge and Secretary of State Frank B. Kellogg sign the Kellogg-Briand Pact in 1929. The treaty, which outlawed war except in cases of national self-defense, did nothing to deter war in the 1930s and 1940s.

Arms Limitation Agreements with the Soviet Union that Jimmy Carter withdrew from the Senate after the Soviet invasion of Afghanistan in 1979.

Proposals have been made to lower the approval requirement to three-fifths or an absolute majority of senators present. Another idea is to prevent any amendments or reservations by senators. Such changes would require a constitutional amendment, and the Senate is unlikely to agree to limitations on its treaty powers.

Treaty obligations can be terminated in a variety of ways. Congress may pass a law inconsistent with the terms of the treaty, and the courts will enforce the law at the expense of the treaty. Congress can pass a joint resolution that directs the President to abrogate, or nullify, a treaty. Or the President can request a Senate resolution consenting to abrogation of a treaty. Finally, the President can abrogate a treaty unilaterally, without obtaining the consent of Congress or the Senate, as Jimmy Carter did in 1978 with the Mutual Defense Treaty of 1954 with the Republic of China (Taiwan).

SEE ALSO
Executive agreements

FURTHER READING
Fisher, Louis. *Constitutional Conflicts between Congress and the President.* Princeton, N.J.: Princeton University Press, 1985.

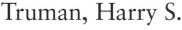

Truman, Harry S.
33RD PRESIDENT

☆ Born: May 8, 1884, Lamar, Mo.
☆ Political party: Democrat
☆ Education: high school
☆ Military service: U.S. Army, 1917–19
☆ Previous government service: road overseer, Jackson County, Mo., 1914; postmaster, Grandview, Mo., 1915; Jackson County judge, 1922–24; Jackson County presiding

judge, 1926–34; U.S. Senate, 1934–45; Vice President, 1945
☆ Succeeded to Presidency, 1945; served, 1945–53
☆ Died: Dec. 26, 1972, Kansas City, Mo.

HARRY TRUMAN was the first President to assume office in the middle of a war. His decision to drop atomic bombs on Japan shortened World War II and reduced U.S. casualties. In the postwar period he presided over the creation of collective security measures (the creation of alliances for mutual defense against aggression) to contain communist expansion in Europe. Although he won an elected term in one of the greatest upsets in U.S. history, subsequent inflation and labor unrest, coupled with his decision to use U.S. troops to defend South Korea, contributed to his unpopularity and his decision not to seek a second elected term.

Truman grew up on a farm near Independence, Missouri. He finished high school and became a railroad worker, mail room boy, bank clerk, and bookkeeper, returning to his grandfather's farm after several years. In World War I he served as a first lieutenant and then captain of artillery, seeing action near the end of the war in the Argonne Forest and at Verdun. In 1919 he married Elizabeth Virginia ("Bess") Wallace. Truman became a partner in a men's haberdashery with an army friend; when the store failed and left him deeply in debt, he refused to declare bankruptcy and spent years paying off creditors.

Truman's political career began after he was introduced to the Democratic boss of Kansas City, Missouri, Tom Pendergast. As a loyal worker in the Pendergast machine, he helped the organization move into rural Jackson County. He became a county judge (an administrative, not a legal, position), and in 1934 the Pendergast machine backed him in a three-way race for the Democratic nomination for U.S. Senate. Truman won the nomination, then campaigned for and won election as a supporter of Franklin Roosevelt's New Deal. In 1940 he again won a three-way race for the Democratic nomination, then won reelection even though Boss Pendergast had been sentenced to prison for income tax evasion and other members of his machine had been convicted of vote fraud. Voters knew that Truman had not been involved in these activities.

In his second term in the Senate, Truman chaired the Special Committee to Investigate the National Defense Program. He uncovered waste, fraud, and corruption and contributed greatly to the successful U.S. war effort.

In 1944 President Franklin Roosevelt dropped Henry Wallace from his ticket and offered the Democratic convention a choice between Harry Truman and Supreme Court justice William O. Douglas. Although a majority of the delegates supported Wallace on the first ballot, they bowed to Roosevelt's wishes and nominated Truman on the second ballot.

President Roosevelt's death on April 12, 1945, elevated Truman to the Presidency. On May 7 Truman announced that the war in Europe had ended. His first important mission was the Potsdam Conference in July 1945, where he met with British prime minister Winston Churchill and Soviet premier Joseph Stalin to negotiate the fate of Eastern Europe. Returning home, Truman won Senate consent to the charter of the United Nations; for the first time, the United States would be part of a world organization. In July he decided to use the atomic bomb against Japan to end the war in the Pacific. Hiroshima was destroyed on August 6, Nagasaki on August 9. On August 14 Japan surrendered.

In September 1945 Truman presented his domestic Fair Deal program to Congress: new initiatives in health care, civil rights, public housing, and rural development. Much of the legislation was stalled by a conservative coalition of Republicans and Southern Democrats, although Congress did pass the Employment Act of 1946, which established the Council of Economic Advisers. With the slogan "Had Enough?" the Republicans won control of Congress in 1946 and began passing their own measures. Truman vetoed the Taft-Hartley Act, a law regulating strikes, because he thought it was antiunion, but Congress passed it over his veto in 1947. It also passed an income tax reduction bill. Truman intervened in railroad and coal strikes in 1946 and 1947, alienating labor and liberals, and his attempt to continue the wartime Fair Employment Practices Committee (set up to outlaw racial discrimination in employment) upset southern conservatives, who abolished it.

In 1948 Truman won the Democratic nomination for President with the support of the urban party bosses. In a brilliant election-year tactic, Truman called the Republican-dominated Congress into special session and challenged it to pass his program. While the Republicans stalled, Truman campaigned for reelection against the "Do-Nothing 80th Congress." He made a whistle-stop railroad tour and crowds chanted "Give 'em Hell, Harry." He proposed major new civil rights legislation, including federal protection against lynchings, voting rights measures, prohibition of discrimination in interstate transportation, and a permanent fair practices commission. In the midst of the campaign Truman issued an executive order ending racial segregation in the armed forces. With overwhelming support from blacks, Truman eked out narrow margins of victory in key northern states and defeated

This kind of atomic bomb, called Fat Man, was detonated over Nagasaki on August 9, 1945. Truman gave the order to drop the bomb after warning the Japanese that they would be destroyed if they did not surrender.

Republican Thomas E. Dewey, Dixiecrat Strom Thurmond, and Progressive Henry Wallace. Truman won less than half the popular vote, in the closest election since 1916.

Truman returned to Washington to savor his victory, proudly holding aloft a copy of the *Chicago Tribune* that carried the election night headline "DEWEY DEFEATS TRUMAN."

Truman's major domestic success after winning reelection was the Housing Act of 1949, which provided for slum clearance and public housing in urban areas. Congress also raised the minimum wage. It stalled, however, on Truman's farm, education, health, labor, and civil rights proposals.

Truman's foreign policy was based on containing communist expansion in Western Europe. Rather than seeking to cultivate the Soviets as allies, Truman believed that they had to "be faced with an iron fist and strong language." Congress created the Defense Department to supervise the Departments of the Army, Navy, and Air Force and established the Joint Chiefs of Staff for military planning. It also created the National Security Council and the Central Intelligence Agency.

In March 1947 the President announced the Truman Doctrine, stating that the United States would "support free peoples who are resisting attempted subjugation by armed minorities or outside pressure." He called for military and

economic aid to Greece and Turkey to prevent communist guerrilla movements from seizing power. Then, in June, Secretary of State George Marshall announced the European Recovery Program (later known as the Marshall Plan). Between 1948 and 1951 more than $12 billion was granted or loaned to European nations to restore their postwar economies. In the spring and summer of 1948 Truman ordered U.S. airplanes to supply West Berlin, breaking a Soviet blockade of the western part of the city. The Point Four foreign aid program of technical assistance began in 1949, the same year that the North Atlantic Treaty Organization (NATO) committed the United States to the defense of Western Europe. Similarly, the Rio Pact and the Anzus Pact committed the United States to the defense of the Western Hemisphere, Australia, and New Zealand. Mutual defense treaties were also signed with the Philippines and Japan. The Soviets tested their first atomic bomb in 1949, so in 1950 Truman permitted development of the powerful hydrogen bomb to proceed. It was successfully tested in 1952.

Truman's policy of containment against communist aggression was put to the test. On June 28, 1950, Truman ordered U.S. air and ground forces to repel a North Korean invasion of South Korea. This "police action" was sanctioned by the United Nations Security Council. Truman's conduct of the war was controversial. On the advice of Secretary of State Dean Acheson, he did not ask Congress for a declaration of war. He allowed General Douglas MacArthur to invade North Korea, but when communist Chinese troops entered the war, Truman refused to allow bombing of North Korean supply bases in China because he feared it might lead to all-out war between the United States and China. On April 11, 1951, Truman fired

Truman (center) meets with Soviet premier Joseph Stalin (right) and British prime minister Clement Attlee at the Potsdam conference in July 1945.

MacArthur for insubordination after the general called for bombing China. MacArthur received a hero's welcome back in the United States and addressed a joint session of Congress.

The Korean War dragged on. Close to 50,000 U.S. troops were killed and 100,000 wounded. The war rekindled inflation and shortages in the economy and contributed to Truman's declining popularity. After Truman seized steel mills on April 8, 1952, during a strike, claiming he had to ensure production as a war measure, the Supreme Court ordered that he return the mills to their owners. This ruling further diminished Truman's popularity.

On March 29, 1952, Truman announced that he would not seek re-election. In his farewell address, he observed that "the President's job is to make decisions. . . . He can't pass the buck to anybody. No one else can do the deciding for him. That's his job." With his job over, he retired to Independence, Missouri, where he wrote his memoirs and oversaw the creation of his Presidential library. "You, more than any man, have saved Western civilization," Winston Churchill told him.

SEE ALSO

Barkley, Alben; Eisenhower, Dwight David; Roosevelt, Franklin D.; Steel seizure; Wallace, Henry

FURTHER READING

Ferrell, Robert H. *Harry S. Truman and the Modern American Presidency.* Boston: Little, Brown, 1983.
McCullough, David. *Truman.* New York: Simon & Schuster, 1992.
Miller, Merle. *Plain Speaking: An Oral Biography of Harry S Truman.* New York: Berkley, 1974.
Truman, Harry S. *Memoirs of Harry S. Truman.* Vol. 1, *Year of Decisions, 1945.* New York: Da Capo, 1986.
Truman, Harry S. *Memoirs of Harry S. Truman.* Vol. 2, *Years of Trial and Hope.* New York: Da Capo, 1987.
Truman, Margaret. *Harry S. Truman.* New York: Morrow, 1973.

12th Amendment

THE 12TH Amendment to the Constitution, ratified in 1804, revised the voting system in the electoral college. The Constitution of 1787 provided that each elector would cast two ballots for President. The person with the most votes would become President and the runner-up would assume the Vice Presidency, provided each received support from a majority of all the electors appointed. If two candidates with such support received an equal number of votes, the House of Representatives was to choose between them.

In the election of 1796, Federalist John Adams received a majority of electoral college votes, but Anti-Federalist Thomas Jefferson was runner-up and became Vice President. In the election of 1800 every Republican elector cast one ballot for Thomas Jefferson and the other for his running mate, Aaron Burr. Because Jefferson and Burr received the same number of votes, the election went into the House of Representatives. Many Federalists preferred Burr to Jefferson, but at the last minute, Alexander Hamilton intervened and on the 36th ballot some Federalists abstained, ensuring Jefferson's election as President. The Senate then elected Burr Vice President, according to the original intentions of the Jeffersonians.

In 1803 Congress passed the 12th Amendment, which was ratified by the states and adopted on September 25, 1804. It provided that each elector would cast a separate ballot for President and Vice President, thus preventing the situation that had occurred in 1800. The new system ensured that the majority that elected a President would also elect his running mate from the same party, preventing a recurrence of the results in 1796.

Because only one ballot can be cast for each office (rather than two for President under the original system), only one candidate can win a majority vote for President, preventing a recurrence of the results in 1800. If no candidate wins an electoral college majority for President, the House chooses from among the top three, with each state casting a single vote. If no candidate wins a majority for the Vice Presidency, the Senate chooses between the top two, with each senator casting one vote. In the event the House fails to elect a President, the person chosen by the Senate as Vice President acts as President until the House does elect a President.

Thomas Jefferson won the 1800 election when the House of Representatives chose him over Aaron Burr, who had received the same number of electoral votes.

SEE ALSO

Burr, Aaron; Electoral college; Jefferson, Thomas; Ticket

FURTHER READING

McCormick, Richard P. *The Presidential Game.* New York: Oxford, 1982.

25th Amendment

THE 25TH Amendment to the Constitution, ratified on February 10, 1967, deals with Presidential disability. If a President is disabled, the 25th Amendment provides that the Vice President acts as President (but does not assume the office of President) until the incumbent can resume the office. The President can declare disability and invite the Vice President to act as President. Or the Vice President, together with a majority of the cabinet, can find the President to be disabled, in which case the Vice President can act as President. In either case the President determines when to resume the duties of the office.

If the Vice President and the cabinet disagree with the President's decision, the final determination is made by Congress. A two-thirds vote by each chamber is required to permit the Vice President to continue to act as President in the event the President wishes to resume the powers of his office. These provisions have not yet been applied to any President.

The 25th Amendment also provides for filling vacancies in the Vice Presidency. The President can nominate a Vice President, who takes office upon confirmation by a majority vote of both chambers of Congress. This provision was used in 1973, when Spiro Agnew resigned from the Vice Presidency and Gerald Ford was nominated by President Richard Nixon and confirmed by Congress. It was also used by Ford to fill the vacancy created when he became President after Nixon's resignation.

Chief Justice Warren Burger administers the oath of office to Vice President Gerald Ford in 1974. Richard Nixon nominated Ford for the position when Vice President Spiro Agnew resigned.

SEE ALSO

Agnew, Spiro T.; Disability, Presidential; Ford, Gerald R.; Health, Presidential; Nixon, Richard M.; Resignation, Presidential; Succession to the Presidency

FURTHER READING

Feerick, John. *From Failing Hands: The Story of Presidential Succession.* New York: Fordham University Press, 1965. Gilbert, Robert E. *The Mortal Presidency.* New York: Basic Books, 1992.

22nd Amendment

THE 22ND Amendment to the Constitution, ratified on February 27, 1951, limits the Presidential term. It provides that no person may be elected President more than twice. No Vice President who succeeded to the office of President, nor any other person in the line of succession who acted as President, and served for more than two years of a term to which someone else had been elected, could be elected to the Presidency more than once.

The wording of the amendment clarifies two situations: When a President dies or leaves office during his term, the Vice President succeeds to the office and becomes President, rather than simply acting as President. On the other hand, anyone else in the line of succession becomes acting President.

Could a former President run for the Vice Presidency, then succeed to the Presidency and serve a third term? The 12th Amendment provides that "no person Constitutionally ineligible to the office of President shall be eligible to that of Vice President of the United States." If a President is deemed to be "ineligible to the office"

A 1940 campaign banner supports a third term for Franklin Roosevelt.

after two terms, this provision would prevent electors in the electoral college from electing that person Vice President.

Could a former President be appointed under provisions of the 25th Amendment to the Vice Presidency, then consented to by Congress? Could he then become President in the event of a vacancy? Again, if a two-term President is deemed "ineligible to the office," Congress could not elect the ex-President to the Vice Presidency.

However, a former President who then was named to the cabinet or who became Speaker of the House or president pro tempore of the Senate would be in the line of succession to become acting President in the event of a double vacancy. Such positions are not covered by the 12th Amendment, which deals only with the election of Vice Presidents.

SEE ALSO

Succession to the Presidency; Term of office; Vice President

Two-term tradition

THE CONSTITUTIONAL Convention of 1787 did not place any limits on the number of terms a President could serve. The two-term tradition was begun by George Washington, although his decision to leave office was made primarily because of criticism in the press. Thomas Jefferson, upon his retirement in 1809, stated that "rotation in office" was his reason for leaving the White House, in order to prevent the danger of a President being reelected for life. The Republican and Democratic Presidents who followed him just assumed that no President should serve more than two terms.

The Whig party carried this one step further and in its 1840 platform stated that a President should not stand

Anti-Roosevelt campaign buttons warn that a President should not be allowed to seek more than two terms.

for reelection. Democratic President James K. Polk pledged in his election campaign that he would serve only one term. Republican Presidents Abraham Lincoln and Ulysses S. Grant reestablished the two-term tradition after the Civil War.

In 1940, faced with the outbreak of war in Europe, Franklin D. Roosevelt decided that the international crisis was too grave for him to leave office, and he decided to run for a third term. Although his Vice President and some other party leaders opposed his decision, Roosevelt was reelected to a third and then a fourth term, putting an end to the two-term tradition. After the war, the Republican-controlled Congress passed the 22nd Amendment to limit Presidents to two elected terms.

SEE ALSO

Jefferson, Thomas; Roosevelt, Franklin D.; Term of office; 22nd Amendment; Washington, George

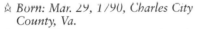

Tyler, John

10TH PRESIDENT

☆ *Born: Mar. 29, 1790, Charles City County, Va.*
☆ *Political party: Democrat, elected on Whig ticket*
☆ *Education: College of William and Mary, B.A., 1807*
☆ *Military service: Virginia militia, 1813*
☆ *Previous government service: Virginia House of Delegates, 1811–16, 1823–25, 1838–40; U.S. House of Representatives, 1817–21; governor of Virginia, 1825–27; U.S. Senate, 1827–36; Vice President, 1841*
☆ *Succeeded to Presidency, 1841; served, 1841–45*
☆ *Died: Jan. 18, 1862, Richmond, Va.*

JOHN TYLER was the first Vice President to succeed to the Presidency. He established the precedent that the successor becomes President and is not the Vice President "acting as President." He also

demonstrated that the constitutional prerogatives of the office can check and balance Congress, even when it is dominated by a party such as the Whigs, who insisted on their right to set national policy.

Tyler came from a family of wealthy Virginia plantation owners. He studied law under his father, practiced briefly, and went into politics. He served in the Virginia legislature and became governor in 1825, then U.S. senator in 1827. Tyler voted against the high tariffs of 1828 and 1832. He supported President Andrew Jackson's veto of internal improvements. But he broke with Jackson over South Carolina's nullification of, or decision not to enforce, federal tariffs, casting the only vote in the Senate against the Force Bill of 1833, which gave Jackson the power to use federal force to ensure compliance with the tariff. Tyler was instrumental in forging the compromise tariff of 1833, which ended the crisis. He voted against the rechartering of the Second Bank of the United States and voted to uphold Jackson's veto of the bill, but he joined in the Senate censure of Jackson over the removal of federal deposits from the Bank. In 1836 he resigned his seat rather than adhere to the instructions of his state legislature to vote to expunge the resolution of censure, and he broke his connections with the Democratic party.

In 1836 Tyler ran for Vice President as a regional Whig candidate but lost to the Democratic ticket. In 1840 he was nominated for the Vice Presidency on the Whig ticket, along with General William Henry Harrison for President. Although opposed to the Bank, the Whigs were attracted to Tyler because they believed correctly that he could help carry southern states.

President Harrison died of pneumonia within a month of taking the oath. John Tyler was in an awkward position. It was not clear from the wording of the

A Whig woodcut produced for the 1840 election uses a log cabin and cider barrel to show that William Henry Harrison and John Tyler were men of the people (even though they had both grown up on aristocratic plantations).

Constitution whether the Vice President succeeded to the office of President or only exercised the "powers and duties" of the office, serving merely as acting President. Tyler took the Presidential oath and issued a statement to the American people couched in the form of an inaugural address. The House promptly passed a resolution referring to him as President, while the Senate defeated a resolution referring to him as Vice President. But much of the nation referred to Tyler as "His Accidency" and did not recognize him as President.

The Whig cabinet moved to take control from the President. At the first cabinet meeting, Secretary of State Daniel Webster told Tyler that his predecessor had settled questions by majority vote of the cabinet. Tyler responded that he alone would be responsible for his administration, and he called for the resignation of anyone who did not accept his view.

Tyler faced a dilemma: Should he allow the Whigs, led by Senator Henry Clay, to pass their economic program? Or should he pursue his own domestic program, which came much closer to the ideas of the Democrats? Tyler did not command a majority in Congress, and the Whigs proceeded to pass their own banking bill, which he vetoed twice. With the help of Democrats, Tyler's vetoes were sustained. The Whig cabinet resigned, and the Whig party issued a

statement disassociating itself from the Tyler administration. Whigs demanded that he resign and be succeeded by the president pro tempore of the Senate—a Whig who would hold office until a special election could be held. Tyler refused and made recess appointments of Democrats to his cabinet. Eventually, the Whigs passed a resolution of censure against Tyler, claiming that his use of the veto on policy grounds was unconstitutional.

Tyler was effective even though he was a President without a party. He resolved Dorr's Rebellion, a civil war between two political factions in Rhode Island. He reorganized the navy. A few days before he left office, Tyler won his most important victory: Congress admitted Texas to the Union.

Tyler was a political failure. He did not win the Democratic Presidential nomination in 1844. Historians generally rate him ineffective because of the deadlock in domestic policies. But he showed that a President without a shred of popular or congressional support could still exercise the power to stalemate congressional majorities.

After leaving the Presidency, Tyler returned to the Democratic party. He supported the Compromise of 1850 and the Kansas-Nebraska Act, both of which were designed to defuse slavery tensions and save the Union. In 1860 he spoke out against secession, believing a new compromise could be reached, and early in 1861 he sponsored the Richmond Convention, a last-ditch attempt to avert war between the regions. After the collapse of that effort, he urged Virginia to secede from the Union. He died on January 18, 1862, shortly after being elected to the Confederate House of Representatives.

SEE ALSO

Harrison, William Henry; Succession to the Presidency

FURTHER READING

Morgan, Robert J. *A Whig Embattled: The Presidency under John Tyler.* Lincoln: University of Nebraska Press, 1954.
Peterson, Norma Lois. *The Presidencies of William Henry Harrison and John Tyler.* Lawrence: University Press of Kansas, 1989.

Van Buren, Martin

8TH PRESIDENT

☆ *Born: Dec. 5, 1782, Kinderhook, N.Y.*
☆ *Political party: Democrat*
☆ *Education: elementary school; read law, 1796–1803*
☆ *Military service: none*
☆ *Previous government service: judge, Columbia County, N.Y., 1811–12; New York Senate, 1813–17; attorney general of New York, 1816–17; U.S. Senate, 1821–28; governor of New York, 1829; U.S. secretary of state, 1829–31; Vice President, 1833–37*
☆ *Elected President, 1836; served, 1837–41*
☆ *Died: July 24, 1862, Kinderhook, N.Y.*

BORN SIX years after the signing of the Declaration of Independence, Martin Van Buren was the first President who was born a citizen of the United States. (All prior Presidents had been born British subjects.) With Andrew Jackson, he founded the Democratic party and developed the ideas that led to the two-party system in the United States. His

Presidency was a failure, in large measure because of monetary policies begun by his predecessor and continued in his own administration.

Van Buren was the son of a tavern keeper whose forebears had come from Holland 150 years before, and Dutch was still spoken in his home. He received no formal education after his local elementary school but read law for seven years in a lawyer's office and began practicing in 1803. Van Buren's wife died in 1819 after bearing four children; he never remarried. He was a successful lawyer, served as attorney general of New York State, and in 1821 organized a convention to write a new constitution for New York. By the 1820s he was being considered for the U.S. Supreme Court. But Van Buren was by instinct a politician whose canny maneuvers gave him the nickname Little Magician, and he was more interested in a political career than serving as a judge.

Van Buren's chief contribution to U.S. politics was the development of the two-party system. In his book *Inquiry into the Origins and Development of Political Parties in the United States* (1867), he argued that the public interest would be best served with two parties (rather than one or many): one would govern and the other would offer the voters an alternative. Prior to Van Buren's time, the Federalists did not believe there should be a Democratic-Republican party, and the Democratic-Republicans did all they could to bury the Federalists. The result was one-party government in the so-called Era of Good Feeling during James Monroe's Presidency. But Van Buren recognized that this was actually an "era of bad feelings" in which sectional animosities had replaced party competition. His goal was the re-creation of the old struggle between Federalists and Democratic-Republicans, with each party containing followers from all across the

Union—and each acknowledging the legitimacy of the other.

Van Buren came to his understanding of two-party politics through his experience in New York. There he led a faction of the Democratic-Republicans who instituted the spoils system—giving government appointments to political allies—by removing a large number of opposition officeholders. After winning election to the U.S. Senate, Van Buren used his patronage powers to create and dominate the Albany Regency—a small group of politicians who organized a political machine and ran the state through the post–Civil War period.

As a U.S. senator, Van Buren renewed the alliance between southern and New York Democratic-Republicans. He opposed the election of John Quincy Adams and the policies of his administration, especially any federal funding of internal improvements such as the Cumberland Road. He also opposed the extension of slavery into Florida. In 1828, while running for governor of New York, he strongly supported Andrew Jackson's second campaign for the White House. After Jackson won, Van Buren became his secretary of state in 1829, resigning the governorship of New York. He was successful in difficult diplomatic negotiations with France, Great Britain, and Turkey. Later, he was denied Senate confirmation to be minister to Great Britain by a single vote.

Between 1828 and 1832 Van Buren and Jackson created the Democratic party. Instead of trying for a single, all-embracing party, with no principles or program, they put together a party that was not all-inclusive. They opposed the national banking system and favored state banks, and they opposed national funding of internal improvements. Moreover, Van Buren pushed Jackson to institute New York's spoils system in the national government, which froze out many politicians. Jackson's opponents united in the 1830s to form the opposition Whig party. Through Van Buren's efforts, the first stable two-party system had been created. In 1832 the first Democratic party convention nominated Van Buren to be Jackson's running mate. As Vice President, he served Jackson well as a political adviser and supported him loyally in the "bank wars." In May 1835, with Jackson's endorsement, Van Buren won the Democratic nomination for the Presidency by a unanimous vote of the convention. In his Presidential campaign Van Buren pledged "to tread generally in the footsteps of President Jackson." He reaffirmed Jackson's opposition to the Second Bank of the United States and pledged to uphold the rights of slave owners where slavery already existed. He won the election against four Whig regional candidates.

In one of his last major decisions Andrew Jackson issued the Specie Circular, which ordered that paper money not be accepted for payment in the sale of government lands. There was a run on specie (metal currency), which flowed from the eastern banks to the western banks that needed it. Then the Treasury withdrew its surplus funds from state banks for distribution to state governments, which further reduced deposits of specie in the state banks, particularly large commercial banks in the Northeast. Soon these banks cut back on loans and extensions of credit needed for businesses all along the Eastern seaboard. In May 1837, two months after Van Buren's

This fake six-cent bank note mocks the small denomination notes issued during the Panic of 1837, when banks suspended payments of metal currency. The panic occurred two months after Van Buren's inauguration and destroyed his popularity.

inauguration, the New York banks suspended payments of specie on demand to their depositors. Within a week banks across the nation followed suit.

Unfortunately for Van Buren, the Panic of 1837, the first serious economic setback the United States had experienced since 1789, destroyed whatever confidence the nation had in his leadership. Of 788 banks, 618 failed when depositors removed their funds. No one could obtain loans or credit, factories closed, and farms were foreclosed, leading to an economic depression. Van Buren refused to endorse a policy of easy money, and he opposed any expansion of credit by the national government. In his inaugural address, he said that "the less Government interferes with private pursuits, the better for general prosperity." The government did intervene minimally to repair the immediate damage: it ended further distribution of surplus revenue from the Treasury and issued $10 million in new Treasury notes to be used to pay government bills and put new funds in circulation. Van Buren refused to spend money on public works to relieve the depression, claiming these expenditures were unconstitutional. His Treasury ran surpluses, which further deflated the currency and weakened the economy.

Van Buren proposed to sever all financial relationships between state banks and the Treasury. He proposed the establishment of an independent treasury system with "subtreasuries" in large cities into which national government funds would be deposited. This would replace Jackson's system in which "pet" banks, owned by state Democratic politicians, controlled federal funds and used them in speculative schemes that had undermined the banking system. The measure, however, would reduce the amount of money available for loans by banks and therefore would further con-

tract the credit system. Whigs argued that the subtreasuries would only make the depression worse. After three years of trying, Van Buren finally won congressional passage of his measure with the argument that the government's funds would be safe only in the government's own bank vaults. Van Buren signed the bill on July 4, 1840, hailing it as the "Second Declaration of Independence." Whigs vowed to make it a campaign issue in the next election.

Van Buren was controversial in handling sectional crises and foreign affairs. He vowed to veto any law changing the status of slavery in the nation's capital (which at that time was legal), leading John Quincy Adams to call him a "northern man with southern feelings." He won over northern Democrats to oppose the abolitionist cause. He got southerners to delay their attempts to annex Texas after Texas requested it in 1837. Like the attempts of other Presidents to keep sectional peace, these efforts only delayed the inevitable conflict between North and South and lost him support in both regions.

In foreign affairs Van Buren kept the nation at peace and its borders secure. He prevented two crises with Great Britain from becoming wars. One involved aid by U.S. citizens to Canadians in rebellion against British rule; British forces sank the *Caroline*, a U.S. boat supplying the rebels. Van Buren issued a proclamation warning Americans not to violate neutrality laws.

The second issue involved the disputed boundary between Maine and the Canadian province of New Brunswick. Timber poachers from New Brunswick crossed over into the disputed territory. The governor of Maine ordered troops to the area. Then British forces went on alert. Van Buren managed to work out a truce between the governors of Maine and New Brunswick, won a withdrawal of the militias, and laid the groundwork for a territorial compromise.

Van Buren continued Jackson's policy of removing southern Indians to Oklahoma, supervising the transfer of 20,000 Cherokee in 1838. In Florida, he fought a long and bloody war against the Seminole Indians, leading to the removal of 3,500 of the 4,000 Indians and the capture of many runaway slaves who had taken refuge with them—all at the cost of 1,500 casualties to U.S. forces.

The hard economic times led to "Martin Van Ruin's" defeat in 1840 at the hands of the popular Whig candidate William Henry Harrison. After leaving the White House, Van Buren devoted his efforts to regaining the Presidency. He was a leading contender for the Democratic nomination in 1844, receiving more than half of the ballots cast but not the necessary two-thirds. He lost the nomination because his stand against the annexation of Texas eroded his support: he correctly foresaw that it would lead to war with Mexico. In 1848 he was nominated by the Free-Soil party, a coalition of New York abolitionists, "conscience" Whigs, and others opposed to the extension of slavery. Van Buren received no electoral college votes but won 10 percent of the popular vote, enough to defeat the Democratic candidate, Lewis Cass, and pave the way for Whig candidate Zachary Taylor to win. Thereafter Van Buren played no role in national politics.

SEE ALSO

Harrison, William Henry; Jackson, Andrew

Martin Van Buren (left), Andrew Jackson (top), Daniel Webster (right), and Henry Clay (bottom) appear together on this 1836 campaign snuffbox. Van Buren and Jackson formed the Democratic party, while Clay and Webster made up the opposition Whig party.

FURTHER READING

Cole, Donald B. *Martin Van Buren and the American Political System.* Princeton, N.J.: Princeton University Press, 1984.
Niven, John. *Martin Van Buren: The Romantic Age of American Politics.* New York: Oxford, 1983.
Wilson, Major. *The Presidency of Martin Van Buren.* Lawrence: University Press of Kansas, 1984.

Veto power

VETO POWER is the right of the executive to reject laws passed by the legislature. The practice of government executives nullifying laws was well known to the framers of the Constitution. In colonial times the king and royal governors often vetoed laws passed by colonial legislatures. Indeed, that was one of the reasons for rebelling mentioned in the Declaration of Independence. After the Revolution, New York State had a Council of Revision made up of the governor, chancellor, and state judges who could nullify laws that seemed to violate the state constitution.

The word *veto* does not appear in the Constitution. However, the framers did provide for Presidential rejection of legislation in order to prevent Congress from encroaching on executive powers and to allow the President to nullify unwise legislation. Article 1, Section 7, of the Constitution provides that all measures that require the concurrence of both chambers are to be presented to the President of the United States. The only exceptions are resolutions to adjourn and constitutional amendments.

The President may sign the measure, allow it to become law if he does not sign it within 10 days, or return it to the chamber in which it originated together with his objections. Congress may pass the law over the President's objection by a two-thirds vote in each chamber. A bill sent to the President by Congress within 10 days of its adjournment is subject to a pocket veto if Congress adjourns before the President can return it. In that case, his failure to sign the bill is the end of it—Congress gets no chance when it reconvenes to pass it over his veto.

A President who sends a bill back to Congress may not change his mind and recall it; Grant attempted to do so twice but Congress refused to return the bills to him.

The Constitution allows for no item-by-item veto. The President may not veto part of a bill and approve the remainder—a power that 43 state governors do have. His veto strikes down the entire measure. In 1877 President Rutherford B. Hayes recommended that the President be given an item veto, and between 1877 and 1888 several such constitutional amendments were introduced in Congress, but none were passed. Presidents Dwight Eisenhower and Ronald Reagan also proposed the item veto for congressional spending bills and were similarly rebuffed. President Bill Clinton also supported the idea, but as part of reforming the budget process, by law, not as a constitutional amendment.

The Constitution does not specify the grounds on which the President may exercise his veto. Initially, many commentators believed that the President could veto legislation only if he believed the measure to be unconstitutional. Prior to 1832, only 6 of 21 vetoes were made for other than constitutional reasons. The issue came to a head when Andrew Jackson vetoed a bill rechartering the Second Bank of the United States. Jackson claimed that he could veto the bill because of policy disagreement, while the opposition Whig party proclaimed that a President could veto a bill only on constitutional grounds. When John Tyler ve-

toed bills of the Whig congressional majority, a select committee of Congress argued that he had misused his power. In 1842 Senator Henry Clay proposed a constitutional amendment to permit Congress to override a President's veto by a majority vote of each chamber. Neither this proposed amendment nor resolutions to impeach Tyler passed the House. Since the Civil War, most vetoes have been exercised because the President believed laws to be unwise rather than unconstitutional.

Senator William Proxmire (left) and Senator Mark Hatfield, chairman of the Senate Appropriations Committee, display the vote tally after the Senate overrode Ronald Reagan's veto on an appropriations bill.

In recent years Presidents have sometimes allowed bills to become law but have indicated that they will not enforce a specific provision they believe to be unconstitutional. President Richard Nixon refused to obey a provision of a 1971 military procurement bill requiring him to declare a cease-fire and negotiate with North Vietnam for a prisoner exchange in return for U.S. withdrawal from Indochina. He claimed that "the so-called Mansfield Amendment is unconstitutional, and without force or effect" because it infringed on his powers as commander in chief.

Presidents have also used "signing statements," which are released when they sign measures passed by Congress, to provide their own interpretation of the law. When President Reagan signed the Beirut Resolution of 1982, authorizing him to keep a marine contingent in Lebanon for peacekeeping, he issued a statement arguing that nothing in the resolution could have the effect of limiting or interfering with his powers as commander in chief to station troops anywhere he wished.

The President is assisted in making decisions about whether to sign or veto bills by the Office of Management and

Budget, which conducts a review of every bill passed by Congress and sent to the President. Often, cabinet secretaries and White House aides comment as well.

The veto power often becomes a threat that the President can use to influence legislation. Because an override requires a two-thirds vote of both houses, fewer than 7 percent of Presidential vetoes have been overridden. So Presidents can intervene early in the legislative process with threats of a veto unless pending legislation is modified to meet their objections, and sometimes more than one-third of a chamber will sign a pledge in advance to back up the President if he vetoes a bill. This makes the White House an integral part of the legislative process from beginning to end.

SEE ALSO

Creation of the Presidency; Jackson, Andrew; Office of Management and Budget; Pocket veto

FURTHER READING

Jackson, Carleton. *Presidential Vetoes: 1792–1945.* Athens: University of Georgia Press, 1967.
Spitzer, Robert. *The Presidential Veto.* Albany: State University of New York Press, 1988.
Zinn, Charles. *The Veto Power of the President.* Washington, D.C.: Government Printing Office, 1951.

Vice President

THE VICE PRESIDENT is the officer designated by the Constitution to succeed to the office of President in case of a vacancy created by the death, disability, impeachment, or resignation of the President.

The Vice Presidency was an afterthought for the Constitutional Convention, put into the document in order to provide for orderly succession without resorting to election of someone from Congress to fill the vacancy. The Vice President is not a member of either the executive or the legislative branch. Constitutionally, the Vice President is not a subordinate of the President, who has no power to issue orders to the Vice President and who cannot remove him from office. (The Vice President can be removed only by impeachment.) But Vice Presidents have found that the way they gain influence in Washington is by subordinating themselves to the President. By doing so they have become, since Dwight Eisenhower's administration, part of the inner circle of senior political advisers to the President.

The Vice President has no constitutional responsibilities other than serving as president of the Senate, presiding over that body (except in Presidential impeachment trials, when the chief justice of the United States presides), and voting to break ties. Rulings by the Vice President may be appealed to the full Senate. Modern Vice Presidents preside about 1 percent of the time the Senate is in session, usually when a tie vote on an important issue is likely to occur. Between 1789 and 1989 they cast 224 tiebreaking votes.

Vice Presidents have only a few statutory duties. Since 1949 they have served on the National Security Council, and they are on the Board of Regents of the Smithsonian Institution (which operates various museums in the capital). They name five cadets to the U.S. Military Academy, U.S. Naval Academy, and Air Force Academy. They appoint senators to various independent commissions, including the Migratory Bird Conservation Commission, the Harry S. Truman Scholarship Foundation, and the Advisory Commission on Intergovernmental Relations.

Vice Presidents are usually assigned by the President to chair various commissions. They generally chair the Space Council; others deal with nondiscriminatory practices in government contracts and efforts at deregulating the economy. They usually serve as the White House liaison with the National Governors Association and the U.S. Conference of Mayors. The Vice President participates in cabinet meetings, a custom established by Warren Harding. Since Eisenhower's time, Vice Presidents have presided over cabinet meetings in the absence of the President; Richard Nixon chaired 20 such meetings during Eisenhower's illnesses and trips.

Until the 1960s, Vice Presidents had their main offices on Capitol Hill near the Senate chamber. President John F. Kennedy asked Lyndon Johnson to take a suite of offices in the Old Executive Office Building, and today the Office of the Vice President is located on the second floor of that building. They have smaller offices in the Capitol and in the West Wing of the White House.

In 1970 the federal budget allocated funds for the first time to the Office of the Vice President under the line item "Special Assistance to the President." More than $2.5 million was spent on the Vice President's staff in 1992.

Units of the Vice President's Office include the chief of staff, scheduling and advance office, domestic policy staff, legal counsel, national security adviser, press office, and speech writers. The office is assisted by the Office of Administration in the White House with support functions such as payroll and personnel. The Vice President's wife has five aides.

Since 1974 the Vice President has had an official residence on Massachusetts Avenue in the District of Columbia, the former Admiral's House at the Naval Observatory. It has 12 rooms on three floors and is situated on 12 landscaped acres. The Vice President receives a $171,500 salary, a taxable expense allowance of $10,000, and $90,000 for entertaining. Six navy stewards serve as the mansion staff. The first Vice President to occupy the residence was Walter Mondale, beginning in 1977. Vice President George Bush and his wife, Barbara, presided over a complete refurbishing of the mansion, using $200,000 in private contributions.

The Vice President receives no additional pay as president of the Senate but does receive more than $1 million in expenses for his office on Capitol Hill. As president of the Senate, the Vice President has 40 additional staff aides. The Vice Presidential plane is known as *Air Force Two*. The Vice Presidential seal is an eagle with spread wings and a claw full of arrows, with a starburst at its head.

Vice Presidents receive protection from the Uniformed Division of the Secret Service. When they leave office, they may be assigned Secret Service protection for six months at the discretion of the new administration. Unlike former Presidents, they have no right to address the Senate or to stay in the residence on Jackson Place.

In modern times the Vice President has generally become the favorite to win his party's Presidential nomination and succeed to the office. Since 1960, Vice Presidents Richard Nixon, Hubert Humphrey, Walter Mondale, and George Bush all won subsequent Presidential nominations.

Gerald Ford (left) meets with Vice President Nelson Rockefeller, a key domestic policy adviser.

SEE ALSO

Cabinet; Disability, Presidential; Electoral college; Executive power; National Security Council; Nominating conventions, Presidential; Secret Service, U.S.; Succession to the Presidency; Ticket; 12th Amendment; 25th Amendment

FURTHER READING

Goldstein, Joel K. *The Modern American Vice Presidency*. Princeton, N.J.: Princeton University Press, 1982.

Light, Paul C. *Vice-Presidential Power: Advice and Influence in the White House*. Baltimore, Md.: Johns Hopkins University Press, 1984.

Moe, Ronald C. "The Institutional Vice Presidency." In *The Presidency in Transition*, edited by James Pfiffner and Gordon Hoxie. New York: Center for the Study of the Presidency, *Proceedings* 6, no. 1 (1989): 391–424.

Natoli, Marie D. *American Prince, American Pauper: The Contemporary Vice Presidency in Perspective*. Westport, Conn.: Greenwood, 1985.

Walch, Timothy, ed. *At the President's Side: The Vice Presidency in the Twentieth Century*. Columbia: University of Missouri Press, 1997.

Young, Donald. *American Roulette: The History and Dilemma of the Vice Presidency*. New York: Viking, 1974.

Wallace, Henry

VICE PRESIDENT

☆ Born: Oct. 7, 1888, Adair County, Iowa

☆ Political party: Republican, then Democrat

☆ Education: Iowa State College, B.S., 1910

☆ Military service: none

☆ Previous government service: secretary of agriculture, 1933–40

☆ Vice President under Franklin D. Roosevelt, 1941–45

☆ Subsequent government service: U.S. secretary of commerce, 1945–46

☆ Died: Nov. 18, 1965, Danbury, Conn.

HENRY WALLACE was associate editor (1911–24) and then editor (1924–33) of the most influential farmers' magazine of his day, *Wallace's Farmer*. He was also president of the Pioneer Hi-Bred Corn Company, which specialized in new, high-yield strains of corn. Although a Republican, he was appointed by Franklin Roosevelt, a Democrat, to be secretary of agriculture in 1933, to help Roosevelt appeal to Midwestern progressives and win their support for his New Deal program. Wallace implemented the New Deal farm policy, developing new programs for soil conservation, production quotas, and farm price supports through the Agricultural Adjustment Administration. In 1936 he became a Democrat.

Roosevelt chose Wallace to be his Vice Presidential nominee in 1940 to retain the farm vote and solidify support on the political left, though he surprised party leaders by not choosing someone from the South for geographic balance. The Democratic convention balked at his choice. But Roosevelt insisted, making Wallace's nomination a condition of his own candidacy, and the delegates backed down. He did ask Wallace not to deliver an acceptance speech to the angry delegates.

As Vice President, Wallace traveled to Latin America as a goodwill ambassador and served as chair of the Economic Defense Board in 1941, renamed the Board of Economic Warfare in 1942. He lost the position of economic defense coordinator in 1943 after frequent battles with Secretary of Commerce Jesse Jones. Opposition to Wallace by leading conservative Democrats in Congress led Roosevelt to drop him from the ticket in 1944. Instead, Roosevelt appointed him secretary of commerce, and newly elected Vice President Harry Truman persuaded key senators to consent to the nomination.

Wallace kept his post when Truman became President but soon broke with him over the President's strong anticommunist stance. In 1946, after making a speech criticizing Truman's "get tough" policy, Wallace was forced by Truman to resign. Two years later Wallace ran for President on the Progressive party ticket, hoping to play a spoiler role and see to Truman's defeat. But he won no electoral votes and could not prevent Truman's reelection.

SEE ALSO
Truman, Harry S.

FURTHER READING
Blum, John M., ed. *The Price of Vision: The Diary of Henry A. Wallace, 1942–46.* Boston: Houghton Mifflin, 1973.
Culver, John C., and John Hyde. *American Dreamer: The Life and Times of Henry A. Wallace.* New York: Norton, 2000.
Markowitz, Norman. *The Rise and Fall of the People's Century: Henry A. Wallace and American Liberalism, 1941–1948.* New York: Free Press, 1973.

War powers

WAR POWERS are the constitutional powers to declare and make war. The Constitution grants to Congress the power to declare war. Except for foreign aggression or invasion, which the President could repel on his own authority as commander in chief, the framers expected that decisions about peace or war would be made by Congress. But of the more than 220 situations in which the armed forces have been used (half of them involving fighting for more than 30 days), only 5 have involved declarations of war: the War of 1812, the Mexican-American War, the Spanish-American War, World War I, and World War II.

In all the other cases Presidents have used the armed forces on their own authority, without congressional authorization. These have included actions against pirates or bandits threatening U.S. foreign commerce, such as President Thomas Jefferson's use of the navy against the Barbary pirates in the Mediterranean Sea in the early 1800s. They have included rescue missions involving the lives and property of Americans, such as President Jimmy Carter's unsuccessful attempt to rescue diplomats held hostage by Iran in 1979. Presidents have ordered retaliatory actions, such as the bombing raid against Libya in 1986, which followed Libyan terrorist attacks against U.S. service personnel in Germany.

Presidents have ordered the military to protect U.S. freedom of the seas, as John Adams did when he ordered U.S. forces into an undeclared naval war with France. They have used the military to temporarily occupy other nations, including Haiti (1915–34), Nicaragua (1912–25), and Cuba (1906–9). Presidents have used force to overthrow unfriendly regimes, such as Ronald Reagan's invasion of Grenada in 1983. They have supported friendly regimes against civil insurrections, such as the use of military advisers in El Salvador during the 1980s. They have used hundreds of thousands of troops to aid friendly nations against external aggression (South Korea in 1950, South Vietnam in 1964, and Kuwait in 1990).

Presidents claim that they can make war on their own constitutional authority as commander in chief. They argue that their duty to see that the laws are faithfully executed gives them an "international police power" to see that other nations pay their debts, protect U.S. lives and property, and abide by international law. In addition, the President executes treaty commitments, and certain treaties require the United States to guarantee the security of other nations. Presidents argue that they can use the armed forces in these cases without waiting for congressional approval. They also argue that their oath of office, the executive

Franklin Roosevelt signs the declaration of war against Japan in 1941.

power, and the commander in chief clause of the Constitution all provide them with the authority to make decisions about peace and war in all other circumstances.

During the cold war, beginning in the late 1940s, when a "balance of terror" seemed to require that the United States and Soviet Union each have the ability to retaliate against a nuclear attack by the other side, Presidents argued that it was unrealistic to assume that Congress could participate in the decision to use nuclear weapons. Presidents argued that only if they had the power to retaliate without waiting for Congress to agree would the other side respect U.S. retaliatory power. Presidential war making becomes controversial if it leads to protracted hostilities, large numbers of dead and wounded, and heavy expenditures. The President risks splitting his own party, and may be forced to withdraw attempts to win renomination and reelection (as Harry Truman did during the Korean War and Lyndon Johnson did during the Vietnam War). On the other hand, a President who wins a quick and decisive military engagement will find his popularity soaring. This happened to Ronald Reagan after the invasion of Grenada and to George Bush after the invasion of Panama and the defeat of Iraqi forces in Kuwait.

If Congress wishes to oppose the President, it can do so in several ways. It can revoke any resolutions supporting the President (as Congress did in 1970 when it revoked the Gulf of Tonkin Resolution

of 1964). Congress can cut off appropriations for Presidential war making. During the Vietnam War, it barred troops from engaging in operations in Thailand and Laos (1969) and from using ground forces in Cambodia (1970) and bombing Cambodia (1973). But usually, Congress votes for appropriations requested by the President as well as other authority (such as drafting troops). It does so, in spite of any doubts, because most members do not want to be vulnerable to charges in an election year that they voted to deny weapons and supplies to troops fighting the enemy.

The federal courts almost always find Presidential war making to be constitutional. Cases brought by soldiers drafted to fight in Presidentially ordered combat are usually decided in favor of the President, on the grounds that his power as commander in chief allows him to send troops into combat. The courts have never ruled that Presidential war making was unconstitutional.

SEE ALSO

Commander in chief; Cuban Missile Crisis; Gulf of Tonkin Resolution; Johnson, Lyndon B.; Lincoln, Abraham; War Powers Resolution

FURTHER READING

Fisher, Louis. *Presidential War Power.* Lawrence: University Press of Kansas: 1995.
Schlesinger, Arthur M., Jr. *The Imperial Presidency.* New York: Popular Library, 1974.

War Powers Resolution

THE WAR POWERS Resolution (WPR) was an act passed by Congress in 1973, over President Richard Nixon's veto, to "insure that the collective judgment of both the Congress and the President will

apply to the introduction of United States armed forces into hostilities." The War Powers Resolution restricted Presidential war making to situations in which Congress had declared war or had given the President specific permission to use the armed forces in hostilities or in which the nation, its territories, possessions, or armed forces had been attacked.

The President was required "in every possible instance" to consult with Congress before introducing U.S. armed forces into hostilities. After every such introduction he was to "consult regularly with the Congress" until the forces had been removed. He was required to report to Congress within 48 hours after the introduction of forces into combat or situations in which hostilities were imminent and to report every six months thereafter.

The President was given a maximum of 60 days to use the armed forces without congressional permission; after that time he would have to obtain a declaration of war, other congressional approval, or an extension of the time limit. If he did not gain congressional approval, he had 30 days to withdraw the forces from hostilities.

Presidents Gerald Ford, Jimmy Carter, Ronald Reagan, and George Bush routinely evaded or ignored provisions of the WPR, arguing that it was an unconstitutional infringement on their powers as commander in chief. President Gerald Ford evacuated Americans and Europeans from South Vietnam, Laos, and Cambodia in 1975, when communist forces seized power in those nations, without invoking the consultation clause of the WPR. He also attempted a rescue of the crew of the merchant ship *Mayaguez* after it was seized by Cambodian communists in 1975, without invoking the resolution. In 1980 President Carter ignored the consultation clauses of the WPR when he ordered military forces to

try to rescue diplomatic hostages held by Iran for more than a year. In 1982 President Ronald Reagan sent marines into Lebanon, where they remained for months exposed to hostile fire, without invoking the 60-day "clock." When he bombed Libya in 1986, he offered members of Congress a briefing while the planes were in midair, rather than consulting with them about whether the bombing should occur.

In 1989, without consulting Congress, President Bush sent forces into Panama to capture General Manuel Noriega and bring him back to the United States to face drug trafficking charges. (Bush did, however, comply with other provisions of the law.) Bush was authorized by Congress to use military force against Saddam Hussein of Iraq, but Congress did not use the provisions of the WPR.

Presidents do not use the WPR if their use of the armed forces involves peacekeeping or antiterrorist actions or for humanitarian assistance, such as the 1992–93 operation in Somalia and the 1993 airdrops of food in Bosnia and Herzegovina, or if covert operations are involved. Presidents never trigger the 60-day clock that starts when they use the armed forces. If Congress wishes to set a time limit, it must do so itself by passing a joint resolution. But that resolution itself is subject to a Presidential veto, which then must be overridden by a two-thirds vote of each house to go into effect. In practice, a President who fails to obey the terms of the WPR can continue using the armed forces until two-thirds of each chamber of Congress decides to force him to withdraw, a most unlikely situation.

The courts have never ordered a President to comply with the WPR. In *Crockett v. Reagan* (1982), a case involving U.S. military advisers in El Salvador, a federal court declined to start

Gerald Ford interrupts a state dinner to take a call regarding the Mayaguez *incident. Ford had sent the military to rescue crewmen from the merchant ship* Mayaguez, *which was in Cambodian custody.*

the WPR's 60-day clock, ruling that it was a "political question" between Congress and the President, not subject to judicial consideration. By the 1990s, many constitutional scholars believed that sooner or later the federal courts would declare some or all of the key provisions of the War Powers Resolution to be unconstitutional.

SEE ALSO
Commander in chief; Gulf of Tonkin Resolution; Nixon, Richard M.; War powers

FURTHER READING
Eagleton, Thomas. *War and Presidential Power.* New York: Liveright, 1974.
Javits, Jacob. *Who Makes War? The President versus Congress.* New York: Morrow, 1973.

Washington, George
1ST PRESIDENT

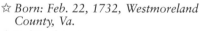

☆ *Born: Feb. 22, 1732, Westmoreland County, Va.*
☆ *Political party: none*
☆ *Education: schooling through age 15*
☆ *Military service: adjutant, Southern District of Virginia, 1752; lieutenant colonel and colonel, Virginia Regiment, 1754; commander of Virginia Military, 1755–58; commander in chief of Continental Army, 1775–83*
☆ *Previous government service: surveyor, Culpeper County, Va., 1749–51; Virginia House of Burgesses, 1759–74; justice of the peace, Fairfax County, Va., 1760–74; First Continental Congress, 1774; Second Continental Congress, 1775; presiding officer, Constitutional Convention, 1787*
☆ *Elected President, 1789; served, 1789–97*
☆ *Died: Dec. 14, 1799, Mount Vernon, Va.*

GEORGE WASHINGTON was the victorious commander in chief of the American military during the Revolutionary War, the presiding officer at the Constitutional Convention of 1787, and the first President of the United States.

Without Washington's leadership the country might have remained a British colony and evolved into a member of the British Commonwealth of Nations. And without Washington's work at the convention there would be no office of the Presidency as we know it today.

George Washington was born on one of six plantations owned by his father, Augustine Washington. George's father died in 1743, leaving the family 10,000 acres and 50 slaves. Thereafter George was raised by his half-brother Lawrence, who was 14 years his senior, at the Epsewasson plantation at Little Hunting Creek, which Lawrence renamed Mount Vernon. His schooling ended at age 15, when he became a plantation supervisor and land surveyor. After Lawrence married a daughter of Colonel William Fairfax, one of the largest and most powerful landowners in Virginia, George was invited to survey Fairfax lands in the Shenandoah Valley, receiving 550 acres in compensation. Between 1749 and 1751 he was surveyor of Culpeper County. In 1752, after Lawrence died, George inherited the 2,500-acre estate (with its 18 slaves) at Mount Vernon, becoming a large plantation owner at age 20.

Washington was soon influential in public affairs. In February 1753 he was named a major and adjutant of the Virginia Militia. In October he was sent by Governor Robert Dinwiddie to the frontier on Lake Erie to warn the French against occupying lands claimed by Great Britain, but the French rejected the ultimatum. The following year he was commissioned a lieutenant colonel and returned to the West. On May 28 he fought an engagement with the French that led to his promotion to colonel. He then constructed Fort Necessity and awaited a French counterattack. On July 4 the superior French forces captured the fort, accepted Washington's surrender, and let him return to Virginia, but only after he signed capitulation papers (written in French) admitting that he had fired on French officers while they had been under a flag of truce—a statement Washington later disavowed, saying he had not understood the language. These battles marked the start of the French and Indian War in the Americas and of the Seven Years War throughout the world.

Washington accompanied General Edward Braddock on an expedition against Fort Duquesne—near where Pittsburgh stands today—in 1755. The general disregarded Washington's advice on how to fight the Indians allied with the French. On July 9 Braddock was killed during the fighting, and Washington prevented the British defeat from becoming a complete rout. "I had four bullets through my coat, and two horses shot under me," Washington later wrote. On his return he was named commander of the Virginia Militia. By 1758 he had defeated the French at Fort Duquesne and renamed it Fort Pitt.

In 1759 Washington resigned his commission with the rank of brigadier general and married a widow named Martha Dandridge Custis, who had two children by her previous marriage and plantations of 15,000 acres, much of the land near Williamsburg, Virginia. Washington resumed tobacco farming, served in the Virginia House of Burgesses, and was a justice of the peace. He began opposing British colonial policies, particularly the Royal Proclamation of 1763, which discouraged settlement in the West (where Washington owned land in the Ohio Valley), and the Stamp Act of 1765, which taxed imports. After the governor disbanded the House of Burgesses for protesting the Stamp Act, Washington played a major role in their unauthorized meetings at

A silhouette of Martha Washington, who was known for her graciousness and charm.

Raleigh Tavern in 1770 (when it drew up resolutions calling on people not to import British goods, so that they would not pay the hated stamp tax) and in 1774 (when it called for a meeting of a continental congress). He was a delegate to the First Continental Congress of 1774, where he declared, "I will raise one thousand men, subsist them at my own expense, and march myself at their head for the relief of Boston." On June 15, 1775, the Second Continental Congress named Washington commander in chief of the Continental Army. He refused to take any pay for the position.

Washington assumed command of his volunteers in Cambridge, Massachusetts, on July 3, 1775, shortly after the Battle of Bunker Hill. He forced the British to evacuate Boston in March 1776 and concentrate their forces in New York. Washington was defeated at the Battle of Long Island in August and at the battles of Manhattan and White Plains. He retreated into New Jersey and then into Pennsylvania. On Christmas night, 1776, he crossed the Delaware River and defeated British forces at Trenton, New Jersey. Then he captured Princeton and Morristown. But British reinforcements forced his withdrawal, and he was defeated at Brandywine Creek and Germantown, leading to the loss of Philadelphia. The Conway Conspiracy, a plot to replace Washington with General Horatio Gates, the hero of the Battle of Saratoga, went nowhere, as Congress reaffirmed its support for the beleaguered commander. Washington's forces regrouped at Valley Forge, Pennsylvania, in October 1777. Three thousand of his troops deserted.

Although badly supplied, the troops who stuck it out during the harsh winter emerged from Valley Forge in the spring of 1778 as a disciplined army with superb morale. And the French had decided to help the Americans.

With the British withdrawing from Philadelphia and regrouping in New York to await the arrival of a French fleet, Washington won the Battle of Monmouth in June 1778. He then surrounded and kept British forces in New York at bay while other military units fought in the South and won in the Northwest. But in 1780 there were new defeats: Charleston, South Carolina, fell and General Gates lost the Battle of Camden. Some troops mutinied when rations were cut.

In 1781 Washington's forces feigned preparations for an attack on New York. He and the French general Rochambeau secretly went south to face the British in Virginia. They joined up with another French general who was commanding American troops, the Marquis de Lafayette, and lay siege to the British. The arrival of a French fleet in the midst of the Yorktown campaign of 1781 forced British general Lord Charles Cornwallis to surrender his 8,000-man force on October 19, 1781. This defeat ended hostilities. Washington then took his army to Newburgh, New York, to await the articles of peace, which were signed in November 1782, to become effective January 20, 1783. On March 15, 1783, Washington quelled a mutiny by senior officers who wished to disperse Congress and name Washington as an American king. His refusal to join the "Newburgh mutiny" and his insistence on preserving civil government made him the most influential political figure in the country.

Washington retired from the army on December 4, 1783, bidding farewell to his officers at Fraunces' Tavern in New York City. He resumed farming at Mount Vernon and toured the lands Congress had given him in the West. In 1785 Mount Vernon was the setting for a conference between representatives from Maryland and Virginia, who set-tled issues involving navigation on the Potomac River. That meeting led to the Annapolis Convention of 1786, which, in turn, called for a new constitutional convention for the following year.

In 1787 James Madison and others prevailed upon Washington to attend the Constitutional Convention in Philadelphia, and on May 25 he was named presiding officer. His participation ensured the success of the enterprise, especially because Washington played the key role in ensuring ratification of the new constitution by Virginia.

By unanimous vote of the electoral college on February 4, 1789, Washington was elected the first President of the United States. On April 30, he was inaugurated on the balcony of Federal Hall in New York City. In his inaugural address to Congress he appealed for a Bill of Rights to be added to the Constitution. He refused to accept a salary as President.

Washington had several goals for his Presidency. The first was to establish precedents, or set examples, that would preserve a republican form of government after his term of office. He also aimed to put the finances of the nation on a sound footing, to normalize relations with the British, and to develop the frontier. The methods that he and his Treasury secretary, Alexander Hamilton, devised to achieve these goals created divisions within his administration.

Hamilton wanted a "strong and energetic executive" who would dominate Congress and take control of policymaking. He wanted to levy taxes on whiskey and other goods to raise revenues and pay government debts. He also wanted an alliance (or at least a treaty of friendship) with the British in order to encourage British investment in new U.S. industries.

The President generally supported Hamilton in his plans for industrialization, assumption of the states' Revolu-

This engraving shows Washington's famous crossing of the Delaware River on December 26, 1776, to defeat and capture the Hessians, who had been hired to fight for the British.

tionary War debts, creation of a national bank, protective tariffs on imported goods to help U.S. industry, excise taxes on whiskey to raise revenue, and strict neutrality in the wars between Great Britain and France. Hamilton was opposed on many of these policies by Secretary of State Thomas Jefferson, who proposed closer relations with the French and disagreed with Hamilton's revenue measures, his idea of a national bank, and his plans to industrialize the nation.

Near the end of his first term, Washington accepted Jefferson's resignation. Now firmly in the camp of the Federalists organized by Hamilton, Washington was reelected by a unanimous vote of the electoral college in February 1793. He then allowed Hamilton to raise revenues through a whiskey excise tax. When Western farmers rebelled against paying the tax, Washington and Hamilton used military force to put down the Whiskey Rebellion in the summer of 1794. Washington cemented the alliance with Great Britain with Jay's Treaty, ratified in 1795. He accepted the resignation of his new secretary of state, Edmund Randolph, because Randolph had been bribed by the French to oppose the treaty. Washington's strong government secured the

West as well: the new frontier state of Kentucky was created in 1792, and Tennessee joined the Union in 1796.

Washington retired after his second term at the age of 64, publishing a farewell address to the nation on September 17, 1796, that warned of the perils of "foreign entanglements" and of "the baneful effects of the spirit of party" in domestic affairs. On July 4, 1798, in the midst of a crisis with France, Congress named him commander in chief of the Army of the United States, but he never took actual command of forces. For the last years of his life he pursued agricultural interests at Mount Vernon and enjoyed his family, especially Martha's grandchildren, two of whom he adopted after the death of their father. He died of pulmonary complications suffered during a snowstorm on December 14, 1799. In Philadelphia, one of his officers, Henry Lee, gave the famous eulogy, "First in war, first in peace, and first in the hearts of his countrymen."

SEE ALSO

Adams, John; Articles of Confederation; Creation of the Presidency; Washington's Farewell Address

FURTHER READING

Brookhiser, Richard. *Founding Father: Rediscovering George Washington.* 1996.

Reprint, New York: Free Press, 1997.

Cunliffe, Marcus. *George Washington: Man and Monument.* Rev. ed. Boston: Little, Brown, 1982.

Flexner, James Thomas. *Washington: The Indispensable Man.* New York: New American Library, 1979.

Ketcham, Ralph. *Presidents above Party: The First American Presidency, 1789–1829.* Chapel Hill: University of North Carolina Press, 1984.

Washington's Farewell Address

WASHINGTON'S FAREWELL Address was the message to the American people published by outgoing President George Washington on September 17, 1796. Washington wrote it during the height of a divisive Presidential campaign. In it he outlined three principles that he believed the new nation should follow in public affairs. First, sectional antagonisms should be put to rest. Second, "the baneful effects of the spirit of party" should be muted, because they threatened liberty by subordinating people to demagogic leaders and hampering the ability of the President to promote the national interest. Third, U.S. diplomacy should "steer clear of permanent alliances" and "trust to temporary alliances for extraordinary emergencies."

The address was controversial. Washington's political opponents, such as James Madison, saw it as nothing more than a defense of Washington's term in office. Politicians took little heed of Washington's advice: in the 19th century the two-party system was established and sectional animosity increased until the Civil War. The United States did follow one piece of his advice: it did not enter into permanent military alliances with other nations until the end of World War II.

SEE ALSO
Washington, George

Watergate investigation

THE WATERGATE scandal from 1972 to 1974 involved an attempt by President Richard M. Nixon to cover up illegal campaign activities by the Committee to Re-Elect the President and several White House aides. These activities included burglary, wiretapping, and dirty campaign tricks aimed at the Democratic Presidential campaign in 1972. The scandal resulted in Nixon's resignation from the Presidency.

On June 7, 1972, five Cubans were caught burglarizing the Democratic National Committee headquarters at the Watergate office complex in Washington, D.C. They named Gordon Liddy, counsel to the Committee to Re-Elect the President, as an accomplice. Liddy, in turn, could be linked to Operation Gemstone, an administration program to investigate and harass political opponents.

To keep Gemstone from becoming public knowledge, Nixon and his two top aides, H. R. Haldeman and John D. Erlichman, decided to get the Central Intelligence Agency to impede the pending FBI investigation of the break-in by having the CIA claim that it was a matter of national security. White House involvement in the burglary and in Gemstone was covered up successfully through the fall of 1972, and Nixon won a landslide victory over his Democratic opponent, George McGovern.

The Watergate burglars were provisionally sentenced to long prison terms by federal judge John Sirica, who hoped to prod them into talking in order to reduce their sentences. John Dean, the White House counsel, realized that he might be implicated, and he confessed his role in the matter to the Justice Department and implicated Nixon's top aides in the cover-up. On April 30, 1973, Nixon accepted the resignations of Haldeman and Erlichman.

The Senate Select Committee on Campaign Activities, chaired by Senator Sam Ervin (Democrat–North Carolina), opened televised hearings. Dean's testimony implicated the President, although he had no evidence. But then an aide to Haldeman, Alexander Butterfield, admitted that the White House had taped conversations in the Oval Office. The Justice Department's special prosecutor, Archibald Cox, demanded that Nixon turn over any recorded conversations involving Watergate. Nixon turned over some of the tapes but told Cox he could not have the rest, citing his right to the confidentiality of conversations in his office, a claim known as executive privilege.

Cox went to court to obtain the evidence, and Nixon ordered his attorney general, Elliot Richardson, to fire Cox. Richardson refused and resigned in protest. Deputy Attorney General William Ruckelshaus also refused and was himself fired by the President; finally, Solicitor General Robert Bork, the next-ranking official in the Justice Department, agreed to carry out Nixon's order. This Saturday Night Massacre unleashed a fire storm of protest. Shortly thereafter the House Judiciary Committee opened an impeachment inquiry. The House committee deliberated until July 24, 1974, when it voted to recommend that the full House pass three articles of impeachment. It accused Nixon of obstruction of justice (his attempt to use the CIA to impede an FBI investigation), abuse of power (misuse of the CIA, FBI, and Internal Revenue Service to harass his political enemies), and refusal to turn over evidence to Congress. It concluded that the President had "acted in a man-

ner contrary to his trust as President and subversive of constitutional government," causing "manifest injury to the people of the United States."

After that vote, the Supreme Court, in *United States* v. *Nixon* (1974), ordered the President to turn over his tapes and other evidence to the federal district court judge who was trying the Watergate crimes, for use by the new special prosecutor, Leon Jaworski. One of the tapes did show that Nixon had engaged in a cover-up and a conspiracy to obstruct justice, which is a federal crime and an impeachable offense.

Shortly afterward a delegation of senior Republican senators, led by Arizona conservative Barry Goldwater, advised Nixon that the Senate would probably convict him if an impeachment trial were held. Nixon resigned from office on August 9, 1974. He was later pardoned for all Watergate-related crimes by his successor, Gerald Ford.

Senator Sam Ervin of North Carolina chaired the committee that investigated the Watergate scandal.

SEE ALSO

Ethics, Presidential; Executive privilege; Ford, Gerald R.; Impeachment; Independent counsel; Nixon, Richard M.

FURTHER READING

Kurland, Philip B. "The Watergate Inquiry, 1973." In *Congress Investigates: A Documented History, 1792–1974,* edited by Arthur M. Schlesinger, Jr., and Roger Bruns. Vol. 5. New York: Bowker, 1975.
Kutler, Stanley L. *The Wars of Watergate.* New York: Knopf, 1990.
Woodward, Bob, and Carl Bernstein. *All the President's Men.* New York: Warner, 1974.

Wheeler, William

VICE PRESIDENT

☆ Born: June 30, 1819, Malone, N.Y.
☆ Political party: Republican

☆ *Education: University of Vermont, 1838–39*
☆ *Military service: none*
☆ *Previous government service: district attorney, Franklin County, N.Y., 1846–49; New York State Assembly, 1850–51; New York Senate, 1858–60; U.S. House of Representatives, 1861–63, 1869–77; president, New York State Constitutional Convention, 1867–68*
☆ *Vice President under Rutherford B. Hayes, 1877–81*
☆ *Died: June 4, 1887, Malone, N.Y.*

WHEN THE Republican party nominated William Wheeler for the Vice Presidency in 1876, he was a political unknown outside of upper New York State. He got the nomination because while in Congress he had not taken part in the graft and corruption that permeated the Capitol during Ulysses S. Grant's Presidency. The Republican ticket, headed by Rutherford B. Hayes, won by a one-vote margin in the electoral college after an election commission awarded the Republicans a number of disputed electoral college votes. Like most 19th-century Vice Presidents, Wheeler claimed no accomplishments during his tenure.

White House

THE WHITE House is the official residence of the President of the United States. Originally called the President's Palace, the President's House, or the Executive Mansion, it was officially proclaimed the White House by President Theodore Roosevelt in 1901.

The site for the White House was determined by George Washington and Pierre L'Enfant, the French architect who developed the master plan for the capital city in 1791. The building was designed by the Irish architect James Hoban, who won a medal worth $500 in a contest judged by three commissioners of the District of Columbia.

The White House cornerstone was laid on October 13, 1792, and the sandstone building was completed in November 1800, just in time for occupancy by John and Abigail Adams. Thomas Jefferson, one of the losers in the design competition, started construction of the East and West Wings during his Presidency, working with architect Benjamin Latrobe. He patterned them after his plantation at Monticello. On August 24, 1814, during the War of 1812, the British burned the White House to the ground. Only the shell—and the kitchen's ironware and stove—remained. James Hoban supervised the rebuilding of the entire structure by September 1817. Hoban built the South Portico during James Monroe's Presidency and the North Portico during Andrew Jackson's tenure. At that time the first plumbing and sewer lines were put in. Martin Van Buren installed a furnace, James Polk installed gas lighting, and Franklin Pierce installed bathrooms with running water in the family quarters. The first telephone was put in by Rutherford Hayes, and Chester Arthur installed an elevator.

The interior was rebuilt in 1902 by architect Charles McKim. The family rooms were enlarged and each bedroom was given its own bath. The West Wing was enlarged and a Presidential office included, and the State Dining Room was enlarged by one-third for diplomatic receptions. Plumbing, heating, and electrical wiring were modernized. An East Wing to accommodate guests at official functions was built. The East Room was redecorated in a colonial revival style for the wedding of Teddy Roosevelt's daughter Alice to Nicholas Longworth. After the work was completed, a time capsule containing memorabilia of the period was placed under the marble floor of the Great Hall entrance.

The next major overhaul took place in Calvin Coolidge's administration in 1927. A third floor with 18 rooms for guests and servants was added, and the roof was replaced. A sun room was built on top of the South Portico. During Franklin Roosevelt's Presidency, the West Wing was rebuilt and underground office space was added. The East Wing was converted to office space for the growing Presidential staff. An indoor swimming pool was added.

From 1949 to 1950, during Harry Truman's Presidency, the entire building was gutted. It was then rebuilt and reinforced with steel beams and a new foundation. Among the improvements were a balcony on the second floor of the South Portico, a grand stairway leading from the family quarters to the first-floor state rooms, and central air-conditioning.

Starting in 1978, the exterior paint was scraped down to wood and stone, and much ornate carving was revealed. The exterior restoration and repainting was completed in 1993.

The White House contains 132 rooms, 29 bathrooms, and 29 fireplaces, all cared for by a chief usher and 96 housekeepers. The National Park Service has 36 workers who take care of its 18.7 acres. The U.S. Secret Service provides protection for White House occupants.

White House furnishings are selected by the curator of the White House (a post established by Lyndon Johnson in 1964) in consultation with the First Family. All furnishings are public property and are inventoried annually. Jacqueline Kennedy created a White House Fine Arts Committee chaired by Henry Francis Du Pont, founder of the Winterthur Museum (a decorative arts museum in Delaware) to advise on the restoration of the state rooms. She also created a Special Committee on Paintings. The White House displays selections from the 444 paintings and sculptures in its permanent collection. Most of the paintings in the collection were done by American artists, but it also includes works by the French painters Paul Cézanne and Claude Monet.

The White House Historical Association and the White House Preservation Committee are private organizations that raise money to preserve furnishings and acquire new pieces. Jimmy and Rosalynn Carter created the White House Endowment Fund, which is supported by private contributions and provides financial support for the maintenance and renovation of first-floor museum rooms.

Ronald and Nancy Reagan spent more than $1 million in private donations to redecorate the second and third floors, using primarily 19th-century American furnishings. Since 1925 Congress has appropriated $50,000 for Presidents to paint and decorate the living quarters at the start of each term.

The first floor contains five state rooms, and Congress requires that it be maintained in "museum character." Patricia Nixon, working with White House curator Clement Conger and the restoration architect Edward Vason Jones, redid the entire first floor in early 18th-century styles.

The original 1792 design for the White House, by architect James Hoban.

A cutaway view of the White House.

The state rooms include the East Room ballroom, 80 feet long and 40 feet wide, where press conferences are held. Seven deceased Presidents lay in state there. President Grover Cleveland was married in the East Room. For his daughter Nellie's wedding Ulysses Grant decorated it in a neoclassic style, with Corinthian columns, heavy wooden mantels, and gilt carved framed mirrors. Today it has a polished oak floor, carved wood paneling, and golden drapes.

The State Dining Room, where official state dinners are held, contains a long centerpiece for the table from the Monroe administration. It has wooden paneling and golden silk draperies. Dinners in the State Dining Room may seat as many as 140 guests. Nancy Reagan created a complete dinnerware set executed by Lenox, which includes 220 place settings of 19 pieces each. (Along with the other White House china, it is displayed in the China Room on the ground floor. The White House silver is located in the Vermeil Room, also on the ground floor.) The Family Dining Room has rarely been used for meals since Jacqueline Kennedy installed a President's Dining Room and kitchen on the second floor in 1961. It serves as a pantry during state dinners.

The Blue Room, a small oval room facing onto the South Portico, is used for small formal dinners and entertaining. It has the original French furniture used in Monroe's day.

The Red Room is used by First Ladies to entertain after dinners and for teas, and Dolley Madison held recep-

Ground Floor
G1 Library
G2 Ground Floor
 Corridor*
G3 Vermeil Room
G4 China Room
G5 Diplomatic
 Reception Room
G6 Map Room

First Floor
F1 East Room*
F2 Green Room*
F3 Blue Room*
F4 South Portico
F5 Red Room*
F6 State Dining
 Room*
F7 Family Dining
 Room
F8 Cross Hall*
F9 Entrance Hall*

*Rooms open to the public

tions there. Rutherford B. Hayes was sworn in as President in the Red Room before his public inauguration ceremony. Eleanor Roosevelt held press conferences there for women reporters. The Green Room was used by Thomas Jefferson for meals and by James Monroe for card games. It became a drawing room for small receptions, teas, or dinners. The carpet is green, as are the silk wall coverings.

The second floor contains the family living quarters. It has 13 rooms, including the Yellow Oval Room, where Presidents receive visitors and entertain guests. It opens onto the balcony and looks over the Mall. Next to it is the President's study, and at the end of the hall is the President's bedroom and dressing room. On the other side is the Treaty Room (which served as the cabinet room in the 19th century), then the Lincoln Bedroom and sitting room (once the Presidential office). The "Queen's Bedroom," which has been occupied by Queen Elizabeth (the queen mother) and Elizabeth II, both of Great Britain, and Queen Wilhelmina of the Netherlands, and sitting room are on the opposite side of the hall. There are three other bedrooms for personal guests. There are no bedrooms for foreign heads of state or other official guests; they stay at Blair House, across the street.

Jacqueline Kennedy did the key restoration of the family quarters. She commissioned New York decorator Sister Parish to design a "country home in the city" on the second floor. An important change was to install a kitchen and dining room opposite the President's bedroom, so the First Family would not have to eat on the first floor.

The third floor contains the White House solarium. It is used as a nursery when the First Family has small children. Teenage children have used it for parties and to entertain their friends—without Secret Service intrusion.

On the lower level are offices for some of the staff of the National Security Council. The White House Communications Agency, also located in the basement, operates the Signal Board, which connects the President with senior staff members, top military commanders, and national security officials.

There are two annexes off the main mansion. The West Wing, containing Presidential offices, was destroyed in a fire in 1929. It was completely rebuilt and now contains the Oval Office, the Cabinet Room, and offices for the President's principal aides. Three dining rooms on the lower level of the West Wing, known as the White House Mess, can serve almost 100 staffers at a time. The Rose Garden, outside the President's office, was created during the Kennedy Presidency.

The East Wing contains staff offices, the Visitors' Office (which coordinates public tours), and the Family Theater. The President's doctor and nurses have a medical suite in the White House residence. The White House garage has military chauffeurs to drive the Presidential limousine and cars for senior aides on official business.

The public may visit the state rooms of the White House on most weekdays. There are also annual spring and fall garden tours, an annual Easter egg roll for children, the lighting of the National Christmas Tree, and three nights of candlelight tours to see Christmas decorations. More than 1.2 million people tour the White House each year. On February 14, 1962, "A Tour of the White House with Mrs. John F. Kennedy," a television program broadcast by CBS, had an estimated audience of 80 million people.

SEE ALSO

Children of Presidents; Executive Office Buildings; First Lady; Kennedy, Jacqueline; Madison, Dolley; Oval Office; Secret Service, U.S.

FURTHER READING

Aikman, Lonnelle. *The Living White House.* Washington, D.C.: White House Historical Association, 1982.

Seale, William. *The White House: The History of an American Idea.* Washington, D.C.: The American Institute of Architects Press, 1992.

White House Office

THE WHITE HOUSE Office is the collective name for the President's assistants. It was created by Reorganization Act No. 1 of 1939, on the recommendation of the Brownlow Commission, a Presidential study group. It concluded that to perform his many functions "the President needs help."

Until 1939 the President had no senior aides on his payroll, though Congress did provide salaries for clerks and for the residence staff. Presidents relied on assistant secretaries, the top-level political appointees of the executive departments, who were informally assigned to handle Presidential business, such as liaison with Congress.

In 1937 the Brownlow Commission recommended that the President be assisted by six senior aides, who ideally would have "a passion for anonymity" in their work. By the end of World War II the number had increased to 45, by the end of Dwight Eisenhower's administration it was up to 400, and there were more than 600 staffers during Richard Nixon's administration.

To run the White House Office, President Eisenhower appointed a chief of staff, assisted by a deputy chief of staff. (John Kennedy and Lyndon Johnson did not follow Eisenhower's innovation, but all Presidents since then have had a chief of staff.) There are also five or six senior political advisers known as "counselors to the President" or "special assistants" who have direct access to him. There are about 50 deputies to these top officials and about 100 assistants to these deputies. These senior aides (including White House speech writers) earn salaries equal to those of under secretaries and assistant secretaries of the departments. The remaining 400 or so staffers serve primarily as managers, secretaries, clerks, or technicians.

The White House Office prepares the President's speeches, does the advance work for the President's public appearances, and handles his schedule and appointments. The Office of Congressional Liaison helps the President persuade Congress to pass his legislative program, and the Office of Intergovernmental Affairs keeps in contact with governors and mayors. The Political Affairs Office keeps the President in close touch with his party's leaders. The Public Liaison Office helps the President gain support from special interest groups and their lobbyists. The Cabinet Secretariat makes sure that department secretaries implement Presidential decisions. The press secretary organizes news conferences and is responsible for preparing the President for questions he may face. The White House counsel ensures that the President is familiar with the legal and constitutional issues involved in decisions he makes.

Other units in the White House include the White House Military Office,

White House employees in the late 1800s.

which handles the "football," a briefcase that contains communications codes that allow the President to launch a nuclear attack; the White House physician, responsible for monitoring the President's physical condition; and the White House Communications Agency, which keeps the President in touch with military, diplomatic, intelligence, and other national security communications networks.

The senior staff works out of the East and West Wings and the basement of the White House itself, and lower-level aides work in the Old Executive Office Building next door.

SEE ALSO

Counsel, Office of; Decision making, Presidential; Executive Office Buildings; Executive Office of the President; Office of Administration; Physician to the President; Press secretary; Speech writers; White House

FURTHER READING

Patterson, Bradley. *The Ring of Power: The White House Staff and Its Expanding Role in Government.* New York: Basic Books, 1988.

Wilson, Henry

VICE PRESIDENT

- ☆ Born: Feb. 16, 1812, Farmington, N.H.
- ☆ Political parties: Whig, Free-Soil, Know-Nothing, Republican
- ☆ Education: no formal education
- ☆ Military service: none
- ☆ Previous government service: Massachusetts Assembly, 1841–44; Massachusetts Senate, 1844–46, 1850–52; U.S. Senate, 1855–73
- ☆ Vice President under Ulysses S. Grant, 1873–75
- ☆ Died: Nov. 22, 1875, Washington, D.C.

HENRY WILSON was a self-made business entrepreneur who parlayed shoe factories into a large fortune. A member of several political parties, he deserted each, in turn, because it did not take a sufficiently strong stand against slavery. He was elected to the Massachusetts Assembly as a Whig in 1840 and to its senate in 1844. He was a founder of the Free-Soil party in 1848 and a member of the Know-Nothing party from 1853 to 1855. In the 1850s he lost three successive elections for governor of Massachusetts. After his election to the Senate in 1855 he joined the Republican party and was a leading member of its abolitionist wing. As chair of the Senate's committee on military affairs, he led the drive for war preparedness and opposed any compromise with the South just prior to the Civil War. After the war he strongly supported the 14th and 15th Amendments to the Constitution, which provided citizenship and voting rights for freed black men.

Wilson was defeated for the Republican Vice Presidential nomination in 1868 but won it in 1872. During Ulysses Grant's second term a series of scandals engulfed the administration, but Wilson was not involved. He accomplished nothing in office, and his failing health kept him from realizing his own Presidential ambitions.

SEE ALSO

Grant, Ulysses S.

FURTHER READING

McKay, Ernest. *Henry Wilson: Practical Radical.* Port Washington, N.Y.: Kennikat Press, 1971.

Wilson, Woodrow

28TH PRESIDENT

- ☆ Born: Dec. 28, 1856, Staunton, Va.
- ☆ Political party: Democrat
- ☆ Education: Davidson College, 1876; College of New Jersey (Princeton), B.A., 1879; University of Virginia Law School, 1880; Johns Hopkins University, Ph.D., 1886

☆ *Military service: none*
☆ *Previous government service:*
   governor of New Jersey, 1911–12
☆ *Elected President, 1912; served,*
   1913–21
☆ *Died: Feb. 3, 1924, Washington, D.C.*

WOODROW WILSON was the only
Democratic President elected between
1896, when William Jennings Bryan was
defeated, and 1932, when Franklin
Roosevelt was elected.
Wilson was a political
scientist who once wrote,
"The President is at lib-
erty, both in law and in
conscience, to be as big a
man as he can." Wilson's
Presidency demonstrated
the validity of his observation: His two terms
were characterized by
successes in instituting a
progressive domestic
program. His foreign policies were
marked by victory in World War I and
military interventions in several nations.

Wilson was born in Virginia and
lived in Georgia and the Carolinas during
the Civil War. His father's church was
used as a temporary hospital for wounded
Confederate soldiers. After attending
Davidson College for a year to study for
the ministry, he withdrew for health
reasons and later went to the College of
New Jersey (Princeton), where he distinguished himself as a debater. After graduating in 1879 he studied law at the University of Virginia and practiced briefly
and without much success in Atlanta
before deciding to study history and
political science at Johns Hopkins University. His doctoral dissertation, which
became a highly regarded book, *Congressional Government*, analyzed the
weakness of the Presidency and the
strength of the standing committees in
Congress. (Wilson is the only President
ever to earn a doctorate and the only one
who was a political scientist.)

Wilson embarked on a career as a
college professor, teaching briefly at Bryn
Mawr College (newly established to
teach women) and Wesleyan University
(where he also served as football coach)
before returning to Princeton in 1890 as
a professor of jurisprudence and political
economy. He published a five-volume
History of the American People. In 1902
Wilson became president of Princeton.

Wilson soon gained a national
reputation for his innovative educational
reforms at Princeton, which were
designed to emphasize academics and
de-emphasize its elitism. In 1908 he
published *Constitutional Government in
the United States*, in which he described
the growth of Presidential power in
Theodore Roosevelt's administration.

Two years later Democratic political
bosses in New Jersey, seeking a candidate with a reputation for honesty and
incorruptibility, visited Wilson at Princeton and offered him the party's nomination for governor. Wilson accepted and
won the election. He broke with the
party bosses who had supported him so
he could establish a reputation as his
own man rather than a follower of the
bosses. Instead, he backed reform laws
to provide for direct primaries for nominations (taking the nominating power
away from the bosses), an ethics law for
elected government officials, workmen's
compensation, a pure food law, and a
commission to regulate such public utili-
ties as electricity.

In 1912 Wilson was a contender, although not the favorite, for the Democratic Presidential nomination. He won
the nomination on the 46th ballot, defeating the favorite, House Speaker
Champ Clark.

With the Republicans split, Wilson
was able to win the Presidency with 42

percent of the popular vote, defeating Theodore Roosevelt and William Howard Taft. The Democrats retained Democratic control of the House and won a six-seat margin in the Senate.

Wilson capped his meteoric rise to the White House by demonstrating energetic leadership and domination of Congress. He influenced the roster of committee members so that supporters of his New Freedom program served on key committees. He imposed party discipline on congressional Democrats, who bound themselves to vote for measures put forward by their President. He broke precedent by giving an address to a special session of Congress called in April 1913, instead of sending the legislature a written annual message, as every President since Thomas Jefferson had done. He held regular news conferences and made every effort to rally public opinion around his legislative proposals.

Wilson won passage of a large number of progressive measures. The Underwood Tariff of 1913 lowered the duties on imported manufactured goods, which benefited consumers. The tariff act also contained a provision for the first income tax limited to wealthy individuals. The Federal Reserve Act of 1913 reorganized the banking system in order to prevent the sort of financial instability that caused panics and depressions. The Federal Trade Commission was established in 1914 to end unfair trade practices. The Clayton Anti-Trust Act of 1914 provided new legal weapons against monopolies (companies that eliminated competition and thus raised prices) while recognizing the rights of workers to organize in labor unions and engage in strikes. In 1916 Wilson got Congress to approve federal land banks to provide low-interest loans to farmers, workmen's compensation for injuries received on the job, an eight-hour day for railroad workers, and laws prohibiting child labor. However, Wilson also promoted racial segregation in government departments in the capital.

In foreign affairs Wilson pursued an interventionist policy against small nations. In 1914 he ordered the military to seize the port of Veracruz, Mexico, to prevent a shipment of German weapons from reaching the revolutionary government of Victoriano Huerta. The crisis ended after European mediators succeeded in getting Huerta to resign. In 1915 the United States occupied the Caribbean island of Haiti and Santo Domingo and took control of their financial affairs in order to pay back banks that had loaned money to these nations. In 1916 Wilson sent General John J. Pershing into Mexico with orders to pursue the guerrilla leader Pancho Villa, who had crossed into U.S. territory and killed 19 Americans. But Pershing's expedition was unsuccessful, and after several clashes with Mexican troops it was withdrawn early in 1917.

In 1914, at the beginning of World War I, Wilson issued a Neutrality Proclamation that stated that the United States would not take sides in the conflict. But Germany's policy of unrestricted submarine warfare caused Wilson to protest and eventually to tilt U.S. policy toward Great Britain and France. Although the British also interfered with U.S. shipping, only the German action resulted in the loss of American lives. On May 17, 1915, the Germans sank a British ocean liner, the *Lusitania,* resulting in the loss of 1,198 lives, among them 128 Americans. Early in 1916 Germany announced it was ending its submarine warfare, and Wilson then campaigned for reelection on the slogan "He kept us out of war." Wilson won a close election against Republican Charles Evans Hughes, receiving 52 percent of the popular vote.

In December 1916 Germany announced its willingness to negotiate an end to the war. Wilson then called for a

In 1917, suffragists demonstrated in front of the White House to demand that Wilson support women's right to vote

peace conference and on January 22, 1917, outlined his ideas for "peace without victory" in Europe. But nine days later, as if in answer, the Germans torpedoed Wilson's initiative by announcing a resumption of unrestricted submarine warfare. On February 3, 1917, Wilson broke off diplomatic relations with Germany. Wilson armed U.S. merchant ships on March 5. On March 18 the Germans sank three U.S. merchant vessels, and on April 6 Congress granted Wilson's request for a declaration of war against Germany. The U.S. expeditionary force under General Pershing broke the long stalemate at the Second Battle of the Marne. (Other troops entered Russia on the side of the anticommunist White Russians fighting the Bolsheviks and remained until 1920.)

As the Allied victory drew near, Wilson announced his Fourteen Points, a set of principles to guide the victors, in an address to Congress on January 8, 1918. He proposed a system of open diplomacy without state secrets, freedom of the seas, arms reductions, and a "general association of nations" to guarantee all nations their independence and secure borders.

Germany acknowledged its defeat and signed an armistice on November 11, 1918. Meanwhile, Wilson had campaigned for Democratic candidates in the 1918 midterm elections on the basis

of his peace proposals, making them a partisan issue. He thus sacrificed the possibility that Republicans would support his plans. Republicans took control of both houses of Congress.

In December 1918 Wilson sailed for the peace negotiations in Paris. He excluded Republican legislators from his delegation, which was a departure from the traditional practice of bipartisan foreign policy. The European allies had already decided to reward themselves with territories and reparations (financial compensation from their defeated enemies), and Wilson was forced to give up most of his Fourteen Points. Nevertheless, he returned with a draft covenant, or constitution, for a League of Nations, which was included in the Treaty of Versailles that the Allies signed on June 28, 1919.

Wilson submitted the treaty to the Republican-controlled Senate for its advice and consent. Some Republican progressives turned isolationist and were prepared to vote against any treaty at all. Other Republicans, led by Senator Henry Cabot Lodge of Massachusetts, would accept a treaty only if it placed strict limitations on the power of the President to commit the United States to peacekeeping duties under Article X of the League of Nations covenant.

Wilson refused to make any concessions. He crossed the nation on a speaking tour in support of the league. On September 25, 1919, in Pueblo, Colorado, he collapsed. He was brought back to Washington, where he suffered a stroke on October 2. For two months Wilson was totally incapacitated. For the remainder of his term, though he understood fully what was happening around him, he was unable to do more than listen, dictate letters, talk for a few minutes, and scrawl his signature. He did not sign acts of Congress, which became laws without his signature. For four months his cabinet did not meet; for another four it met without him. Cabinet secretaries were unable to discuss government business with him. His wife and the White House physician controlled all access to him. When Secretary of State Robert Lansing inquired if the President was so disabled he should resign, they vigorously denied it. No one in government wanted Vice President Thomas Marshall, whom they considered incompetent, to take over.

Paralyzed and totally dependent on his wife as his link to the outside world, Wilson was in no position to control the outcome of the struggle for the Treaty of Versailles. The Senate approved it with a series of "reservations" sponsored by Senator Lodge. Wilson called on his supporters to vote against that version of the treaty. In November, a coalition of Republicans who opposed any version of the treaty and Democrats defeated Lodge's version. (In 1921, by a simple resolution, Congress declared the war with Germany over.)

Wilson was awarded the Nobel Peace Prize in December 1920, but that prize was small consolation for his political defeat. After his retirement from office, he remained in Washington, D.C., but he was too ill to take part in public affairs. On Armistice Day, 1923, he made his last public speech, in which he foretold eventual U.S. participation in the League of Nations. "I have seen fools resist Providence before," he warned. "That we shall prevail is as sure as God reigns." He died in Washington on February 3, 1924. The United States never joined the League of Nations, though Wilson's goal was ultimately realized when the country took the lead in creating the United Nations at the end of World War II.

SEE ALSO
Checks and balances; Disability, Presidential; Health, Presidential; Marshall, Thomas; New Freedom; Roosevelt,

Theodore; State of the Union address; Taft, William Howard; Treaty of Versailles; Treaty powers

FURTHER READING
Levin, N. Gordon. *Woodrow Wilson and World Politics.* New York: Oxford, 1970.
Link, Arthur S. *Woodrow Wilson and the Progressive Era, 1910–1917.* New York: Harper & Row, 1954.
Smith, Gene. *When the Cheering Stopped: The Last Years of Woodrow Wilson.* New York: Morrow, 1964.

Women in the executive branch

EVEN BEFORE the 19th Amendment was passed in 1920, many women lobbied for reform as members of clubs or as social workers. When President Franklin D. Roosevelt's New Deal made social welfare a priority of the federal government, many of these female reformers began to work at the national level. This new governmental focus coupled with the lobbying efforts of Eleanor Roosevelt and Molly Dewson, the head of the Women's Division of the Democratic National Committee, meant that more women than ever before helped shape U.S. policy in the 1930s.

Mary Anderson, an organizer of the Women's Trade Union League (WTUL, founded in 1903), was made assistant director of the wartime government bureau Women in Industry Service. When this bureau was replaced by the Women's Bureau of the Department of Labor in 1920, Anderson became its first director, improving women's access to employment, fair wages, and the vote.

Roosevelt gave another labor advocate, Frances Perkins, a place in his administration: she served as secretary of labor from 1933 to 1945, becoming the first female cabinet member and

exercising great influence over labor legislation during her tenure. In addition, Roosevelt appointed Mary McLeod Bethune, the child of former slaves, to direct the Division of Negro Affairs of the National Youth Administration. Bethune's experience as an educator and founder of a school for black women made her the ideal manager of this New Deal agency, which worked to increase educational opportunities for African Americans. When Ruth Bryan Owen became Roosevelt's minister to Denmark in 1933, she made history as the first female U.S. ambassador.

Women continued to hold a range of positions in the executive branch in the period during and after World War II. The journalist and parliamentary expert Oveta Culp Hobby organized a military unit for women as director of the Women's Interest Section of the War Department in 1941. As the first American female colonel, she became head of the Women's Auxiliary Army Corps (WAAC) in 1942, which became the Women's Army Corps (WAC) in 1943. Her public service continued after the war: from 1952 to 1955, Hobby served as the first secretary of the Department of Health, Education, and Welfare, making her the only woman to serve in

President Dwight D. Eisenhower's cabinet. Beginning in the 1980s Elizabeth Dole held two different cabinet posts, exemplifying the range of positions newly available to women. As the first female secretary of transportation, she increased automobile safety regulations and led the campaign to raise the drinking age to 21 under Ronald Reagan's administration. As secretary of labor under President George Bush, she began the "Glass Ceiling Study" to examine barriers to job promotion for women and minorities.

Women continue to perform key executive branch functions as cabinet secretaries. By the time of the 2000 elections, Donna Shalala had become the longest-serving secretary of health and human services in U.S. history, having begun her work under President Bill Clinton in January 1993. She was instrumental in directing and implementing welfare reform during her seven years as secretary. Alexis Herman was sworn in as the 23rd secretary of labor on May 1, 1997, becoming the first African American to hold the position. She had served previously as assistant to the President, as director of the White House Public Liaison Office, and as deputy director of the Presidential Transition Office in 1992.

Under President Clinton, Janet Reno and Madeleine Albright served in positions once considered the sole domain of men. Reno became the first female attorney general on March 12, 1993, just 33 years after she was denied a position in one of Miami's biggest law firms because of her sex. When Clinton made Albright the 64th secretary of state in 1997, she became the highest-ranking woman in the U.S. government. During Clinton's first term, Albright had served as U.S. representative to the United Nations and as a member of the National Security Council.

As of 1998, according to government figures, the representation of women in the permanent executive branch work force exceeded their percentage representation in directly comparable occupations in the regular civilian work force, in 10 of 22 of the executive branch independent agencies.

Yacht, Presidential

THE FIRST yacht placed into official service was the U.S.S. *Mayflower,* assigned to President Theodore Roosevelt in 1902. It was used by Roosevelt, William Howard Taft, Warren Harding, and Calvin Coolidge to entertain personal and government guests. President Herbert Hoover ordered the yacht moth-balled in the interest of economy, and it sank in a Philadelphia naval yard in 1931.

President Franklin D. Roosevelt used the U.S.S. *Sequoia,* which was placed in service in 1933, and the U.S.S. *Potomac,* put in service in 1936. The U.S.S. *Williamsburg,* put in service in 1945, was used by Roosevelt and Harry Truman. A 64-foot cabin cruiser used by Presidents from Truman through Lyndon Johnson was renamed by each succeeding President for someone in his family. It was taken out of service in 1969.

To symbolize a more austere Presidency, President Jimmy Carter sold the *Sequoia* in 1977. A private group, the Presidential Yacht Trust, bought it from a private owner and has refitted it, though no President has accepted the Trust's offer to sail it again.

A Presidential yacht is owned by the U.S. government. Its expenses are part of the navy budget, and its crew consists of naval personnel.

John Kennedy holds his 1963 birthday celebration on board the Sequoia.

PRESIDENTIAL ELECTION RESULTS

YEAR	NAME	PARTY	POPULAR VOTE	ELECTORAL COLLEGE VOTE
1789	George Washington	Federalist	—	69
1792	George Washington	Federalist	—	132
1796	John Adams	Federalist	—	71
	Thomas Jefferson	Democratic-Republican	—	68
1800	Thomas Jefferson	Democratic-Republican	—	73
	John Adams	Federalist	—	65
1804	Thomas Jefferson	Democratic-Republican	—	162
	Charles C. Pinckney	Federalist	—	14
1808	James Madison	Democratic-Republican	—	122
	Charles C. Pinckney	Federalist	—	47
1812	James Madison	Democratic-Republican	—	128
	George Clinton	Federalist	—	89
1816	James Monroe	Democratic-Republican	—	183
	Rufus King	Federalist	—	34
1820	James Monroe	Democratic-Republican	—	231
	John Quincy Adams	Democratic-Republican	—	1
1824	John Quincy Adams	Democratic-Republican	108,740	84
	Andrew Jackson	Democratic-Republican	153,544	99
	William Crawford	Democratic-Republican	46,618	41
	Henry Clay	Democratic-Republican	47,136	37
1828	Andrew Jackson	Democrat	647,286	178
	John Quincy Adams	National Republican	508,064	83
1832	Andrew Jackson	Democrat	687,502	219
	Henry Clay	National Republican	530,189	49
	Electoral votes not cast			2
1836	Martin Van Buren	Democrat	765,483	170
	William Henry Harrison	Whig	550,816	73
	Hugh White	Whig	146,107	26
	Daniel Webster	Whig	41,201	14
	Total for the 3 Whigs		739,795	113
1840	William Henry Harrison	Whig	1,274,624	234
	Martin Van Buren	Democrat	1,127,781	60
1844	James K. Polk	Democrat	1,338,464	170
	Henry Clay	Whig	1,300,097	105
1848	Zachary Taylor	Whig	1,360,967	163
	Lewis Cass	Democrat	1,222,342	127
	Martin Van Buren	Free-Soil	291,263	—
1852	Franklin Pierce	Democrat	1,601,117	254
	Winfield Scott	Whig	1,385,453	42
	John P. Hale	Free-Soil	155,825	—
1856	James Buchanan	Democrat	1,832,955	174
	John Frémont	Republican	1,339,932	114
	Millard Fillmore	Whig-American	871,731	8

YEAR	NAME	PARTY	POPULAR VOTE	ELECTORAL COLLEGE VOTE
1860	Abraham Lincoln	Republican	1,865,593	180
	John C. Breckinridge	Democratic	848,356	72
	Stephen Douglas	Democrat	1,382,713	12
	John Bell	Constitutional Union	592,906	39
1864	Abraham Lincoln	Unionist (Republican)	2,206,938	212
	George McClellan	Democrat	1,803,787	21
	Electoral votes not cast			81
1868	Ulysses S. Grant	Republican	3,013,421	214
	Horatio Seymour	Democrat	2,706,829	80
	Electoral votes not cast		23	
1872	Ulysses S. Grant	Republican	3,596,745	286
	Horace Greeley	Democrat	2,843,446	
	Thomas Hendricks	Democrat	—	42
	Benjamin Brown	Democrat	—	18
	Charles Jenkins	Democrat	—	2
	David Davis	Democrat	—	1
1876	Rutherford B. Hayes	Republican	4,036,572	185
	Samuel Tilden	Democrat	4,284,020	184
	Peter Cooper	Greenback	81,737	—
1880	James A. Garfield	Republican	4,453,295	214
	Winfield S. Hancock	Democrat	4,414,082	155
	James B. Weaver	Greenback-Labor	308,578	—
1884	Grover Cleveland	Democrat	4,879,507	219
	James G. Blaine	Republican	4,850,293	182
	Benjamin Butler	Greenback-Labor	175,370	—
	John St. John	Prohibition	150,369	—
1888	Benjamin Harrison	Republican	5,447,129	233
	Grover Cleveland	Democrat	5,537,857	168
	Clinton Fisk	Prohibition	249,506	—
	Anson Streeter	Union Labor	146,935	—
1892	Grover Cleveland	Democrat	5,555,426	277
	Benjamin Harrison	Republican	5,182,690	145
	James B. Weaver	People's	1,029,846	22
	John Bidwell	Prohibition	264,133	—
1896	William McKinley	Republican	7,102,246	271
	William J. Bryan	Democrat	6,492,559	176
	John Palmer	National Democratic	133,148	—
	Joshua Levering	Prohibition	132,007	—
1900	William McKinley	Republican	7,218,491	292
	William J. Bryan	Democrat	6,356,734	155
	John C. Wooley	Prohibition	208,914	—
	Eugene V. Debs	Socialist	87,814	—
1904	Theodore Roosevelt	Republican	7,628,461	336
	Alton B. Parker	Democrat	5,084,223	140
	Eugene V. Debs	Socialist	402,283	—
	Silas Swallow	Prohibition	258,536	—
	Thomas Watson	People's	117,183	—
1908	William Howard Taft	Republican	7,675,320	321
	William J. Bryan	Democrat	6,412,294	162
	Eugene V. Debs	Socialist	420,793	—
	Eugene Chafin	Prohibition	253,840	—

YEAR	NAME	PARTY	POPULAR VOTE	ELECTORAL COLLEGE VOTE
1912	Woodrow Wilson	Democrat	6,296,547	435
	William Howard Taft	Republican	3,486,720	8
	Theodore Roosevelt	Progressive	4,118,571	86
	Eugene V. Debs	Socialist	900,672	—
	Eugene Chafin	Prohibition	206,275	—
1916	Woodrow Wilson	Democrat	9,127,695	277
	Charles E. Hughes	Republican	8,533,507	254
	A. L. Benson	Socialist	585,113	—
	J. Frank Hanly	Prohibition	220,506	—
1920	Warren Harding	Republican	16,143,407	404
	James M. Cox	Democrat	9,130,328	127
	Eugene V. Debs	Socialist	919,799	—
	P. P. Christensen	Farmer-Labor	265,411	—
	Aaron Watkins	Prohibition	189,408	—
1924	Calvin Coolidge	Republican	15,718,211	382
	John W. Davis	Democrat	8,385,283	136
	Robert La Follette	Progressive	4,831,289	13
1928	Herbert C. Hoover	Republican	21,391,993	444
	Alfred E. Smith	Democrat	15,016,169	87
	Norman Thomas	Socialist	267,835	
1932	Franklin D. Roosevelt	Democrat	22,809,638	472
	Herbert C. Hoover	Republican	15,758,901	59
	Norman Thomas	Socialist	881,951	—
	William Foster	Communist	102,785	—
1936	Franklin D. Roosevelt	Democrat	27,752,869	523
	Alfred M. Landon	Republican	16,674,665	8
	William Lemke	Union	882,479	—
	Norman Thomas	Socialist	187,720	—
1940	Franklin D. Roosevelt	Democrat	27,307,819	449
	Wendell Willkie	Republican	22,321,018	82
1944	Franklin D. Roosevelt	Democrat	25,606,585	432
	Thomas E. Dewey	Republican	22,014,745	99
1948	Harry S. Truman	Democrat	24,179,345	303
	Thomas E. Dewey	Republican	21,991,291	189
	Strom Thurmond	Dixiecrat	1,176,125	39
	Henry Wallace	Progressive	1,157,326	—
	Norman Thomas	Socialist	139,572	—
	Claude A. Watson	Prohibition	103,900	—
1952	Dwight D. Eisenhower	Republican	33,936,234	442
	Adlai Stevenson II	Democrat	27,314,992	89
	Vincent Hallinan	Progressive	140,023	—
1956	Dwight D. Eisenhower	Republican	35,590,472	457
	Adlai Stevenson II	Democrat	26,022,752	73
	T. Coleman Andrews	States' Rights	111,178	—
	Walter B. Jones	Democrat	—	1
1960	John F. Kennedy	Democrat	34,226,731	303
	Richard M. Nixon	Republican	34,108,157	219
	Harry Byrd	Democrat	—	15

YEAR	NAME	PARTY	POPULAR VOTE	ELECTORAL COLLEGE VOTE
1964	Lyndon B. Johnson	Democrat	43,129,566	486
	Barry Goldwater	Republican	27,178,188	52
1968	Richard M. Nixon	Republican	31,785,480	301
	Hubert H. Humphrey	Democrat	31,275,166	191
	George Wallace	American Independent	9,906,473	46
1972	Richard M. Nixon	Republican	47,170,179	520
	George McGovern	Democrat	29,171,791	17
	John Hospers	Libertarian	—	1
1976	Jimmy Carter	Democrat	40,830,763	297
	Gerald R. Ford	Republican	39,147,793	240
	Ronald Reagan	Republican	—	1
1980	Ronald Reagan	Republican	43,904,153	489
	Jimmy Carter	Democrat	35,483,883	49
	John Anderson	Independent candidacy	5,719,437	—
1984	Ronald Reagan	Republican	54,455,074	525
	Walter F. Mondale	Democrat	37,577,137	13
1988	George Bush	Republican	48,881,278	426
	Michael Dukakis	Democrat	41,805,374	111
	Lloyd Bentsen	Democrat	—	1
1992	Bill Clinton	Democrat	43,727,625	370
	George Bush	Republican	38,165,180	168
	Ross Perot	Independent candidacy	19,236,411	0
1996	Bill Clinton	Democrat	45,628,667	379
	Bob Dole	Republican	37,869,435	159
	Ross Perot	Independent candidacy	7,874,283	0
2000	George W. Bush	Republican	49,820,518	271
	Albert Gore, Jr.	Democrat	50,158,094	267

NOTES

• In 1872, the Democratic Presidential nominee, Horace Greeley, died after the popular votes were cast but before the electors had met. Because the Democrats had lost the election to the Republican candidate, President Ulysses S. Grant, the Democratic electors felt no need to unite behind a single candidate. Instead, they split their votes among four Democratic politicians who had not run for the Presidency or received any popular votes in the election.

• In 1956 a Stevenson elector cast his ballot for Walter B. Jones.

• In 1960 Senator Harry Byrd of Virginia won the electoral votes in his state from an uncommitted slate of electors that had won the popular vote, and he also picked up an electoral vote in Oklahoma from a Nixon elector.

• In 1968 a Nixon elector voted for George Wallace.

• In 1972 a Nixon elector voted for John Hospers.

• In 1976 a Ford elector voted for Ronald Reagan.

• In 1988 a Dukakis elector voted for Lloyd Bentsen for President, even though Bentsen was running on the Democratic ticket for Vice President.

SOURCES

The statistics given here are the best estimates available based on currently accepted data; election statistics vary widely from source to source. 1789–1968 data from U.S. Bureau of the Census. *Historical Statistics of the United States, Colonial Times to 1970*. Washington, D.C.: Government Printing Office, 1975; 1972–1988 data from *Presidential Elections Since 1789*. 5th ed. Washington, D.C.: Congressional Quarterly, 1991.

APPENDIX 2

PRESIDENTIAL TERMS

PRESIDENT	TERM OF SERVICE	VICE PRESIDENT
George Washington	Apr. 30, 1789–Mar. 4, 1793	John Adams
George Washington	Mar. 4, 1793–Mar. 4, 1797	John Adams
John Adams	Mar. 4, 1797–Mar. 4, 1801	Thomas Jefferson
Thomas Jefferson	Mar. 4, 1801–Mar. 4, 1805	Aaron Burr
Thomas Jefferson	Mar. 4, 1805–Mar. 4, 1809	George Clinton
James Madison	Mar. 4, 1809–Mar. 4, 1813	George Clinton
James Madison	Mar. 4, 1813–Mar. 4, 1817	Elbridge Gerry
James Monroe	Mar. 4, 1817–Mar. 4, 1821	Daniel Tompkins
James Monroe	Mar. 4, 1821–Mar. 4, 1825	Daniel Tompkins
John Quincy Adams	Mar. 4, 1825–Mar. 4, 1829	John C. Calhoun
Andrew Jackson	Mar. 4, 1829–Mar. 4, 1833	John C. Calhoun
Andrew Jackson	Mar. 4, 1833–Mar. 4, 1837	Martin Van Buren
Martin Van Buren	Mar. 4, 1837–Mar. 4, 1841	Richard M. Johnson
William Henry Harrison	Mar. 4, 1841–Apr. 4, 1841	John Tyler
John Tyler	Apr. 6, 1841–Mar. 4, 1845	
James K. Polk	Mar. 4, 1845–Mar. 4, 1849	George Dallas
Zachary Taylor	Mar. 4, 1849–July 9, 1850	Millard Fillmore
Millard Fillmore	July 10, 1850–Mar. 4, 1853	
Franklin Pierce	Mar. 4, 1853–Mar. 4, 1857	William King
James Buchanan	Mar. 4, 1857–Mar. 4, 1861	John C. Breckinridge
Abraham Lincoln	Mar. 4, 1861–Mar. 4, 1865	Hannibal Hamlin
Abraham Lincoln	Mar. 4, 1865–Apr. 15, 1865	Andrew Johnson
Andrew Johnson	Apr. 15, 1865–Mar. 4, 1869	
Ulysses S. Grant	Mar. 4, 1869–Mar. 4, 1873	Schuyler Colfax
Ulysses S. Grant	Mar. 4, 1873–Mar. 4, 1877	Henry Wilson
Rutherford B. Hayes	Mar. 4, 1877–Mar. 4, 1881	William Wheeler
James A. Garfield	Mar. 4, 1881–Sept. 19, 1881	Chester Alan Arthur
Chester Alan Arthur	Sept. 20, 1881–Mar. 4, 1885	
Grover Cleveland	Mar. 4, 1885–Mar. 4, 1889	Thomas Hendricks
Benjamin Harrison	Mar. 4, 1889–Mar. 4, 1893	Levi Morton
Grover Cleveland	Mar. 4, 1893–Mar. 4, 1897	Adlai Stevenson
William McKinley	Mar. 4, 1897–Mar. 4, 1901	Garret Hobart
William McKinley	Mar. 4, 1901–Sept. 14, 1901	Theodore Roosevelt
Theodore Roosevelt	Sept. 14, 1901–Mar. 4, 1905	
Theodore Roosevelt	Mar. 4, 1905–Mar. 4, 1909	Charles Fairbanks
William Howard Taft	Mar. 4, 1909–Mar. 4, 1913	James Sherman
Woodrow Wilson	Mar. 4, 1913–Mar. 4, 1917	Thomas Marshall
Woodrow Wilson	Mar. 4, 1917–Mar. 4, 1921	Thomas Marshall
Warren G. Harding	Mar. 4, 1921–Aug. 2, 1923	Calvin Coolidge
Calvin Coolidge	Aug. 3, 1923–Mar. 4, 1925	
Calvin Coolidge	Mar. 4, 1925–Mar. 4, 1929	Charles Dawes
Herbert C. Hoover	Mar. 4, 1929–Mar. 4, 1933	Charles Curtis
Franklin D. Roosevelt	Mar. 4, 1933–Jan. 20, 1937	John Nance Garner
Franklin D. Roosevelt	Jan. 20, 1937–Jan. 20, 1941	John Nance Garner
Franklin D. Roosevelt	Jan. 20, 1941–Jan. 20, 1945	Henry Wallace
Franklin D. Roosevelt	Jan. 20, 1945–Apr. 12, 1945	Harry S. Truman
Harry S. Truman	Apr. 12, 1945–Jan. 20, 1949	
Harry S. Truman	Jan. 20, 1949–Jan. 20, 1953	Alben Barkley
Dwight D. Eisenhower	Jan. 20, 1953–Jan. 20, 1957	Richard M. Nixon
Dwight D. Eisenhower	Jan. 20, 1957–Jan. 20, 1961	Richard M. Nixon
John F. Kennedy	Jan. 20, 1961–Nov. 22, 1963	Lyndon B. Johnson
Lyndon B. Johnson	Nov. 22, 1963–Jan. 20, 1965	
Lyndon B. Johnson	Jan. 20, 1965–Jan. 20, 1969	Hubert H. Humphrey
Richard M. Nixon	Jan. 20, 1969–Jan. 20, 1973	Spiro T. Agnew
Richard M. Nixon	Jan. 20, 1973–Aug. 9, 1974	Spiro T. Agnew
		Gerald R. Ford
Gerald R. Ford	Aug. 9, 1974–Jan. 20, 1977	Nelson Rockefeller
Jimmy Carter	Jan. 20, 1977–Jan. 20, 1981	Walter F. Mondale
Ronald Reagan	Jan. 20, 1981–Jan. 20, 1985	George Bush
Ronald Reagan	Jan. 20, 1985–Jan. 20, 1989	George Bush
George Bush	Jan. 20, 1989–Jan. 20, 1993	J. Danforth Quayle
Bill Clinton	Jan. 20, 1993–Jan. 20, 2001	Albert Gore, Jr.
George W. Bush	Jan. 20, 2001–	Richard Cheney

IMPORTANT DATES IN THE DEVELOPMENT OF THE PRESIDENCY

The Articles of Confederation, 1776–77
Plan for confederation submitted to Congress with no plan for an executive (July 12, 1776).

Continental Congress adopts Articles of Confederation and Perpetual Union with no provision for an executive (Nov. 15, 1777).

The Constitutional Convention, 1787
Between June and September, the Constitutional Convention voted to include the following provisions in the new Constitution:

A single executive will head the government; Congress has power to declare war; President is commander in chief of the armed forces; there will be no religious test for Presidency; Presidential selection is by the electoral college for a term of four years; President may be impeached by House for "High crimes and misdemeanors"; Senate tries cases of impeachment; President is granted the "Executive Power" of the United States; Presidential veto of legislation can be overridden by two-thirds vote of Congress.

1789
Electoral college chooses George Washington as first President.

1793
First use of term *cabinet* to describe Presidential meeting with department secretaries.

1794
Washington, commanding the state militias, crushes Whiskey Rebellion protesting national government taxing power.

1796
Washington refuses to let House of Representatives see papers relating to the negotiations over a treaty; establishes precedent of Presidential secrecy in foreign policy.

Washington declines third term, sets precedent for two-term limit.

1798
Congress forces President John Adams into undeclared naval war with France. Supreme Court decides that "undeclared" wars are constitutional.

1801
House of Representatives chooses Thomas Jefferson for Presidency after electoral college deadlock.

John Adams turns over Presidency peacefully to leader of opposition party, Thomas Jefferson.

1804
12th Amendment to Constitution modifies electoral college voting to provide for separate ballots for President and Vice President.

1809
Cabinet begins practice of voting on Presidential decisions.

1812
James Madison asks Congress for its first declaration of war (against Great Britain).

1823
James Monroe proclaims the Monroe Doctrine.

1825
House of Representatives chooses John Quincy Adams over popular vote winner Andrew Jackson.

1828
Size of electorate has quadrupled since 1824 as states end property qualifications for voting. Most states now choose electors to electoral college by popular election rather than state legislative selection. Popular vote winner Andrew Jackson is elected.

1829
Jackson removes some civil servants and replaces them with party followers, as he institutes the "spoils system" in the civil service.

1832
Jackson vetoes a law, the first time a President has done so on policy grounds.

Jackson fires secretary of the Treasury, until then an official considered accountable only to Congress.

Vice President John C. Calhoun resigns from office.

1833
Jackson issues proclamation warning South Carolina that it must implement federal laws or face the consequences.

1834
Senate censures Jackson for assuming "authority and power not conferred by the Constitution and laws." Jackson responds with "protest" message. (Senate "expunges" its censure resolution of Jackson in 1837.)

1841
William Henry Harrison is the first President to die in office. John Tyler assumes the Presidency, refuses to consider himself "acting President."

1842
First effort in Congress to impeach a President (John Tyler) fails.

1847
James K. Polk becomes the first President to supervise preparation of executive department budget estimates before they are sent to Congress; also supervises military strategy and tactics in Mexican War.

1861
Abraham Lincoln calls for 75,000 volunteers and imposes a naval blockade on the South without a declaration of war; also suspends writ of habeas corpus, withdraws money from Treasury, and enlarges army and navy without congressional assent.

1862
Lincoln declares martial law. Military courts begin to try rebel sympathizers for treason.

1863
Lincoln emancipates slaves in areas ruled by Confederacy.

In the *Prize Cases* the Supreme Court upholds the constitutionality of the blockade against the South without a congressional declaration of war.

1865
Lincoln is the first President to be assassinated.

1867
Congress passes Tenure of Office Act, limiting Presidential power to fire cabinet officers.

Andrew Johnson fires the secretary of war. The House impeaches Johnson, but he is acquitted by one vote in the Senate.

1905
Theodore Roosevelt mediates Russo-Japanese War and wins Nobel Peace Prize for 1906.

1913
Woodrow Wilson addresses Congress in person and delivers State of the Union address.

1920
Wilson suffers a stroke. Mrs. Wilson and White House aides run the government.

1921
Warren Harding signs Budget and Accounting Act, which creates a Bureau of the Budget to prepare an executive branch budget.

1924
Supreme Court decides in *Myers* v. *United States* that the President has the constitutional power to remove officials in the executive departments.

1933
Franklin D. Roosevelt begins series of "fireside chats" on radio.

1936
Supreme Court decides in *Humphrey's Executor* v. *United States* that the President does not have the power to remove officials of independent regulatory agencies.

Supreme Court in *United States* v. *Curtiss-Wright Export Corp.* recognizes vast Presidential foreign affairs powers.

1937
Franklin D. Roosevelt's court-packing plan is defeated by Congress.

1939
The White House Office is created. The Bureau of the Budget is transferred from the Treasury Department to the Executive Office of the President.

1940
Franklin D. Roosevelt wins third term in office, shattering tradition of the two-term Presidency.

Roosevelt exchanges U.S. destroyers for British military bases, using an executive agreement and bypassing the Senate treaty powers.

1942
Roosevelt orders the evacuation of Japanese Americans from the West Coast and demands their internment in concentration camps.

1944
Roosevelt elected to unprecedented fourth term.

1946
The Council of Economic Advisers is created.

1947
The National Security Council is created.

1950
Harry Truman goes to war in Korea without obtaining a congressional declaration of war.

1951
Congress passes the 22nd Amendment, limiting the President to two elected terms.

Truman seizes the steel mills. The Supreme Court orders him to return the mills to the owners in *Youngstown Sheet and Tube* v. *Sawyer.*

1954
Dwight Eisenhower is the first President to invoke executive privilege, refusing Senator Joseph McCarthy's request for military personnel records.

1955
Eisenhower and Vice President Richard Nixon sign agreement on Presidential disability in office.

1962

Cuban Missile Crisis: John F. Kennedy forces Soviet Union to withdraw missiles from Cuba and becomes the first President to threaten the Soviets with nuclear attack.

1964

Congress passes Gulf of Tonkin Resolution, which Lyndon B. Johnson uses as the equivalent of declaration of war to begin military buildup in Vietnam.

1967

25th Amendment ratified, providing for congressional election of Vice President in case of death or resignation and procedures for Vice President to act as President in case of Presidential disability.

1969

Council on Environmental Quality is created.

1970

Richard Nixon invades Cambodia, then orders the bombing of Cambodia to be kept secret from Congress and the public.

1971

Nixon impounds funds appropriated by Congress. Federal courts later declare these impoundments illegal.

Federal Election Campaign Act regulates eligibility of Presidential candidates for federal funds.

1973

Congress passes War Powers Resolution, attempting to regulate President's powers as commander in chief.

1974

Congress passes Budget and Impoundment Control Act to regulate Presidential attempts to impound funds.

Supreme Court in *Nixon* v. *United States* orders Nixon to turn over Watergate tapes to special prosecutor, rejecting White House claims of "executive privilege" in ordinary criminal prosecutions.

Nixon becomes the first President to resign from office. President Gerald Ford pardons Nixon for all Watergate crimes.

Federal Election Commission is established.

1976

Supreme Court in *Buckley* v. *Valeo* says that Congress is prohibited from appointing "officers of the United States." Congress rewrites campaign law to provide for President to appoint all members of Federal Election Commission.

1978

Jimmy Carter abrogates treaty with Taiwan. Supreme Court in *Goldwater* v. *Carter* (1979) allows Presidential abrogation of treaties without congressional participation to stand.

Ethics in Government Act establishes Office of Ethics in the White House and provides for appointment of independent counsel to investigate alleged crimes of President and others.

1980

Executive agreement with Iran ends hostage crisis; it limits the rights of U.S. companies to sue Iran in U.S. courts. Supreme Court upholds the agreement in *Dames and Moore* v. *Regan*.

1981

Use of "early reconciliation" mechanism in budget process allows Ronald Reagan to dominate congressional budget process.

1982

Reagan orders U.S. forces on peacekeeping mission in Lebanon. Congress uses the War Powers Resolution for the first time and backs his initiative.

1985

Gramm-Rudman-Hollings Budget Act requires President to act to reduce deficits.

1986

Reagan orders arms delivered to Iran. Proceeds of arms sales are diverted to Nicaraguan Contras in violation of laws passed by Congress. The attempt by the administration to bypass congressional appropriations and laws is uncovered and Congress holds hearings.

1990

The Budget Enforcement Act sets limits on domestic and defense spending.

1993

Bill Clinton creates National Economic Council.

1998–99

House of Representatives impeaches Bill Clinton for perjury and obstruction of justice in a private lawsuit. Senate failure to convict sets precedent that these charges are not "high crimes."

2001

The 2000 election race between George W. Bush and Al Gore, Jr. goes to Bush after the U.S. Supreme Court overturns a Florida Supreme Court ruling for a ballot recount in that state, giving Bush the deciding electoral college votes.

APPENDIX 4

PRESIDENTIAL HISTORIC SITES AND LIBRARIES

All Presidents

The White House
1600 Pennsylvania Avenue
Washington, D.C. 20500
Tel. 202-456-1414
www.whitehouse.gov

Hours for visits: Tuesday through Saturday, 10:00 to 12:00, no charge. Closed New Year's Day, Thanksgiving, and Christmas Day.

John Adams and John Quincy Adams

John Adams and John Quincy Adams
    Birthplace
Quincy Historical Society
133–141 Franklin Street
Quincy, Mass. 02269
Tel. 617-773-1177

Adams National Historic Site
135 Adams Street
Quincy, Mass. 02269
Tel. 617-770-1175
www.nps.gov/adam

Chester Alan Arthur

Chester A. Arthur Historic Site
(birthplace replica)
Fairfield, Vt. 05455
Tel. 802-828-3051

James Buchanan

Wheatland, home of James Buchanan
1120 Marietta Avenue
Lancaster, Pa. 17603
Tel. 717-392-8721
www.wheatland.org

George Bush

George Bush Presidential Library and
    Museum
Texas A&M University
1000 George Bush Drive West
College Station, Tex. 77843
Tel. 409-260-9552
http://bushlibrary.tamu.edu

Jimmy Carter

Jimmy Carter Library
One Copenhill Avenue
Atlanta, Ga. 30307
Tel. 404-331-3942
http://carterlibrary.galileo.peachnet.edu

Grover Cleveland

Grover Cleveland Birthplace
207 Bloomfield Avenue
Caldwell, N.J. 07006
Tel. 201-226-1810

Calvin Coolidge

Calvin Coolidge Homestead
Route 100A
Plymouth Notch, Vt. 05056
Tel. 802-672-3773

Dwight David Eisenhower

Dwight D. Eisenhower Library
SE Fourth Street
Abilene, Kans. 67410
Tel. 913-263-4751/1-877-RINGIKE
www.eisenhower.utexas.edu

Eisenhower Birthplace State Historic Site
208 East Day Street
Denison, Tex. 75020
Tel. 903-465-8908
www.eisenhowerbirthplace.org

Eisenhower National Historic Site
Gettysburg National Military Park
97 Taneytown Road
Gettysburg, Pa. 17325
Tel. 717-338-9114
www.nps.gov/eise/home

Millard Fillmore

Fillmore Glen State Park
(replica of birthplace)
Moravia, N.Y. 13118
Tel. 315-497-0130

Millard Fillmore House
24 Shearer Avenue
East Aurora, N.Y. 14052
Tel. 716-652-8875

Gerald R. Ford

Gerald R. Ford Library
1000 Beal Avenue
Ann Arbor, Mich. 48109-2114
Tel. 734-741-2218
www.ford.utexas.edu

Gerald Ford Museum
303 Pearl Street
Grand Rapids, Mich. 49504
Tel. 616-451-9263
www.ford.utexas.edu

James A. Garfield

James A. Garfield National Historic Site
Lawnfield
8095 Mentor Avenue
Mentor, Ohio 44060
Tel. 440-255-8722
www.nps.gov/jaga

Ulysses S. Grant

Grant's Birthplace State Memorial
U.S. 52 and State Route 232
Point Pleasant, Ohio 45163
Tel. 513-553-4911

U.S. Grant's Home State Historic Site
500 Bouthillier Street
Galena, Ill. 61036
Tel. 815-777-3310

Appomattox Court House National
   Historic Park
McLean House
Appomattox, Va. 24522
Tel. 804-352-8987
www.nps.gov/apco

General Grant National Memorial
Grant's Tomb
Riverside Drive and 122nd Street
New York, N.Y. 10024
Tel. 212-666-1640
www.nps.gov/gegr

Warren G. Harding

Harding Home and Museum
380 Mount Vernon Avenue
Marion, Ohio 43302
Tel. 740-387-9630
www.ohiohistory.org/places/harding

Benjamin Harrison

President Benjamin Harrison Memorial
   Home
1230 North Delaware Street
Indianapolis, Ind. 46202
Tel. 317-631-1888

William Henry Harrison

William Henry Harrison Museum
Grouseland
3 West Scott Street
Vincennes, Ind. 47591
Tel. 812-882-2096

Rutherford B. Hayes

Rutherford B. Hayes Center
Spiegel Grove
Fremont, Ohio 43420
Tel. 419-332-2081/1-800-998-7737
www.rbhayes.org

Herbert C. Hoover

Herbert Hoover Library–Museum
Parkside Drive
West Branch, Iowa 52358
Tel. 319-643-5301
http://hoover.nara.gov

Herbert Hoover National Historic Site
Parkside Drive and Main Street
West Branch, Iowa 52358
Tel. 319-643-2541
www.hooverassoc.org

Andrew Jackson

The Hermitage, home of Andrew Jackson
4580 Rachel's Lane
Hermitage, Tenn. 37076
Tel. 615-889-2941
www.thehermitage.com

Thomas Jefferson

Monticello, home of Thomas Jefferson
Thomas Jefferson Memorial Foundation
Charlottesville, Va. 22902
Tel. 804-984-9822
www.monticello.org

Jefferson Memorial
The Mall
Washington, D.C.

Andrew Johnson

Andrew Johnson National Historic Site
College and Depot Streets
Greeneville, Tenn. 37743
Tel. 423-638-3551
www.nps.gov/anjo

Lyndon B. Johnson

Lyndon Baines Johnson Library and
   Museum
University of Texas
2313 Red River Street
Austin, Tex. 78705-5702
Tel. 512-916-5137
www.lbjlib.utexas.edu

John F. Kennedy

John Fitzgerald Kennedy Library and
    Museum
Columbia Point
Boston, Mass. 02125
Tel. 617-929-4500
www.cs.umb.edu/jfklibrary/

John Fitzgerald Kennedy National Historic
    Site
83 Beals Street
Brookline, Mass. 02146
Tel. 617-566-7937

Abraham Lincoln

Lincoln Birthplace National Historic Site
2995 Lincoln Farm Road
Hodgenville, Ky. 42748
Tel. 270-358-3137
www.nps.gov/abli

Abraham Lincoln Library and Museum
Highway 25 East
Harrogate, Tenn. 37752
Tel. 423-869-6235
www.Imunet.edu/Museum

Lincoln Boyhood National Memorial
Lincoln City, Ind. 47552
Tel. 812-937-4541
www.nps.gov/libo

Lincoln Home National Historic Site
426 South Seventh Street
Springfield, Ill. 62701
Tel. 217-492-4241, ext. 221
www.nps.gov/liho

Lincoln's Tomb State Historic Site
Oak Ridge Cemetery
Springfield, Ill. 62702
Tel. 217-782-2717

Ford's Theatre National Historic Site
511 10th Street, N.W.
Washington, D.C. 20004
Tel. 202-426-6924
www.nps.gov/foth/index2

Lincoln Memorial
23rd Street, N.W.
Washington, D.C.
www.nps.gov/linc/home

James Madison

Montpelier, home of James Madison
Route 20
Orange County, Va. 22957
Tel. 540-672-2728
www.montpelier.org

Octagon House
1799 New York Avenue, S.W.
Washington, D.C. 20006
Tel. 202-638-3105

William McKinley

National McKinley Birthplace Memorial
40 North Main Street
Niles, Ohio 44446
Tel. 330-652-1704
www.mckinley.lib.oh.us/memorial

James Monroe

James Monroe Museum and Memorial
    Library
908 Charles Street
Fredericksburg, Va. 22401
Tel. 540-654-1043

Ash Lawn–Highland, home of
    James Monroe
Albemarle County, Route 795
Charlottesville, Va. 22901
Tel. 804-293-9539
http://monticello.avenue.org/ashlawn

Richard M. Nixon

Richard Nixon Presidential Library and
    Birthplace
Yorba Linda, Calif. 92686
Tel. 714-993-3393
www.nixonfoundation.org

Franklin Pierce

Franklin Pierce Homestead
Routes 31 and 9
Hillsboro, N.H. 03244
Tel. 603-478-3165
www.conknet.com/hillsboro/historic/
    homestead

The Pierce Manse
14 Penacook St.
Concord, N.H. 03301
Tel. 603-225-2068/603-224-7668
www.newww.com/free/pierce

James K. Polk

Ancestral Home of James Knox Polk
301 West 7th Street
Columbia, Tenn. 38401
Tel. 931-388-2354
www.jameskpolk.com

Ronald Reagan

Ronald Reagan Birthplace
Main Street
Tampico, Ill.

Ronald Reagan Presidential Library
40 Presidential Drive
Simi Valley, Calif. 93065
Tel. 805-522-8444
www.reagan.utexas.edu

Franklin D. Roosevelt

Franklin D. Roosevelt Library
259 Albany Post Road
Hyde Park, N.Y. 12538
Tel. 914-229-8114
www.academic.marist.edu/fdr/

Home of Franklin D. Roosevelt National
Historic Site
Route 9
Hyde Park, N.Y. 12538
Tel. 914-229-9115
www.nps.gov/hofr

Little White House Historic Site
Highway 85 West
Warm Springs, Ga. 31830
Tel. 706-655-5870

Franklin D. Roosevelt Memorial
900 Ohio Drive, S.W.
Washington, D.C. 20242
www.nps.gov/fdrm/home

Theodore Roosevelt

Theodore Roosevelt Birthplace National
Historic Site
28 East 20th Street
New York, N.Y. 10003
Tel. 212-260-1616
www.nps. gov/thrb

Sagamore Hill National Historic Site
20 Sagamore Hill
Oyster Bay, N.Y. 11771
Tel. 516-922-4788
www.nps.gov/sahi

Theodore Roosevelt Island National
Memorial
Washington, D.C.
www.nps.gov/this/

William Howard Taft

William Howard Taft National Historic
Site
2038 Auburn Avenue
Cincinnati, Ohio 45202
Tel. 513-684-3262
www.nps.gov/wiho/

Zachary Taylor

Zachary Taylor National Cemetery
4701 Brownsboro Road
Louisville, Ky. 40202

Harry S. Truman

Harry S. Truman Library and Museum
U.S. Highway 24 and Delaware Street
Independence, Mo. 64050
Tel. 816-833-1400
www.trumanlibrary.org

Harry S. Truman Birthplace State
Historic Site
1009 Truman Avenue and 11th Street
Lamar, Mo. 64759
Tel. 417-682-2279
www.mostateparks.com/trumansite

Harry S. Truman National Historic Site
223 Main Street
Independence, Mo. 64050
Tel. 816-254-9929
www.nps.gov/hstr

John Tyler

Sherwood Forest Plantation
Route 5
Charles City, Va. 23020
Tel. 804-829-5377
www.sherwoodforest.org

Martin Van Buren

Martin Van Buren National Historic Site
(Lindenwald)
1013 Old Post Road
Kinderhook, N.Y. 12106
Tel. 518-758-9689
www.nps.gov/mava

George Washington

Mount Vernon, home of George Washington
George Washington Parkway South
Mt. Vernon, Va. 22121
Tel. 703-780-2000
www.mountvernon.org

Washington Monument
The Mall
Washington, D.C.

Valley Forge Historical Society Museum
Route 23
Valley Forge, Pa. 19481
Tel. 610-783-0535
www.ushistory.org/valleyforge

Woodrow Wilson

Wilson Birthplace
20 North Coalter Street
Staunton, Va. 24401
Tel. 703-885-0897

Woodrow Wilson Museum
2340 S Street, N.W.
Washington, D.C. 20008
Tel. 202-387-4062

Other Sources of Information about Presidents

Center for the Study of the Presidency
208 East 75th Street
New York, N.Y. 10021
Tel. 212-249-1200
The center publishes Presidential Studies Quarterly, *a scholarly magazine containing articles on the Presidency.*

The White House Office
1600 Pennsylvania Avenue, N.W.
Washington, D.C. 20500
Tel. 202-456-1414
This is the address and the telephone number that you can use to let the President know your opinions.

White House Historical Association
740 Jackson Place, N.W.
Washington, D.C. 20503
Tel. 202-737-8292
www.whitehousehistory.org/whha/

FURTHER READING

Books about the Presidency for Young Adults

Beard, Charles, and Detlev Vagts. *Presidents in American History.* 2d ed. Englewood Cliffs, N.J.: Julian Messner, 1989.

Bernstein, Richard B., and Jerome Agel. *The Presidency: Into the Third Century.* New York: Walker, 1989.

Phillips, Louis. *Ask Me Anything about the Presidents.* New York: Avon, 1992.

Pious, Richard M. *The American Presidency.* Englewood Cliffs, N.J.: Silver Burdett, 1991.

Scriabine, Christine Brendel. *The Presidency.* New York: Chelsea House, 1988.

General References about the Presidency

Burns, James McGregor. *Presidential Government: The Crucible of Leadership.* Boston: Houghton Mifflin, 1966.

Congressional Quarterly staff. *The Presidency A to Z.* Washington, D.C.: Congressional Quarterly, 1992.

Graff, Henry F., ed. *The Presidents: A Reference History.* New York: Scribners, 1984.

Grossman, Mark. *Encyclopedia of the United States Cabinet.* 3 vols. Santa Barbara, Calif.: ABC-CLIO, 2000.

Kane, Joseph N. *Facts about the Presidents.* 5th ed. New York: H. W. Wilson, 1989.

Levy, Leonard W., and Louis Fisher, eds. *Encyclopedia of the American Presidency.* 4 vols. New York: Simon & Schuster, 1993.

Nelson, Michael. *Congressional Quarterly Guide to the Presidency.* Washington, D.C.: Congressional Quarterly, 1989.

Pious, Richard M. *The Presidency.* Boston: Allyn & Bacon, 1995.

Schick, Frank L. *The Records of the Presidency: Presidential Papers & Libraries from Washington to Reagan.* Phoenix, Ariz.: Oryx, 1989.

Anecdotal Treatments of the Presidency

Boller, Paul F., Jr. *Presidential Anecdotes.* New York: Penguin, 1989.

Boller, Paul F., Jr. *Presidential Campaigns.* New York: Oxford, 1985.

Frank, Sid, and Arden Melick. *The Presidents: Tidbits and Trivia.* Rev. ed. New York: Hammond, 1990.

Hay, Peter. *All the Presidents' Wives: Anecdotes of the Women behind the Men in the White House.* New York: Penguin, 1989.

Brief Biographical Treatments

Armbruster, Maxim E. *The Presidents of the United States.* New York: Horizon Press, 1982.

Bailey, Thomas A. *Presidential Saints and Sinners.* New York: Free Press, 1981.

Bailey, Thomas A. *The Pugnacious Presidents: White House Warriors on Parade.* New York: Free Press, 1980.

Freidel, Frank. *The Presidents of the United States of America.* 12th ed. Washington, D.C.: White House Historical Association, 1989.

Magill, Frank N., ed. *The American Presidents: The Office and the Men.* 3 vols. Danbury, Conn.: Grolier, 1989.

Pictorial Histories

The American Heritage Pictorial History of the Presidents. New York: Simon & Schuster, 1968.

Durant, John, and Alice Durant. *Pictorial History of the American Presidents.* New York: A. S. Barnes, 1969.

Presidential Elections

Fischer, Roger A. *Tippecanoe and Trinkets Too: The Material Culture of American Presidential Campaigns, 1828–1984.* Urbana: University of Illinois Press, 1988.

Jamieson, Kathleen Hall. *Packaging the Presidency: A History and Criticism of Presidential Campaign Advertising.* 2nd ed. New York: Oxford, 1992.

McCormick, Richard P. *The Presidential Game.* New York: Oxford, 1982.

McGinnis, Joe. *The Selling of the President.* New York: Penguin, 1988.

Melder, Keith. *Hail to the Candidate: Presidential Campaigns from Banners to Broadcasts.* Washington, D.C.: Smithsonian Institution Press, 1992.

Polsby, Nelson W., and Aaron Wildavsky. *Presidential Elections: Contemporary Strategies of American Electoral Politics.* 7th ed. New York: Free Press, 1988.

Reinsche, J. Leonard. *Getting Elected: From Radio and Roosevelt to Television and Reagan.* New York: Hippocrene, 1988.

Schlesinger, Arthur M., Jr., and Fred L. Israel, eds. *The Coming to Power: Critical Presidential Elections in American History.* New York: Chelsea House, 1981.

Schlesinger, Arthur M., Jr., ed. *History of American Presidential Elections, 1789–1984.* 5 vols. New York: Chelsea House, 1986.

Tugwell, Rexford G. *How They Became President.* New York: Simon & Schuster, 1964.

Wayne, Stephen J. *The Road to the White House: The Politics of Presidential Elections.* New York: St. Martin's, 1992.

The Development of the Presidency

Barrileaux, Ryan J. *The Post-Modern Presidency: The Office after Ronald Reagan.* New York: Praeger, 1988. A study of recent Presidential prerogatives.

Berman, Larry. *The New American Presidency.* Boston: Little, Brown, 1987. A history of the modern Presidency, with prescriptions for reforming the office.

King, Gary, and Lyn Ragsdale. *The Elusive Executive: Discovering Statistical Patterns in the Presidency.* Washington, D.C.: Congressional Quarterly, 1988. Statistical tables and analysis.

Koh, Harold. *The National Security Constitution.* New Haven: Yale University Press, 1991. An examination of the Iran-Contra case and its aftermath.

Leuchtenberg, William E. *In the Shadow of FDR: From Harry Truman to Ronald Reagan.* Rev. ed. Ithaca, N.Y.: Cornell University Press, 1985.

Lowi, Theodore. *The Personal President: Power Invested, Promise Unfulfilled.* Ithaca, N.Y.: Cornell University Press, 1985. An examination of the excesses of the post-Watergate Presidency.

Milkis, Sidney, and Michael Nelson. *The American Presidency.* Washington, D.C.: Congressional Quarterly, 1990.

Pious, Richard M. *The American Presidency.* New York: Basic Books, 1979. A theory of Presidential power as constitutional prerogative.

Riccards, Michael P. *A Republic If You Can Keep It: The Foundations of the American Presidency, 1700–1800.* Westport, Conn.: Greenwood, 1987. Traces the history of self-government in the colonies and states.

Rose, Richard. *The Postmodern President.* Chatham, N.J.: Chatham House, 1989. Discusses how changes in American economic power have changed the role of the President in world politics.

Rossiter, Clinton. *The American Presidency.* New York: Harcourt Brace & World, 1956. Classic account of the duties of the President.

Rossiter, Clinton. *Constitutional Dictatorship.* New York: Harcourt Brace & World, 1963. A study of Lincoln's use of power during the Civil War.

Rubin, Richard. *Press, Party, and Presidency.* New York: Norton, 1981. Discusses changes in Presidential leadership of public opinion and relations with media.

Schlesinger, Arthur M., Jr. *The Imperial Presidency.* Boston: Houghton Mifflin, 1973. Examines how Truman, Eisenhower, Kennedy, and Johnson paved the way for Nixon's abuses of power.

Tulis, Jeffrey. *The Rhetorical Presidency.* Princeton, N.J.: Princeton University Press, 1987. A study of Presidential speech making.

Presidential Decision Making

Barber, James David. *The Presidential Character.* 4th ed. Englewood Cliffs, N.J.: Prentice-Hall, 1992. Psychological studies of modern Presidents.

Graff, Henry F. *The Tuesday Cabinet.* Englewood Cliffs, N.J.: Prentice-Hall, 1970. An account of Lyndon Johnson's advisers during the Vietnam War.

Greenstein, Fred. *The Hidden-Hand Presidency.* New York: Basic Books, 1982. Discusses the techniques used by Eisenhower to win political victories.

May, Ernest R., ed. *The Ultimate Decision.* New York: George Braziller, 1960. Examines the decisions Presidents make to go to war.

Neustadt, Richard. *Presidential Power and the Modern Presidents.* New York: Free Press, 1990. Discusses the way Presidents use power and influence to get others to do what they want.

Pyle, Christopher, and Richard M. Pious, eds. *The President, Congress, and the Constitution.* New York: Free Press, 1984. An examination of constitutional law cases involving Presidential power.

Sorensen, Theodore. *Decision-Making in the White House.* New York: Columbia University Press, 1963. Discusses crisis decision making in the Kennedy White House.

Leadership

Burns, James MacGregor. *Leadership.* New York: Harper & Row, 1978. A study of great leaders and what made them so.

Patterson, Bradley. *The Ring of Power.* New York: Basic Books, 1990. A discussion of the operations of the White House, by a former aide.

Reedy, George. *The Twilight of the Presidency.* New York: New American Library, 1970. Discusses the dangers of a large Presidential staff, by a former press secretary.

Presidents on the Presidency

Carter, Jimmy. *Keeping Faith: Memoirs of a President.* New York: Bantam, 1982.

Eisenhower, Dwight D. *The White House Years.* Garden City, N.Y.: Doubleday, 1965.

Ford, Gerald R. *A Time to Heal.* New York: Harper & Row, 1979.

Hoover, Herbert. *Memoirs.* 3 vols. 1951–52. Reprint. New York: Garland, 1979.

Johnson, Lyndon B. *The Vantage Point.* New York: Holt, Rinehart & Winston, 1971.

Nixon, Richard M. *RN: The Memoirs of Richard Nixon.* New York: Grosset & Dunlap, 1978.

Reagan, Ronald. *An American Life.* New York: Simon & Schuster, 1990.

Roosevelt, Theodore. *An Autobiography.* New York: Macmillan, 1919.

Taft, William Howard. *Our Chief Magistrate and His Powers.* New York: Columbia University Press, 1916.

Truman, Harry S. *Memoirs.* 2 vols. Garden City, N.Y.: Doubleday, 1955.

Wilson, Woodrow. *Constitutional Government in the United States.* New York: Columbia University Press, 1908.

First Ladies on Life in the White House

Carter, Rosalynn. *First Lady from Plains.* Boston: Houghton Mifflin, 1984.

Ford, Betty. *The Times of My Life.* New York: Harper & Row, 1978.

Reagan, Nancy, and William Novak. *My Turn: The Memoirs of Nancy Reagan.* New York: Random House, 1988.

Roosevelt, Eleanor. *This I Remember.* 1949. Reprint. Westport, Conn.: Greenwood, 1975.

INDEX

Richard M. Pious is Adolph and Effie Ochs Professor and Chair of the Department of Political Science at Barnard College. His books include *The American Presidency* and *The President, Congress, and the Constitution.* He edited the centennial volume of the Academy of Political Science, *The Power to Govern,* and its public affairs volume for the 1992 election year, *Presidents, Elections, and Democracy.* He has published articles in *Political Science Quarterly,* the *Wisconsin Law Review,* the *Journal of International Affairs,* the *Journal of Armed Forces and Society,* and *Constitution Magazine.* He has also written articles on the Presidency for the Soviet Union's press agency Novosti and for the Russian newspaper *Za Rubeshom,* for the Russian Academy of Sciences, and for the *Journal des Elections* in France. He has written several books for younger readers, including *Richard M. Nixon: A Political Life* and *The American Presidency.*

Dr. Pious has been a consultant in several Presidential election campaigns and an adviser to congressional committees dealing with Presidential–congressional relations. He has lectured on the war powers of Presidents at the United States Military Academy at West Point. Most recently he has been an adviser to the Hungarian Academy of Sciences, advising on the transition from communist rule to a democratic system of government, a consultant to the Russian Academy of Sciences Institute for the U.S.A. and Canada on Presidential powers, and a consultant to the commission that wrote the constitution for the new Russian Republic. He is on the board of advisers of the Center for Presidential Studies, which is organizing the George Bush Presidential Library, and the editorial board of *Political Science Quarterly.* He has appeared in public-service videos promoting voter education produced for MTV.